PERSONAL AND SOCIAL ETHICS
Moral Problems with Integrated Theory

PERSONAL AND SOCIAL ETHICS
Moral Problems with
Integrated Theory

VINCENT BARRY

Bakersfield College

Wadsworth Publishing Company, Inc., Belmont, California

Philosophy Editor: Kenneth King
Production Editors: Joanne Cuthbertson, Connie Martin
Designer: Nancy Benedict
Copy Editor: Paul Monsour
Cover Illustrator: Alan May

Printed in the United States of America
  3 4 5 6 7 8 9 10—82 81 80 79

Library of Congress Cataloging in Publication Data

Barry, Vincent E.
  Personal and social ethics

  Includes bibliographies and index.
  1. Social ethics. 2. United States—Moral conditions
I. Title.
HM216.B18   170'.2   77–22463
ISBN 0–534–00533–0

CONTENTS

v

PREFACE

One of the main problems that I have found in teaching ethics is weaving theory with practice. Trying to provide students with some theoretical framework while not avoiding moral application invariably consumes much of my teaching preparation time and energies. And, sad to say, textbooks often offer little help.

Frequently an introductory ethics is either a reader or a text. If a reader, it likely takes a strict issues approach to ethics. Unfortunately, such an approach can leave too many students unable to go beyond the issue discussed to see the broader philosophical and ethical questions involved.

On the other hand, ethics texts generally satisfy those wishing a more theoretical approach. But too often with these, the theory becomes heavy and obtuse, losing readers in a fog of abstraction. Even the glaring exceptions to these generalities, and there are many such publications, are often unable to integrate theory and practice in any other way than to present an issue in one chapter, a theory in the next. The result: readers can easily develop a fragmented, incoherent, and sometimes mistaken notion of what ethics involves.

Personal and Social Ethics is an attempt to introduce ethics in a balanced mix of theory and practice that is unified and coherent, engaging and compelling. But I think an introductory ethics should do more than this. It also should assist readers (1) to see the moral overtones in their own lives, (2) to feel the urgency of ethics, the pressing personal and social need to perceive and confront the moral dimensions of everyday experiences, and (3) to understand, analyze, and resolve moral dilemmas for themselves. To throw some light on how *Personal and Social Ethics* aims to accomplish these ends, let's consider its structure, style, organization, and special features.

First, the structure. Intending to help instructors avoid the reader-or-text decision or some version of it, *Personal and Social Ethics* is a combination text-reader. The text of each chapter develops a theoretical aspect of ethics but in a practical, applied way, using various devices. The readings immediately follow.

Specifically, each chapter opens with an actual case study of contemporary interest, drawn primarily from newspapers and magazines. These cases function as springboards to the chapter's theoretical content. Since there is a tendency to abandon practical concerns once theory has been launched, each chapter contains a running dialogue between everyday people involved in a situation similar to the one the case study describes. In this way I hope that readers, while learning ethical theory, never stray far from its practical implications.

Two reading selections follow each textual exposition. These selections generally relate directly to the practical issue that the chapter raises. In some instances the selections are fiction. I hope this has the effect of further rooting ethics in real-life situations. To facilitate understanding, each selection is preceded by a short introduction that focuses the reader's attention.

This is roughly how *Personal and Social Ethics* is structured. But I should add a few remarks here to ensure understanding about the nature of the cases, dialogues, and readings.

The cases were not necessarily selected because they were the ones that best illustrated the theory under discussion. In fact, I thought that a preoccupation with this quality could give the book a "canned" flavor that would leave readers vaguely skeptical about its application to issues other than the model. For example, the morality of scientific experimentation is raised in the chapter dealing with utilitarianism. Clearly, any number of issues could have been considered: social justice, war, civil disobedience, even premarital sex. This is an important point to realize at the outset—that any number of ethical issues can serve to illustrate a theory. In fact, I believe that it is important for readers to learn to spot the many theoretical dimensions of an ethical problem, for in a real sense our ability to resolve moral dilemmas depends on our ability to throw as much ethical light on an issue as possible. For this reason I have chosen some cases that may be related to a theory in a less obvious way than another case might be. There was also a practical reason—I wished to include as many different issues as possible without repeating any. This necessitated something of a juggling act in terms of which issue would go with which theory.

You will also note that no attempt has been made to resolve these cases or the issues they raise. This lies outside the parameters of this work. The primary function of the cases and issues in this introductory text is to elicit interest in moral matters and ease moral understanding. Ultimately, of course, I would hope that readers pursue these issues and resolve them for themselves.

Like the cases, the purpose of the dialogues is to ease and ensure understanding. In addition, I hope they make the reader's introduction to ethics more enjoyable by making it more readable. Finally, it would be nice if these dialogues somehow helped readers to detect ethical problems in everyday contexts and, of course, to deal with them within a moral framework.

Before leaving the structure of *Personal and Social Ethics*, I should mention at least three important criteria I used in selecting the readings: appropriateness, readability, and contrast. By *appropriateness* I mean that the reading is directly related to a main concern of the chapter, usually to the practical issue raised. By *readability* I mean that the reading is understandable to an ethical novice. Granting that this criterion may be uncomfortably subjective, I hope I have not missed the mark by too much. By *contrast* I mean that the readings are either opposed in viewpoints or, if agreed, opposed in approaches or justification. One caution: the selections are not necessarily the most rational and compelling treatments of an issue available. Sometimes, as in the case of Dalton Trumbo's *Johnny Got His Gun,* the appeal springs more from the gut than the head. But because moral appeals are not always the most logical, it seems that readers should gain some experience in analyzing all sorts of appeals. In the majority of cases, however, I have selected readings that have received wide recognition for their ethical scholarship.

So much for the structure of *Personal and Social Ethics.* As to its style, I have intentionally attempted to be informal, as free of ethical jargon as pedagogically advisable. I hope this style is not offensive, but so facilitates a general grasp of ethical thought that readers ultimately may feel confident enough to engage ethical classics without fear and trembling.

With respect to the organization of *Personal and Social Ethics,* I wished to provide some logical order for the chapters while leaving the arrangement loose enough for personal tastes. The result is that, apart from doing chapter 1 first and chapter 10 last, readers may safely consider chapters in whatever order they choose. For those preferring a linear development, however, it's there. Let's briefly see how.

The text opens with an exposition of what ethical and moral justification involve. Because the issues of freedom/determinism and absolutism/relativism provide the bases for important ethical assumptions, these subjects are considered in chapters 2 and 3, before any normative positions are raised. Chapters 4 through 9 are equally divided between moral positions that rely on a consideration of consequences and those that rely on factors other than consequences. Specifically, chapters 4 and 5 deal with egoism and utilitarianism, and chapter 6 with situational ethics. Chapter 7 deals with single-rule non-consequential (deontological) theories, chapter 8 with prima facie duties, and chapter 9 with social justice and with one theory in particular—the maximin principle. Chapter 10 stresses the importance of personal commitment, autonomy, and the need for decision making. In addition, it attempts to formulate some basic ethical principles and negative obligations. So, although readers may read chapters in whatever order they wish, e.g., according to issue preference, there is a clear linear organization to *Personal and Social Ethics.*

Finally, I should say a word about some special features. The Selections for Further Reading section after each chapter contains titles appropriate to both the theory and the practical issue raised. In addition, the first chapter emphasizes the need for moral justification. This is not intended to be a formal analysis of the connection between logic and ethics. It is simply intended to make readers aware of what is often overlooked—that an ethical position that is not justified is essentially irrational. I have attempted to use the handful of common fallacies raised here in criticizing ethical theories elsewhere and also in the Exercises for Analysis section that follows each chapter. I hope all of this makes readers a bit more perceptive in evaluating and formulating ethical positions.

Special note should be made of chapters 9 and 10. Chapter 9, in dealing primarily with the maximin principle theory of social justice, is an attempt to introduce readers to a contemporary theory of social justice by John Rawls. The chapter is by no means comprehensive, but should familiarize readers with a current attempt to tackle serious social problems. Chapter 10 tries to salvage readers from the ethical limbo that I'm afraid they often find themselves in at the conclusion of an introductory ethics. In this chapter I tried to be nondogmatic while at the same time giving readers some guidelines for charting their ethical courses.

Finally, some of the issues raised in *Personal and Social Ethics* are unusual: plagiarism, premarital sex, scientific experimentation, confidentiality and privacy, and reverse discrimination. Of course, there are more traditional issues: civil disobedience, euthanasia, abortion, and war, all of which I trust are handled in an imaginative and intelligent way.

The number of novel features in *Personal and Social Ethics* leaves me especially indebted to those who gave encouragement, counsel, and criticism along the way. Chief among these is Wadsworth philosophy editor, Ken King, whose solid instincts and sound judgment influenced the book's conception and development.

Many ideas were gleaned from feedback from the publisher's readers. I am especially indebted to Peter List of Oregon State University, S. M. Le of West Valley College, and Richard Wasserstrom of U.C.L.A. for their detailed critiques of the manuscript. The book is much improved through their efforts. Any errors of fact or omission are, of course, my responsibility.

1

CIVIL DISOBEDIENCE
of doing good by serving time
ETHICAL REASONING

In the late 1950s and early 1960s, America's brew of racial unrest, which had been heating up for so long, finally boiled over. "Justice too long delayed is justice denied"; "We will overcome"; "Freedom now!": these cries for racial equality echoed throughout the land. "Freedom riders," persons who traveled the roads of America's South to demonstrate opposition to racial inequalities, became as commonplace on television screens as the nightly news. So did the face of their leader, the velvet-voiced, inspirational president of the Southern Christian Leadership Conference, the Reverend Martin Luther King.

At the height of this period of vigorous racial protest, King was arrested in Birmingham, Alabama. Charge: "parading without a permit." Immediately some were reminded of the contrived charges brought against such historic figures as Socrates and Jesus. Others praised the Birmingham commissioner of public safety, Eugene "Bull" Connor, for keeping order and preventing violence. Among those applauding Connor were eight of King's fellow clergymen, who published a statement attacking King's action as unwise and untimely. King, confined in the city jail, responded in what has become known as his "Letter from Birmingham Jail."*

At least two aspects of King's reply make it a lively springboard to a study of ethics. First, it illustrates an important aspect of an individual's value system, the moral aspect. Second, it illustrates moral reasoning in action.

A word about the moral aspect. Although there is great debate about the precise nature of values, we may define a *value* simply as an assessment of worth. Clearly, we humans exhibit a variety of values. In automobiles, some of us value snappy sports models, others conservative sedans. In books, some prefer fiction, others nonfiction. Politically, some people value a democratic form of government, others a constitutional monarchy. On it goes: values in religion, art, politics, education—values in every area of human affairs. Most important, it seems that humans are the only animals that can formulate and

---

*Martin Luther King, "Letter from Birmingham Jail," in *The Norton Reader*, rev. ed. (New York: Norton, 1969), pp. 556–70.

express a value, ads for cat food notwithstanding.

One aspect of our values is what we value in the realm of human conduct; that is, moral values. Some people, for example, might value justice. They might contend that a person should always do the just thing and refrain from doing the unjust thing. Others might value civil order. They might argue that we should always act in a way that promotes civil order and refrain from acting in a way that will produce disorder. Of course, we could speak of other moral values that people hold: honesty, truth, loyalty, love, and so on. People cherish any number of moral values, as we will discover in the pages ahead. But how do we know which values to hold? This is a tough question to answer, perhaps impossible. The study of ethics partially involves a search for the answer.

Complicating the question of what moral values to hold is the inevitable situation of conflicting values. King was involved in precisely this dilemma. Should he prefer justice or order? By parading without a permit, King clearly stated that in the area of racial equality he valued justice over order. In other words, King believed that intentionally breaking the law was the right and proper way to behave in that instance because such behavior would dramatize the inequities of racial injustice. King had chosen a moral value; having chosen it, he acted in accordance with that decision. How do we know that King acted rightly? Another difficult question to answer. Again, the study of ethics partially involves a search for what constitutes morally right human conduct.

In deciding his course of action, King realized that it was not enough to express a moral value, to prefer justice over order in the case of racial inequality. He had to justify it; he had to demonstrate why racial justice was a superior value to civil order. This suggests the second aspect that makes King's reply worthy of our consideration: it is a moral stand justified through rational procedures.

So often today people hold views without really knowing why. They may be against abortion and capital punishment, for euthanasia and premarital sex, or against governmental invasion of individual privacy and scientific experimentation without informed consent. Name an issue and you will find plenty of people willing to give you a position. But justifications for their positions are rare. Without justification a belief has little meaning, an action no rational basis. Thus, this opening chapter emphasizes moral reasoning and justification. Of course, we shall talk about the meaning and nature of ethics, what ethics involves, and some of the problems peculiar to ethics. But mostly we will stress the need to justify our moral beliefs, to provide reasons for maintaining the moral values that we hold and the moral actions that we undertake. And we will rely heavily on King to help us do this.

A final point before we begin. Discussing Martin Luther King's moral justification for his behavior will undoubtedly provoke thinking about civil disobedience. Civil disobedience is the willful breaking of a law in order to dramatize its alleged injustice. We do not intend to determine the morality of civil disobedience here, nor even to air the issue completely. Rather, we are using the civil disobedience issue to make practical what otherwise could remain only theoretical. Ethics is nothing if not practical, concrete, and useful. So, even though this chapter is not intended to debate the civil disobedience issue, begin thinking seriously about it, begin applying what you glean from this chapter not only to the civil disobedience issue but to all moral issues. In other words, begin making this study a part of your life.

To assist you, at the end of this chapter appear a number of arguments commonly raised for and against civil disobedience. Read them; think about them; pick out the flaws. Following these arguments are two readings that should further advance informed discussion on civil disobedience. When you have finished, you should not only have some idea where you stand on the civil disobedience issue, but *why*.

ETHICS

In the chapters ahead we focus on values that govern what is called good and bad human conduct. *The study of what constitutes good and bad human conduct, including related action and values, is called ethics.*

The term *ethics* is sometimes used synonymously with *morals*. It would be more accurate, though, to use the terms *morals* and *moral* to refer to the conduct itself, and the terms *ethics* and *ethical* to refer to the study of moral conduct or to the code one follows. So, when we use the word *moral*, we refer to an action or person insofar as either is considered right or good. When we use the word *immoral*, we refer to an action or person insofar as either one is considered wrong or bad.

Sometimes in ethics the word *amoral* occurs. *Amoral* refers to something outside the sphere of moral concern. For example, whether your new sports car will "top out" at 120 or 130 mph is an amoral question; it is not a moral issue. But whether you should "top it out" on Main Street on a Wednesday at high noon would probably be a moral question.

In ethics we are concerned with questions of right and wrong, duty and obligation, and moral responsibility. When ethicists use words like *good* or *right* to describe a person or action, they generally mean that the person or action conforms with some moral standard. A good person or action has desirable qualities or possesses qualities desirable to humans. Ethicists often disagree about the nature of these qualities and follow different paths in hopes of discovering them. For purposes of understanding, though, we can view ethics as divided into two main classifications—normative ethics and meta-ethics.

NORMATIVE ETHICS AND META-ETHICS

Normative ethics involves an attempt to determine precisely what moral standards to follow so that our actions may be morally right or good. For most of us, ethical action springs from some standard: "Do unto others as you would have them do unto you"; "Act in such a way that you bring about the greatest good for the greatest number"; "Always act in your own best interests." Whatever it is, when we think about why we choose to act the way we do, we can usually discover some principle with which we agree. *Normative ethics is the reasoned search for principles of human conduct, including a critical study of the major theories about what things are good, what acts are right, and what actions are blameworthy.*

But in the twentieth century, many philosophers have relegated ethical questions primarily to language clarification. These philosophers are called meta-ethicists. *Meta-ethics is the highly technical discipline of the meaning of ethical terms, including a critical study of how ethical statements can be verified.* In short, meta-ethicists are more concerned with the meaning of the word *good* or *bad* than with what we think is good or bad. For example, to someone who maintained that King's behavior was "right," the meta-ethicist might reply: "Just what do you mean by 'right'? Do you mean that the majority of citizens approved King's action? That King's action squared with some divine law? Perhaps you mean simply that you yourself approved of King's action?"

There are several reasons that this book is devoted to normative ethics, although along the way we will touch upon some meta-ethical concerns. First, as noted, most of us approach ethics normatively. We want to determine for ourselves some principles or standards of moral behavior. Although language analysis helps to clarify ethical issues, in the last analysis, if one seeks principles and standards, as most do, then one must investigate normative ethics. Another reason is that normative ethics traditionally has occupied the thinking of ethicists. So in becoming familiar with normative ethics, we necessarily are exposed to some of the most profound of ethical inquiries. Third, in recent years ethicists have begun to rekindle their historic interest in normative ethics. Perhaps the crunch of today's moral issues has caused this. Civil disobedience, war, abortion, euthanasia, sex, privacy—are all areas and issues fraught with ethical questions that seem to beg for immediate and adequate resolution.

Normative positions generally break down into either (1) those that consider only the consequences of actions as determining the morality of the action and agent (the person performing the action) or (2) those that consider factors other than consequences, such as rules or principles. The King case is a good example of a moral decision made primarily on the basis of a rule or principle rather than consequences.

Thus, King is not primarily concerned with the good or bad results his action may have. For King, laws that discriminate racially are in themselves immoral and should not be obeyed, regardless of the consequences of such disobedience. To understand his position it is necessary to consider the reasoning behind his stand. That, in turn, requires some familiarity with the reasoning process.

REASONING

Note in the definition of normative ethics the word *reasoned*. Since this book focuses almost exclusively on normative ethics, we must understand what "reasoned search" involves. In general, *reason* is the capacity to think reflectively and make judgments. When we reason, we frequently draw conclusions based on evidence. *Reasoning, therefore, is the process of following relationships from one thought to another and thereby discovering, when we perform this process correctly, what must follow if the evidence is true.*

Reasoning often takes the form of argument. In logic, the study of correct reasoning, an argument is not considered a fight. *An argument is a group of true or false statements (called propositions), one of which (called the conclusion) is said to follow from the others (called the premises).* Here is a simple example of an argument:

If a person is a mother, the person is a female.

Fran is a mother.

Therefore, Fran is a female.

Notice that the first two statements, the premises, entail the last statement, the conclusion. In other words, given the first two premises, the conclusion must logically follow.

With respect to civil disobedience, consider these arguments:

If an action violates the law, it is wrong.

Civil disobedience violates the law.

So, civil disobedience is wrong.

If an action violates the will of the majority, the action is wrong.

Civil disobedience violates the will of the majority.

Therefore, it is wrong.

If an action is an expression of one's commitment to a higher law, the action is moral.

Civil disobedience can be an expression of one's commitment to a higher law.

Thus, civil disobedience can be moral.

If an action is the only practical alternative in a situation, the action is right.

Civil disobedience may be the only practical alternative in a situation.

Therefore, civil disobedience may be right.

These represent a wide range of arguments in opposition to or defense of civil disobedience. Notice that each of these contains a moral judgment. *Let's define a moral judgment as a conclusion about the moral worth of a person or action.* Thus, "King's action was good," "King's action was bad," "King was right," and "King was wrong" are all moral judgments. So are the conclusions in the preceding arguments about civil disobedience. Notice in all these judgments the presence of what we can call moral words: *good, bad, right, wrong.* Although not all judgments using such words are moral judgments (e.g., "Martin Luther King was a good speaker"), frequently these words do indicate the presence of moral judgments. So do *ought, duty, responsibility,* and similar words.

Nevertheless, in the absence of such words a moral judgment could still be present. For example, if someone was clearly suggesting moral disapproval in the statement "King broke the law!" that statement would be expressing a moral judgment. So, a statement's context, its physical and rhetorical surroundings, is important to consider in determining the presence of a moral judgment.

A judgment, by definition, is a conclusion we form on the basis of some data. Therefore, any judgment should have a logical basis; we should have reasonable grounds for holding it. Ethical judgments are no exception. Thus, Martin Luther King had to provide justification for his judgment that he was morally right to disobey the Birmingham ordinance that forbade parading without a permit. This concept of justification is important to grasp in understanding the nature of ethical discourse.

JUSTIFICATION

When we justify any position, we provide reasons for it and demonstrate the reasoning process we have followed to arrive at it. In justifying the conclusion of an argument, it is important to keep in mind at least these two criteria: (1) that the premises logically entail the conclusion and (2) that the premises are true. Arguments that satisfy the first criterion are said to be valid. A valid argument is one whose premises logically necessitate their conclusion. We have already seen one valid argument:

If a person is a mother, the person is a female.

Fran is a mother.

Therefore, Fran is a female.

The conclusion of this argument must logically follow the stated premises. In other words, assuming that the premises are true, the conclusion must logically follow. But be careful. A valid argument may contain false premises, as in:

If a person is a female, the person is a mother.

Fran is a female.

Therefore, Fran is a mother.

This argument is valid; that is, when we assume its premises are true, its conclusion necessarily follows. But we should not be persuaded by this argument, because not all females are mothers. So, validity and truth are separate and distinct concepts. Validity applies to arguments, truth to the premises of arguments.

It is possible to have validity without truth; it is also possible to have truth without validity, as in this example:

If a person is a mother, the person is a female.

Rosalynn Carter is a female.

Therefore, Rosalynn is a mother.

Each of these statements is true, but we should not accept this conclusion based on these premises. If we did, then we should accept the preposterous conclusion of this argument of the same form:

If a person is a mother, the person is a female.

My infant sister is a female.

Therefore, my infant sister is a mother.

So, it is important that an argument be valid before we are persuaded by it. But it is equally important that we ensure that the argument's premises are true. These are the two criteria to remember in justification.

Although philosophers frequently debate the meaning and nature of truth, let us define *truth as that characteristic of a proposition that is present when the proposition describes an actual state of affairs*. By state of affairs is meant any event, condition, or circumstance.

Thus, "Water boils at 212 degrees Fahrenheit at sea level" and "Washington, D.C., is the capital of the United States" are true statements because they describe actual states of affairs. Put another way, we can prove or verify these statements. But such verification does not seem directly applicable to moral statements, such as "Civil disobedience is moral" or "King's action was good." How can you prove these statements? To understand the dimensions of the problem, consider again this argument:

If an action violates the law, it is wrong.

Civil disobedience violates the law.

Therefore, civil disobedience is wrong.

Now, there's no problem verifying the second premise ("Civil disobedience violates the law.") But what about the first? How can you prove that an action that violates a law is indeed morally wrong? Yet it seems we must be able to do just that if we are to evaluate the truth of the conclusion. (There's no question that the conclusion is valid.)

The nature of moral statements is hotly debated. Some argue that they can be verified, others that they cannot. Even if we assume that moral statements cannot be verified the way other statements can, the fact remains that we still must deal with them. You and I daily must make moral judgments whether we want to or not. Simply to say that, since moral statements cannot be verified, we therefore should not and need not formulate any moral judgments, is to avoid reality. Such an attitude takes a most narrow and perhaps dangerous view of human experience. So, we still must deal with moral judgments. Just what can we do to throw some light on moral statements, to help determine their reliability, if not truth?

A simple but useful answer to this question is: attempt to justify them. In other words, when encountering a moral argument that assumes that an action violating a law is wrong, get at the reasons for this assumption. Why is such an action wrong? What does the speaker mean by *wrong*? By *law*? The replies to these questions will undoubtedly launch a full-scale ethical debate that will likely air some principle or standard that the speaker is using to judge moral behavior. This principle, in turn, can then be put to the test of human experience. Having done this, you are in a much better position to evaluate the statement "If an action violates a law, it is wrong" than you were initially. Granted, at the end you may not be in possession of an indubitable truth. But you will have the assurance that scientists have who test a hypothesis and conclude that, although the explanation is still far from certain, all the evidence suggests that they are on the right track.

Of course, the study of logic is an extremely helpful tool in helping us evaluate any argument, including a moral one. Logic provides us with a certain analytical methodology that enables us to detect flaws in the reasoning process. Obviously we cannot provide logical training here. But what we can do is to become familiar with some of the more common devices people use to warp the content of arguments and thereby undermine the truth or reliability of their own arguments. These devices are called *logical fallacies*. Even an acquaintance with them will help you to detect glaring deficiencies in moral arguments and avoid these pitfalls in your own moral justification. In the chapters that follow, we will frequently refer to these fallacies in analyzing the ethical theories we consider.

FALLACIES

Broadly defined, a fallacy is an incorrect way of reasoning. A fallacy is also any attempt to persuade emotionally or psychologically, but not logically. For example, a U.S. senator once voted against the Equal Rights Amendment, which among other things would have forbidden sexual discrimination. He justified his vote by saying that the bill was being sponsored by a "small band of braless bubble-heads." The senator did not rely on reason but on name-calling to justify his view. This is a fallacy; it is called the *ad hominem* appeal. *The ad hominem is the fallacy of attacking the person rather than the person's argument.* Instead of attacking weaknesses and shortcomings of the Equal Rights Amendment, the senator attacked some of the sponsors. The ad hominem is one of the many ways that people reason incorrectly. Knowing the more common of these fallacies should help us in analyzing and formulating ethical arguments.

To illustrate some of these fallacies, let's fictionalize a civil disobedience case not too different from the one that involved Martin Luther King. This one concerns the highly controversial subject of forced busing. Some believe that in order to racially integrate and balance school enrollments, children should be bused to schools outside their neighborhoods. Others say that this is illegal as well as immoral.

In our fictitious case, Maria Josephson is for forced busing. So much does she favor it that, like King, she is organizing and planning to lead a demonstration in the heart of a major U.S. city without first obtaining a license to demonstrate. She hopes that by being arrested she and other demonstrators will dramatize to the country the injustice of racially unbalanced schools and the moral obligation to remedy that imbalance through forced busing. City officials are trying to dissuade Josephson from her proposed course. Charged with this responsibility is the city chief of police, Robert Dillon. The conversation that follows occurs when Dillon visits Josephson in hopes of preventing the demonstration:

Dillon: I can't impress on you enough, Ms. Josephson, that what you're about to do is wrong.
Josephson: I disagree with you. Not only is it right, but it is absolutely obligatory.
Dillon: You realize what will happen to you, don't you?
Josephson: Of course I do. That doesn't frighten me. I've got right on my side.
Dillon: And I've got the law on mine.
Josephson: I disagree. If you really understood it, you would see that the law was on my side.

Unless Maria and the chief quickly start defining their terms, their conversation will rapidly founder for lack of clarity. Terms like *wrong, right,* and *law* all need definition before Dillon and Josephson can hope to reach any accord. Take just one word, *law*. Clearly, by *law* Dillon means statutes, human-made prescriptions for behavior. Josephson may mean the U.S. Constitution, or she may be appealing to some higher law, perhaps what she considers a principle of human rights, perhaps even some kind of divine prescription. It is hard to say. But they seem to be coming from different directions on this one point alone. In short, ambiguity is present.

1. Ambiguity

The fallacy of ambiguity occurs when we use a word or phrase in such a way that its meaning is not clear. Take, for example, the word *wrong* in Dillon's statement "What you're about to do is wrong." Probably by *wrong* Dillon means "against the law." On the other hand, Josephson understands wrong in a moral context. Undoubtedly she would agree that she is breaking the law, but she would contend that she is not doing "wrong," that is, something immoral. But even used in a moral sense, a word like *wrong* is still ambiguous.

Consider the possible meanings that *wrong* could have in the statement "Civil disobedience is wrong." It may mean that the speaker disapproves of civil disobedience. It may mean that society disapproves of civil disobedience, or possibly it could mean that God, speaking through some pious book like the Bible or the Koran, disapproves of civil disobedience.

So, in evaluating ethical arguments it is important to try to determine what people mean by their ethical terms. Of course, it is just as important to define other terms that may appeal in ethical discourse. Thus, if someone argues that abortion is wrong because it is the willful taking of an innocent human life, it is essential to define *human life* and *innocent* before attempting to evaluate that argument. This may seem like a tedious task, but in the long run it is the only way to avoid the fallacy of ambiguity.

2. Invincible Ignorance

Josephson: Do you believe that racial segregation is immoral?
Dillon: Ms. Josephson, I'm not here to debate the merits of your proposed demonstration. My job is merely to enforce the law.
Josephson: But you can't separate law from morality that easily.
Dillon: Perhaps you can't, but that's not the issue.
Josephson: It appears that nothing I can say could convince you that this demonstration may be needed and is right.
Dillon: Nothing at all.

Dillon will not be moved. He is so entrenched in his position that he will not even entertain another view. He is guilty of invincible ignorance.

Perhaps you have heard someone argue, "I don't care what the President has done, he is still the President and therefore should not be impeached," or "No matter what medical authorities say, no one can convince me that cigarette smoking causes lung cancer." Such arguments rely on invincible ignorance. *Invincible ignorance is the fallacy of insisting on the legitimacy of an idea or principle despite contradictory facts.* The attitude of invincible ignorance is captured in the statement "Don't confuse me with facts. My mind is already made up."

The phrase "I don't care what you say" is a dead giveaway for invincible ignorance. It indicates that the arguer does not wish to confuse the issue with facts. Chief Dillon seems to be taking such a position. He admits that nothing Maria Josephson could say would alter his law enforcement principle, even if the law might be contributing to an unjust or immoral condition. Note, however, that this does not mean that Dillon's position is unjustifiable. It simply means that the way he has attempted to justify it, by relying on invincible ignorance, is fallacious.

Moral arguments frequently rely on invincible ignorance. For example: "I don't care what you say, lying is always wrong"; "It doesn't matter what anyone thinks, abortion isn't right"; "I admit that there are more good reasons to remain sexually faithful than not. But I always do what I feel like."

3. Questionable Claim

Dillon: You're really convinced that what you're doing is right, aren't you?

Josephson: If I weren't I wouldn't be here.
Dillon: Well tell me—how can you be so sure?
Josephson: Because racial injustice is wrong and forced busing is the only way to correct it.
Dillon: The *only* way?
Josephson: That's right.
Dillon: I doubt that.

Dillon doubts that forced busing is the *only* way to right racial injustice. He probably thinks that Josephson has overstated her case. Frequently we make such expansive claims that they lose credibility. Consider these two advertising claims, for example: "Dial is the most effective deodorant soap you can buy" and "Zest makes you feel cleaner than soap." Each of these statements involves the fallacy of questionable claim. *A questionable claim is one that cannot stand up under investigation because of the breadth of its assertion.* In other words, an argument posited on questionable claim founders for lack of demonstrative evidence. Words like *most* and *best* and other superlatives frequently signal questionable claim fallacies.

In the moral sphere, persons frequently rely on unquestioned assumptions as the foundations of their ethical codes. Thus: "What I believe is right *is* right"; "Whatever the Bible forbids is necessarily wicked"; "Whatever is good for society is always the right thing to do." Obviously these assumptions are morally controversial and need thoughtful examination before acceptance. Without justification, they are questionable claims.

There's a particular version of the questionable claim fallacy that is common. It is the inconsistency. *The fallacy of inconsistency occurs when we contradict ourselves in word or action without justification for the change of mind.* A political example of the inconsistency fallacy occurred during the 1976 presidential primaries. President Ford claimed that Ronald Reagan was too conservative to be president of the United States. Asked afterwards whether he could conceive of Reagan running on the Republican ticket as a vice-presidential candidate, Ford refused to rule out the possibility. How Reagan could be too conservative to be president and yet be put within a "heartbeat" of the presidency needed justification. There was one. Ford was being inconsistent.

In the moral sphere, parents frequently tell children it is wrong to lie or cheat, and yet they themselves turn around and do precisely that. More seriously, some people seem to act inconsistently when they contend that they believe in the golden rule (doing unto others as you'd have them do unto you) while actually operating in their own best interests.

One ethicist, whom we will meet later, so highly regarded logical consistency that he established his ethical code using it as the main principle. Of course, there is no virtue in being consistent for consistency's sake. In the words of the poet, "a foolish consistency is the hobgoblin of small minds." Naturally, when we have good and compelling reasons to change our minds, we obviously should. But when we do not have good reasons or when the reasons are not expressed or apparent, then inconsistency is present.

4. Begging the Question

Josephson: I think the demonstration is right because the goal is right.
Dillon: I don't mean to be rude, Ms. Josephson, but how do you know your goal is right?
Josephson: Chief Dillon, if you have to ask a question like that, you shouldn't be in charge of law enforcement in this city.

Josephson has begged the question. *Begging the question is the fallacy of answering a question with a variation of the very question asked, or of answering a question in such a way that the original question goes unanswered.* When one begs the question, one assumes that the very statement to be proved is true in order to make it look more plausible. Consider this exchange:

A: How do you know God exists?
B: Because it says so in the Bible.
A: But how do you know the Bible speaks the truth?
B: Because it's the inspired word of God.

Notice the circularity in the argument: God exists because it says so in the Bible, which is the inspired word of God. Josephson is guilty of begging the question when she claims that the demonstration is right because the goal is right. But then she must prove that the goal is right. When Dillon asks her to do this, she again begs his question by telling him he should not be a police chief. Whether he should or not is irrelevant to his question, which deserves an answer.

In the moral sphere, circular reasoning frequently undermines arguments. For example:

A: Lying in this instance is the right thing to do because it will produce the most good for the most people.
B: But how do you know that what produces the most good for the most people is the right thing to do?
A: Because that contention is consistent with the greatest happiness principle.

This sounds good until you realize that the greatest happiness principle is that the moral act is the one that produces the most good for the most people. So, what produces the most good for the most people is not only consistent with the greatest happiness principle, it is the principle! A is guilty of circularity, or begging the question.

5. Argument from Ignorance

Dillon: The fact is that you cannot prove that the demonstration is right.
Josephson: I'm sure I can't in any way that will satisfy you, because you've already made up your mind. But what if I can't? What does that prove?
Dillon: To me it proves that what you're about to do is wrong.

It is tempting to think that because something cannot be proved that it must not be the case. This is Chief Dillon's erroneous conviction, an argument from ignorance. *The argument from ignorance is the fallacy of insisting that a statement is true until proved false or false until proved true.* Perhaps you have heard someone argue like this: "Until you prove that God exists, he does not"; "Since no convincing evidence was brought against the senator, the senator obviously did not break any law"; "Women have never shown themselves to be as fast sprinters as men, so clearly they are not." All of these are arguments from ignorance.

In morality, the argument from ignorance is tempting because of the seeming non-empirical character of ethical statements. Thus, someone argues that the doctrine that one should always act in one's own best long-term interests cannot be proven; therefore, we should reject it. Or: since the doctrine that we have a moral obligation to honor our promises cannot be proved, it is all right to break promises. Worse still: since no moral statement can be empirically verified, then no moral truth exists.

6. False Appeal to Authority

Dillon: Besides, people don't want forced busing in this city.
Josephson: What does that have to do with it?
Dillon: Everything. It means that the majority of people disagree with you. They don't approve of what you're doing.
Josephson: But I don't see how the views of the people affect the rightness or wrongness of racial integration.
Dillon: Because this is a democracy. And in a democracy the will of the majority rules.
Josephson: But that doesn't make the will of the majority right.
Dillon: Doesn't it? When an overwhelming number of people are opposed to something, to me that's proof positive that that thing is wrong.

Chief Dillon's appeal is a species of the false appeal to authority. *Authority is an expert source outside the agent and on whom the agent is resting his or her claim to knowledge.* A simple example: "Cigarette smoking is hazardous to health because the surgeon general says so." In this claim to knowledge, the surgeon general is used as the authority, the expert outside the agent making the claim. Here the claim is legitimate, because the authority is indeed an expert in the area and there is general agreement among the experts. When these two criteria are present—expertise and general agreement among experts—you can feel secure in your appeal to authority. But when either is absent, then you've a false appeal to authority.

Suppose, for example, someone is drinking milk because a celebrity has endorsed it. Probably the celebrity is not a nutritionist or in any way qualified to speak about the virtues of milk drinking. So the celebrity is *not* an expert in the field. Moreover, there is disagreement about the value of milk drinking: milk is not good for everyone. So, the claim that you should drink milk because the celebrity endorses milk drinking would be a *false appeal to authority*.

The false appeal to authority frequently crops up in ethics. The following appeals are probably false because of disagreement among experts: "Civil disobedience is an evil practice because civic authorities condemn it"; "Killing is wrong because it says so in the Bible"; "Wiretapping is moral because the President approves of it." Frequently the false appeal to authority takes a version called *popularity*, or *democracy*, as in the conversation here.

The fallacy of popularity, or democracy, is a false appeal to authority that relies on numbers alone to support its claim. Thus: "Fifty million people have seen this film. Shouldn't you?"; "This LP has already sold one million copies. Get yours today!" Because we are so influenced by popular appeals, for some such an appeal may imply a conclusion, as in: "The latest polls indicate that most Americans believe that abortion on demand is right." Possibly implied conclusion: "So it must be!"

Occasionally the false appeal to authority takes the form of the appeal to traditional wisdom. *Traditional wisdom is the fallacy of relying exclusively on the past to justify the present.* The phrase "This is how it has always been done" signals the traditional wisdom appeal. Thus, a woman who insists on keeping her maiden name after marrying might be told that she cannot because it has never been done. In expressing his opposition to the Equal Rights Amendment, Senator Sam Ervin relied on traditional wisdom when he explained that because the bill had lain around Congress for over 40 years without being passed, that was conclusive proof it should not be passed at all. On moral issues, someone might argue, "Traditionally in this society, individuals have always had the right to determine the size of their families. So, it's immoral for the government to tell them how many children they can have."

Undoubtedly, if we pursued the conversation between Maria Josephson and Chief Dillon, we would spot more fallacies. In addition to the ones we have already mentioned are the four frequently occurring fallacies listed below.

7. Provincialism

Provincialism is the fallacy of seeing things exclusively through the eyes of your own group, organization, or affiliation. Thus: "This automobile must be good because it's made in America." The fallacy of provincialism is especially evident in moral doctrines that insist the good act is the one that a particular group of people approves of. Evident in such reasoning is also an appeal to popularity or democracy.

8. Hasty Conclusion

As its name implies, *the fallacy of hasty conclusion occurs when we make a judgment based on insufficient evidence.* Thus: "The last three teachers in the room were males. So all teachers at this college must be males"; "Since only 42 percent of those eligible actually voted, this proves that the majority of voters are apathetic." In ethics, someone may use atypical cases as a basis for a conclusion. Thus: "Since it is right to lie under a direct and immediate threat to your life, it is unwise to hold to a rule that considers lying immoral."

9. Two-Wrongs-Make-a-Right

The fallacy of two-wrongs-make-a-right is the fallacy of defending what is considered wrongdoing by pointing to an instance of similar behavior. Thus, a traffic officer stops you for speeding. Your defense: "Why stop me? A Jaguar just passed me as if I were standing still." Perhaps a Jaguar did, but that does not justify your speeding.

Frequently we rely not on a single instance to justify wrongdoing but on a great number of instances. Thus: "Everybody is speeding! I'm just trying to keep up with traffic!" *When we rely on numbers of instances to justify wrongdoing, we are guilty of a common-practice appeal.* Here are some examples of the common-practice appeal in moral arguments: "Cheating on your income tax is all right because just about everyone else does it"; "Premarital sex is moral because it has become pretty much an accepted practice"; "Political corruption is not necessarily immoral, for there is such a wide occurrence of it."

10. Slippery Slope

The slippery slope fallacy is the fallacy of objecting to something because you erroneously assume it will inevitably lead to an undesirable consequence. Thus, someone argues, "I'm not going to vote for national health insurance, because if that passes then it won't be long before the railroads and steel mills are nationalized and we have out-and-out socialism in the United States." The speaker is not objecting to national health insurance as much as to the socialism he assumes it will inevitably lead to. But this is not inevitable. The fact is that the passage of national health insurance does not necessitate socializing railroads, steel mills, or anything else for that matter. Each of these is a separate issue and must be advanced independently of a national health insurance program. True, one socialistic program may leave people psychologically disposed toward another socialistic program, but that is another issue.

The way to detect the slippery slope appeal is simply to ask yourself, "Must A inevitably lead to B?" If the answer is no, if the supposedly inevitable chain can be broken at any one link along the way, then the slippery slope fallacy is present.

Sometimes the slippery slope finds its way into moral issues. Thus, someone argues, "Euthanasia should not be legalized because that will lead to the murder of the mentally retarded, the congenitally diseased, the incorrigibly criminal, and all sorts of so-called socially undesirable elements." The fact is that legalized mercy deaths for the incurably ill and suffering do not necessarily lead to such morally dubious consequences at all.

Although avoiding these and other fallacies will help us keep ethical discourse on a rational level, it alone does not justify moral positions. Obviously Maria Josephson believes that demonstrating without a permit is in this instance moral, if not legal. But we really do not know why she believes this. Evidently her belief is connected with her conviction that racially unbalanced schools are immoral. She must justify this claim, after which she must then justify that intentionally breaking a law is moral. This she must do without relying on fallacies.

A similar problem faced Martin Luther King and faces all who must make a moral decision. It is one thing to claim, as King did, that segregationist laws are immoral; it is another to justify that claim. Opinions, beliefs, feelings, hunches, even convictions are relatively cheap commodities in the marketplace of ideas. But sound justification for them is rare. King attempted to provide such justification. Since his situation so closely resembles her own, Maria Josephson would do well to consider it. We would as well, for King's thinking exhibits an appreciation of three principles that characterize the moral reasoning and attitude of all ethicists. For simplicity, let's call these the *three don'ts of moral reasoning*.

THE THREE DON'TS OF MORAL REASONING

1. Don't Rely on Emotionalism

With a kind of sweet reasonableness, King outlines for his fellow clergymen the events leading up to Birmingham, how he and his supporters took steps prior to direct action, and why the criticisms of the clergymen are unfounded. It is true that there are moments in the letter when King relies on emotion, as when he recalls the impossibility of explaining to his six-year-old daughter why she can't go to the public amusement park that has just been advertised on television, and the agony he feels when he sees "tears welling up in her eyes when she is told that Funtown is closed to colored children, and . . . ominous clouds of inferiority beginning to form in her little mental sky."* But these emotional moments are rare and, sad to say, based on fact, not fantasy. More important, King uses such dramatic appeal to demonstrate the righteousness of his cause— that racial discrimination poisons a person's self-image and eventually relegates the person to the status of a thing. His is not emotionalism for emotionalism's sake; it is not merely an attempt to win minds by moving hearts.

Emotionalism is poison to almost any argument, certainly to moral ones. When we cast reason aside, we almost always becloud and distort ethical issues. This suggests a curious dimension about ethical judgments. For many of us, ethical judgments precede their reasons, because most of us inherit our moral positions. We generally adopt the moral postures of our parents, religions, societies, peer groups, and other influential social forces without query or quarrel. In this sense our ethics are based primarily on authorities. The result may be that in effect we are living others' lives; we are living according to a value system that we have never really examined and justified for ourselves. Because these forces are so much a part of our lives, we can very easily emotionalize moral positions that run against what we have been influenced to believe. And we can just as easily forget the second don't of moral reasoning.

---

*Martin Luther King, "Letter from Birmingham Jail," in *The Norton Reader*, rev. ed. (New York: Norton, 1969), p. 560.

2. Don't Rely on Popular Feeling to Determine Morality

We have already mentioned the fallacy of popularity. It bears underscoring. Implied in King's stand is the belief that we must never allow popular feeling or sentiment to decide what is morally right. In the case of segregationist laws, the overwhelming majority, including many church leaders in states practicing discrimination, openly or tacitly favored such laws. But this alone didn't make such laws moral. Popular opinion does not determine morality. Neither does a law that may be based on popular consent. We will say more of this shortly.

3. Don't Do Wrong

As do all moralists, King insists that once persons determine what is right they must do it and avoid wrong. Thus he writes, "I have heard numerous southern religious leaders admonish their worshipers to comply with a desegregation decision because it is the law, but I have longed to hear white ministers declare: 'Follow this decree because integration is morally right and because the Negro is your brother.'"* So, no matter what people will think of us or how they'll treat us, we must never do what is morally wrong.

These three features seem to characterize all moral reasoning: (1) avoid emotionalism, (2) avoid basing a moral decision only on popular sentiment, and (3) avoid wrong, no matter what the consequences. Admittedly, these are most general. Spelling them out in specific situations is often difficult. Let's see how King does it.

KING'S MORAL JUSTIFICATION OF CIVIL DISOBEDIENCE

The core of the King case is civil disobedience, his willful breaking of a city ordinance in order to dramatize its inequity and the inequity of racial segregation laws. The question is, Is King morally justified in breaking the ordinance? He believes that he is. More important, he thinks he can justify that belief.

At the outset King attempts to clarify, to avoid ambiguity. Thus, in providing his justification, King distinguishes between two types of law: just and unjust. He says, "I would be the first to advocate obeying just laws. One has not only a legal but a moral responsibility to obey just laws. Conversely, one has a moral responsibility to disobey unjust laws."† At this point, you may wish to question this assumption. If not, you must still wonder what is the difference between a just and an unjust law. This is the crux of the civil disobedience issue. It is a question that Maria Josephson and all engaging in civil disobedience must ultimately answer. King realizes this.

---

*King, "Letter from Birmingham Jail," p. 560.
†Ibid.

In distinguishing between a just and unjust law, King provides four criteria. By so doing he provides grounds for a rational discussion of the civil disobedience issue, which, like most moral questions, could otherwise founder in emotionalism.

First, King contends that the just law is a human-made code that squares with the law of God. An unjust law does not. Again, you might question this contention; certainly you would if you did not believe in God. King further argues that a law that uplifts human personality is just and that a law that degrades human personality is unjust. Since all segregation laws, according to King, degrade human personality, they are unjust. We could construct King's first argument this way:

If a law does not uplift personality, it is unjust.

A segregation law does not uplift personality.

Therefore, a segregation law is unjust.

King further describes a just law as one that a majority compels a minority to obey and also binds itself to obey. Segregation laws are the opposite of this. They bind a minority but not the majority that has formulated them. So, they are unjust. Thus, we can represent King's second argument:

If a majority formulates a law to bind a minority but not itself, that law is unjust.

Segregation laws are laws that a majority formulates to bind a minority but not itself.

Therefore, segregation laws are unjust.

In addition, King characterizes an unjust law as one that is inflicted on a minority that, as a result of being denied the right to vote, had no voice in the law's devising or enactment. Again, since segregation laws are of this kind, they are unjust. Thus, King's third argument is:

If a law is inflicted on a minority that, as a result of being denied the right to vote, had no voice in formulating it, then that law is unjust.

Segregation laws are inflicted on a minority that, as a result of being denied the right to vote, had no voice in formulating them.

Therefore, segregation laws are unjust.

Finally, King argues that a just law can be unjust in its application. This is crucial in this case because it is on this basis that he feels justified in willfully breaking the Birmingham ordinance. Remember: King has been arrested on a charge of parading without a permit. There is nothing intrinsically wrong with such an ordinance. But when the ordinance is used to deny citizens the First

Amendment privilege of peaceful assembly and protest, and thereby to maintain segregation, then it is unjust. King's argument might be constructed to read:

> If a law, which is intrinsically just, is used to deny citizens constitutional rights, then it is an unjust law.
>
> Birmingham's parading without a permit ordinance is a law that, on its face, is just, but in this case is being used to deny citizens constitutional rights.
>
> Therefore, Birmingham's parading without a permit ordinance in this case is an unjust law.

Of course, what is implied in King's stand is the third characteristic of all moral reasoning—that we should never do what is wrong. Obviously King believes that what is unjust is wrong. Therefore, he must not obey the law. To do so would be to act immorally. Conversely, to disobey it would be to act morally. Thus, his demonstration.

At this point we may wonder about some of the assumptions King makes. For example, in his first argument King assumes that if a law uplifts personality, then it is just. But why is a law that uplifts personality necessarily just? We could also wonder precisely what *uplifting personality* means. We could ask similar questions about the assumptions King makes in the next three arguments. In doing so we are beginning to wonder how basic ethical judgments and principles are to be justified. After all, the first statement in each of King's arguments is an assumption. On what basis are these assumptions themselves to be justified? If they are not justified, then they are questionable claims.

In his essay it is clear that King is using a law of God as the basis for his assumptions. But not all ethical judgments are so defended. Some ethicists would agree with King's decision, but for different reasons. They might argue that segregation laws are immoral because they are not in the best long-term interests of all people. Others might claim that what King did was immoral because his action was not in his own best long-term interests. Still others might argue that his action was moral because it was in his own best long-term interests. Furthermore, meta-ethicists would probably wonder precisely what the words *just* and *unjust* mean to begin with. When we raise such questions, we inevitably engage in full-scale philosophical debate about moral issues.

SUMMARY AND CONCLUSIONS

This concludes our opening remarks about ethics and ethical discourse. We now know what ethics is—the study of what constitutes good and bad human conduct, including related actions and values. We know that ethics divides into normative ethics and meta-ethics, and that the remainder of this book will concentrate on normative ethics. *Normative ethics* is the reasoned search for principles of human conduct. We paid particular attention to the phrase *reasoned search* in this definition.

Intimately connected with any reasoned search is the idea of justification. By *justification* we mean the reasons or defense for a position or belief. We saw that it is important to justify our moral beliefs, that is, to provide the reasons and demonstrate the reasoning process that go into them. Justification is particularly important in moral discourse because moral statements are unusual in the sense that they do not seem verifiable the way other statements are. As a result, the credibility of our moral views and actions frequently stands or falls on the soundness of our reasoning. When our reasoning is both valid and true, we can feel safe in our conclusions. Frequently undermining reasoning, however, are fallacies—incorrect ways of reasoning that often persuade for emotional or psychological reasons, but not for logical ones. Steering clear of fallacies will help us reason soundly.

As an example of one person's attempt to justify a moral stand, we considered Martin Luther King's "Letter from a Birmingham Jail." We noted in King's thinking three cautions to all who would attempt to formulate and justify moral beliefs: (1) don't be emotional, (2) don't appeal to popular feeling, and (3) don't do wrong.

Although King's defense for his civil disobedience leaves some questions unanswered, it nevertheless illustrates the most important point of this chapter. When we attempt to justify our ethical judgments, when we provide reasons for our moral positions, we stand a good chance of defining, exposing, clarifying, and examining the bases of our beliefs. Such exploration may provoke further ponderings, perhaps insoluble ones, but this should not frighten us. After all, in moral affairs it is unlikely that we can ever be certain of the truth of our beliefs. But there is inestimable consolation and strength in knowing that, as well as we can humanly determine, a particular value is a sound one and one worth living by.

Forsaking the attempt to justify our moral values, we seem destined to live with a chronic low-grade self-deceit: we will live according to values that are not essentially ours. In effect, we will live others' value systems.

Chief Dillon is perhaps a good example of this self-deceit. Evidently he has given the civil disobedience issue little thought. Rather, he chooses to base his stand on what appears to be a blind allegiance to the law. Maria Josephson, despite her apparent failure to think through the issue, at least perceives that what is legal is not necessarily moral. If nothing else, this insight impels her to a personal confrontation with the civil disobedience issue. This element of personal confrontation with moral issues is vital if we are to develop and justify our own ethical codes.

An important part of this process of reaching our own decision is familiarizing ourselves with the facets of an issue. The more we know about an issue, the better the basis for justifying our views. Civil disobedience is no exception.

EXERCISES FOR ANALYSIS

EXERCISE 1

Each of the following passages contains some sort of poor reasoning or arguing. Determine which of the fallacies discussed in chapter 1 occur in each item, and explain why you think so. Remember that there may be more than one fallacy present and that the material is open to interpretation.

1. "One of the most respected persons who ever lived was a civil disobedient—Mahatma Gandhi. I think that's proof positive that social protest is moral."

2. "The clearest demonstration that civil disobedience is at least sometimes right is that most people would agree it was."

3. **A:** Why do you think King was morally wrong at Birmingham?
   B: Because he broke the law.
   A: But why is law breaking necessarily morally wrong?
   B: Because to break a law is to disregard a rule by which people agree to live, and that's wrong.

4. "Some claim that terroristic activities are immoral. But I insist that if the opposition uses ruthless, brutal tactics to suppress dissent, then we are justified in reacting in kind."

5. "Since King was justified in protesting against racial injustice, it seems to me that civil disobedience is moral."

6. "Civil disobedience is wrong because it invariably leads to disorder and violence."

EXERCISE 2

Each of the following statements is a condensed general argument against or for the morality of civil disobedience.* Determine whether the justification provided for each conclusion is adequate. If it is not, why isn't it? Looking for fallacies would be a good place to begin your analysis.

Arguments against Civil Disobedience

1. A democracy by definition is a form of government in which the people rule. Ideally, in a democratic state laws should reflect the view of every citizen. Obvi-

---

*These have been inspired by, and reflect the sentiment of, those presented by Carl Wellman, *Morals & Ethics* (Glenview, Ill.: Scott, Foresman, 1975, pp. 6–13).

ously, it does not work out this way. People often disagree. So, democratic societies must approximate the ideal of democracy by following the will of the majority of their citizens. In practice, this means that some people, the minority, will labor under laws with which they do not agree. But for this minority to attempt to overthrow the rule of the majority would divert the state even further from its democratic ideal. Therefore, the minority, although disagreeing with a law, has a moral obligation to obey it. (Is there an appeal to popularity here? Does the arguer assume that an action which violates the will of the majority in a democracy is wrong?)

2. If an action encourages law breaking and violence, it produces serious social evils and is therefore wrong. Civil disobedience is an action that encourages law breaking and violence. This is particularly true if the civil disobedient happens to be someone that people admire and respect. Moreover, even though civil disobedients may not intend violence by their actions, they do intend to arouse a response to their cause, and those responding are not likely to practice the self-restraint that the original civil disobedients did. The result is inevitably violence. So, civil disobedience is wrong because it produces serious social evils by encouraging law breaking and violence. (Are there any questionable claims here? What about ambiguities?)

3. Civil disobedience is law breaking and law breaking is wrong. This is clear when you realize that, as members of society, all citizens have obligations stemming from an implied contractual agreement between individual and state. The nature of any society is that individuals form a political union for the purposes of safety, security, and prosperity. In exchange for these assurances, they willingly give up certain personal rights and assume certain obligations. Obeying the law would be one of these obligations. When people willfully break the law, as in civil disobedience, they violate the contractual agreement between individual and state. And this is always wrong.

4. No one says that a democracy is perfect. Certainly changes are always needed, even changes in laws. But a democracy by definition provides the machinery for change in terms of the rights of free speech, assembly, petition, even demonstration. These rights are available to minority and majority alike. Where these rights are available, civil disobedience is unnecessary. It is doing more than is required to effect change; it is needless tearing at the fabric of democracy. And since acts of unnecessary evil are wrong, civil disobedience is wrong.

5. Surely a cardinal principle in any ethical code is the recognition that any individual act is right only if every act that is exactly the same is also right. Thus, if an action is right, it can be universalized. Individual acts of civil disobedience cannot be universalized. Therefore, civil disobedience is not right. (To draw out this argument, consider this illustration of what the argument maintains. Suppose that it is right for a mother of a schoolchild to demonstrate at noon in a major city to protest forced busing. Then it must also be right for every mother of a schoolchild who finds herself in similar circumstances to do the same. In other words, the mother's action must be universalizable, that is, it can become a universal rule of human behavior. But imagine the social catastrophe that would result if every mother of a schoolchild appeared at high noon in downtown Boston.)

Arguments for Civil Disobedience

1. A person must always avoid what the person feels is wrong. Sometimes civil disobedience is the only effective way of avoiding evil. So, civil disobedience is sometimes right. (Can you think of an example to illustrate this argument?)

2. Civil disobedience is sometimes the only realistic way to remove a social evil. Therefore, civil disobedience is sometimes right. (To illustrate, consider the racist laws that persisted in the U.S. long after the Civil War, and in some cases persist today. An integral part of those laws was to deny the very ones victimized by them constitutional redress. The arguer would probably conclude that without the racial protest movement of the 1960s, legalized racism would have likely remained unchecked.)

3. Josephson: I think the strongest argument in favor of the rightness of civil disobedience is that it can be the only effective way of checking governmental authority over the individual.
Dillon: What do you mean?
Josephson: Well, what recourse does anyone have when they sincerely believe that the government has no legal or moral right to do what it's doing? Social protest, that's all. And, as far as I'm concerned, when social protest is calculated to curb excessive governmental power, it is right.

4. Of course there are many ways to voice opposition to what one views as wrong: speeches, letters to editors, running for office. But the history of social protest indicates that no method is more likely to capture the imagination and support of the people than civil disobedience. Today, when the media play such an influential role in molding public opinion, the dramatic appeal of civil disobedience is even more apparent. Thus, if by generating wide attention an action hastens the death of social evils, then it is right. Civil disobedience is an action that by generating widespread attention hastens the death of social evils. Therefore, civil disobedience is sometimes right.

SELECTIONS FOR FURTHER READING

Ethical Reasoning

Castaneda, H. N. *The Structure of Morality.* Springfield, Ill.: Thomas, 1973.

Grice, G. R. *The Grounds of Moral Judgment.* Cambridge: Cambridge University Press, 1962.

Richards, D. A. *A Theory of Reasons for Actions.* Oxford: Clarendon Press, 1971.

Taylor, Richard. *Good and Evil: A New Direction*. New York: Macmillan, 1970.

Toulmin, Stephen. *An Examination of the Place of Reason in Ethics*. Cambridge: Cambridge University Press, 1950.

Civil Disobedience

Bedau, H. A., ed. *Civil Disobedience: Theory and Practice*. New York: Pegasus, 1969.

Camus, Albert. *The Rebel*. Translated by A. Bower. New York: Knopf, 1954.

Cohen, Carl. *Civil Disobedience*. New York: Columbia University Press, 1971.

Hall, Robert Tom. *Morality of Civil Disobedience*. New York: Harper & Row, 1971.

Murphy, Jeffrie, ed. *Civil Disobedience and Violence*. Belmont, Calif.: Wadsworth, 1971.

Singer, Peter. *Democracy and Disobedience*. Oxford: Oxford University Press, 1973.

Zinn, Howard. *Disobedience and Democracy: Nine Fallacies in Law and Order*. New York: Random House, 1968.

READING

PLATO/ *The Crito*

Unlike many philosophers, Plato (427–347) wrote well. Using a dialogue technique, he devised conversations to illuminate philosophical questions. Playing a prominent role in these dialogues was Plato's teacher, Socrates.

Socrates (469–399) was eventually put to death for having "corrupted" the youth of Athens. One of the more fascinating aspects of Socrates' execution was that he could have avoided it. But rather than escape from prison, Socrates chose to remain and die. Why? Out of loyalty to the state that had raised and educated him. Socrates' is clearly a case of a person choosing a moral value and, in this case, dying for it.

In his dialogue entitled The Crito, *Plato demonstrates precisely how Socrates comes to his decision. The dialogue is set in prison while Socrates is awaiting execution and being urged by Crito, one of his students, to escape. Note as you read the dialogue how Socrates builds his argument for refusing to escape, how he justifies his moral decision. Socrates' argument hinges on what he views as an essential part of civil disobedience—that in breaking a law, even an unjust one, a person must be prepared to accept punishment for it. Would King have agreed with Socrates? Do you?*

Socrates: Why have you come at this hour, Crito? It must be quite early?

Crito: Yes, certainly.

Socrates: What is the exact time?

Crito: The dawn is breaking.

Socrates: I wonder that the keeper of the prison would let you in.

Crito: He knows me, because I often come, Socrates; moreover, I have done him a kindness.

Socrates: And are you only just arrived?

Crito: No, I came some time ago.

Socrates: Then why did you sit and say nothing, instead of at once awakening me?

Crito: I should not have liked myself, Socrates, to be in such great trouble and unrest as you are—indeed I should not: I have been watching with amazement your peaceful slumbers; and for that reason I did not awake you, because I wished to minimize the pain. I have always thought you to be of a happy disposition; but never did I see anything like the easy, tranquil manner in which you bear this calamity.

Socrates: Why, Crito, when a man has reached my age he ought not to be repining at the approach of death.

Crito: And yet other old men find themselves in similar misfortunes, and age does not prevent them from repining.

Socrates: That is true. But you have not told me why you come at this early hour.

Crito: I come to bring you a message

From Plato, *The Crito*, trans. B. Jowett, 3rd ed. (Oxford: Clarendon Press, 1892).

which is sad and painful; not, as I believe, to yourself, but to all of us who are your friends, and saddest of all to me.

Socrates: What? Has the ship come from Delos, on the arrival of which I am to die?

Crito: No, the ship has not actually arrived, but she will probably be here to-day, as persons who have come from Sunium tell me that they left her there; and therefore to-morrow, Socrates, will be the last day of your life.

Socrates: Very well, Crito; if such is the will of God, I am willing; but my belief is that there will be a delay of a day.

Crito: Why do you think so?

Socrates: I will tell you. I am to die on the day after the arrival of the ship.

Crito: Yes; that is what the authorities say.

Socrates: But I do not think that the ship will be here until to-morrow; this I infer from a vision which I had last night, or rather only just now, when you fortunately allowed me to sleep.

Crito: And what was the nature of the vision?

Socrates: There appeared to me the likeness of a woman, fair and comely, clothed in bright raiment, who called to me and said: O Socrates, 'The third day hence to fertile Phthia shalt thou go.'*

Crito: What a singular dream, Socrates!

Socrates: There can be no doubt about the meaning, Crito, I think.

Crito: Yes; the meaning is only too clear. But, oh! my beloved Soc-

rates, let me entreat you once more to take my advice and escape. For if you die I shall not only lose a friend who can never be replaced, but there is another evil: people who do not know you and me will believe that I might have saved you if I had been willing to give money, but that I did not care. Now, can there be a worse disgrace than this—that I should be thought to value money more than the life of a friend? For the many will not be persuaded that I wanted you to escape, and that you refused.

Socrates: But why, my dear Crito, should we care about the opinion of the many? Good men, and they are the only persons who are worth considering, will think of these things truly as they occurred.

Crito: But you see, Socrates, that the opinion of the many must be regarded, for what is now happening shows that they can do the greatest evil to any one who has lost their good opinion.

Socrates: I only wish it were so, Crito; and that the many could do the greatest evil; for then they would also be able to do the greatest good—and what a fine thing this would be! But in reality they can do neither; for they cannot make a man either wise or foolish; and whatever they do is the result of chance.

Crito: Well, I will not dispute with you; but please to tell me, Socrates, whether you are not acting out of regard to me and your other friends: are you not afraid that if you escape from prison we may get into trouble with the inform-

---

*Homer, *Il* ix. 363.

ers for having stolen you away, and lose either the whole or a great part of our property; or that even a worse evil may happen to us? Now, if you fear on our account, be at ease; for in order to save you, we ought surely to run this, or even a greater risk; be persuaded, then, and do as I say.

Socrates: Yes, Crito, that is one fear which you mention, but by no means the only one.

Crito: Fear not—there are persons who are willing to get you out of prison at no great cost; and as for the informers, they are far from being exorbitant in their demands—a little money will satisfy them. My means, which are certainly ample, are at your service, and if you have a scruple about spending all mine, here are strangers who will give you the use of theirs; and one of them, Simmias the Theban, has brought a large sum of money for this very purpose; and Cebes and many others are prepared to spend their money in helping you to escape. I say, therefore, do not hesitate on our account, and do not say, as you did in the court, that you will have a difficulty in knowing what to do with yourself anywhere else. For men will love you in other places to which you may go, and not in Athens only; there are friends of mine in Thessaly, if you like to go to them, who will value and protect you, and no Thessalian will give you any trouble. Nor can I think that you are at all justified, Socrates, in betraying your own life when you might be saved; in acting thus you are playing into the hands of your enemies, who are hurrying on your destruction. And further I should say that you are deserting your own children; for you might bring them up and educate them; instead of which you go away and leave them, and they will have to take their chance; and if they do not meet with the usual fate of orphans, there will be small thanks to you. No man should bring children into the world who is unwilling to persevere to the end in their nurture and education. But you appear to be choosing the easier part, not the better and manlier, which would have been more becoming in one who professes to care for virtue in all his actions, like yourself. And indeed, I am ashamed not only of you, but of us who are your friends, when I reflect that the whole business will be attributed entirely to our want of courage. The trial need never have come on, or might have been managed differently; and this last act, or crowning folly, will seem to have occurred through our negligence and cowardice, who might have saved you, if we had been good for anything; and you might have saved yourself, for there was no difficulty at all. See now, Socrates, how sad and discreditable are the consequences, both to us and you. Make up your mind then, or rather have your mind already made up, for the time of deliberation is over, and there is only one thing to be done, which must be done this very night, and if we delay at all will be no longer practicable or possible; I beseech you therefore, Socrates, be persuaded by me, and do as I say.

Socrates: Dear Crito, your zeal is invaluable, if a right one; but if wrong, the greater the zeal the greater the danger; and therefore we ought to consider whether I shall or shall not do as you say. For I am and always have been one of those natures who must be guided by reason, whatever the reason may be which upon reflection appears to me to be the best; and now that this chance has befallen me, I cannot repudiate my own words: the principles which I have hitherto honoured and revered I still honour, and unless we can at once find other and better principles, I am certain not to agree with you; no, not even if the power of the multitude could inflict many more imprisonments, confiscations, deaths, frightening us like children with hobgoblin terrors. What will be the fairest way of considering the question? Shall I return to your old argument about the opinions of men?—we were saying that some of them are to be regarded, and others not. Now were we right in maintaining this before I was condemned? And has the argument which was once good now proved to be talk for the sake of talking—mere childish nonsense? That is what I want to consider with your help, Crito:— whether, under my present circumstances, the argument appears to be in any way different or not; and is to be allowed by me or disallowed. That argument, which, as I believe, is maintained by many persons of authority, was to the effect, as I was saying, that the opinions of some men are to be regarded, and of other men not to be regarded. Now you, Crito, are not going to die tomorrow—at least, there is no human probability of this—and therefore you are disinterested and not liable to be deceived by the circumstances in which you are placed. Tell me then, whether I am right in saying that some opinions, and the opinions of some men only, are to be valued, and that other opinions, and the opinions of other men, are not to be valued. I ask you whether I was right in maintaining this?

Crito: Certainly.

Socrates: The good are to be regarded, and not the bad?

Crito: Yes.

Socrates: And the opinions of the wise are good, and the opinions of the unwise are evil?

Crito: Certainly.

Socrates: And what was said about another matter? Is the pupil who devotes himself to the practice of gymnastics supposed to attend to the praise and blame and opinion of every man, or of one man only—his physician or trainer, whoever he may be?

Crito: Of one man only.

Socrates: And he ought to fear the censure and welcome the praise of that one only, and not of the many?

Crito: Clearly so.

Socrates: And he ought to act and train, and eat and drink in the way which seems good to his single master who has understanding, rather than according to the opinion of all other men put together?

Crito: True.

Socrates: And if he disobeys and disregards the opinion and approval of the one, and regards the opinion of the many who have no understanding, will he not suffer evil?

Crito: Certainly he will.

Socrates: And what will the evil be, whither tending and what affecting, in the disobedient person?

Crito: Clearly, affecting the body; that is what is destroyed by the evil.

Socrates: Very good; and is not this true, Crito, of other things which we need not separately enumerate? In questions of just and unjust, fair and foul, good and evil, which are the subjects of our present consultation, ought we to follow the opinion of the many and to fear them; or the opinion of the one man who has understanding? ought we not to fear and reverence him more than all the rest of the world: and if we desert him shall we not destroy and injure that principle in us which may be assumed to be improved by justice and deteriorated by injustice;—there is such a principle?

Crito: Certainly there is, Socrates.

Socrates: Take a parallel instance:— if, acting under the advice of those who have no understanding, we destroy that which is improved by health and is deteriorated by disease, would life be worth having? And that which has been destroyed is—the body?

Crito: Yes.

Socrates: Could we live, having an evil and corrupted body?

Crito: Certainly not.

Socrates: And will life be worth having, if that higher part of man be destroyed, which is improved by justice and depraved by injustice? Do we suppose that principle, whatever it may be in man, which has to do with justice and injustice, to be inferior to the body?

Crito: Certainly not.

Socrates: More honourable than the body?

Crito: Far more.

Socrates: Then, my friend, we must not regard what the many say of us: but what he, the one man who has understanding of just and unjust, will say, and what the truth will say. And therefore you begin in error when you advise that we should regard the opinion of the many about just and unjust, good and evil, honourable and dishonourable.—"Well," someone will say, "but the many can kill us."

Crito: Yes, Socrates; that will clearly be the answer.

Socrates: And it is true: but still I find with surprise that the old argument is unshaken as ever. And I should like to know whether I may say the same of another proposition—that not life, but a good life, is to be chiefly valued?

Crito: Yes, that also remains unshaken.

Socrates: And a good life is equivalent to a just and honourable one—that holds also?

Crito: Yes, it does.

Socrates: From these premises I proceed to argue the question whether I ought or ought not to try and escape without the consent of the Athenians: and if I am clearly right in escaping, then I will make the attempt; but if not, I will abstain. The other considerations which you mention, of money and loss of character and the duty of educating one's children, are, I fear, only the doctrines of the multitude, who would be as ready to restore people to life, if they were able, as they are to put them to death—and with as little reason. But now, since the argument has thus far prevailed, the only question which remains to be considered is, whether we shall do rightly either in escaping or in suffering others to aid in our escape and paying them in money and thanks, or whether in reality we shall not do rightly; and if the latter, then death or any other calamity which may ensue on my remaining here must not be allowed to enter into the calculation.

Crito: I think that you are right, Socrates; how then shall we proceed?

Socrates: Let us consider the matter together, and do you either refute me if you can, and I will be convinced; or else cease, my dear friend, from repeating to me that I ought to escape against the wishes of the Athenians: for I highly value your attempts to persuade me to do so, but I may not be persuaded against my own better judgment. And now please to consider my first position, and try how you can best answer me.

Crito: I will.

Socrates: Are we to say that we are never intentionally to do wrong, or that in one way we ought and in another way we ought not to do wrong, or is doing wrong always evil and dishonourable, as I was just now saying, and as has been already acknowledged by us? Are all our former admissions which were made within a few days to be thrown away? And have we, at our age, been earnestly discoursing with one another all our life long only to discover that we are no better than children? Or, in spite of the opinion of the many, and in spite of consequences whether better or worse, shall we insist on the truth of what was then said, that injustice is always an evil and dishonour to him who acts unjustly? Shall we say so or not?

Crito: Yes.

Socrates: Then we must do no wrong?

Crito: Certainly not.

Socrates: Nor when injured injure in return, as the many imagine; for we must injure no one at all?

Crito: Clearly not.

Socrates: Again, Crito, may we do evil?

Crito: Surely not, Socrates.

Socrates: And what of doing evil in return for evil, which is the morality of the many—is that just or not?

Crito: Not just.

Socrates: For doing evil to another is the same as injuring him?

Crito: Very true.

Socrates: Then we ought not to retaliate or render evil for evil to any one, whatever evil we may have suffered from him. But I would have you consider, Crito, whether you really mean what you are saying. For this opinion has never been held, and never will be held, by any considerable number of persons; and those who are agreed and those who are not agreed upon this point have no common ground, and can only despise one another when they see how widely they differ. Tell me, then, whether you agree with and assent to my first principle, that neither injury nor retaliation nor warding off evil by evil is ever right. And shall that be the premise of our argument? Or do you decline and dissent from this? For so I have ever thought, and continue to think; but, if you are of another opinion, let me hear what you have to say. If, however, you remain of the same mind as formerly, I will proceed to the next step.

Crito: You may proceed, for I have not changed my mind.

Socrates: Then I will go on to the next point, which may be put in the form of a question:—Ought a man to do what he admits to be right, or ought he to betray the right?

Crito: He ought to do what he thinks right.

Socrates: But if this is true, what is the application? In leaving the prison against the will of the Athenians, do I wrong any? or rather do I not wrong those whom I ought least to wrong? Do I not desert the principles which were acknowledged by us to be just—what do you say?

Crito: I cannot tell, Socrates; for I do not know.

Socrates: Then consider the matter in this way:—Imagine that I am about to play truant (you may call the proceeding by any name which you like), and the laws and the government come and interrogate me: "Tell us, Socrates," they say; "what are you about? are you not going by an act of yours to overturn us—the laws, and the whole state, as far as in you lies? Do you imagine that a state can subsist and not be overthrown, in which the decisions of law have no power, but are set aside and tramped upon by individuals?" What will be our answer, Crito, to these and the like words? Any one, and especially a rhetorician, will have a good deal to say on behalf of the law which requires a sentence to be carried out. He will argue that this law should not be set aside; and shall we reply, "Yes; but the state has injured us and given an unjust sentence." Suppose I say that?

Crito: Very good, Socrates.

Socrates: "And was that our agreement with you?" the law would answer; "or were you to abide by the sentence of the state?" And if I were to express my astonishment at their words, the law would probably add: "Answer, Socrates, instead of opening your eyes—you are in the habit of asking and answering questions. Tell us,—What complaint have you to make against us which justifies you in attempting to destroy us and the state? In the first place did we not bring you into existence? Your father married your mother by our aid and begat you. Say whether you have any objection to urge against those of us who regulate marriage?'' None, I should reply. ''Or against those of us who after birth regulate the nurture and education of children, in which you also were trained? Were not the laws, which have the charge of education, right in commanding your father to train you in music and gymnastics?'' Right, I should reply. ''Well then, since you were brought into the world and nurtured and educated by us, can you deny in the first place that you are our child and slave, as your fathers were before you? And if this is true you are not on equal terms with us; nor can you think that you have a right to do to us what we are doing to you. Would you have any right to strike or revile or do any other evil to your father or your master, if you had one, because you have been struck or reviled by him, or received some other evil at his hands?—you would not say this? And because we think right to destroy you, do you think that you have any right to destroy us in return, and your country as far as in you lies? Will you, O professor of true virtue, pretend that you are justified in this? Has a philosopher like you failed to discover that our country is more to be valued and higher and holier far than mother or father or any ancestor, and more to be regarded in the eyes of the gods and of men of understanding? also to be soothed, and gently and reverently entreated when angry, even more than a father, and either to be persuaded, or if not persuaded, to be obeyed? And when we are punished by her, whether with imprisonment or stripes, the punishment is to be endured in silence; and if she lead us to wounds or death in battle, thither we follow as is right; neither may any one yield or retreat or leave his rank, but whether in battle or in a court of law, or in any other place, he must do what his city and his country order him; or he must change their view of what is just: and if he may do no violence to his father or mother, much less may he do violence to his country.'' What answer shall we make to this, Crito? Do the laws speak truly, or do they not?

Crito: I think that they do.

Socrates: Then the laws will say; ''Consider, Socrates, if we are speaking truly that in your present attempt you are going to do us an injury. For, having brought you into the world, and nurtured and educated you, and given you and every other citizen a share in every good which we had to give, we further proclaim to any Athenian by the liberty which we allow him, that if he does not like us when he has become of age and has seen the ways of the city, and made our acquaintance, he may go where he pleases and take his goods with him. None of us laws will forbid him or interfere with him. Any one who does not like us and the city, and who wants to emigrate to a colony or to any other city, may go where he likes, retaining his property. But he who has experience of the manner in which we order justice and administer the state, and still remains, has entered into an implied contract that he will do as we command him. And he who disobeys us is, as we maintain, thrice wrong; first, because in disobeying us he is disobeying his parents; secondly, because we are the authors of his education; thirdly, because he has made an agreement with us that he will duly obey our command; and he neither obeys them or convinces us that our commands are unjust; and we do not rudely impose them, but give him the alternative of obeying or convincing us;—that is what we offer, and he does neither.

"These are the sort of accusations to which, as we were saying, you, Socrates, will be exposed if you accomplish your intentions; you, above all other Athenians." Suppose now I ask, why I rather than anybody else? they will justly retort upon me that I above all other men have acknowledged the agreement. "There is clear proof," they will say, "Socrates, that we and the city were not displeasing to you. Of all Athenians you have been the most constant resident in the city, which, as you never leave, you may be supposed to love. For you never went out of the city either to see the games, except once when you went to Isthmus, or to any other place unless when you were on military service; nor did you travel as other men do. Nor had you any curiosity to know other states or their laws: your affections did not go beyond us and our state; we were your special favourites, and you acquiesced in our government of you; and here in this city you begat your children, which is a proof of your satisfaction. Moreover, you might in the course of the trial, if you had liked, have fixed the penalty at banishment; the state which refuses to let you go now would have let you go then. But you pretended that you preferred death to exile, and that you were not unwilling to die. And now you have forgotten these fine sentiments, and pay no respect to us the laws, of whom you are the destroyer; and are doing what only a miserable slave would do, running away and turning your back upon the compacts and agreements which you made as a citizen. And first of all answer this very question: Are we right in saying that you agreed to be governed according to us in deed, and not in word only? Is that true or not?" How shall we answer, Crito? Must we not assent?

Crito: We cannot help it, Socrates.

Socrates: Then will they not say: "You, Socrates, are breaking the covenants and agreements which you made with us at your leisure, not in any haste or under any compulsion or deception, but after you have had seventy years to think of them, during which time you were at liberty to leave the city, if we were not to your mind, or if our covenants appeared to you to be unfair. You had your choice, and might have gone either to Lacedaemon or Crete, both which states are often praised by you for their good government, or to some other Hellenic or foreign state. Whereas you, above all other Athenians, seemed to be so fond of the state, or, in other words, of us her laws (and who would care about a state which has no laws?), that you never stirred out of her; the halt, the blind, the maimed were not more stationary in her than you were. And now you run away and forsake your agreements. Not so, Socrates, if you will take our advice; do not make yourself ridiculous by escaping out of the city.

"For just consider, if you transgress and err in this sort of way, what good will you do either to yourself or to your friends? That your friends will be driven into exile and deprived of citizenship, or will lose their property, is tolerably certain; and you yourself, if you fly to one of the neighbouring cities, as, for example, Thebes or Megara, both of which are well governed, will come to them as an enemy, Socrates, and their government will be against you, and all patriotic citizens will cast an evil eye upon you as a subverter of the laws, and you will confirm in the minds of the judges the justice of their own condemnation of you. For he who is a corrupter of the laws is more than likely to be a corrupter of the young and foolish portion of mankind. Will you then flee from well-ordered cities and virtuous men? and is existence worth having on these terms? Or will you go to them without shame, and talk to them, Socrates? And what will you say to them? What you say here about virtue and justice and institutions and laws being the best things among men? Would that be decent of you? Surely not. But if you go away from well-governed states to Crito's friends in Thessaly, where there is great disorder and licence, they will be charmed to hear the tale of your escape from prison, set off with ludicrous particulars of the manner in which you were wrapped in a goatskin or some other disguise, and metamorphosed as the manner is of runaways; but will there be no one to remind you that in your old age you were not ashamed to violate the most sacred laws from a miserable desire of a little more life? Perhaps not, if you keep them in a good temper; but if they are out of temper you will hear many degrading things; you will live, but how?— as the flatterer of all men, and the servant of all men; and doing what?—eating and drinking in Thessaly, having gone abroad in order that you may get a dinner. And where will be your fine sentiments about justice and virtue? Say that you wish to live for the sake of your children—you want to bring them up and educate them—will you take them into Thessaly and deprive them of Athenian citizenship? Is this the benefit which you will confer upon them? Or are you under the impression that they will be better cared for and educated here if you are still alive, although absent from them; for your friends will take care of them? Do you fancy that if you are an inhabitant of Thessaly they will take care of them, and if you are an inhabitant of the other world that they will not take care of them? Nay; but if they who call themselves friends are good for anything, they will—to be sure they will.

"Listen, then, Socrates, to us who have brought you up. Think not of life and children first, and of justice afterwards, but of justice first, that you may be justified before the princes of the world below. For neither will you nor any that belong to you be happier or holier or juster in this life, or happier in another, if you do as Crito bids. Now you depart in innocence, a sufferer and not a doer of evil; a victim, not of the laws but of men. But if you go forth, returning evil for evil, and injury for injury, breaking the covenants and agreements which you have made with us, and wronging those whom you ought least of all to wrong, that is to say, yourself, your friends, your country, and us, we shall be angry with you while you live, and our brethren, the laws in the world below, will receive you as an enemy; for they will know that you have done your best to destroy us. Listen, then, to us and not to Crito."

This, dear Crito, is the voice which I seem to hear murmuring in my ears, like the sound of the flute in the ears of the mystic; that voice, I say, is humming in my ears, and prevents me from hearing any other. And I know that anything more which you may say will be vain. Yet speak, if you have anything to say.

Crito: I have nothing to say, Socrates.

Socrates: Leave me then, Crito, to fulfil the will of God, and to follow whither he leads.

THOREAU/ *Civil Disobedience*

It seems that all self-respecting civil disobedients eventually do time. The American author and poet Henry David Thoreau (1817–1862) was no exception. Thoreau believed that the U.S. government had exceeded its constitutional power in waging a war against Mexico. He also believed the government had acted immorally by not abolishing slavery. So, he decided to protest by not paying his taxes. As a result, Thoreau ended up in jail.

Unlike Socrates, Thoreau was anarchic in his thinking: he believed that the best government is the one that governs least; a person's primary loyalty is to one's own nature. He claimed that unjust laws should not be obeyed and that conscience, not popular feeling, should be the basis of law. He developed his theory of civil disobedience in a work appropriately entitled Civil Disobedience (1849), *from which a selection follows.*

Follow Thoreau's line of argument and detect, if you can, any fallacies that he commits. Although both Socrates and Thoreau believe civil disobedience can be moral, at what points do you think their justifications differ?

I heartily accept the motto,—"That government is best which governs least;" and I should like to see it acted up to more rapidly and systematically. Carried out, it finally amounts to this, which also I believe,—"That government is best which governs not at all;" and when men are prepared for it, that will be the kind of government which they will have. Government is at best but an expedient; but most governments are usually, and all governments are sometimes, inexpedient. The objections which have been brought against a standing army, and they are many and weighty, and deserve to prevail, may also at last be brought against a standing government. The standing army is only an arm of the standing government. The government itself, which is only the mode which the people have chosen to execute their will, is equally liable to be abused and perverted before the people can act through it. Witness the present Mexican war, the work of comparatively a few individuals using the standing government as their tool; for, in the outset, the people would not have consented to this measure.

This American government,—what is it but a tradition, though a recent one, endeavoring to transmit itself unimpaired to posterity, but each instant losing some of its integrity? It has not the vitality and force of a single living man; for a single man can bend it to his will. It is a sort of wooden gun to the people themselves. But it is not the less necessary for this; for the people must have some complicated machinery or

Abridged from Henry David Thoreau, *Civil Disobedience* (Boston: 1849).

other, and hear its din, to satisfy that idea of government which they have. Governments show thus how successfully men can be imposed on, even impose on themselves, for their own advantage. It is excellent, we must all allow. Yet this government never of itself furthered any enterprise, but by the alacrity with which it got out of its way. *It* does not keep the country free. *It* does not settle the West. *It* does not educate. The character inherent in the American people has done all that has been accomplished; and it would have done somewhat more, if the government had not sometimes got in its way. For government is an expedient by which men would fain succeed in letting one another alone; and, as has been said, when it is most expedient, the governed are most let alone by it. Trade and commerce, if they were not made of India-rubber, would never manage to bounce over the obstacles which legislators are continually putting in their way; and, if one were to judge these men wholly by the effects of their actions and not partly by their intentions, they would deserve to be classed and punished with those mischievous persons who put obstructions on the railroads.

But, to speak practically and as a citizen, unlike those who call themselves no-government men, I ask for, not at once no government, but *at once* a better government. Let every man make known what kind of government would command his respect, and that will be one step toward obtaining it.

After all, the practical reason why, when the power is once in the hands of the people, a majority are permitted, and for a long period continue, to rule is not because they are most likely to be in the right, nor because this seems fairest to the minority, but because they are physically the strongest. But a government in which the majority rule in all cases cannot be based on justice, even as far as men understand it. Can there not be a government in which majorities do not virtually decide right and wrong, but conscience?—in which majorities decide only those questions to which the rule of expediency is applicable?

Must the citizen ever for a moment, or in the very least degree, resign his conscience to the legislator? Why has every man a conscience, then? I think that we should be men first, and subjects afterward. It is not desirable to cultivate a respect for the law, so much as for the right. The only obligation which I have a right to assume is to do at any time what I think right. It is truly enough said, that a corporation has no conscience; but a corporation of conscientious men is a corporation *with* a conscience. Law never made men a whit more just; and, by means of their respect for it, even the well-disposed are daily made the agents of injustice. A common and natural result of an undue respect for law is, that you may see a file of soldiers, colonel, captain, corporal, privates, powder-monkeys, and all, marching in admirable order over hill and dale to the wars, against their wills, ay, against their common sense and consciences, which makes it very steep marching indeed, and produces a palpitation of the heart. They have no doubt that it is a damnable business in which they are concerned; they are all peaceably inclined. Now, what are they? Men at all? Or small movable forts and magazines, at the service of some unscrupulous man in power? Visit the Navy-yard, and behold a marine, such a man as an American government can make, or such as it can make a man with its black arts,—a mere shadow and reminiscence of humanity, a man laid out alive and standing, and already, as one may say, buried under arms with funeral accompaniments, thought it may be,—

Not a drum was heard, not a funeral note,
　As his corse to the rampart we hurried;
Not a soldier discharged his farewell shot
　O'er the grave where our hero we
　　buried.

The mass of men serve the state thus, not as men mainly, but as machines, with their bodies. They are the standing army, and the militia, jailors, constables, posse comitatus, etc. In most cases there is no free exercise whatever of the judgment or of the moral sense; but they put themselves on a level with wood and earth and stones; and wooden men can perhaps be manufactured that will serve the purpose as well. Such command no more respect than men of straw or a lump of dirt. They have the same sort of worth only as horses and dogs. Yet such as these even are commonly esteemed good citizens. Others—as most legislators, politicians, lawyers, ministers, and office-holders—serve the state chiefly with their head; and, as they rarely make any moral distinctions, they are as likely to serve the Devil, without *intending* it, as God. A very few, as heroes, patriots, martyrs, reformers in the great sense, and *men*, serve the state with their consciences also, and so necessarily resist it for the most part; and they are commonly treated as enemies by it. A wise man will only be useful as a man, and will not submit to be "clay," and "stop a hole to keep the wind away," but leave that office to his dust at least:—

I am too high-born to be propertied,
To be a secondary at control,
Or useful serving-man and instrument
To any sovereign state throughout the
　world.

He who gives himself entirely to his fellow-men appears to them useless and selfish; but he who gives himself partially to them is pronounced a benefactor and philanthropist.

How does it become a man to behave toward this American government to-day? I cannot for an instant recognize that political organization as *my* government which is the *slave's* government also.

All men recognize the right of revolution; that is, the right to refuse allegiance to, and to resist, the government, when its tyranny or its inefficiency are great and unendurable. But almost all say that such is not the case now. But such was the case, they think, in the Revolutions of '75. If one were to tell me that this was a bad government because it taxed certain foreign commodities brought to its ports, it is most probable that I should not make an ado about it, for I can do without them. All machines have their friction; and possibly this does enough good to counterbalance the evil. At any rate, it is a great evil to make a stir about it. But when the friction comes to have its machine, and oppression and robbery are organized, I say, let us not have such a machine any longer. In other words, when a sixth of the population of a nation which has undertaken to be the refuge of liberty are slaves, and a whole country is unjustly overrun and conquered by a foreign army, and subjected to military law, I think that it is not too soon for honest men to rebel and revolutionize. What makes this duty the more urgent is the fact that the country so overrun is not our own, but ours is the invading army. . . .

Unjust laws exist: shall we be content to obey them, or shall we endeavor to amend them, and obey them until we have succeeded, or shall we transgress them at once? Men generally, under such a government as this, think that they ought to wait until they have persuaded the majority to alter them. They think that, if they should resist, the remedy would be worse than the evil. But it is the fault of the government itself that the remedy *is* worse than the evil. *It* makes it worse. Why is it not more apt to anticipate and provide for reform? Why does it not cherish its wise minority? Why does it cry and resist before it is hurt? Why does it not encourage its citizens to be on the alert to point out its faults and *do* better than it would have them? Why does it always crucify Christ, and excommunicate Copernicus and Luther, and pronounce Washington and Franklin rebels?

One would think, that a deliberate and practical denial of its authority was the only offense never contemplated by government; else, why has it not assigned its definite, its suitable and proportionate penalty? If a man who has no property refuses but once to earn nine shillings for the state, he is put in prison for a period unlimited by any law that I know, and determined only by the discretion of those who placed him there; but if he should steal ninety times nine shillings from the state, he is soon permitted to go at large again.

If the injustice is part of the necessary friction of the machine of government, let it go, let it go; perchance it will wear smooth,—certainly the machine will wear out. If the injustice has a spring, or a pulley, or a rope, or a crank, exclusively for itself, then perhaps you may consider whether the remedy will not be worse than the evil; but if it is such a nature that it requires you to be the agent of injustice to another, then, I say, break the law. Let your life be a counter friction to stop the machine. What I have to do is to see, at any rate, that I do not lend myself to the wrong which I condemn.

As for adopting the ways which the state has provided for remedying the evil, I know not of such ways. They take too much time, and a man's life will be gone. I have other affairs to attend to. I came into this world, not chiefly to make this a good place to live in, but to live in it, be it good or bad. A man has not everything to do, but something; and because he cannot do *everything*, it is not necessary that he should do *something* wrong. It is not my business to be petitioning the Governor or the Legislature any more than it is theirs to petition me; and if they should not hear my petition, what should I do then? But in this case the state has provided no way: its very Constitution is the evil. This may seem to be harsh and stubborn and unconciliatory; but it is to treat with the utmost kindness and consideration the only spirit that can appreciate or deserves it. So is all change for the better, like birth and death, which convulse the body.

I do not hesitate to say, that those who call themselves Abolitionists should at once effectually withdraw their support, both in person and property, from the government of Massachusetts and not wait till they constitute a majority of one, before they suffer the right to prevail through them. I think that it is enough if they have God on their side, without waiting for that other one. Moreover, any man more right than his neighbors constitutes a majority of one already.

I meet this American government, or its representative, the state government, directly, and face to face, once a year—no more—in the person of its tax-gatherer; this is the only mode in which a man situated as I am necessarily meets it; and it then says distinctly, Recognize me; and the simplest, most effectual, and, in the present posture of affairs, the indispensablest mode of treating with it on this head, of expressing your little satisfaction with and love for it, is to deny it then. My civil neighbor, the tax-gatherer, is the very man I have to deal with,—for it is, after all, with men and not with parchment that I quarrel,—and he has voluntarily chosen to be an agent of the government. How shall he ever know well what he is and does as an officer of the government, or as a man, until he is obliged to consider whether he shall treat me, his neighbor, for whom he has respect, as a neighbor and well-disposed man, or as a maniac and disturber of the peace, and see if he can get over this obstruction to his neighborliness without a ruder and more

impetuous thought or speech corresponding with his action. I know this well, that if one thousand, if one hundred, if ten men whom I could name,—if ten *honest* men only,—ay, if *one* HONEST man, in this State of Massachusetts, *ceasing* to *hold* slaves, were actually to withdraw from this copartnership, and be locked up in the county jail therefor, it would be the abolition of slavery in America. For it matters not how small the beginning may seem to be: what is once well done is done forever. But we love better to talk about it: that we say is our mission. Reform keeps many scores of newspapers in its service, but not one man. If my esteemed neighbor, the State's ambassador, who will devote his days to the settlement of the question of human rights in the Council Chamber, instead of being threatened with the prisons of Carolina, were to sit down the prisoner of Massachusetts, that State which is so anxious to foist the sin of slavery upon her sister,— though at present she can discover only an act of inhospitality to be the ground of a quarrel with her,—the Legislature would not wholly waive the subject the following winter.

Under a government which imprisons any unjustly, the true place for a just man is also a prison. The proper place to-day, the only place which Massachusetts has provided for her freer and less desponding spirits, is in her prisons, to be put out and locked out of the State by her own act, as they have already put themselves out by their principles. It is there that the fugitive slave, and the Mexican prisoner on parole, and the Indian come to plead the wrongs of his race should find them; on that separate, but more free and honorable ground, where the State places those who are not *with* her, but *against* her,—the only house in a slave State in which a free man can abide with honor. If any think that their influence would be lost there, and their voices no longer afflict the ear of the State, that they would not be as an enemy within its walls, they do not know by how much truth is stronger than error, nor how much more eloquently and effectively he can combat injustice who has experienced a little in his own person. Cast your whole vote, not a strip of paper merely, but your whole influence. A minority is powerless while it conforms to the majority; it is not even a minority then; but it is irresistible when it clogs by its whole weight. If the alternative is to keep all just men in prison, or give up war and slavery, the State will not hesitate which to choose. If a thousand men were not to pay their tax-bills this year, that would not be a violent and bloody measure, as it would be to pay them, and enable the State to commit violence and shed innocent blood. This is, in fact, the definition of a peaceable revolution, if any such is possible. If the tax-gatherer, or any other public officer, asks me, as one has done, "But what shall I do?" my answer is, "If you really wish to do anything, resign your office." When the subject has refused allegiance, and the officer has resigned his office, then the revolution is accomplished. But even suppose blood should flow. Is there not a sort of blood shed when the conscience is wounded? Through this wound a man's real manhood and immortality flow out, and he bleeds to an everlasting death. I see this blood flowing now. . . .

When I converse with the freest of my neighbors, I perceive that, whatever they may say about the magnitude and seriousness of the question, and their regard for the public tranquillity, the long and the short of the matter is, that they cannot spare the protection of the existing government, and they dread the consequences to their property and families of disobedience to it. For my own part, I should not like to think that I ever rely on the protection of the State. But, if I deny the authority of the State when it presents its tax-bill, it will soon take and waste all my property, and so harass me and my children without end. This is hard. This makes it possible for a man to live honestly, and at the same time comfortably, in outward respects. It will not be worth the while to accumulate property; that would be sure to go again. You must hire or squat somewhere, and raise but a small crop, and eat that soon. You must live within yourself, and depend upon yourself always tucked up and ready for a start, and not have many affairs. A man may grow rich in Turkey even, if he will be in all respects a good subject of the Turkish government. Confucius said: "If a State is governed by the principles of reason, poverty and misery are subjects of shame; if a state is not governed by the principles of reason, riches and honors are the subjects of shame." . . . It costs me less in every sense to incur the penalty of disobedience to the State than it would to obey. I should feel as if I were worth less in that case. . . .

Thus, the State never intentionally confronts a man's sense, intellectual or moral, but only his body, his senses. It is not armed with superior wit or honesty, but with superior physical strength. I was not born to be forced. I will breathe after my own fashion. Let us see who is the strongest. What force has a multitude? They only can force me who obey a higher law than I. They force me to become like themselves. I do not hear of *men* being *forced* to live this way or that by masses of men. What sort of life were that to live? When I meet a government which says to me, "Your money or your life," why should I be in haste to give it my money? It may be in a great strait, and not know what to do: I cannot help that. It must help itself; do as I do. It is not worth the while to snivel about it. I am not responsible for the successful working of the machinery of society. I am not the son of the engineer. I perceive that, when an acorn and a chestnut fall side by side, the one does not remain inert to make way for the other, but both obey their own laws, and spring and grow and flourish as best they can, till one, perchance, overshadows and destroys the other. If a plant cannot live according to its nature, it dies; and so a man.

2

EUTHANASIA
of dignity and death
DEFINITIONS, ABSOLUTISM, RELATIVISM

On an April night in 1975, shortly after drinking a gin and tonic with friends, twenty-one-year-old Karen Ann Quinlan mysteriously collapsed. Earlier she had taken some tranquilizers. The combination caused her to "nod out" according to one of her friends, who took her back to a house she was visiting. There he attempted but failed to revive her.

A year later, in a hospital in New Jersey, Karen Quinlan lay curled in a fetal position and fell to less than half of her normal 120 pounds. Her eyes were open but she did not see. Every few seconds her body convulsed slightly as an artificial respirator connected to her windpipe forced her lungs to work, which enabled her to maintain what doctors described as a "chronic vegetative state." Her heart beat; her brain, though permanently damaged, emitted faint but steady signals visible on an electroencephalogram (EEG).

Karen's case raises medical and legal problems that have been complicated by our technological ability to keep gravely injured and irreparably damaged persons at a minimal state of survival. At what point, if any, does an incurable illness become a living death? Is it permissible for someone's life to be deliberately terminated? Who, if anyone, should make such a decision?

It is helpful here to distinguish between active and passive as well as involuntary and voluntary euthanasia. Active euthanasia refers to the process by which one kills another by direct means, such as injecting a poison into the veins. Passive euthanasia is the process by which a person is allowed to die as a result of the removal of artificial life support systems or the failure to provide such systems. Clearly, passive euthanasia is involved in the Quinlan case.

The kind of euthanasia that most moralists advocate today is voluntary euthanasia. This means that a person desires and freely consents to either active or passive euthanasia. Involuntary euthanasia, on the other hand, is when the person has not expressed a desire for or does not freely consent to either active or passive euthanasia. In what follows, *euthanasia* will be used in the voluntary sense.

Some argue that the morality of euthanasia depends solely on definitions, that it is first necessary to define what it means for a human to be alive. This is seldom easy. Until recently, two elements were considered in rulings of life or death: whether the heart was beating and whether the individual could breathe sporadically. Today, however, most medical authorities place at least as much importance on the condition of the brain. If there is (1) no spontaneous respiration, (2) no reflexive response to external stimuli or to pain, and (3) no brain activity recorded on an EEG as checked by one observer and then by another twenty-four hours later, the patient is considered dead, even though a machine may be keeping the person "alive." Some might argue that if a definition of life is formulated and the patient's condition satisfies that definition, then the patient is a living human and it is immoral to kill such a person. Conversely, if the patient's condition does not satisfy the definition, then the person is not a living human; therefore, it is moral to terminate the person's vegetative state. Though strictly logical, these conclusions, like most in the moral sphere drawn from definitional assumptions, are morally controversial.

To illustrate, suppose a society of blue-eyed individuals decided that a defining characteristic of being human is having blue eyes. Anyone without blue eyes by definition is nonhuman and therefore does not enjoy the conventional moral proprieties that blue-eyed individuals extend toward fellow humans. Since by definition brown-eyed individuals are not humans, the blue-eyed population decides to exterminate them. Is their behavior moral?

Of course, this example is not analogous to cases like Karen Quinlan's. But it does illustrate the danger of drawing conclusions based on assumptions. Any definition is an assumption in the sense that individuals agree to understand an entity in the same way. History records the tragic consequences of such thinking, perhaps the best example being Hitler's systematic attempt to exterminate the Jews. Based on Hitler's definition, Jews simply were not human. It followed that the moral conventions one human extended to another did not apply to a Nazi with respect to a Jew.

Again, Nazi treatment of Jews is not analogous to euthanasia cases. Nevertheless, it focuses on a key question in the euthanasia issue: is the morality of mercy killing simply a definitional matter? Having defined human life, can a society infer that any behavior consistent with maintaining human life as defined is automatically moral? For example, if a patient does not satisfy any of the three agreed-upon criteria of human life except with the assistance of machinery, can we conclude that shutting down that machinery is not immoral?

Those who say yes frequently defend their stand by maintaining that morality is a matter of social convention to begin with. In short, what a group of people *believes* is right *is* right. This position is called *moral relativism*. Thus, if euthanasia is *thought* to be morally right, it *is* morally right; if it is thought to be wrong, it is wrong. Since moral relativism frequently is the basis for moral positions, we should closely consider it. But to understand moral relativism, we must understand its theoretical opposite, moral absolutism. Moral absolutism is the position of those who maintain that no matter what anyone thinks is right, there is an objective standard of right that determines the morality of an action. Thus, if euthanasia is wrong, it is wrong regardless of what anyone thinks; if it is right, it is right regardless of what anyone thinks.

One point before analyzing these positions. Moral relativism and absolutism are two very broad moral classifications that ease ethical understanding. Although opposed in theory, in practice moral relativists and absolutists could find themselves in agreement in much the same way that political liberals and conservatives might on political positions. For example, both moralists might claim that euthanasia is moral, but for different reasons. At the same time, relativists could disagree among themselves on an issue, and so could absolutists.

So, using euthanasia as a moral issue, in this chapter we zero in on a most fundamental ethical concern: does there exist a moral standard or code regardless of what anyone thinks, or is a moral standard synonymous with social convention? (Recall again what we said at the outset: any number of issues could be used to air a theoretical matter like relativism/absolutism. We have simply chosen euthanasia.)

ABSOLUTISM VERSUS RELATIVISM

To air the absolutistic and relativistic positions, let's hop aboard an early morning commuter special shuttling between Bridgeport, Connecticut, and New York City. On the train are two men, neither of whom is an ethicist; so, the terms *ethical absolutism* and *relativism* are not part of their vocabularies. But they are thoughtful and sensitive individuals who have been particularly moved by the Karen Quinlan case, which has occupied the news headlines for some weeks. The Supreme Court has rendered its decision; the men are curious about it. This curiosity is about to pitch them knee-deep into the absolutism/relativism debate.

George: You know, it's a funny thing. Another state court might have ruled differently. They could have denied the appeal.

Walter: Laws vary, George, and so do interpretations.

George: I know. But it just seems funny that what's wrong in one state is right in another.

Walter: It's all a matter of law, George.

George: No, I don't mean what's *legally* right or *socially* right. I mean what's *morally* right.

Walter: But what's morality other than what people agree is moral? If Montanans agree that euthanasia is immoral, then it's immoral. If New Jerseyans decide it's moral, then it's moral. I think it's that simple.

George: I can't see that. To me it's like saying if New Jerseyans believe that eating mushrooms is a cure for cancer then it is, and if Montanans believe that eating mushrooms is not a cure for cancer, then it's not.

Walter: I don't think it's like that at all. Science can prove if eating mushrooms can cure cancer. So, regardless of what anyone thinks, mushrooms are either a cure or not a cure for cancer.

George: But that's my point. Why shouldn't the same principle apply to ethics? It seems to me that euthanasia is either morally right or it's not right, regardless of what anyone thinks.

Clearly there's a fundamental difference between the thinking of Walter and George with respect to the nature of morality. George suggests that a moral law must exist that is independent of personal feelings. He's an absolutist. *Ethical absolutism is the ethical position which contends that there exists one and only one moral code.* Absolutists like George maintain that this code applies to everyone at all times everywhere. What is a duty for me must also be a duty for you. What's a duty for an aborigine must also be a duty for an Asian, Australian, or European. If euthanasia is wrong, it is wrong in Montana as well as in New Jersey, in Africa as well as Europe, in China as well as South America. The fact that a people may see nothing wrong with euthanasia or lying or cannibalism in no way affects the rightness or wrongness of such actions. According to absolutism, there is not one standard of moral behavior for Americans, another for Asians, and another for Europeans. There is but one code, one law, one standard, one morality for all persons. Not only does this standard have universal application, but it is not restricted by any considerations of time or period. What is right now was right thousands of years ago and will be right thousands of years hence, for all people everywhere.

A final point about ethical absolutism. Ethical absolutists are not necessarily committed to the position that their interpretation of the absolute standard is the true and valid one. Obviously they would *believe* that it is. But theoretically they must admit that they could be wrong, that another interpretation could be the correct one. All that absolutists are committed to is the position that there exists a true moral code and that this code is the same for all people in all ages.

In contrast to George, Walter appears to be a relativist. This does not mean that incest runs in Walter's family. *Ethical relativism may simply and generally be defined as the ethical position which denies that there is a single moral standard that is universally applicable to all people at all times.* Relativists deny that there exists only one moral code, law, principle, or standard. They insist that there are many moral codes that take root in diverse social soils and environments. As their name implies, relativists insist that any morality is relative to the time, place, and circumstances in which it occurs. In no way is such a code absolute.

Frequently people misunderstand ethical relativism and reduce it to a platitude. The platitude stems from the observation that the moral code of Orientals is obviously different from Europeans, which in turn is obviously different from New Guineans. Thus the platitude: history records the existence of many obviously different and often contradictory moral codes. Such an observation is a sociological fact, and although it may lend support to the relativistic thesis, it is not the thesis itself. Relativists like Walter are not merely saying that what is *thought* right in one part of the world is frequently thought wrong in another, which even absolutists would admit. What moral relativists assert is that precisely the same action that *is* right in one society at one time can be wrong in another. Putting to death anyone over eighty years old can be right in the jungles of New Guinea and wrong in the United States. This startling claim is entirely different from saying that putting octogenarians to death is *thought* to be right in one place and wrong in another.

For relativists, what is *thought* right *is* right. What Vietnamese think right is right for Vietnamese; what Hindus think wrong is wrong for Hindus. But again, it is easy to misinterpret this point. Relativists are not asserting that there exists an objective moral standard in Vietnam and a different objective standard in India, and that Vietnamese and Indian thought, opinions, and behavior inform us about these objective standards. The relativistic point is to deny entirely the existence of an objective moral standard on either a universal or local level. All standards, claim Walter and other relativists, are *subjective;* they originate from the personal feelings of people at a particular time, in a particular place, under particular circumstances.

So, the absolutist/relativist debate reduces to two major points of disagreement:

1. Absolutists assert that there is a single universal moral standard that obliges everyone at all times everywhere. Relativists deny this, insisting that there are only local, changing, and diverse standards.

2. Absolutists assert that there is a difference between what is *thought* right and what *is* right. Relativists deny this, insisting that what is *thought* moral by a group of people at a particular time *is* in fact moral.

The absolutism/relativism controversy grows more provocative with further investigation. So let us rejoin Walter and George on the commuter special as they react to each other's positions. In the following conversation, Walter raises some common objections to absolutism.

OBJECTIONS TO ABSOLUTISM

1. *There is no evidence to support the claim that there is a universal moral code.*

Walter: You seem to be saying that however the court ruled in the Quinlan case, there exists an objectively right thing to do.

George: I guess I am. I suppose what I'm saying is that no matter what the courts say, or anyone else for that matter, there is a right and a wrong.

Walter: But what evidence do you have for saying that?

George: Just good common sense, I guess.

Walter: I'd think common sense would suggest just the opposite. Since there are so many different moral viewpoints, that to me suggests that there can't be any such thing as an absolute right or wrong.

George: I see what you mean, but I think you should consider the fact that these moral viewpoints often are not only different, they're contradictory.

Walter: So what?

George: In any case of contradiction, we readily admit that one position must be incorrect. If I said that this object in my hand is a newspaper and you said that it was not a newspaper, then surely one of us would be incorrect.

Walter: Of course. That's just logic.

George: Well, it seems to me the same logic applies to Karen's case. If I say that allowing Karen to die is morally wrong and you say that it's morally right, it seems to me that one of us is incorrect.

Walter: But there's a big difference. When you say that one of us is incorrect with respect to the newspaper, you're saying that, according to what we agree a newspaper is, one of our judgments is not true.

George: Right.

Walter: And when you say that one of us is incorrect about the morality of allowing Karen to die, then you're saying that, according to our definition of what's moral, one of our judgments is not true.

George: Agreed.

Walter: What I want is your basis for defining morality in absolute terms. It can't be like our definition of a newspaper, because that relies on things like shape, size, content, texture, and a lot of other things we can experience.

George: Of course it can't. Morality isn't something that can be quantified the way that something physical can be.

Walter: Then what evidence do you have for saying that there must be an absolute right or wrong?

If we were speaking philosophically, we'd say that Walter is an empiricist. *Empiricism is the doctrine that all knowledge originates in sense experience.* In general, empiricists do not accept as true any statement that cannot be verified, that is, that cannot be proven to describe an actual state of affairs. (There are some exceptions. An empiricist would accept as true a statement like "The white chalk is white" or "My brother is a male" because such statements are self-evident, that is, their predicates repeat their subjects in whole or in part.) Thus, Walter is asking for evidence to support the statement "There exists an absolute standard or code of morality."

Antiabsolutists like George argue that there is no such evidence. George would be a rationalist. This does not mean he is the kind of person who would pour five pounds of sugar in your gas tank, then give you a good reason for doing it. *Rationalism is the doctrine which contends that at least some knowledge is possible without sense experience.* For example, without sense experience it is possible to know that if X is greater than Y and Y is greater than Z, then X must be greater than Z. We know this, claim rationalists, by reason alone. So, rationalists insist that reason alone is sufficient to arrive at some knowledge. The empiricism/rationalism debate is one that provocatively threads its way through the history of philosophy, although it probably would not make for an exciting movie. A commuter special is not the most appropriate place to detail the controversy, but distinguishing these two positions is helpful in understanding a chief objection to absolutism.

In brief, Walter wants evidence for George's absolutistic claim. Until Walter can verify the claim through sense experience, as he can judgments about the newspaper, he is not willing to accept it. A newspaper, Walter claims, can be defined in terms of sense experiences. Thus, for Walter, the definition of a newspaper is grounded in fact: the definition corresponds with a state of affairs. But what evidence is there for George's definition of morality? Apparently George can't point to the same kind of concrete sense information to justify his definition. Therefore, Walter is not prepared to accept the assumption that there is an absolute standard of behavior that obligates all people at all times everywhere. Consequently, he's not prepared to accept any judgment using George's absolutistic definition as a basis. Speaking in terms of logic, Walter will not accept as sound the conclusion of an argument whose premise cannot be verified.

George might argue that we can arrive at such a definitional assumption without any sense experience on the basis of what he calls "common sense." Rationalists would call such knowledge "a priori," that is, *knowledge which is rooted solely in reason and which comes prior to sense experience.* Rationalists might hold that statements like "Every event has a cause" or "A thing cannot be in two places at the same time" represent a priori knowledge. It's true that George would support his claim by pointing to analogies from the world of sense experience, as he does with the newspaper. But because analogies never in themselves prove or verify a claim, ultimately George would rely on what he would view as the necessity of his assumption based on reason. For George, the assumption is necessary because of a law of logic which contends that something cannot both be and not be at the same time: euthanasia cannot be both right and not right at the same time, any more than an entity can be a newspaper and not a newspaper at the same time.

But there is implied in Walter's objections a second criticism of absolutism.

2. *There is no methodology to discover and verify a universal moral code.* If there is an ultimate moral principle that is applicable to all humans, then presumably there exists a method of discovering this ultimate moral law and thus a method of determining whether a moral belief is true or false. What is this method?

Many absolutists are hard pressed to define their method. But they insist that simply because a method cannot be presented does not mean that one does not exist; such a contention is an argument from ignorance. For them, it is like saying that there is no cure for cancer since we don't know of one. The absolutists' defense of their position, then, is parallel to one we might take regarding all empirical or scientific beliefs. Just because societies may maintain different beliefs about the causes of a particular disease would hardly lead us to conclude that there is no true cause. On the contrary, we'd insist that there was a true cause, despite our ignorance of it.

Clearly we have two major objections to the theoretical scaffolding of absolutism: (1) lack of evidence to support the claim that there is a universal moral code and (2) the absence of methodology to discover and verify the code. These objections of absolutist theory lead to a related objection to the application of absolutism.

3. *It is difficult or impossible to know that one's interpretation of the universal code is correct or to resolve conflicts.*

Walter: You know that because you can't verify your claim you have an obvious problem.

George: What's that?

Walter: The fact that you never know for sure who's right. I mean how do you know for sure that cannibalism is wrong? Maybe it's right. Maybe some aborigine headhunters are morally right in their behavior and we Americans are wrong. How do you ever know for sure?

George: I don't think that's the point. Just because we don't know for sure doesn't necessarily mean there isn't a right way to behave, any more than not knowing for sure whether there's life in deep space means that there is not.

Walter: But at least we know what we'd have to do to find out: go out into deep space and have a look around. At least we can tell the disputants what they'd have to do to check their claims. But what can you offer along those lines, George? Tell me how I can verify that cannibalism is morally wrong. What should I do to prove that allowing Karen to live is morally right or wrong?

Obviously the lack of hard evidence and the absence of methodology to verify their claims lead to tough problems for absolutists when they apply their belief. Walter is asking a legitimate question: how do we know that our individual interpretation of the absolutistic creed is the correct one? He's wondering further how conflicting interpretations are to be resolved. Although George accurately insists that the absence of such resolution does not disprove that there is a universal moral code, his reply does little to satisfy Walter's appetite for some empirical rod by which to measure the truth of moral judgments. Apparently Walter believes that relativism provides such a device. Although relativism may be on firmer ground with respect to verification, it is hardly an airtight case.

OBJECTIONS TO RELATIVISM

1. *Sociological relativism is no guarantee of moral relativism.* One of the popular arguments set forth in defense of moral relativism is based on sociological relativism, the fact that various moral codes exist. Anthropologists have shown that there exist a mind-boggling number of moral codes. From the jungles of New Guinea to the steppes of Siberia, from the deserts of Australia to the jungles of Africa, humans practice a welter of contradictory and exotic moral beliefs. Thus, it seems that there is nothing that has been considered morally good by all people everywhere. This fact, that values, customs, ways of life, and moral codes vary tremendously, frequently serves as the basis for moral relativism, the claim that there is no absolute moral code.

But the antirelativist argues that no matter how many examples of diverse value systems anthropology may unearth, it is erroneous to conclude that there is no universal moral standard. On the contrary, absolutists would contend that the moral variability leads to only one legitimate conclusion: people just do not know what the true moral code is. But simply because they do not know what it is does not mean that it doesn't exist; to make such a claim is to argue from ignorance.

2. *There is no solid evidence to support the claim that there is no universal moral code.* A related objection to the first one is that it is impossible to know that people's feelings, in which morality has its source, are themselves morally right. This is a tough objection for the empirically minded relativist to answer, for feelings are hardly a firm basis for claims to knowledge. Yet the relativist is saying, "Because society *feels* that this conduct is right, I *know* that it is right." This appears to be a blatant appeal to popularity. On the other hand, if relativists choose to anchor society's feelings in sound reasons, then presumably they are establishing a standard that might read: "Society's feelings are right if they are based on sound evidence." What "sound evidence" is, of course, is debatable, and the relativistic argument can quickly become circular if it is contended that sound evidence is what society feels is right. Absolutists would argue that it is precisely because of the mistaken notion that morality should be founded on feeling or custom that there are so many divergent ethical codes. They would further argue that when relativists claim, "There is no universal moral code," they are themselves proposing a universal standard as much as the absolutists are when they claim, "There is a universal moral code."

So, two major criticisms of the conceptual framework of moral relativism are (1) evidence for sociological relativism does not logically imply the soundness of moral relativism and (2) there is no solid evidence to verify the relativist's claim that there is no universal moral standard—the claim itself is an absolutistic one. These objections to moral relativity lead to criticisms of its application.

3. *There is no way to compare meaningfully the moral standards of one society with those of another.*

George: When you claim that the moral standards of a particular social group are the only standards that exist, then you make absurd any statement that tries to compare various moral codes.
Walter: I don't follow.
George: Well, I remember a day on this train a few years ago when you were deploring the My Lai incident.
Walter: I remember. It seemed to me a clear case of ruthless, unwarranted killing.
George: Let me ask you this. Suppose that such behavior was considered perfectly moral in Vietnam.
Walter: But it wasn't.
George: A lot of people would disagree with you. Let's just for argument's sake suppose that it was.

Walter: All right. Let's say that murdering civilians was considered moral in a society, so what?

George: How would you compare the morals of that society with one that disapproved of murdering civilians?

Walter: I'd probably say that a society that murdered people capriciously was uncivilized.

George: Would you say or think that their ethical ideas are better or worse than those of a society that doesn't practice that behavior?

Walter: I'd probably say it was morally inferior.

George: But to make such a comparative judgment implies that you've a common standard that can be applied to any society or civilization.

In effect, George is charging Walter with inconsistency. The heart of George's criticism is in the area of moral comparisons. We are constantly comparing one society with another and judging the moral code found in them as better or worse. We would probably say, for example, that the moral code of Nazi Germany was worse than the moral code of many other societies or that the moral code of a cannibalistic tribe in, say, New Guinea is worse than the moral code of a society that disapproves of cannibalism. But such statements become meaningless in the light of ethical relativism. For to make such comparisons presupposes a common standard applicable to various civilizations, and relativism denies the existence of such a standard. It follows that relativists must treat all statements of moral comparison as meaningless or at best always founded on provincialism.

4. *There is no way of logically determining the standard of moral behavior without individuals' making their own standards.*

Walter: Look, even though there's no way of proving that one society's ethics are better than another's, that doesn't mean that you can't make judgments within your own particular group.

George: All right, let's make one on the Karen Quinlan case. What factors will determine the moral decision to make in her case?

Walter: The values of the society of which she's a part.

George: Which society is that? Do you decide on the basis of her being a New Jerseyan? A Catholic? An American? It seems to me that if you're going to be consistent, you'd have to allow each individual the prerogative of determining their own moral code based on their own feelings.

Walter: I don't see why that follows.

George: Once you reject all of humanity as the area covered by a single moral standard, then what makes up the area that will serve as the standard? Is it a race? A nation? A state? A family? Just what is it? It seems to me that if you're to be consistent, you must allow the individual to be his or her own determinant of moral standards.

On the practical level, this is perhaps the strongest objection that George could raise. It seems that relativists would contend that moral judgments are meaningful about individuals who are subject to the same moral code. But surely there always have been and no doubt will continue to be individuals whose standards of morality on particular issues are different from their society's. Why shouldn't the standard of morality be whatever an individual feels is right? Of course, there is a good, practical reason. If such were the case, moral chaos would probably result; individuals would become moral rules unto themselves. But if relativists are not willing to allow such a possibility, then it seems they are actually relying on a standard after all—the good of society. They seem to have formulated a rule like the one mentioned previously: act in such a way that your action conforms to the accepted code of your society.

There are additional points we might garner from eavesdropping further on George and Walter's conversation. But we have enough now to understand the absolutistic/relativistic debate and how it relates directly to moral questions such as euthanasia.

SUMMARY

Moral Theories

Moral Absolutism: the belief that there is a universal moral code that applies to all people at all times everywhere

Objections

1. lack of evidence to support the absolutistic doctrine

2. absence of methodology to discover the universal moral code

3. inability to verify one's own interpretation of the universal code and the incapacity to resolve conflicting interpretations of the universal code

Moral Relativism: the belief that there is no single valid and true moral code, that there are many moral codes, and that these codes spring from the feelings and customs of societies

1. sociological relativism no guarantee of moral relativism

2. lack of evidence to support the contention that there is no universal moral standard; the absolutistic nature of such a claim

3. meaningless rendering of all statements that compare the ethical values of one society with another's

4. impossibility of logically determining a standard of moral behavior apart from each individual's feelings

CONCLUSIONS

Although fundamentally at odds, both ethical absolutism and relativism share a number of features that may suggest points of synthesis. Through such a synthesis we may make our own ethical framework more useful in dealing with euthanasia and other moral issues.

First, both absolutism and relativism make needed contributions to ethical theory. With its emphasis on rational knowledge, absolutism applies a desirable touch of logic to ethical debate. Surely any attempt to illuminate the euthanasia issue must take the form of a coherent argument rooted in a definition of human life. At the same time, any definition of human life must be grounded solidly in human experience. This is where relativism makes its contribution. With its stress on empiricism, relativism seems to provide such an experiential grounding.

Second, both views lack conclusive evidence to verify their claims. Consequently, a commitment to either, in theory, must be based on likelihood. This means that, in theory, we must admit that the ethical position we hold may ultimately be no better or worse than another's, or that it might be incorrect altogether. Realizing this, we should approach the euthanasia issue open-mindedly.

But, paradoxically, a commitment to either position seems to work out in practice as a commitment to a moral code. A third feature that both share, therefore, is a belief in some kind of standard. The absolutist openly admits this. But the relativists, in maintaining that there is no universal code of human conduct, in effect have established this denial as a standard. Furthermore, for all intents and purposes, in binding everyone to some local standard regarding euthanasia, for instance, relativists have universalized that standard; they have obliged everyone within the group. If the standard happens to be each individual's own, then each individual could be looked upon as a universe populated by one and bound by that individual's (or universe's) moral standards.

Fourth, at the same time, both relativism and absolutism seem to leave to the individual the ultimate decision about a moral standard. Relativism clearly does so. But in admitting that they can never verify their own interpretations of the universal standard, in practice absolutists leave individuals with the same uncertainty that relativists do—in fact, maybe more. At least with relativism, individuals are not haunted by the thought that their ethical codes could be wrong. For absolutists this is a real possibility: euthanasia—despite what a law reads or does not read, what a group of people thinks or does not think—is either right or wrong.

In the last analysis, it seems that we know what is right and what is wrong by first introducing all the data that bear directly on the issue at hand. In the case of euthanasia, this must include the social, cultural, and historical contexts in which the decision must be made, as well as whether the euthanasia is voluntary or involuntary. If involuntary, who will decide the costs of maintaining life, and who will shoulder the costs and the prospects of improvement in the physical condition? To these data we then rigorously apply sound reasoning, which consists of weighing not only the pros and cons, but also our intentions and the means we will use. Even then the decision is never easy and hardly ever palatable. Yet, it seems that in this way we use the best of what ethical absolutism and relativism offer. We use the rational procedures of absolutism, but ground them in our experience. We are reasoning not from a self-evident moral standard, but from the stuff of our experience. Reasoning this way, we probably improve our chances of resolving questions like euthanasia.

EXERCISES FOR ANALYSIS

EXERCISE 1

Each of the following passages is a condensed version of a common argument for or against euthanasia. Determine whether the justification provided for each conclusion is adequate. If it is not, why isn't it? As always, look for fallacious appeals.

Arguments for Euthanasia

1. If you don't think voluntary euthanasia is right and moral, visit a hospital some time. Take a look at terminally ill patients. Observe the excruciating physical pain they're feeling and the psychological pain that must come from recognizing that things can only get worse. Observe also the comatose who are being kept alive artificially. Humans have duties to help relieve the suffering and hopelessness of fellow humans. In such cases we are surely acting morally in extending pain-relieving and humility-ending death, as we mercifully do to nonhuman animals.

2. Any law that prohibits voluntary euthanasia that is decided upon by a patient and the patient's physician violates the fundamental and natural right to privacy. Why? Because such a law disregards the intimate relation between patients and their physicians, a relation that the law recognizes as inviolable. Such a law also invades the relation between patients and their families. But most important, an antieuthanasia law interferes with an individual's most intimate decision—whether to end one's life when the consequences of existing are agonizing and humiliating. Antieuthanasia laws deny these rights and are therefore wrong and should be abolished.

3. Wife of terminally ill patient: Doctor, you have a moral obligation to let my husband die.

Doctor: I don't believe that. In fact, I think I have an obligation to keep him alive.

Wife: But don't you realize the immeasurable harm you are causing me and my children? I'm not only talking about our pain of seeing him suffer and degenerate before our very eyes, but also the incalculable financial harm you're doing to us. Do you realize that we will be in debt for years to come?

That long after he dies, we will be trying to recover financially from the prolonged dying that you have subjected him and us to?

4. Euthanasia is simply a matter of definition. Define life. Once you've done that, simply see if the patient's status meets that definition. If it doesn't, then it certainly can't be immoral to *allow* the person to die, because the person isn't actually alive to begin with.

Arguments against Euthanasia

1. Surely involuntary euthanasia is always immoral. After all, no right is more fundamental than one's right to one's own life. In cases where individuals have done absolutely nothing to relinquish that right except to become so tragically ill or injured that they are unable to indicate whether they wish to live or die, no one has the right to make that decision for them. In fact, to do so, under any circumstances, is immoral.

2. Believer: God is the giver and taker of life. We don't have the right to take it.
   Skeptic: But we take life all the time—in self-defense, war, capital punishment.
   Believer: But that's different. Those are exceptions that are in keeping with traditional interpretation of the law of God, interpretation that has compelling religious, historical, cultural, and legal traditions for it. But there's no such justification for euthanasia.

3. Voluntary euthanasia is really just a form of suicide. So, approving of euthanasia is a tacit approval of suicide. But consider the implications. To approve of suicide in the form of voluntary euthanasia is to encourage individuals to take what is often the easy way out of their problems. But this is dangerous because the strength of a society lies in the willingness of its members to cope with and overcome their problems, both physical and psychological. So, in legalizing voluntary euthanasia, we're really undermining the foundations of society, and that's immoral.

4. Just imagine what will happen if even voluntary euthanasia is allowed. Why, it won't be long before someone other than the recipient will be deciding who dies and when. The specter that this presents is frightening. Today the deciding parties may choose to kill some hopelessly comatose patient, but who can be sure that tomorrow they will not extend that decision to the mentally retarded, the congenitally diseased, or the less productive members of society? So, even voluntary euthanasia is immoral, because it will lead to the arbitrary taking of human life.

EXERCISE 2

In 1976, California became the first state in the United States to pass a law that in effect legalizes voluntary euthanasia. Do you think that such a law in any way affects the *morality* of voluntary euthanasia? In replying, introduce the concepts of moral absolutism versus relativism.

SELECTIONS FOR FURTHER READING

Absolutism/Relativism

Everett, Millard S. *Ideals of Life*. New York: Wiley, 1954.

Ginsberg, Morris. *On the Diversity of Morals*. New York: Macmillan, 1956.

Nietzsche,Friedrich. *"Birth of Tragedy" and "The Genealogy of Morals."* Translated by Francis Gollfing. New York: Doubleday, 1956.

Sidgwick, Henry. *An Outline of the History of Ethics*. 6th ed. London: Macmillan, 1937.

Warnock, Mary. *Ethics since 1900*. London: Oxford University Press, 1960.

Westermarck, Edvard A. *Ethical Relativity*. New York: Harcourt, Brace, 1932.

Euthanasia

Choron, Jacques. *Death and Western Thought*. New York: Collier, 1963.

Cutler, D. R., ed. *Updating Life and Death*. Boston: Beacon Press, 1969.

Downing, A. B., ed. *Euthanasia and the Right to Die*. Los Angeles: Nash, 1969.

Fletcher, Joseph. *Morals and Medicine*. Boston: Beacon Press, 1960.

Kübler-Ross, Elisabeth. *On Death and Dying*. New York: Macmillan, 1969.

———. *Questions and Answers on Death and Dying*. New York: Macmillan, 1974.

KAMISAR/ *Some Non-Religious Views against Proposed 'Mercy-Killing' Legislation*

Even cases of patients requesting euthanasia to escape from incurable, unceasing pain are not easy to handle. One complication is that no two cases are ever precisely the same. The result: making general rules to cover all cases often raises additional problems.

In "Some Non-Religious Views against Proposed 'Mercy-Killing' Legislation," Yale Kamisar raises two such problems: the possibility of a medical practitioner making a mistake when given a wide range of freedom in determining even voluntary euthanasia, and the possibility that voluntary euthanasia could become a precedent for legalizing involuntary euthanasia. Along the way, Kamisar raises objections to these fears.

Do you think Kamisar adequately meets the objections he raises to his own beliefs? By the end of the essay, are you convinced that even voluntary euthanasia should not be permitted?

A recent book, Glanville Williams' *The Sanctity of Life and the Criminal Law,* once again brings to the fore the controversial topic of euthanasia, more popularly known as "mercy-killing." In keeping with the trend of the euthanasia movement over the past generation, Williams concentrates his efforts for reform on the *voluntary* type of euthanasia, for example, the cancer victim begging for death; as opposed to the *involuntary variety,* that is, the case of the congenital idiot, the permanently insane, or the senile.

As an ultimate philosophical proposition, the case for voluntary euthanasia is strong. Whatever may be said for and against suicide generally, the appeal of death is immeasurably greater when it is sought not for a poor reason or just any reason, but for "good cause," so to speak; when it is invoked not on behalf of a "socially useful" person, but on behalf of, for example, the pain-racked "hopelessly incurable" cancer victim. *If* a person is *in fact* (1) presently incurable, (2) beyond the aid of any respite which may come along in his life expectancy, suffering (3) intolerable and (4) unmitigable pain and of a (5) fixed and (6) rational desire to die, I would hate to have to argue that the hand of death should be stayed. But abstract propositions and carefully formed hypotheticals are one thing; specific proposals designed to

From Yale Kamisar, "Some Non-Religious Views against Proposed 'Mercy-Killing' Legislation," *Minnesota Law Review,* 42 (1958). Reprinted by permission. Footnotes omitted.

cover everyday situations are something else again.

In essence, Williams' proposal is that death be authorized for a person in the above situation "by giving the medical practitioner a wide discretion and trusting to his good sense." This, I submit, raises too great a risk of abuse and mistake to warrant a change in the existing law. That a proposal entails risk of mistake is hardly a conclusive reason against it. But neither is it irrelevant. Under any euthanasia program the consequences of mistake, of course, are always fatal. As I shall endeavor to show, the incidence of mistake of one kind or another is likely to be quite appreciable. If this indeed be the case, unless the need for the authorized conduct is compelling enough to override it, I take it the risk of mistake *is* a conclusive reason against such authorization. I submit too, that the possible radiations from the proposed legislation, *e.g.*, involuntary euthanasia of idiots and imbeciles (the typical "mercy-killings" reported by the press) and the emergence of the legal precedent that there are lives not "worth living," give additional cause to pause.

I see the issue, then, as the need for voluntary euthanasia versus (1) the incidence of mistake and abuse; and (2) the danger that legal machinery initially designed to kill those who are a nuisance to themselves may someday engulf those who are a nuisance to others.

The "freedom to choose a merciful death by euthanasia" may well be regarded, as does Professor Harry Kalven in a carefully measured review of another recent book urging a similar proposal, as "a special area of civil liberties far removed from the familiar concerns with criminal procedures, race discrimination, and freedom of speech and religion." The civil liberties angle is definitely a part of Professor Williams' approach:

If the law were to remove its ban on euthanasia, the effect would merely be to leave this subject to the individual conscience. This proposal would . . . be easy to defend, as restoring personal liberty in a field in which men differ on the question of conscience. . . .

On a question like this there is surely everything to be said for the liberty of the individual.

I am perfectly willing to accept civil liberties as the battlefield, but issues of "liberty" and "freedom" mean little until we begin to pin down *whose* "liberty" and "freedom" and for *what* need and at *what* price. This paper is concerned largely with such questions.

It is true also of journeys in the law that the place you reach depends on the direction you are taking. And so, where one comes out on a case depends on where one goes in.

So it is with the question at hand. Williams champions the "personal liberty" of the dying to die painlessly. I am more concerned about the life and liberty of those who would needlessly be killed in the process or who would irrationally choose to partake of the process. Williams' price on behalf of those who are *in fact* "hopeless incurables" and *in fact* of a fixed and rational desire to die is the sacrifice of (1) some few, who, though they know it not, because their physicians know it not, need not and should not die;

(2) others, probably not so few, who, though they go through the motions of "volunteering," are casualties of strain, pain, or narcotics to such an extent that they really know not what they do. My price on behalf of those who, despite appearances to the contrary, have some relatively normal and reasonably useful life left in them, or who are incapable of making the choice, is the lingering on for awhile of those who, if you will, *in fact* have no desire and no reason to linger on.

A CLOSE-UP VIEW OF VOLUNTARY EUTHANASIA: THE EUTHANASIAST'S DILEMMA AND WILLIAMS' PROPOSED SOLUTION

As if the general principle they advocate did not raise enough difficulties in itself, euthanasiasts have learned only too bitterly that specific plans of enforcement are often much less palatable than the abstract notions they are designed to effectuate. In the case of voluntary euthanasia, the means of implementation vary from (1) the simple proposal that mercy-killings by anyone, typically relatives, be immunized from the criminal law; to (2) the elaborate legal machinery contained in the bills of the Voluntary Euthanasia Legalisation Society (England) and the Euthanasia Society of America for carrying out euthanasia.

The English Society would require the eligible patient, *i.e.*, one over twenty-one and "suffering from a disease involving severe pain and of an incurable and fatal character," to forward a specially prescribed ap-plication—along with two medical certificates, one signed by the attending physician, and the other by a specially qualified physician—to a specially appointed Euthanasia Referee "who shall satisfy himself by means of a personal interview with the patient and otherwise that the said conditions shall have been fulfilled and that the patient fully understands the nature and purpose of the application"; and, if so satisfied, shall then send a euthanasia permit to the patient; which permit shall, seven days after receipt, become "operative" in the presence of an official witness; unless the nearest relative manages to cancel the permit by persuading a court of appropriate jurisdiction that the requisite conditions have not been met.

The American Society would have the eligible patient, *i.e.*, one over twenty-one "suffering from severe physical pain caused by a disease for which no remedy affording lasting relief or recovery is at the time known to medical science," petition for euthanasia in the presence of two witnesses and file same, along with the certificate of an attending physician, in a court of appropriate jurisdiction; said court to then appoint a committee of three, of whom at least two must be physicians, "who shall forthwith examine the patient and such other persons as they deem advisable or as the court may direct and within five days after their appointment, shall report to the court whether or not the patient understands the nature and purpose of the petition and comes within the [act's] provisions"; whereupon, if the report is in the affirmative, the court shall—"unless there is some reason to believe that the report is erroneous or untrue"—grant the petition; in which event euthanasia is to be administered in the presence of the committee, or any two members thereof.

As will be seen, and as might be expected, the simple negative proposal to remove "mercy-killings" from the ban of the criminal law is strenuously resisted on the ground that it offers the patient far too little protection from not-so-necessary or not-so-merciful killings. On the other hand, the elaborate affirmative proposals of the euthanasia societies meet much pronounced eye-blinking, not a few guffaws, and sharp criticism that the legal machinery is so drawn-out, so complex, so formal, and so tedious as to offer the patient far too little solace. . . .

Nothing rouses Professor Williams' ire more than the fact that opponents of the euthanasia movement argue that euthanasia proposals offer either inadequate protection or over-elaborate safeguards. Williams appears to meet this dilemma with the insinuation that because arguments are made in the antithesis *they must each be invalid, each be obstructionist, and each be made in bad faith.*

It just may be, however, that each alternative argument is quite valid, that the trouble lies with the euthanasiasts themselves in seeking a goal which is *inherently inconsistent:* a procedure for death which *both* (1) provides ample safeguards against abuse and mistake; and (2) is "quick" and "easy" in operation. Professor William meets the problem with more than bitter comments about the tactics of the opposition. He makes a brave try to break through the dilemma:

The reformers might be well advised, in their next proposal, to abandon all their cumbrous safeguards and to do as their opponents wish, giving the medical practitioner a wide discretion and trusting to his good sense.

The essence of the bill would then be simple. It would provide that no medical practitioner should be guilty of an offense in respect of an act done intentionally to accelerate the death of a patient who is seriously ill, unless it is proved that the act was not done in good faith with the consent of the patient and for the purpose of saving him from severe pain in an illness believed to be of an incurable and fatal character. Under this formula it would be for the physician, if charged, to show that the patient was seriously ill, but for the prosecution to prove that the physician acted from some motive other than the humanitarian one allowed to him by law. . . .

Evidently, the presumption is that the general practitioner is a sufficient buffer between the patient and the restless spouse or overwrought or overreaching relative, as well as a depository of enough general scientific know-how and enough information about current research developments and trends, to assure a minimum of error in diagnosis and anticipation of new measures of relief. Whether or not the general practitioner will accept the responsibility Williams would confer on him is itself a problem of major proportions. Putting that question aside, the soundness of the underlying premises of Williams' "legislative suggestion" will be examined in the course of the discussion of various aspects of the euthanasia problem.

THE "CHOICE"

Under current proposals to establish legal machinery, elaborate or otherwise, for the administration of a quick and easy death, it is not enough that those authorized to pass on the question decide that the patient, in effect, is "better off dead." The patient must concur in this opinion. Much of the appeal in the current proposal lies in this so-called "voluntary" attribute.

But is the adult patient really in a position to concur? Is he truly able to make euthanasia a "voluntary" act? There is a good deal to be said, is there not, for Dr. Frohman's pithy comment that the "voluntary" plan is supposed to be carried out "only if the victim is both sane and crazed by pain."

By hypothesis, voluntary euthanasia is not to be resorted to until narcotics have long since been administered and the patient has developed a tolerance to them. *When,* then, does the patient make the choice? While heavily drugged? Or is narcotic relief to be withdrawn for the time of decision? But if heavy dosage no longer deadens pain, indeed, no longer makes it bearable, how overwhelming is it when whatever relief narcotics offer is taken away, too? . . .

Undoubtedly, some euthanasia candidates will have their lucid moments. How they are to be distinguished from fellow-sufferers who do not, or how these instances are to be distinguished from others when the patient is exercising an irrational judgment is not an easy matter. Particularly is this so under Williams' proposal, where no specially qualified persons, psychiatrically trained or otherwise, are to assist in the process.

Assuming, for purposes of argument, that the occasion when a euthanasia candidate possesses a sufficiently clear mind can be ascertained and that a request for euthanasia is then made, there remain other problems. The mind of the pain-racked may occasionally be clear, but is it not also likely to be uncertain and variable? This point was pressed hard by the great physician, Lord Horder, in the House of Lords debate:

During the morning depression he [the patient] will be found to favor the application under this Bill, later in the day he will think quite differently, or will have forgotten all about it. The mental clarity with which noble Lords who present this Bill are able to think and to speak must not be thought to have any counterpart in the alternating moods and confused judgments of the sick man.

The concept of "voluntary" in voluntary euthanasia would have a great deal more substance to it if, as is the case with voluntary admission statutes for the mentally ill, the patient retained the right to reverse the process within a specified number of days after he gives written notice of his desire to do so—but unfortunately this cannot be. The choice here, of course, is an irrevocable one. . . .

Even if the patient's choice could be said to be "clear and incontrovertible," do not other difficulties remain? Is this the kind of choice, assuming that it can be made in a fixed and rational manner, that we want to offer a gravely ill person? Will we not sweep up, in the process, some who are not really tired of life, but think others are tired of them; some who do not really want to die, but who feel they should not live on, because to do so when there looms the legal alternative of euthanasia is to do a selfish or a cowardly act? Will not some feel an obligation to have themselves "eliminated" in order that funds allocated for their terminal care might be better used by their families or, financial worries aside, in order to relieve their families of the emotional strain involved?

It would not be surprising for the gravely ill person to seek to inquire of those close to him whether he should avail himself of the legal alternative of euthanasia. Certainly, he is likely to wonder about their attitude in the matter. It is quite possible, is it not, that he will not exactly be gratified by any inclination on their part—however noble their motives may be in fact—that he resort to the new procedure? . . .

At such a time, . . . members of the family are not likely to be in the best state of mind, either, to make this kind of decision. Financial stress and conscious or unconscious competition for the family's estate aside:

The chronic illness and persistent pain in terminal carcinoma may place strong and excessive stresses upon the family's emotional ties with the patient. The family members who have strong emotional attachment to start with are most likely to take the patient's fears, pains, and fate personally. Panic often strikes them. Whatever guilt feelings they may have toward the patient emerge to plague them.

If the patient is maintained at home, many frustrations and physical demands may be imposed on the family by the advanced illness. There may develop extreme weakness, incontinence, and bad odors. The pressure of caring for the individual under these circumstances is likely to arouse a resentment and, in turn, guilt feelings on the part of those who have to do the nursing.

Nor should it be overlooked that while Professor Williams would remove the various procedural steps and the various personnel contemplated in the American and English Bills and bank his all on the "good sense" of the general practitioner, no man is immune to the fear, anxieties, and frustrations engendered by the apparently helpless, hopeless patient. Not even the general practitioner:

Working with a patient suffering from a malignancy causes special problems for the physician. First of all, the patient with a malignancy is most likely to engender anxiety concerning death, even in the doctor. And at the same time, this type patient constitutes a serious threat or frustration to medical ambition. As a result, a doctor may react more emotionally and less objectively than in any other area of medical practice. . . . His deep concern may make him more pessimistic than is necessary. As a result of the feeling of frustration in his wish to help, the doctor may have moments of annoyance with the patient. He may even feel almost inclined to want to avoid this type of patient.

The only Anglo-American prosecution involving an alleged mercy-killing physician seems to be the case of Dr. Herman Sander. The state's testimony was to the effect that, as Sander had admitted on various occasions, he finally yielded to the persistent pleas of his patient's husband and pumped air into her veins "in a weak moment." Sander's version was that he finally "snapped" under the strain of caring for the cancer victim, bungled simple tasks, and became "obsessed" with the need to "do something" for her—if only to inject air into her *already* dead body. Whichever side one believes—and the jury evidently believed Dr. Sander—the case well demonstrates that at the moment of decision the tired practitioner's "good sense" may not be as good as it might be. . . .

The boldness and daring which characterizes most of Glanville Williams' book dims perceptibly when he comes to involuntary euthanasia proposals. As to the senile, he states:

At present the problem has certainly not reached the degree of seriousness that would warrant an effort being made to change traditional attitudes toward the sanctity of life of the aged. Only the grimmest necessity could bring about a change that, however cautious in its approach, would probably cause apprehension and deep distress to many people, and inflict a traumatic injury upon the accepted code of behaviour built up by two thousand years of the Christian religion. It may be, however, that as the problem becomes more acute it will itself cause a reversal of generally accepted values.

To me, this passage is the most startling one in the book. On page 348 Williams invokes "traditional attitudes towards the sanctity of life" and "the accepted code of behaviour built up by two thousand years of the Christian religion" to check the extension of euthanasia to the senile, but for 347 pages he had been merrily rolling along debunking both. Substitute "cancer victim" for "the aged" and Williams' passage is essentially the argument of many of his *opponents* on the voluntary euthanasia question.

The unsupported comment that "the problem [of senility] has certainly not reached the degree of seriousness" to warrant euthanasia is also rather puzzling, particularly coming as it does after an observation by Williams on the immediately preceding page that "it is increasingly common for men and women to reach an age of 'second childishness and mere oblivion,' with a loss of almost all adult faculties except that of digestion."

How "serious" does a problem have to be to warrant a change in these "traditional attitudes"? If, as the statement seems to indicate, "seriousness" of a problem is to be determined numerically, the problem of the cancer victim does not appear to be as substantial as the problem of the senile. For example, taking just the 95,837 first admissions to "public prolonged-care hospitals" for mental diseases in the United States in 1955, 23,561—or one fourth—were cerebral arteriosclerosis or senile brain disease cases. I am not at all sure that there are 20,000 cancer patients per year who die *unbearably painful* deaths. Even if there were, I cannot believe that among their ranks are some 20,000 per year who, when still in a rational state, so long for a quick and easy death that they would avail themselves of legal machinery for euthanasia.

If the problem of the incurable cancer victim "has reached the degree of seriousness that would warrant an effort being made to change traditional attitudes toward the sanctity of life," as Williams obviously thinks it has, then so has the problem of senility. In any event, the senility problem will undoubtedly soon reach even Williams' requisite degree of seriousness:

A decision concerning the senile may have to be taken within the next twenty years. The numbers of old people are increasing by leaps and bounds. Pneumonia, "the old man's friend" is now checked by antibiotics. The effects of hardship, exposure, starvation, and accident are now minimized. Where is this leading us? . . . What of the drooling, helpless, disorientated old man or the doubly incontinent old woman lying log-like in bed? Is it here that the real need for euthanasia exists?

If, as Williams indicates, "seriousness" of the problem is a major criterion for euthanatizing a category of unfortunates, the sum total of mentally deficient persons would appear to warrant high priority, indeed.

When Williams turns to the plight of the "hopelessly defective infants," his characteristic vim and vigor are, as in the senility discussion, conspicuously absent:

While the Euthanasia Society of England has never advocated this, the Euthanasia Society of America did include it in its original program. The proposal certainly escapes the chief objection to the similar proposal for senile dementia: it does not create a sense of insecurity in society, because infants cannot, like adults, feel anticipatory dread of being done to death if their condition should worsen. Moreover, the proposal receives some support on eugenic grounds, and more importantly on humanitarian grounds— both on account of the parents, to whom the child will be a burden all their lives, and on account of the handicapped child itself. (It is not, however, proposed that any child should be destroyed against the wishes of its parents.) Finally, the legalization of euthanasia for handicapped children would bring the law into closer relation to its practical administration, because juries do not regard parental mercy-killing as murder. For these various reasons the proposal to legalize humanitarian infanticide is put forward from time to time by individuals. They remain in a very small minority, and the proposal may at present be dismissed as politically insignificant.

It is understandable for a reformer to limit his present proposals for change to those with a real prospect of success. But it is hardly reassuring for Williams to cite the fact that only "a very small minority" has urged euthanasia for "hopelessly defective infants" as the *only* reason for not pressing for such legislation now. If, as Williams sees it, the only advantage voluntary euthanasia has over the involuntary variety lies in the organized movements on its behalf, that advantage can readily be wiped out.

In any event, I do not think that such "a very small minority" has advocated "humanitarian infanticide." Until the organization of the English and American societies led to a concentration on the voluntary type, and until the byproducts of the Nazi euthanasia program somewhat embarrassed, if only temporarily, most proponents of involuntary euthanasia, about as many writers urged one type as another. Indeed, some euthanasiasts have taken considerable pains to demonstrate the superiority of defective infant euthanasia over incurably ill euthanasia. . . .

Nor do I think it irrelevant that while public resistance caused Hitler to yield on the adult euthanasia front, the killing of malformed and idiot children continued unhindered to the end of the war, the definition of "children" expanding all the while. Is it the embarrassing experience of the Nazi euthanasia program which has rendered destruction of defective infants presently "politically insignificant"? If so, is it any more of a jump from the incurably and painfully ill to the unorthodox political thinker than it is from the hopelessly defective infant to the same "unsavory character"? Or is it not so much that the euthanasiasts are troubled by the Nazi experience as it is that they are troubled that the public is troubled by the Nazi experience?

THE PARADE OF HORRORS

Look, when the messenger cometh, shut the door, and hold him fast at the door; is not the sound of his master's feet behind him?

This is the "wedge principle," the "parade of horrors" objection, if you will, to voluntary euthanasia. Glanville Williams' peremptory retort is:

This use of the 'wedge' objection evidently involves a particular determination as to the meaning of words, namely the words 'if raised to a general line of conduct.' The author supposes, for the sake of argument, that the merciful extinction of life in a suffering patient is not in itself immoral. Still it is immoral, because if it were permitted this would admit 'a most dangerous wedge that might eventually put all life in a precarious condition.' It seems a sufficient reply to say that this type of reasoning could be used to condemn any act whatever, because there is no human conduct from which evil cannot be imagined to follow if it is persisted in when some of the circumstances are changed. All moral questions involve the drawing of a line, but the "wedge principle" would make it impossible to draw a line, because the line would have to be pushed farther and farther back until all action became vetoed.

I agree with Williams that if a first step is "moral" it is moral wherever a second step may take us. The real point, however, the point that Williams sloughs, is that whether or not the first step is precarious, is perilous, is worth taking, rests in part on what the second step is likely to be.

It is true that the "wedge" objection can always be advanced, the horrors can always be paraded. But it is no less true that on some occasions the objection is much more valid than it is on others. One reason why the "parade of horrors" cannot be too lightly dismissed in this particular instance is that Miss Voluntary Euthanasia is not likely to be going it alone for very long. Many of her admirers, as I have endeavored to show in the preceding section, would be neither surprised nor distressed to see her joined by Miss Euthanatize the Congenital Idiots and Miss Euthanatize the Permanently Insane and Miss Euthanatize the Senile Dementia. And these lasses—whether or not they themselves constitute a "parade of horrors"—certainly make excellent majorettes for such a parade:

Some are proposing what is called euthanasia; at present only a proposal for killing those who are a nuisance to themselves; but soon to be applied to those who are a nuisance to other people.

Another reason why the "parade of horrors" argument cannot be too lightly dismissed in this particular instance, it seems to me, is that the parade *has* taken place in our time and the order of procession has been headed by the killing of the "incurables" and the "useless":

Even before the Nazis took open charge in Germany, a propaganda barrage was directed against the traditional compassionate nineteenth-century attitudes toward the chronically ill, and for the adoption of a utilitarian, Hegelian point of view. . . . Lay opinion was not neglected in this campaign. Adults were propagandized by motion pictures, one of which, entitled "I Accuse," deals entirely with euthanasia. This film depicts the life history of a woman suffering from multiple sclerosis; in it her husband, a doctor, finally kills her to the accompaniment of soft piano music rendered by a sympathetic colleague in an adjoining room. Acceptance of this ideology was implanted even in the children. A widely used high-school mathematics text . . . included problems stated in distorted terms of the cost of caring for and rehabilitating the chronically sick and crippled. One of the problems asked, for instance, how many new housing units could be built and how many marriage-allowance loans could be given to newly wedded couples for the amount of money it cost the state to care for "the crippled, the criminal, and the insane. . . ." The beginnings at first were merely a subtle shift in emphasis in the basic attitude of the physicians. *It started with the acceptance of the attitude, basic in the euthanasia movement, that there is such a thing as life not worthy to be lived.* This attitude in its early stages concerned itself merely with the severely and chronically sick. Gradually the sphere of those to be included in this category was enlarged to encompass the socially unproductive, the ideolog-

ically unwanted, the racially unwanted, and finally all non-Germans. But it is important to realize that the infinitely small wedged-in lever from which this entire trend of mind received its impetus was the attitude toward the non-rehabilitatable sick.

The apparent innocuousness of Germany's "small beginnings" is perhaps best shown by the fact that German Jews were at first excluded from the program. For it was originally conceived that "the blessing of euthanasia should be granted only to [true] Germans."

Relatively early in the German program, Pastor Braune, Chairman of the Executive Committee of the Domestic Welfare Council of the German Protestant Church, called for a halt to euthanasia measures "since they strike sharply at the moral foundations of the nation as a whole. The inviolability of human life is a pillar of any social order." And the pastor raised the same question which euthanasia opponents ask today, as well they might, considering the disinclination of many in the movement to stop at voluntary "mercy-killings": Where do we, how do we, draw the line? The good pastor asked:

How far is the destruction of socially unfit life to go? The mass methods used so far have quite evidently taken in many people who are to a considerable degree of sound mind. . . . Is it intended to strike only at the utterly hopeless cases—the idiots and imbeciles? The instruction sheet, as already mentioned, also lists senile diseases. The latest decree by the same authorities requires that children with serious congenital disease and malformation of every kind be registered, to be collected and processed in special institutions. This necessarily gives rise to grave apprehensions. Will a line be drawn at the tubercular? In the case of persons in custody by court order euthanasia measures have evidently already been initiated. Are other abnormal or antisocial persons likewise to be included? Where is the borderline? Who is abnormal, antisocial, hopelessly sick?

Williams makes no attempt to distinguish or minimize the Nazi Germany experience. Apparently he does not consider it worthy of mention in a euthanasia discussion. There are, however, a couple of obvious arguments by which the Nazi experience can be minimized.

One goes something like this: It is silly to worry about the prospects of a dictatorship utilizing euthanasia "as a pretext for putting inconvenient citizens out of the way. Dictatorships have no occasion for such subterfuges. The firing squad is less bother." One reason why this counter argument is not too reassuring, however, if again I may be permitted to be so unkind as to meet speculation with a concrete example to the contrary, is that Nazi Germany had considerable occasion to use just such a subterfuge.

Thus, Dr. Leo Alexander observes:

It is rather significant that the German people are considered by their Nazi leaders more ready to accept the exterminations of the sick than those for political reasons. It was for that reason that the first exterminations of the latter group were carried out under the guise of sickness. So-called "psychiatric experts" were dispatched to survey the inmates of camps with the specific order to pick out members of racial minorities and political offenders from occupied territories and to dispatch them to killing centers with specially made diagnoses such as that of "in-

veterate German hater" applied to a number of prisoners who had been active in the Czech underground.

A large number of those marked for death for political or racial reasons were made available for 'medical experiments involving the use of involuntary human subjects.'

The "hunting season" in Germany officially opened when Hitler signed on his own letterhead a secret order dated September 1, 1939, which read:

Reichsleiter Bouhler and Dr. Brandt, M.D., are charged with the responsibility of enlarging the authority of certain physicians, to be designated by name, in such a manner that persons who, according to human judgment, are incurable can, upon a more careful diagnosis of their condition of sickness, be accorded a mercy death.

Physicians asked to participate in the program were told that the secrecy of the order was designed to prevent patients from becoming "too agitated" and that it was in keeping with the policy of not publicizing home front measures in time of war.

About the same time that aged patients in some hospitals were being given the "mercy" treatment, the Gestapo was also "systematically putting to death the mentally deficient population of the Reich."

The courageous and successful refusal by a Protestant pastor to deliver up certain cases from his asylum well demonstrates that even the most totalitarian governments are not always indifferent to the feelings of the people, that they do not always feel free to resort to the firing squad. Indeed, vigorous protests by other ecclesiastical personalities and some physicians, numerous requests of various public prosecutors for investigation of the circumstances surrounding the mysterious passing away of relatives, and a generally aroused public opinion finally caused Hitler to yield, if only temporarily, and in August of 1941 he verbally ordered the discontinuance of the adult euthanasia program. Special gas chambers in Hadamar and other institutions were dismantled and shipped to the East for much more extensive use on Polish Jews.

Perhaps it should be noted, too, that even dictatorships fell prey to the inertia of big government:

It is . . . interesting that there was so much talk against euthanasia in certain areas of Germany, particularly in the region of Wiesbaden, that Hitler in 1943 asked Himmler to stop it. But, it had gained so much impetus by 1943 and was such an easy way in crowded concentration camps to get rid of undesirables and make room for newcomers, that it could not be stopped. The wind had become a whirlwind.

Another obvious argument is that it just can't happen here. I hope not. I think not.

But then, neither did I think that tens of thousands of perfectly loyal native-born Americans would be herded into prison camps without proffer of charges and held there for many months, even years, because they were of "Japanese blood" and, although the general who required these measures emitted considerable ignorance and bigotry, his so-called military judgment would be largely sustained by the highest court of the land. The Japanese-American experience of World War II undoubtedly fell somewhat short of first-class

Nazi tactics, but we were getting warm. I venture to say it would not be too difficult to find American citizens of Japanese descent who would maintain we were getting very warm indeed.

A FINAL REFLECTION

There have been and there will continue to be compelling circumstances when a doctor or relative will violate The Law On The Books and, more often than not, receive protection from The Law In Action. But this is not to deny that there are other occasions when The Law On The Books operates to stay the hand of all concerned, among them situations where the patient is in fact (1) presently incurable, (2) beyond the aid of any respite which may come along in his life expectancy, suffering (3) intolerable and (4) unmitigable pain and of a (5) fixed and (6) rational desire to die. That any euthanasia program may only be the opening wedge for far more objectionable practices, and that even within the bounds of a "voluntary" plan such as Williams' the incidence of mistake or abuse is likely to be substantial, are not much solace to one in the above plight.

It may be conceded that in a narrow sense it is an "evil" for such a patient to have to continue to suffer— if only for a little while. But in a narrow sense, long-term sentences and capital punishment are "evils," too. If we can justify the infliction of imprisonment and death by the state "on the ground of the social interests to be protected" then surely we can similarly justify the postponement of death by the state. The objection that the individual is thereby treated not as an "end" in himself but only as a "means" to further the common good was, I think, aptly disposed of by Holmes long ago. "If a man lives in society, he is likely to find himself so treated."

READING

CADY / *The Burning*

What would you do if your best friend was trapped inside the burning cab of a truck? In "The Burning," author Jack Cady portrays what one truck driver does, while at the same time raising what is the most common argument presented in behalf of legalized euthanasia—the end of suffering. Clearly, fiction should not be held as rigorously accountable to the laws of sound reasoning as pure argument should be. Nevertheless, some fiction is decidedly less emotive than other fiction, although it forcefully makes its point. In reading "The Burning," ask yourself whether the author has remained reasonably dispassionate in raising the euthanasia issue. Do you think that Manny's behavior is morally justifiable?

Sunlight gleamed as Singleton and I walked down the hill to the charred wreckage of what had been a truck. Gates was dead, and the breeze lifted sooty material that mixed with the valley smells of weeds, flowers, and diesel stink. Manny was in jail. Nothing more could be done for Gates, but now Manny was sitting in his own fire, burning because he was kind, because he was gentle.

Traffic was moving as usual on the long slopes; only an occasional car slowed, its occupants looking over the scene of last night's fire. The truck drivers would know all about the trouble, and they did not want to see. Besides, there was a hill to climb on either side of the valley. They could not afford to lose speed. I knew that by now the word of the burning had spread at least a hundred miles. As far as Lexington, drivers would be leaning against counters listening, with wildness spreading in them. Singleton and I had not slept through the long night. We revisited the scene because we felt it was the final thing we could do for both men.

Close-up the sunlight played on bright runs of metal where someone had pulled the cab apart hoping to recover enough of Gates's remains for burial. An oil fire, when the oil is pouring on a man, doesn't leave much. Only the frame and other heavy structural members of the truck remained.

"If he had only been knocked out or killed before the fire got to him . . ." We were both thinking the words. Either might have said them.

"His company's sending an investigator." Singleton told me. "But since we're here, let's go over it. They'll be sure to ask."

"Are you going to pull?"

"No." He shook his head and ran his hand across his face. "No. Next week maybe or the week after. I'm not steady. I called for three drivers. That's one for your rig too."

"Thanks. I've got vacation coming. I'm taking it."

The road surface along the wreck was blackened, and the asphalt waved and sagged. It was a bad spot. The state should have put up signs. Forty-seven feet of power and payload; now it seemed little there in the ditch, its unimportance turning my stomach. I wanted to retch. I felt lonely and useless.

We walked to the far hill to look at the tire marks. Narrow little lines which swung wide across the other lane and then back in, suddenly breaking and spinning up the roadway. Heavy black lines were laid beside them where the driver of the car being passed had ridden his brakes and then gone on up the hill. Coming down were the marks Gates made, and they showed that he had done what a trucker is supposed to do. He had avoided at all costs. The marks ran off the road.

I never knew him. Manny, tall, sandy-haired, and laughing, was my good friend, but I did not know Gates. I did not know until later that Singleton knew him.

We had picked Gates up twenty miles back on the narrow two-lane that ran through the Kentucky hills. We rode behind him figuring to pass when he got a chance to let us around. It was early, around 3 a.m., but there was still heavy vacation-season traffic. Manny was out front behind Gates. My rig was second behind him, and Singleton was behind me. Our three freights were grossing less than fifty thousand so we could go.

Gates's tanker must have scaled at around sixty thousand. Even with that weight you can usually go, but his gas-powered tractor was too light.

It slowed us to be laying back, but there was no reason to dog it. He was making the best time he could. He topped the hill by June's Stop and ran fast after he crested on the long slope down. He had Manny by maybe two hundred yards because Manny had signaled into June's.

When he signaled I checked my mirrors. Singleton kept pulling so I kept pulling. When he saw us coming on, Manny cancelled the signal and went over the top behind Gates. It allowed enough of a lag for Gates to get out front, and it kept Manny from being killed.

We took the hill fast. You have to climb out the other side. I was a quarter mile back, running at forty-five and gaining speed, when I saw the headlights of the little car swing into the lane ahead of Gates's tanker. The driver had incorrectly estimated the truck's speed or the car's passing power.

It was quick and not bad at first. The tanker went into the ditch. The car cut back in, broke traction, and spun directly up the roadway. It came to a stop next to Manny's rig, almost brushing against his drive axle and not even bending sheet metal, a fluke. The car it had passed went onto the shoulder and recovered. The driver took it on up the hill to get away from the wreck and involvement.

Manny was closer. He had perhaps a second more to anticipate the wreck. He had stopped quicker than I believed possible. It was about a minute before the fire started. I was running with my extinguisher when I saw it, and I knew I would be too late.

"I wish he'd exploded," Singleton said. He kicked up dust along the roadway. He was too old for this, and he was beat-out and shaken. The calmness of resignation was trying to take him, and I hoped it would. I wondered to myself if those clear eyes that had looked down a million and a half miles of road had ever looked at anything like this.

"Exploded? Yes, either that or got out."

"He was hurt. I think he was hurt bad." He looked at me almost helplessly. "No sense wishing; let's go back up."

After the wreck Singleton had backed his rig over the narrow two-lane, following the gradual bend of the road in the dark. He had taken the two girls from the small car into his cab.

I had stayed a little longer until Gates's burning got really bad. Then I brought the little car in, feeling the way I feel in any car: naked, unprotected, and nearly blind. I was shaking from weakness. The road was blocked above. There was no oncoming beyond the pot flares. The cop with the flashlight had arrived ten or fifteen minutes after the wreck. Behind me the fire rose against the summer blackness and blanketed the valley with the acrid smell of number-two diesel. Because of the distance, Manny's rig seemed almost in the middle of the fire and silhouetted against the burning, though I knew he had stopped nearly fifty yards up the roadway. My own rig was pulled in behind him; its markers stood pale beside the bigger glow. As I was about to go past the cop, he waved me over.

"Where you taking it?"

"Just to the top," I told him. "The girls were pretty shaken up. Don't

worry, they won't go anywhere."

"Think they need an ambulance?" He paused, uncertain. "Christ," he said. "Will that other cruiser ever get here?"

"What about Manny?" I asked.

"In there." He nodded to where Manny sat in the cruiser. The lights were out inside. He could not be seen. "I'll take a statement at the top. You'll see him at the top."

I wanted to call to Manny, but there was nothing I could do. I took the car on to June's Stop. Rigs were starting to pile in, even stacking up along the roadway. Cars were parked around and between them, blacked out and gleaming small and dull in the lights from the truck markers. Most of the guys had cut their engines. It would be a long wait.

Singleton's truck was down by the restaurant. Inside around the counter, which formed a kind of box, drivers were sitting and talking. A few were standing around. They were excited and walked back and forth. I wanted coffee, needed it, but I could not go in. At least not then. A driver came up behind me.

"You Wakefield?" he asked. He meant did I drive for Wakefield. My name is Arnold.

I told him yes.

"Your buddy took the girls to Number Twelve. He said to come."

"As if we didn't have enough trouble . . ."

"He's got the door open." The guy grinned. He was short with a light build and was in too good a mood. I disliked him right away. "Listen," he said. "They say there's going to be a shakedown."

"Who says?"

"Who knows? That's just the

word. If you left anything back there, you'd better get it out. Check it with June."

He meant guns and pills. A lot of companies require them in spite of the law. A lot of guys carry them on their own, the guns I mean. Pills are Benzedrine, Bennies, or a stronger kind called footballs. Only drivers who don't know any better use them to stay awake or get high on.

"I've got it right here," I told him, and patted my side pocket. "I'll hang onto it myself."

"Your funeral," he said, grinning. He gave me a sick feeling. He was a guy with nose trouble, one who spreads his manure up and down the road, a show-off to impress waitresses. "Thanks," I said, and turned to go to the motel room.

"Hey," he yelled, "what do you think will happen to him?"

"You figure it out." I went over to the motel, found Twelve, and went inside.

The room had twin beds. Singleton was sitting on one, facing the two girls on the other. One was kind of curled up. The other was leaning forward still crying. Vassar, I thought. No, nothing like that on 25 south; University of Kentucky likely, but the same sorry type. I edged down beside Singleton. "Why do you bother?" I asked him. "To hell with them." The girl bawling looked up hard for a moment and started bawling worse.

"I had room," she bawled.

We were all under a strain. The diesel smell was bad, but the other smell that I would never forget had been worse. Even away from the fire I seemed still to smell it.

"You thought you had room!" I yelled at her.

"No, really. I was all right. I had room." She was convinced, almost righteous. At some other time she might have been pretty. Both were twenty or twenty-one. The curled-up one was sort of mousy-looking. The one who was bawling was tall with long hair. I thought of her as a thing.

"No—really," I yelled at her; "you had no room, but keep lying to yourself. Pretty soon that'll make everything OK."

"Leave it, Arn," Singleton told me. "You're not doing any good."

He went to the sink to wet a towel, bringing it to the girl. "Wipe your face," he told her. Then he turned to me. "Did you bring their car?"

"I brought it—just a minute. You can have them in just a minute." I was still blind angry. "Old, young, men, women, we've seen too many of their kind. I just want to say it once." I looked directly at her. "How much have you driven?"

For a moment it didn't take; then she understood.

"Five years."

"Not years. Miles."

"Why—I guess—I don't know. Five years."

"Five thousand a year? Ten thousand? That would be plenty; you haven't driven that much. Five years times ten is fifty thousand. That's six to eight months' work for those guys down there. *You had no room!*" I bit it out at her. She just looked confused, and I felt weak. "I'm ready to leave it now," I told Singleton. "I should have known. Remember, we've got a friend down there."

"I've got two."

He looked different than ever before. He sat slouched on the bed and leaned forward a little. His hands were in his lap, and the lines and creases in his face were shadowed in the half-light from the floor lamp.

"Who was he?" I asked.

He looked at me. I realized with a shock that he had been fighting back tears, but his eyes were gray and clear as always. The silver hair that had been crossed with dark streaks as long as I had known him now seemed a dull gray. The hands in his lap were steady. He reached into a pocket.

"Get coffee." He looked at the girls. "Get two apiece for everybody."

"Who was it, Singleton?"

"Get the coffee. We'll talk later." He looked at the girl who was curled up. "She's not good."

"Shock?"

"Real light. If it was going to get worse, I think it would have. Maybe you'd better bring June." He got up again and tried to straighten the curled-up girl. He asked her to turn on her back. She looked OK. She tried to fight him. "Help him," I told the one who had been bawling.

The restaurant was better than a hundred yards off. A hillbilly voice was deviling a truck song. June was in the kitchen. I told her I needed help, and she came right away. Business is one thing, people are another. She has always been that way. She brought a Silex with her, and we walked back across the lot. In the distance there was the sound of two sirens crossing against each other.

"The other police car."

"That and a fire truck," she told me.

June is a fine woman, once very pretty but now careless of her appearance and too heavy. It is always sad and a little strange to see a nice-looking woman allow herself to slide. There must be reasons, but not the kind that bear thinking about. She had a good hand with people, a good way. She ran a straight business. When we came to the room, she asked us to leave and started mothering the girls. We went outside with the coffee and sat on the step.

"I'm sorry," I told him. "I shouldn't have blown up, but for a minute I could have killed them. I hate every fool like them."

"It's their road too."

"I know."

"Everybody makes mistakes. You—me—nobody has perfect judgment."

"But not like that."

"No. No, we're not like that, but she won't ever be again either. She has to live with that."

I understood a little more about him. He was good in his judgments. It was suddenly not a matter for us to forgive. There was the law. It had nothing to do with us.

We sat listening to the muffled sounds from the room behind us. Soon, off at the downhill corner of the lot, headlights appeared coming from the wreck. The state car cruised across the lot. It stopped at the end of the motel row. Singleton stood up and motioned to him. The car moved toward us, rolling in gently. The cop got out. Manny was sitting in the back seat. He was slumped over and quiet. When the cop slammed the door, he did not look up.

He was an older cop, too old to be riding a cruiser. In the darkness and excitement there had been no way to tell much about him. He was tired and walked to us unofficially. We made room for him on the step. He sat between us, letdown, his hands shaking with either fatigue or nervousness.

"Charles," he said to Singleton, "who was he?"

"You'd better have some coffee," Singleton told him. He reached over and put his hand on the cop's shoulder. I poured coffee from the Silex, and he drank it fast.

"Gates," said Singleton. "Island Oil. When Haber went broke, I pulled tanks for two years." He stopped as if reflecting. "He was pretty good. I broke him in."

The cop pointed to the car. "Him?"

"Manley, Johnny Manley."

"You're taking him in," I said. "What's the charge?"

"I don't know," the cop told me. "I wouldn't even know what would stick. His rig's half in one lane. If you're going to say I need a charge, then I'll take him in for obstructing the road."

"I didn't mean that. I'm not trying to push you. I just wanted to see how you felt."

"Then ask straight out. I don't know what I think myself till I get the whole story."

Singleton walked to the car. He leaned through the window to call softly to Manny. Manny did not move, and Singleton leaned against the car for a little while as the cop and I sat and watched. A couple of drivers came by, curious but respectfully silent, and the cop ran them off. June came out with a chair and sat beside the steps. The two girls came out and stood quietly. I looked at them. They were both young, pretty, and in the present circumstances useless and destructively ignorant. I could no longer hate them.

"Is that him?" one of them whispered.

"Yes." I felt like whispering myself. It seemed wrong to be talking about him when he was no more than ten yards off, but I doubted that he was listening to anyone. He was looking down, his face, which was never very good-looking, was drawn tight around his fixed eyes, and his hands were not visible. Perhaps he held them in his lap.

"They can't prove nothing," the cop said. "I bet he gets off." He stood up. "Let's get it over with; we've wasted time."

Singleton came back then. "Tell me," the cop said to him.

"He won't be driving again. I don't know what the law will do, but I know what Manny can't do. He won't take another one out. You can take her statement on the accident"— he pointed at one of the girls—"and his"—he pointed at me. "I was just over the crest—couldn't see it very well. What I can tell you about is afterward, but"—he turned to the girls— "I want to tell you something first maybe you ought to know. I've known that man yonder seven, eight years. He's a quiet guy. Doesn't say much; really not hard to get to know. He likes people, has patience with them. Sometimes you think he'd be more sociable if he just knew how to start." He hesitated as if searching for words.

"I don't know exactly how to tell it. Instead of talking, he does nice things. Always has extra equipment to spare if the scales are open and the ICC's checking, or maybe puts a bag of apples in your cab before you leave out. Kid stuff—yes, that's it, kid stuff a lot of the time. Sometimes guys don't understand and joke him.

"When he finally got married, it was to a girl who started the whole thing, not him. She was wild. Silly, you know, not especially bad but not the best either. She worked at a stop in Tennessee and quit work after she married instead of going back like she planned. The guy has something. He did good for that girl. I don't know what's going to happen to them now, and it's none of our business I guess, but I just thought you ought to know."

He turned back to the cop. "I came over the crest and saw Manny's and Arnie's stoplights and saw Arnie's trailer jump and pitch sideways till he corrected and got it stopped. I pulled in behind them, and they were both already out and running. Before I got there, I saw the fire. He could tell you more about how it started." He looked at me. I was thinking about it. I nodded for him to go on because it was very real to me, still happening. I wondered if maybe I could get out of having to describe it. I knew there would have to be a corroborative statement, so as Singleton told it I thought along with him.

He did a good job of the telling. He had gotten there only a minute or so after Manny and I were on the scene. Manny jumped from his cab, dodged around the car with the girls in it, and ran to the wreck. I took only enough time to grab my extinguisher. When I got there, Manny was on top of the wreck trying to pull Gates out and holding the door up at the same time.

The tanker had gone in hitting the ditch fast but stretching out the way you want to try to hit a ditch. It had made no motion to jackknife. The ditch had been too deep, and instead it had lain over on its side. All along there—for that matter, all through those hills—the roadside is usually an outcropping of limestone, slate, and coal. In the cuts and even in the valleys there is rock. Until the truck was pulled off, there would be no way to know. It was likely that the tank and maybe his saddle tank had been opened up on an outcrop of rock. There was a little flicker of fire forward of the cab. Gasoline, I had thought, but it did not grow quick like gasoline. The diesel from his tank was running down the ditch and muffled it some at first.

I went for it with the extinguisher, but it was growing and the extinguisher was a popgun. Manny started yelling to come help him, and I whirled and climbed up over the jutting wheel. Singleton was suddenly there, grabbing me, boosting me up. I took the cab door and held it up, and Gates started to yell.

Manny had him under the shoulders pulling hard, had him about halfway out, but he was hung up. I believe Gates's leg was pinched or held by the wheel. Otherwise Manny would not have gotten him out that far. Manny knew though. He knelt down beside him staring into the wrecked cab.

The fire was getting big behind me, building with a roar. It was flowing down the ditch but gaining backward over the surface rapidly. I gave Manny a little shove and closed the door over Gates's head so we could both reach him through the window. He was a small chunky man—hard to grasp. We got him under the arms and pulled hard, and he screamed again. The heat was close now. I was terrified, confused. We could not pull harder. There was no way to get him out.

Then I was suddenly alone. Manny jumped down, stumbling against Singleton, who tried to climb up and was driven back, his face lined and desperate in the fire glow. Manny disappeared running into the darkness. Where I was above the cab, the air was getting unbearably hot. The fire had not yet worked in under the wreck. I tugged hopelessly until I could no longer bear the heat and jumped down and rolled away. Singleton helped me up and pulled me back just as the screams changed from hurt to fear; high weeping, desperate and unbelieving cries as the heat but not the fire got to him.

I was held in horrified disbelief of what was happening. Outside the cab and in front of it were heavy oil flames. Gates, his head and neck and one hand outside the window, was leaning back away from them, screaming another kind of cry because the fire that had been getting close had arrived. The muscles of his neck and face were cast bronze in the fire glow, and his mouth was a wide black circle issuing cries. His eyes were closed tight, and his straining hand tried to pull himself away.

Then there was a noise, and he fell back and disappeared into the fire, quietly sinking to cremation with no further sound, and we turned to look behind us. Manny was standing helplessly, his pistol dropping from his shaking hand to the ground, and then he too was falling to the ground, covering his eyes with his hands and rolling on his side away from us.

"If I'd known, I wouldn't have stopped him," Singleton told the cop. "Of all the men I know, he's the only one who could have done that much."

He hesitated, running his hand through his graying hair. "I didn't help, you understand—didn't help." He looked pleading. "Nothing I could do, no use—Arn didn't help. Only Manny."

The girls and June were sobbing. The sky to the eastward was coming alive with light. The cop who was too old to be riding a cruiser looked blanched and even older in the beginning dawn. I felt as I had once felt at sea after battling an all-night storm. Only Singleton seemed capable of further speech, his almost ancient features passive but alive.

He looked at the patrol car where Manny still slumped. "They can't prove he killed a man. There's nothing to prove it with. They can't even prove the bullet didn't miss, and in a way that's the worst thing that can happen. You see, I know him. You think maybe he'll change after a while—maybe it will dull down and let him live normal. It won't. I sat with him before you came and did what I could, and it was nothing. Do they electrocute in this state or use gas? If they were kind, the way he is kind, they'd do one or the other."

3

PLAGIARISM
of term papers unlimited
FREEDOM VERSUS DETERMINISM

"Although it is hard to quantify the actual increase in student plagiarism, the rapid growth of the ghost-writing industry suggests that such theft has been substantial."* So writes Fred M. Hechinger, coauthor of *Growing Up in America*, a social history of America viewed through the perspective of education. "Last year, to cite a disconcerting example," Hechinger goes on, "two students at a prestigious university were found to have submitted, quite independently of each other, a little-known piece of published scholarship as their own senior theses. The coincidence of their unwitting choice of the same plagiarized material led to their discovery. But when the department chairman recommended against allowing the offenders to graduate with their class and asked instead that they be made to prove themselves by repeating the course the following semester, the institution's administrative machinery went into high gear—not to punish the violators but to overrule the chairman."†

Picture the scene: the office of a university dean. Call him Dean Evans. He sits behind a wide glass-topped mahogany desk reading a manuscript. The tall, thick, smoked glass window behind him frames a portion of the campus that remains curiously silent, despite the visible bustle of students going about their business. The lighting is soft, the floors are carpeted, the walls are crammed with books and plastered with plaques. When anyone speaks, the room seems to strengthen and deepen the words, to turn the prosaic precious.

Dean Evans closes the manuscript and returns it to Professor Anna Roth, who, all the while he was reading it, sat by with the glum expression of one facing a distasteful task. "That," says Evans, "is the best paper I've seen in years."

"It should be," says Roth. "The author's a leading authority in the field."

Dean Evans clears his throat once and says, "Do you mean that the student didn't author this?"

---

*Fred M. Hechinger, "What is Happening to Ethical Standards in Education?", *Saturday Review*, 1 November 1975, p. 56.
†Hechinger, pp. 56–57.

"I'm afraid he didn't."

"This is most serious, Anna. What do you propose we do?"

"Do we have a choice? A senior thesis is a requirement for graduation. The student did not fulfill the requirement. Draw your own conclusion."

Dean Evans smiles kindly and says, "As always, your logic is impeccable." Then he adds, "But logic often needs to be tempered by mercy if justice is to be served."

"What are you suggesting?"

Before Dean Evans can reply, his telephone rings. He is on the phone no more than a few seconds, and he only says three words, "Send her in." When he hangs up he explains to Professor Roth that he has invited Marge Triplett, the student's counselor, to join them. Although Professor Roth doesn't object, she fails to see what purpose will be served.

Counselor Triplett enters carrying a yellow portfolio bulging with papers. The three exchange cordialities, after which Dean Evans abruptly turns the conversation to the issue. "I thought, Anna, that Marge might give us some insight into the kind of person Ron is, not that that will in any way lessen the gravity of what he's done. But . . . well, it might give us a slant on why he did it."

"Is that so important?" Roth asks.

"I think it might be," says Counselor Triplett. "It might help us deal with him more fairly."

"You make it sound as if he's not quite responsible for what he did," says Roth.

"I'm sorry, Anna, I don't mean to imply that. It's just that he may not be as inexcusably responsible as he now seems."

"In which case we may wish to deal with him differently," adds the dean.

For a few seconds Professor Roth says nothing. She merely stares at her hands folded in her lap. Then, without raising her eyes, she says, "Proceed."

As Counselor Triplett tells it, Ron Turner is the product of an upper middle class family. His father is a dentist, his mother a librarian. He has a brother and sister, both older, and both quite successful. His brother is currently enrolled in Harvard Law School. Ron's sister has just begun medical school, hoping to specialize in gynecology and obstetrics. Achievement has always been a hallmark of the Turner family, and as a child Ron could recall his parents' rewarding academic achievement with appropriate gifts, privileges, and prerogatives. In some cases the Turner children even received money.

From all indications Ron was an average student, certainly not the equal of his siblings. As a result he never achieved as they did, nor was he rewarded the way they were.

More than once one of his parents said to Ron, "Well, I guess we know who has the brains in this family," or, "Well, don't you worry about it, Ron, you have other talents." But Ron never discovered what those other talents were. He tried his hand at sports but failed; he took up dramatics for a while, but never got more than bit parts; he even applied to the armed forces when he graduated from high school but was rejected because of a heart murmur. He once told

Counselor Triplett that he didn't think he would ever marry. When asked why, he said that he couldn't imagine anyone ever loving him.

For Ron, college has been a struggle, a thoroughly unenjoyable experience. He is barely maintaining a 2.5 grade point average on a 4-point system and has spent several semesters of his four years on probation, but he is determined to complete his college education. Counselor Triplett suggested to him in his sophomore year that perhaps he'd be happier in the liberal arts, perhaps in history or literature. But he insisted on being a science major. Evidently out of a competitiveness with his brother and sister, he expressed hope of one day going to medical school. Triplett informed him that his plans were probably unrealistic in light of his achievements, but he was adamant. "In fact," she tells Dean Evans and Professor Roth, "he became rather indignant and remarked that he was going to show a lot of people some day just what he was capable of."

"And now he has," says Professor Roth, "in a most tragic way." After a moment Roth speaks again, "It seems to me, Marge, that you are suggesting that the pressure to succeed became too great for Ron Turner to handle. That, in fact, he thought himself incapable of completing the senior thesis in a satisfactory way, much as he believes that no one can love him. And, thinking thus, he cracked under the strain."

Neither the dean nor the counselor says anything. Professor Roth searches their faces for even the hint of an answer. When none comes, she says softly, "If you are suggesting that, Marge, then you are suggesting that Ron Turner is not responsible for what he did. In which case he is not deserving of punishment."

The room is silent.

Plagiarism in education is certainly a moral issue, as much as embezzlement in banking or figure juggling in accounting. But it is hardly the only one that prevails in academia. Student cheating of all sorts; instructors' chronic failure to meet classes, prepare material adequately, and personally discharge responsibilities to their students; the hiring and maintaining of incompetent staff by administrators and boards of education—these and many more would probably fall under the heading of morality in education. Often the underlying justification for such questionable moral behavior is pressure—the pressure to pass courses, the pressure to get grades in order to gain admittance into graduate schools, the pressure to keep up with peers, the pressure to publish or perish, the pressure to satisfy governmental regulations, the pressure to maintain image. Those justifying such behavior say that they are not solely to blame for what they're doing, that they'd actually prefer to behave otherwise but can't given the circumstances of their lives. In so justifying their actions, they raise what is a most crucial question in morality: how responsible are we for what we do? Put another way: just how free is any of us to make moral decisions?

This chapter concerns the question of freedom and moral responsibility, a recurring topic in the history of humanity. Adolf Eichmann, who was ultimately hanged for his role in Nazi atrocities, pleaded that he could not have acted otherwise than he did, that he was following orders. In the 1970s Lt. William Calley, who was convicted of the deliberate and unprovoked slaying of civilians at My Lai, Vietnam, claimed that he too was following orders. In Calley's defense many argued that given his background, conditioning, and indoctrination, Calley could not help but do what he did. Similarly, those involved in the notorious Watergate affair and its related illegalities almost without exception claimed that they were victims of an unconscionable system. One of the principals, Jeb Stuart Magruder, in his book *One Man's Watergate,* contends that it was inconceivable to him that the president of the United States could ask him to do something wrong. In the 1976 Patty Hearst trial, defense attorney F. Lee Bailey's main line of defense was that Patty was coerced or brainwashed into breaking the law and therefore was not responsible for what she did.

In dealing with the issue of moral freedom and responsibility, it is tempting to concentrate exclusively on such sensational issues as these, for they often throw the problem into high relief. But at the same time, the bigger-than-life nature of these cases can remove the freedom issue from everyday lives, from the more common moral dilemmas that face people. For what is under discussion is this question: given our genetic and cultural backgrounds, how free are any of us to accept moral responsibility—*any* moral responsibility, not just that evident in the prominent news stories of the day? Each of the preceding celebrated cases evidences obvious restraints on personal freedom. But the question we raise here is: does any moral freedom exist to begin with? In order to throw light on this issue, it seems advisable to avoid the more dramatic issues where restricted freedom is obvious and focus instead on cases with less apparent constraints. In this way we will be better able to maintain an objective attitude. In brief, if there is no moral freedom, then Ron Turner ultimately is no more free than any of the more celebrated persons mentioned.

Moreover, if there is no moral freedom, then the basis for punishing people for the wrong that they apparently do bears reexamination, for we have traditionally based this practice on the belief that individuals could have acted otherwise. If they can never act otherwise, then by what right do we hold them morally responsible? Consider Ron Turner's case. No one disputes that Ron broke a rule, while other people, perhaps the majority, kept the rule. The issue is whether he or any of them could have acted differently given all the circumstances of their lives. To examine this question we must begin by examining the doctrine of determinism, which has proved so influential in the twentieth century.

DETERMINISM

The advance and increasing influence of science in the twentieth century has highlighted the question of freedom and moral responsibility, because central to scientific inquiry is the doctrine of determinism. Simply put, *determinism is the principle that every event has a cause.* In other words, nothing happens in the universe without a cause. Note that determinists do not say whether the cause is mental or physical, whether it is due to organisms, inorganic nature, or God. For determinists, the cause can be anything. Determinists do not argue that they know the cause of every event in the universe, nor all the causes of human behavior. They simply argue that, although we may be ignorant of such causes, these causes nevertheless exist.

Most recently deterministic principles have influenced the disciplines of psychology, sociology, and anthropology. These social sciences have made substantial progress in explaining why we think, feel, and act the way we do. As their influence increases, so does the view that humans, like everything else, are subject to causal laws. They are products of their pasts—their sociocultural environment, family, and genetic inheritance.

This view has received impetus from psychological behaviorism, a school of psychology that restricts the study of humans to what can be objectively observed—namely, human behavior. Founded by John B. Watson and popularized by B. F. Skinner, psychological behaviorism is not concerned with human motives and goals, or the purpose of speech or action. In effect, it maintains that human beings are assembled organic machines ready to run. As a result, behaviorists view all humans as empty organisms equipped with the same neural apparatus to be conditioned and programmed. Phenomena such as *will*—which we can define as the capacity to choose freely from among alternatives—find no place in psychological behaviorism. This view does not distinguish between humans and other aspects of nature, for human phenomena are as much the products of material forces as are inorganic and organic phenomena. In essence we are not free but determined.

In short, behaviorists would claim that Ron Turner was not free to do other than what he did—plagiarize his senior thesis. Determinists would argue further that, since he was not free, he is no more morally responsible for his actions than any other human is. As B. F. Skinner puts it, "The free man who is held responsible for the behavior of the external biological organism is only a prescientific substitute for the kinds of cause which are discovered in the course of a scientific analysis. All these alternatives lie outside the individual."*

So, some argue that moral freedom and responsibility are not compatible with the doctrine of determinism. They say that if we believe that humans are morally responsible agents, then we can't believe in scientific determinism, which, by definition, would not allow humans to be morally free when making a choice. If we maintain that humans are morally responsible, then, they contend, we must believe in *indeterminism, the doctrine that at least some events in the realm of human actions are entirely independent of prior causes.* Yet, indeterminism seems to run contrary to tried and proven scientific methodology.

The issue of whether or not Ron Turner is morally responsible for what he has done, therefore, has implications that extend beyond the walls of Dean Evans's office. For the heart of the moral responsibility question is the issue of determinism itself and whether the doctrine of determinism is true. But this

---

*B. F. Skinner, *Science and Human Behavior* (New York: Free Press, 1965), p. 285.

question far exceeds the parameters of ethics. What does not, however, and what must concern us is whether or not freedom is compatible with determinism. There are forceful arguments on both sides. But before giving these, let's try to throw some light on the concept of freedom.

FREEDOM

We can speak of all kinds of freedom—freedom of religion, freedom of speech, freedom of thought, freedom of political expression. *But in ethics we take freedom in its broadest sense to mean that characteristically human capacity to exercise some power of choice between options.* Notice the phrase *some power.* Obviously no one is *absolutely* free in the sense that one's freedom is totally unlimited. So, when we speak of freedom, we are referring to relative freedom, not absolute. For example, the court-martial board decided that William Calley was free in this sense to act other than the way he did. Similarly, a San Francisco jury decided that Patty Hearst was relatively free to have not acted in concert with the Symbionese Liberation Army during her captivity. And Professor Roth would argue that Ron Turner was free to plagiarize or not to plagiarize. In understanding this notion of freedom, it helps to realize the conditions under which someone's behavior is generally excused, for under such conditions the persons are not considered free to have acted other than the way they did. Let's return to the dean's office to see what these conditions are.

Roth: Marge, you realize that Ron was perfectly aware of the consequences of his action?
Triplett: Yes, I do.
Roth: And that he was not being coerced to plagiarize?
Triplett: Not in the way that I think you mean.
Evans: What Professor Roth means, I think, is that no one was forcing him to do what he did in the sense of threatening him. Am I right, Professor?
Roth: Precisely. Furthermore, he is the one who went to this organization, contracted for the work, and submitted it as his own. All the while having an alternative: to submit his own.

Roth has amplified the concept of freedom by indicating the general conditions under which we generally excuse behavior. They are: (1) justifiable ignorance of consequences, (2) constraints that force the person to behave in a prescribed way, (3) inability or incapacity to control the circumstances surrounding the act, and (4) the absence of the ability and/or opportunity to perform an optional act.* Since all of these conditions were absent in Ron's case, Professor Roth concludes he must have been free; therefore, he is responsible.

---

*See Paul Taylor, *Problems of Moral Philosophy,* 2nd ed. (Belmont, Calif.: Dickenson, 1973), p. 277.

Triplett: Anna, I agree with you. Everything you say is so.

Roth: Then Ron Turner's responsible for what he did.

Triplett: But I'm afraid I don't agree with that.

Roth: I don't understand.

Triplett: Given what we know about Ron Turner—I mean everything—I don't think he could have acted other than the way he did.

Roth: But you said yourself that he was free of coercion. That no one or thing was forcing him to do what he did.

Triplett: No *one* thing or *one* person, perhaps. But I believe there was a whole nexus of things operating.

Roth: A nexus?

Evans: What Marge means, I think, is that given everything in Ron's life prior to what he did, he couldn't help himself.

Having thrown some light on the concept of freedom, let's now see why many contend that determinism precludes personal freedom.

FREEDOM AS INCOMPATIBLE WITH DETERMINISM

In arguing their case, determinists frequently focus on the second criterion under which we generally excuse behavior, constraints. Like Marge Triplett they argue that even though individuals themselves may not be aware of any internal or external constraints influencing their behavior, they are only deluding themselves if determinism is a fact. Thus, before we knew anything about laws of gravity, things still behaved according to those principles. Likewise, psychological determinists argue that even though we may not know why we are behaving the way we do, we are no more free to exercise free choice than we are to leap a mile into the air under our own physical power. In other words, what any of us does is the only thing that we can do, because our behavior is governed by causal laws. And if, like Ron Turner, we cannot have acted otherwise, then morally we cannot be held responsible for what we do. Those who argue like Marge Triplett that determinism and moral responsibility are incompatible are called *incompatibilists* or *hard determinists*.

As a result of this argument, many ethicists argue that if there is to be moral responsibility, there cannot be behavioral determinism. They insist that humans cannot be explained solely in scientific terms, that humans do exercise free choice, that when faced with what we call *moral problems,* humans are rightly termed *moral agents.* In other words they advance an indeterminism doctrine.

In a famous essay on the subject, Professor C. A. Campbell argues that moral responsibility requires what he calls a *contra-causal type of freedom.* By a *contra-causal freedom,* he means a freedom that is not compatible with the doctrine of determinism. Campbell states his position succinctly.

If we say that A ought to have done X, we imply that in our opinion he could have done X. But we assign moral blame to a man only for failing to do what we think he morally ought to have done. Hence if we morally blame A for not having done X, we imply that he could have done X even though in fact he did not. In other words, we imply that A could have acted otherwise than he did. And that means that we imply, as a necessary condition of man's being morally blameworthy, that he enjoyed a freedom of a kind not compatible with unbroken causal continuity.*

But the behavioral determinist is likely to argue that this is begging the question, that the whole point is that humans should not be morally blameworthy because they could not have acted otherwise. They would argue that, whereas our knowledge of causes is daily increasing and lends hope to the belief that ultimately we will know the causes of human actions although we might not know them now, there is no evidence for indeterminism of this sort—there's no evidence to believe that some events are uncaused. Therefore, to conclude that even some events are uncaused is a hasty conclusion. True, there may be an area of events *not known* to be caused, but this area seems to be dwindling rather than increasing. To posit indeterminism because every single cause has not been established is an argument from ignorance. Furthermore, determinists object that if indeterminism is true, then we can't be free, because if even some acts are uncaused, we can never know if they originate with us. We can't know that they are *ours* if they could be uncaused by us.

Other philosophers, not wishing to be stranded on the shaky limb of indeterminism, argue that determinism and freedom are compatible.

FREEDOM AS COMPATIBLE WITH DETERMINISM

In contrast with hard determinism and indeterminism is the school of thought called *soft determinism*. A soft determinist is not a hard determinist who has lost his nerve. On the contrary, in trying to solve the freedom/determinism problem, soft determinists recognize that genetic and environmental influences predispose us to behave in certain ways; such factors may incline Ron Turner to plagiarize. But, in the last analysis, soft determinists maintain that Ron Turner need not necessarily plagiarize, that none of us must make the choices we do. None of us is, to use existentialist Jean-Paul Sartre's words, a "kind of moss, or a fungus, or a cauliflower." Indeed, "we are our choices. Man is freedom."† Professor Roth appears to be of this mind.

---

*C. A. Campbell, "Is Free Will a Pseudo Problem?" in *Problems of Moral Philosophy*, ed. Paul W. Taylor (Belmont, Calif.: Dickenson, 1972), p. 303.

†Jean-Paul Sartre, "Existentialism is a Humanism," in *Existentialism from Dostoevsky to Sartre*, ed. Walter Kaufman (New York: World, 1965), p. 291.

Roth: I'm well aware that to a great degree Ron Turner, like all of us, is a product of his experience.

Evans: I think Marge is saying no more than this, Anna.

Roth: I disagree, Dean Evans. I think that she's saying quite a bit more when she says that because of his experiences Ron could not have behaved other than he did.

Triplett: I don't believe he could have.

Roth: I couldn't disagree more.

Triplett: Are you suggesting that what Ron did was uncaused?

Roth: Of course not. It most certainly was caused.

Triplett: Then why hold him responsible?

Roth: Because he himself, it seems to me, is a significant part of the cause of his behavior. And by that I simply mean that he could have acted otherwise. He could have chosen not to plagiarize.

Notice that Professor Roth does not deny the doctrine of determinism. She admits that Ron's act was caused. But she insists that he was part of that cause. This is a soft deterministic position. *Soft determinism, or compatabilism, argues that determinism is consistent with moral responsibility.*

According to most soft determinists, when we call an action *free*, we don't mean that it was uncaused. We mean that the person performing the action was not forced to perform it. But the freedom that the soft determinists assume is not the contra-causal kind that indeterminists say is incompatible with determinism. It is the freedom that springs from exercising a choice among alternatives. True, the choices are caused, but soft determinists argue that we ourselves are at least part of the cause, that some of our actions, such as moral judgments, are caused by our own desires and choices. For this reason they say we are morally responsible for what we do.

In the Ron Turner case, soft determinists might observe the following:

1. Ron could have done otherwise.

2. Ron tried to write his own paper.

3. Ron read several books relating to the topic of his choice, jotted down a few of his own ideas on paper, formulated three different outlines for the paper, etc.

4. Ron could not but plagiarize.

It seems that soft determinists would then be interested in showing that (1) can be argued on the basis of (2) or (3), and that given (2) or (3), it is justifiable to claim (1). If such is the case, to argue (4) while knowing (1) is justifiable would be difficult.

Critics of soft determinism insist that we don't formulate desires and choices, that these too are caused by forces outside our control. Some even insist that it is meaningless to suggest that such personality and character traits could be different.

Evans: I think it's important here to ask, or at least speculate, about why the student did what he did. ,

Triplett: Because of his personality and character, because of years of conditioning at home, in school, and in society. And over these he had no control.

Evans: So he wasn't responsible for the plagiarism?

Triplett: I don't see how he could be.

Roth: But you conveniently ignore that Ron Turner preferred to plagiarize rather than not to.

Triplett: But his preferences and desires were also caused by his past. So in reality he wasn't exercising free choice at all.

Roth: You make it sound as if none of us can change a desire. Yet experience contradicts that. How many people, for example, suppress the desire to smoke? Indeed, many give up smoking after having engaged in it for many years.

Triplett: I'm one of them. But I don't take any credit for that.

Evans: Believe me, you should. I've been trying for years and can't break the habit.

Triplett: I think that's only because I have within me the ability to stop smoking and you don't. But neither one of us is responsible for having or not having the ability. Maybe as a child I was trained to have more self-discipline than you; maybe because my father and uncle, both heavy smokers, died of lung cancer. I don't know. But I don't think it's anything I should take credit for having done or that you should take the blame for not having done, Dean Evans.

Roth: I think you're warping my position. I never said that you're free with respect to everything. I can easily agree that many things are outside our abilities. My only point is that we are free with respect to some things—that freedom exists.

Triplett: But even if that's so, how do you know when you are exercising freedom?

Roth: When you perform an action in the absence of coercion, pressure, or duress.

Triplett: But that's the point. Perhaps no pressure is evident. Perhaps we can't experience the constraints. But from what psychology teaches us they could easily be influencing us on a subconscious level.

Philosopher Richard Taylor makes an observation similar to Triplett's. Says Taylor:

> Whether a desire which causes my body to behave in a certain way is inflicted upon me by another person, for instance, or derived from hereditary factors, or indeed from anything at all, matters not the least. In any case, if it is in fact the cause of my bodily behavior, I cannot but act in accordance with it. Wherever it came from, whether from personal or impersonal origins, it was entirely caused or determined, and not within my control. Indeed if determinism is true . . . all those inner states which cause my body to behave in whatever ways it behaves must arise from circumstances that existed before I was born; for the chain of causes and effects is

infinite, and none could have been the least different, given those that preceded.*

Taylor's observation bears directly on Ron Turner's moral responsibility.

Evans: It seems to me that the only way we can hold Ron Turner responsible is by also believing that if everything else were the same, he could have acted otherwise.

Roth: What do you mean by *everything else?*

Evans: I mean if any of us chooses freely, that seems to imply that given precisely the same circumstances—I mean if we could replicate conditions that prevailed when we made the first decision—we could choose and do other than what we did.

Triplett: I don't believe that we could act otherwise.

Roth: I think we could.

At this point it seems that Professor Roth is being unfaithful to her determinism. This is hardly grounds for divorce, but it is inconsistent. Part and parcel of the deterministic doctrine is that given a set of circumstances, a particular action would occur and recur if the circumstances were replicated. But it seems that we can retain the concepts of obligation and guilt as ethical ideas only if we can also believe that actions could have been other than they were, even though everything else had remained the same. How to reconcile these incompatible doctrines? It seems that soft determinists must explain this apparent inconsistency in their position.

In raising this evident inconsistency we have returned to the central problem: how can human freedom exist together with determinism? Obviously there is no simple answer. But understanding the problem should reveal a dimension to morality that sometimes goes sadly unexplored. In grasping the freedom/ determinism problem, notice that the many objections to hard determinism, indeterminism, and soft determinism reside in the controversial but logical implications of these doctrines. Many consider these implications to be questionable claims that their respective doctrines spawn.

SUMMARY

Doctrine

Hard Determinism: the doctrine that every event has a cause, including all human behavior

Objections

1. It logically follows that there can be no moral freedom.

---

*Richard Taylor, *Metaphysics,* 2nd ed. (Englewood Cliffs, N.J.: Prentice-Hall, 1974), p. 46.

Doctrine	Objections
	2. It logically follows that at least in theory there is no basis for holding persons morally responsible for what they do.
Indeterminism: the doctrine that at least some events, those in the area of human behavior, occur by chance	**1.** There is insufficient evidence to hold to indeterminism.
	2. It logically follows that humans can never be sure when they have chosen freely and when they have not.
	3. It logically follows that at least in theory there is no basis for holding persons morally responsible, since it is impossible in a given circumstance to establish that responsibility.
Soft Determinism: the doctrine that although everything is caused, human choice is one of those causes	**1.** If everything is caused, then it follows that human choice must also be caused, in which event it cannot be free choice; thus, the doctrine is inconsistent.
	2. The social sciences are almost daily revealing new findings that indicate underlying reasons, such as subconscious and unconscious motivation, for human choices.
	3. The doctrine is inconsistent because on the one hand it espouses determinism, which contends that identical conditions will produce identical results, while endorsing moral freedom and responsibility, which presupposes that identical conditions would not necessarily produce identical results.

CONCLUSIONS

There is no question of the weighty evidence for behavioristic determinism. Humans do feel the press of genetic and environmental influences. These obviously severely limit personal freedom, including moral freedom. In some cases causal influences may become so intense that individuals could not have acted other than they did. But still, because in a given situation they perhaps acted in the only way they could have does not lead to the conclusion that in *all* cases humans can act in one and only one way. The issue is whether humans can *ever* act other than they do.

As Jean-Paul Sartre points out in *Being and Nothingness,* although brute things can from the start limit our freedom of action, the extent of their limit is determined by freedom itself, which constitutes the framework within which these things will work their influences. To understand this observation it is necessary to realize that, philosophically, to be free does not mean to obtain what you wish but rather to attempt to obtain it. In short, success is not necessary for freedom.

For example, during her captivity Patty Hearst may very well have been unable to escape from her captors. But it is more difficult to imagine that she could never have tried to escape. In the sense that she was unable to succeed, she was not free. But in the sense that she still could try, she was free. By *trying* is meant that, whatever our condition, we can project a change and discover the value of our projection by undertaking some action. If we look at freedom philosophically, as the autonomy of choice, we seem to be on much firmer ground for pleading freedom's case than if we view freedom in a sociopolitical context as solely the attainment of ends.

Perhaps Ron Turner could not have written his own senior thesis. But it seems that he could have tried. Some would argue that given the circumstances of his life, he could not even have tried. But this would presuppose that he was not even aware of the alternatives, for if he were aware of the alternatives, he would have been aware that one of them was to submit his own work. But to understand what submitting his own work meant, Ron would necessarily realize that it entailed doing his own work, which in turn required an effort on his part. If upon attempting the thesis he could not accomplish it, then it is clear that he was not free to attain his goal any more than a human is free to leap a tall building in a single bound. But both Ron and the human are free to make the attempt, as long as they have the capacity to conceive of that alternative. Of course, lacking that capacity, it is hard to imagine in what sense they would be free or held morally responsible. But excluding cases of obviously profound and irreparable brain damage, it is very difficult to imagine situations in which humans cannot conceive of such basic alternatives as acting or refraining from acting in a certain way.

EXERCISES FOR ANALYSIS

EXERCISE 1

In the following passages, determine whether the reasons given for the positions stated or implied are adequate. Look for fallacies.

1. "There's nothing wrong with my buying a term paper from a term paper mill and submitting it as my own. After all, it *is* my own. I paid good money for it. I didn't steal or plagiarize it. Since I purchased it, I own it and can do with it whatever I want."

2. "Of course plagiarism is moral. Everyone does it."

3. "Sure plagiarism is wrong. But submitting work that someone has freely given you isn't plagiarism, and I don't think that doing that is always wrong. For example, suppose a person just had to pass a particular course. In the middle of the term, the professor assigns a term paper. The person just doesn't have the time to meet the assignment without jeopardizing other courses. I think that under those circumstances the person would be justified in submitting as his own a paper that someone else has given him."

4. Debbie is in a bind. Time is short and she must write two term papers, one for criminology and one for sociology. She can't do both without great personal inconvenience. So, she decides to write just one and so fashion it that it satisfies both course requirements, despite her instructors' directions to the contrary. Debbie is convinced that there's nothing wrong with her action. (An interesting aspect of this—whether or not the instructors' directives against submitting one paper for several courses are fair and reasonable.)

5. You're working as a teacher's assistant. One day while completing some routine chores in the teacher's office, you stumble across a test that will be given in a class that you are taking. You read the test, reasoning that you would be doing yourself a disservice if you did not.

6. **Dean:** Professor, I think that your habit of arriving for class ten minutes late is morally wrong.
Professor: Why? I know I can cover the material in the abbreviated session.
Dean: That's not the point. Everyone else must be to class on time. You shouldn't be an exception. Why, before we know it, no instructor will be showing up for classes at all. They'll simply cover material by making reading assignments.

(Does an instructor have a moral obligation to be punctual?)

7. **Professor:** I think the idea of assigning courses strictly on the basis of who has been in the department the longest is immoral. Just think of it: no consideration is given to qualifications. A teacher could be utterly incompetent in a subject, yet teach it simply because he or she has seniority.

Chairperson: In theory you may be right, Professor. But in practice you are dead wrong. Do you know why? Because, if nothing else, experience informs one of one's strengths and weaknesses. No instructor would choose a subject in which he or she were utterly incompetent.

(Is a chairperson under a moral obligation to assign courses primarily on the basis of subject matter qualifications?)

8. **Teacher:** Don't you know that cheating is wrong?
   Student: I wasn't cheating.
   Teacher: But I saw you looking directly at Cribsheet's paper.
   Student: You don't understand. Cribsheet and I have an agreement to share answers. I wasn't taking anything from him. Cribsheet was freely giving me his answers.

9. Elmer Fudd is taking a "Mickey Mouse" course. The course is offered in an amphitheatre to 223 students known to the professor only by numbers. It's common knowledge that nobody ever flunks the course, its being just one of those courses that everyone must take to graduate. Fudd attends all the lectures, passes all the tests, and now needs only to pass the final exam to receive a passing grade. There's little doubt that Fudd will pass the test, but it's being offered at a time that conflicts with a most important job interview that cannot be rescheduled. Everyone must take the test at the appointed time, no exceptions. So, Fudd decides to send in fraternity brother Magoo to take the test. Magoo passes the test, but just barely. Indeed, Fudd ends up with a grade considerably lower than he probably would have if he himself had taken the test. But at the same time, he got the job that he interviewed for.

EXERCISE 2

How you view the morality of punishment relates directly to the freedom/ determinism issue. One view of punishment, the *retributivist,* contends that the only moral standard for administering punishment is the law, by which all people are treated equally and get precisely what they deserve. The *deterrent* view, on the other hand, contends that the function of punishment is to dissuade people from acting in a way thought to be undesirable. Finally, the *therapeutic* view of punishment argues that the function of punishment must be to rehabilitate, that is, to help restore an offender to a functional social role. With which views of freedom—hard determinism, soft determinism, or indeterminism— would you associate these concepts of punishment? (Begin by stating assumptions each view must make about personal freedom in order to support its conclusion. In other words, in order to claim that punishment is only moral when viewed as administering to people exactly what they *deserve,* the retributivist view must assume something about personal freedom. What is that assumption? That we are ultimately free? Not free?)

EXERCISE 3

Should Ron Turner be punished? If so, why? (Remember that not allowing him to graduate is the same treatment that someone who failed to turn in a thesis paper would receive. Can this treatment, therefore, be considered punishment? Is it really deferring a reward?)

SELECTIONS FOR FURTHER READING

Freedom/Determinism

Berlin, Isaiah. *Historical Inevitability.* London: Oxford University Press, 1954.

Campbell, C. A. *In Defense of Free Will.* New York: Humanities Press, 1967.

Dworkin, G., ed. *Determinism, Free Will and Moral Responsibility.* Englewood Cliffs, N.J.: Prentice-Hall, 1970.

Glover, J. *Responsibility.* New York: Humanities Press, 1970.

Hook, Sidney, ed. *Determinism and Freedom in the Age of Modern Science.* New York: New York University Press, 1958.

Sartre, Jean-Paul. *Being and Nothingness.* Translated by H. E. Barnes. New York: Philosophical Library, 1956.

Punishment

Acton, H. B., ed. *The Philosophy of Punishment.* London: Macmillan, 1969.

Beccaria, C. B. *On Crimes and Punishments.* Translated by H. Paolucci. Indianapolis: Bobbs-Merrill, 1963.

Fitzgerald, P. J. *Criminal Law and Punishment.* Oxford: Clarendon Press, 1962.

Hart, H. L. A. *Punishment and Responsibility.* Oxford: Oxford University Press, 1968.

Henderich, T. *Punishment: The Supposed Justifications.* London: Hutchinson, 1969.

SARTRE/*Being and Nothingness*

Perhaps the most vocal and influential exponent of personal freedom is existentialist philosopher Jean-Paul Sartre. Being and Nothingness, *from which two portions follow, contains Sartre's classic defense of freedom.*

In the first portion, "Freedom and facticity: the situation," Sartre makes the point that to be free does not mean, as is commonly thought, that we are able to obtain what we wish. In other words, success is not necessary for freedom. Rather, freedom means autonomy of choice, that is, the ability to intend something, not just to act on an intention or to achieve what is intended. In effect, as long as we are able to choose to choose ("by oneself to determine oneself to wish"), we are free.

In the second portion, "Freedom and responsibility," Sartre discusses the implications of his contention that we are free. The chief implication is that we are acutely responsible for our decisions, even, of course, for our decision to decide. At the same time, we have no certain directives, no absolute moral guidelines, to follow. Thus, we are "condemned to be free." Do you think Sartre's contentions would tend to make people more or less moral? Why?

FREEDOM AND FACTICITY: THE SITUATION

The decisive argument which is employed by common sense against freedom consists in reminding us of our impotence. Far from being able to modify our situation at our whim, we seem to be unable to change ourselves. I am not "free" either to escape the lot of my class, of my nation, of my family, or even to build up my own power or my fortune or to conquer my most insignificant appetites or habits. I am born a worker, a Frenchman, an hereditary syphilitic, or a tubercular. The history of a life, whatever it may be, is the history of a failure. The coefficient of adversity of things is such that years of patience are necessary to obtain the feeblest result. Again it is necessary "to obey nature in order to command it"; that is, to insert my action into the network of determinism. Much more than he appears "to make himself," man seems "to be made" by climate and the earth, race and class, language, the history of the collectivity of which he is a part, heredity, the individual circumstances of his childhood, acquired habits, the great and small events of his life.

This argument has never greatly troubled the partisans of human freedom. Descartes, first of all, recognized both that the will is infinite and that it is necessary "to try to conquer ourselves rather than fortune." Here certain distinctions ought to be made.

Many of the facts set forth by the determinists do not actually deserve to enter into our considerations. In particular the coefficient of adversity in things can not be an argument against our freedom, for it is *by us*—i.e., by the preliminary positing of an end—that this coefficient of adversity arises. A particular crag, which manifests a profound resistance if I wish to displace it, will be on the contrary a valuable aid if I want to climb upon it in order to look over the countryside. In itself—if one can imagine what the crag can be in itself—it is neutral; that is, it waits to be illuminated by an end in order to manifest itself as adverse or helpful. Again it can manifest itself in one or the other way within an instrumental-complex which is already established. Without picks and piolets, paths already worn, and a technique of climbing, the crag would be neither easy nor difficult to climb; the question would not be posited, it would not support any relation of any kind with the technique of mountain climbing. Thus although brute things (what Heidegger calls "brute existents") can from the start limit our freedom of action, it is our freedom itself which must first constitute the framework, the technique, and the ends in relation to which they will manifest themselves as limits. Even if the crag is revealed as "too difficult to climb," and if we must give up the ascent, let us note that the crag is revealed as such only because it was originally grasped as "climbable"; it is therefore our freedom which constitutes the limits which it will subsequently encounter.

Of course, even after all these observations, there remains an unnamable and unthinkable residuum which belongs to the in-itself considered and which is responsible for the fact that in a world illuminated by our freedom, this particular crag will be more favorable for scaling and that one not. But this residue is far from being originally a limit for freedom; in fact, it is thanks to this residue—that is, to the brute in-itself as such—that freedom arises as freedom. Indeed common sense will agree with us that the being who is said to be *free* is the one who can *realize* his projects. But in order for the act to be able to allow a *realization*, the simple projection of a possible end must be distinguished *a priori* from the realization of this end. If conceiving is enough for realizing, then I am plunged in a world like that of a dream in which the possible is no longer in any way distinguished from the real. I am condemned henceforth to see the world modified at the whim of the changes of my consciousness; I can not practice in relation to my conception the "putting into brackets" and the suspension of judgment which will distinguish a simple fiction from a real choice. If the object appears as soon as it is simply conceived, it will no longer be chosen or merely wished for. Once the distinction between the simple wish, the representation which I could choose, and the choice is abolished, freedom disappears too. We are free when the final term by which we make known to ourselves what we are is an end; that is, not a real existent like that which in the supposition which we have made could fulfill our wish, but an object which does not yet exist. But consequently this end can be transcendent only if it is separated from us at the same time that it is accessible. Only an ensemble of real existents can separate us from this end—in the same way that this end can be conceived only as a state-to-come of the real existents which separate me from it. It is nothing but the outline of an order of existents—that is, a series of dispositions to be assumed by existents on the foundation of their actual relations. By the internal negation, in fact, the for-itself illuminates the existents in their mutual relations by means of the end which it posits, and it projects this end in terms of the determinations which it apprehends in the existent. There is no circle, as we have seen, for the upsurge of the for-itself is effected at one stroke. But if this is the case, then the very order of the existents is indispensable to freedom itself. It is by means of them that freedom is separated from and reunited to the end which it pursues and which makes known to it what it is. Consequently the resistance which freedom reveals in the existent, far from being a danger to freedom, results only in enabling it to arise as freedom. There can be a free for-itself only as engaged in a resisting world. Outside of this engagement the notions of freedom, of determinism, of necessity lose all meaning.

In addition it is necessary to point out to "common sense" that the formula "to be free" does not mean "to obtain what one has wished" but rather "by oneself to determine oneself to wish" (in the broad sense of choosing). In other words success is not important to freedom. The discussion which opposes common sense to philosophers stems here from a misunderstanding: the empirical and popular concept of "freedom" which has been produced by historical, political, and moral circumstances is equivalent to "the ability to obtain the ends chosen." The technical and philosophical concept of freedom, the only one which we are considering here, means only the autonomy of choice. It is necessary, however, to note that the choice, being identical with acting, supposes a commencement of realization in order that the choice may be distinguished from the dream and the wish. Thus we shall not say that a prisoner is always free to go out of prison, which would be absurd, nor that he is always free to long for release, which would be an irrelevant truism, but that he is always free to try to escape (or get himself liberated); that is, that whatever his condition may be, he can project his escape and learn the value of his project by undertaking some action. Our description of freedom, since it does not distinguish between choosing and doing, compels us to abandon at once the distinction between intention and the act. The intention can no more be separated from the act than thought can be separated from the language which expresses it; and as it happens that our speech informs us of our thought, so our act will inform us of our intentions—that is, it will enable us to disengage our intentions, to schematize them, and to make objects of them instead of limiting us to living them.

FREEDOM AND RESPONSIBILITY

Although the considerations which are about to follow are of interest primarily to the ethicist, it may nevertheless be worthwhile after these descriptions and arguments to return to the freedom of the for-itself and try to understand what the fact of this freedom represents for human destiny.

The essential consequence of our earlier remarks is that man being condemned to be free carries the weight of the whole world on his shoulders; he is responsible for the world and for himself as a way of being. We are taking the word "responsibility" in its ordinary sense as "consciousness (of) being the incontestable author of an event or of an object." In this sense the responsibility of the for-itself is overwhelming since he is the one by whom it happens that *there is* a world; since he is also the one who makes himself be, then whatever may be the situation in which he finds himself, the for-itself must wholly assume this situation with its peculiar coefficient of adversity, even though it be insupportable. He must assume the situation with the proud consciousness of being the author of it, for the very worst disadvantages or the worst threats which can endanger my person have meaning only in and through my project; and it is on the ground of the engagement which I am that they appear. It is therefore senseless to think of complaining since nothing foreign has decided what we feel, what we live, or what we are.

Furthermore this absolute responsibility is not resignation; it is simply the logical requirement of the consequences of our freedom. What happens to me happens through me, and I can neither affect myself with it nor revolt against it nor resign myself to it. Moreover, everything which happens to me is mine. By this we must understand first of all that I am always equal to what happens to me *qua* man, for what happens to a man through other men and through himself can only be human. The most terrible situations of war, the worst tortures do not create a non-human state of things; there is no non-human situation. It is only through fear, flight, and recourse to magical types of conduct that I shall decide on the non-human, but this decision is human, and I shall carry the entire responsibility for it. But in addition the situation is mine because it is the image of my free choice of myself and everything which it presents to me is mine in that this represents me and symbolizes me. Is it not I who decide the coefficient of adversity in things and even their unpredictability by deciding myself?

Thus there are no accidents in a life; a community event which suddenly bursts forth and involves me in it does not come from the outside. If I am mobilized in a war, this war is *my* war; it is in my image and I deserve it. I deserve it first because I could always get out of it by suicide or by desertion; these ultimate possibilities are those which must always be present for us when there is a question of envisaging a situation. For lack of getting out of it, I have chosen it. This can be due to inertia, to cowardice in the face of public opinion or because I prefer certain other values to the value of the refusal to join the war (the good opinion of my relatives, the honor of my family, etc.). Anyway you look at it, it is a matter of choice. This choice will be repeated later on again and again without a break until the end of the war. Therefore we must agree with the statement by J. Romains, "In war there are no innocent victims." If therefore I have preferred war to death or to dishonor, everything takes place as if I bore the entire responsibility for this war. Of course others have declared it, and one might be tempted perhaps to consider me as a simple accomplice. But this notion of complicity has only a juridical sense, and it does not hold here. For it depended on me that for me and by me this war should not exist, and I have decided that it does exist. There was no compulsion here, for the compulsion could have got no hold on a freedom. I did not have any excuse; for as we have said repeatedly in this book, the peculiar character of human reality is that it is without excuse. Therefore it remains for me only to lay claim to this war.

But in addition the war is *mine* because by the sole fact that it arises in a situation which I cause to be and that I can discover it there only by engaging myself for or against it, I can no longer distinguish at present the choice which I make of myself from the choice which I make of the war. To live this war is to choose myself through it and to choose it through my choice of myself. There can be no question of considering it as "four years of vacation" or as a "reprieve," as a "recess," the essential part of my responsibilities being elsewhere in my married, family, or professional life. In this war which I have chosen I choose myself from day to day, and I make it mine by making myself. If it is going to be four empty years, then it is I who bear the responsibility for this.

Finally, as we pointed out earlier, each person is an absolute choice of self from the standpoint of a world of knowledges and of techniques which this choice both assumes and illumines; each person is an absolute upsurge at an absolute date and is perfectly unthinkable at another date. It is therefore a waste of time to ask what I should have been if this war had not broken out, for I have chosen myself as one of the possible meanings of the epoch which imperceptibly led to war. I am not distinct from this same epoch; I could not be transported to another epoch without contradiction. Thus I am this war which restricts and limits and makes comprehensible the period which preceded it. In this sense we may define more precisely the responsibility of the for-itself if to the earlier quoted statement, "There are no innocent victims," we add the words, "We have the war we deserve." Thus, totally free, undistinguishable from the period for which I have chosen to be the meaning, as profoundly responsible for the war as if I had myself declared it, unable to live without integrating it in my situation, engaging myself in it wholly and stamping it with my seal, I must be without remorse or regrets as I am without excuse; for from the instant of my upsurge into being, I carry the weight of the world by myself alone without anything or any person being able to lighten it.

Yet this responsibility is of a very particular type. Someone will say, "I did not ask to be born." This is a naive way of throwing greater emphasis on our facticity. I am responsible for everything, in fact, except for my very responsibility, for I am not the foundation of my being. Therefore everything takes place as if I were compelled to be responsible. I am abandoned in the world, not in the sense that I might remain abandoned and passive in a hostile universe like a board floating on the water, but rather in the sense that I find myself suddenly alone and without help, engaged in a world for which I bear the whole responsibility without being able, whatever I do, to tear myself away from this responsibility for an instant. For I am responsible for my very desire of fleeing responsibilities. To make myself passive in the world, to refuse to act upon things and upon Others is still to choose myself, and suicide is one mode among others of being-in-the-world. Yet I find an absolute responsibility for the fact that my facticity (here the fact of my birth) is directly inapprehensible and even inconceivable, for this fact of my birth never appears as a brute fact but always across a projective reconstruction of my for-itself. I am ashamed of being born or I am astonished at it or I rejoice over it, or in attempting to get rid of my life I affirm that I live and I assume this life as bad. Thus in a certain sense I choose being born. This choice itself is integrally affected with facticity since I am not able not to choose, but this facticity in turn will appear only in so far as I surpass it towards my ends. Thus facticity is everywhere but inapprehensible. I never encounter anything except my responsibility. That is why I can not ask, "Why was I born?" or curse the day of my birth or declare that I did not ask to be born, for these various attitudes toward my birth—i.e., toward the fact that I realize a presence in the world—are absolutely nothing else but ways of assuming this birth in full responsibility and of making it mine. Here again I encounter only myself and my projects so that finally my abandonment—i.e., my facticity—consists simply in the fact that I am condemned to be wholly responsible for myself. I am the being which is in such a way that in its being its being is in question. And this "is" of my being is as present and inapprehensible.

Under these conditions since every event in the world can be revealed to me only as an opportunity (an opportunity made use of, lacked, neglected, etc.), or better yet since everything which happens to us can be considered as a chance (i.e., can appear to us only as a way of realizing this being which is in question in our being) and since others as transcendences-transcended are themselves only opportunities and chances, the responsibility for the for-itself extends to the entire world as a peopled-world. It is precisely thus that the for-itself apprehends itself in anguish; that is, as a being which is neither the foundation of its own being nor of the Other's being nor of the in-itselfs which form the world, but a being which is compelled to decide the meaning of being—within it and everywhere outside of it. The one who realizes in anguish his condition as being thrown into a responsibility which extends to his very abandonment has no longer either remorse or regret or excuse; he is no longer anything but a freedom which perfectly reveals itself and whose being resides in this very revelation.

HOSPERS/ *What Means This Freedom?*

In direct contrast with Sartre's contention that humans are free is John Hospers's hard deterministic position in "What Means This Freedom?" Hospers attempts to discover under what conditions a person should be held morally accountable. Having listed several criteria, he then proceeds to demonstrate how each of these can easily be outside the individual's control. The result is a paradox in which we hold people morally responsible under conditions whose presence they are not responsible for.

Does Hospers convince you that freedom is little more than illusion? Do you detect any questionable claims in his analysis?

Under precisely what conditions is a person to be held morally responsible for an action? Disregarding here those conditions that have to do with a person's *ignorance* of the situation or the effects of his action, let us concentrate on those having to do with his "inner state." There are several criteria that might be suggested:

1. The first idea that comes to mind is that responsibility is determined by the presence or absence of *premeditation*—the opposite of "premeditated" being, presumably, "unthinking" or "impulsive." But this will not do—both because some acts are not premeditated but responsible, and because some are premeditated and not responsible.

Many acts we call responsible can be as unthinking or impulsive as you please. If you rush across the street to help the victim of an automobile collision, you are (at least so we would ordinarily say) acting responsibly; but you did not do so out of premeditation; you saw the accident, you didn't think, you rushed to the scene

without hesitation. It was like a reflex action. But you acted responsibly: unlike the knee jerk, the act was the result of past training and past thought about situations of this kind; that is why you ran to help instead of ignoring the incident or running away. When something done originally from conviction or training becomes habitual, it becomes *like* a reflex action. As Aristotle said, virtue should become second nature through habit: a virtuous act should be performed *as if* by instinct; this, far from detracting from its normal worth, testifies to one's mastery of the desired type of behavior; one does not have to make a moral effort each time it is repeated.

There are also premeditated acts for which, I would say, the person is not responsible. Premeditation, especially when it is so exaggerated as to issue in no action at all, can be the result of neurotic disturbance or what we sometimes call "block," which the person inherits from long-past situations. In Hamlet's revenge on his uncle (I use this example because it is

From *Determinism and Freedom in the Age of Modern Science*, ed. Sidney Hook. Copyright © 1958 by New York University Press. Reprinted by permission.

familiar to all of us), there was no lack, but rather a surfeit, of premeditation; his actions were so exquisitely premeditated as to make Freud and Dr. Ernest Jones look more closely to find out what lay behind them. The very premeditation camouflaged unconscious motives of which Hamlet himself was not aware. I think this is an important point, since it seems that the courts often assume that premeditation is a criterion of responsibility. If failure to kill his uncle had been considered a crime, every court in the land would have convicted Hamlet. Again: a woman's decision to stay with her husband in spite of endless "mental cruelty" is, if she is the victim of an unconscious masochistic "will to punishment," one for which she is not responsible; she is the victim and not the agent, no matter how profound her conviction that she is the agent; she is caught in a masochistic web (of complicated genesis) dating back to babyhood, perhaps a repetition of a comparable situation involving her own parents, a repetition-compulsion that, as Freud said, goes "beyond the pleasure principle." Again: a criminal whose crime was carefully planned step by step is usually considered responsible, but as we shall see in later examples, the overwhelming impulse toward it, stemming from an unusually humiliating ego defeat in early childhood, was as compulsive as any can be.

2. Shall we say, then, that a person is not responsible for his act unless he can *defend it with reasons?* I am afraid that this criterion is no better than the previous one. First, intellectuals are usually better at giving reasons than non-intellectuals, and according to this criterion would be more responsible than persons acting from moral conviction and not implemented by reasoning; yet it is very doubtful whether we should want to say that the [former] are the more responsible. Second, the giving of reasons itself may be suspect. The reasons may be rationalizations camouflaging unconscious motives of which the agent knows nothing. Hamlet gave many reasons for not doing what he felt it was his duty to do: the time was not right, his uncle's soul might go to heaven, etc. His various "reasons" contradict one another, and if an overpowering compulsion had not been present, the highly intellectual Hamlet would not have been taken in for a moment by these rationalizations. The real reason, the Oedipal conflict that made his uncle's crime the accomplishment of his own deepest desire, binding their fates into one and paralyzing him into inaction, was unconscious and of course unknown to him. One's intelligence and reasoning power do not enable one to escape from unconsciously motivated behavior; it only gives one greater facility in rationalizing that behavior; one's intelligence is simply used in the interests of the neurosis—it is pressed into service to justify with reasons what one does quite independently of the reasons.

If these two criteria are inadequate, let us seek others.

3. Shall we say that a person is responsible for his actions unless it is the *result of unconscious forces* of which he knows nothing? Many psychoanalysts would probably accept this criterion. If it is not largely reflected in the language of responsibility as ordinarily used, this may be due to ignorance of fact: most people do not

know that there are such things as unconscious motives and unconscious conflicts causing human beings to act. But it may be that if they did, perhaps they would refrain from holding persons responsible for certain actions.

I do not wish here to quarrel with this criterion of responsibility. I only want to point out the fact that if this criterion is employed a far greater number of actions will be excluded from the domain of responsibility than we might at first suppose. Whether we are neat or untidy, whether we are selfish or unselfish, whether we provoke scenes or avoid them, even whether we can exert our powers of will to change our behavior—all these may, and often do, have their source in our unconscious life.

4. Shall we say that a person is responsible for his act unless it is *compelled?* Here we are reminded of Aristotle's assertion (*Nicomachean Ethics,* Book III) that a person is responsible for his act except for reasons of either ignorance or compulsion. Ignorance is not part of our problem here (unless it is unconsciously induced ignorance of facts previously remembered and selectively forgotten—in which case the forgetting is again compulsive), but compulsion is. How will compulsion do as a criterion? The difficulty is to state just what it means. When we say an act is compelled in a psychological sense, our language is metaphorical—which is not to say that there is no point in it, or that, properly interpreted, it is not true. Our actions are compelled in a literal sense if someone has us in chains or is controlling our bodily movements. When we say that the storm compelled us to jettison the cargo of the ship (Aristotle's example), we have a less literal sense of compulsion, for at least it is open to us to go down with the ship. When psychoanalysts say that a man was compelled by unconscious conflicts to wash his hands constantly, this is also not a literal use of "compel": for nobody forced his hands under the tap. Still, it is a typical example of what psychologists call *compulsive* behavior: it has unconscious causes inaccessible to introspection, and moreover nothing can change it—it is as inevitable for him to do it as it would be if someone were forcing his hands under the tap. In this it is exactly like the action of a powerful external force; it is just as little within one's conscious control.

In its area of application this interpretation of responsibility comes to much the same as the previous one. And this area is very great indeed. For if we cannot be held responsible for the infantile situations (in which we are after all passive victims), then neither, it would seem, can we be held responsible for compulsive actions occurring in adulthood that are inevitable consequences of those infantile situations. And, psychiatrists and psychoanalysts tell us, actions fulfilling this description are characteristic of all people some of the time and some people most of the time. Their occurrence, once the infantile events have taken place, is inevitable, just as the explosion is inevitable once the fuse has been lighted; there is simply more "delayed action" in the psychological explosions than there is in physical ones.

(I have not used the word "inevitable" here to mean "causally determined," for according to such a definition every event would be inevitable if one accepted the causal principle in some form or other; and probably nobody except certain philosophers use "inevitable" in this sense. Rather, I use "inevitable" in its ordinary sense of "cannot be avoided." To the extent, therefore, that adult neurotic manifestations *can* be avoided, once the infantile patterns have become set, the assertion that they are inevitable is not true.)

5. There is still another criterion, which I prefer to the previous ones, by which a man's responsibility for an act can be measured: the degree to which that act can (or could have been) *changed by the use of reasons*. Suppose that the man who washes his hands constantly does so, he says, for hygienic reasons, believing that if he doesn't do so he will be poisoned by germs. We now convince him on the best medical authority, that his belief is groundless. Now, the test of his responsibility is whether the changed belief will result in changed behavior. If it does not, as with the compulsive hand washer, he is not acting responsibly, but if it does, he is. It is not the *use* of reasons, but their *efficacy in changing behavior*, that is being made the criterion of responsibility. And clearly in neurotic cases no such change occurs; in fact, this is often made the defining characteristic of neurotic behavior: it is unchangeable by any rational considerations.

I have suggested these criteria to distinguish actions for which we can call the agent responsible from those for which we cannot. Even persons with extensive knowledge of psychiatry do not I think, use any of these criteria to the exclusion of the others; a conjunction of two or more may be used at once. But however they may be combined or selected in actual application, I believe we can make the distinction along some such lines as we have suggested.

But is there not still another possible meaning of "responsibility" that we have not yet mentioned? Even after we have made all the above distinctions, there remains a question in our minds whether we are, in the final analysis, *responsible for any of our actions at all*. The issue may be put this way: How can anyone be responsible for his actions, since they grow out of his character, which is shaped and molded and made what it is by influences—some hereditary, but most of them stemming from early parental environment—that were not of his own making or choosing? This question, I believe, still troubles many people who would agree to all the distinctions we have just made but still have the feeling that "this isn't all." They have the uneasy suspicion that there is a more ultimate sense, a "deeper" sense, in which we are *not* responsible for our actions, since we are not responsible for the character out of which those actions spring. . . .

Let us take as an example a criminal who, let us say, strangled several persons and is himself now condemned to die in the electric chair. Jury and public alike hold him responsible (at least they utter the words "he is responsible"), for the murders were planned down to the minutest detail, and the defendant tells the jury exactly how he planned them. But now we find out how it all came about; we learn of parents who rejected him from babyhood, of the childhood spent in one foster home after another, where it was always plain to him that he was not wanted; of the constantly frustrated early desire for affection, the hard shell of nonchalance and bitterness that he assumed to cover the painful and humiliating fact of being unwanted, and his subsequent attempts to heal these wounds to his shattered ego through defensive aggression.

The criminal is the most passive person in this world, helpless as a baby in his motorically inexpressible fury. Not only does he try to wreak revenge on the mother of the earliest period of his babyhood; his criminality is based on the inner feeling of being incapable of making the mother even feel that the child seeks revenge on her. The situation is that of a dwarf trying to annoy a giant who superciliously refuses to see these attempts. . . . Because of his inner feeling of being a dwarf, the criminotic uses, so to speak, dynamite. Of that the giant must take cognizance. True, the "revenge" harms the avenger. He may be legally executed. However the primary inner aim of forcing the giant to acknowledge the dwarf's fury is fulfilled.

The poor victim is not conscious of the inner forces that exact from him this ghastly toll; he battles, he schemes, he revels in pseudo-aggression, he is miserable, but he does not know what works within him to produce these catastrophic acts of crime. His aggressive actions are the wriggling of a worm on a fisherman's hook. And if this is so, it seems difficult to say any longer, "He is responsible." Rather, we shall put him behind bars for the protection of society, but we shall no longer flatter our feeling of moral superiority by calling him personally responsible for what he did.

Let us suppose it were established that a man commits murder only if, sometime during the previous week, he has eaten a certain combination of foods—say, tuna fish salad at a meal also including peas, mushroom soup, and blueberry pie. What if we were to track down the factors common to all murders committed in this country during the last twenty years and found this factor present in all of them, and only in them? The example is of course empirically absurd; but may it not be that there is some combination of factors that regularly leads to homicide, factors such as are described in general terms in the above quotation? (Indeed the situation in the quotation is less fortunate than in our hypothetical example, for it is easy to avoid certain foods once we have been warned about them, but the situation of the infant is thrust on him; something has already happened to him once and for all, before he knows it has happened.) When such specific factors are discovered, won't they make it clear that it is foolish and pointless, as well as immoral, to hold human beings responsible for crimes? Or, if one prefers biological to psychological factors, suppose a neurologist is called in to testify at a murder trial and produces X-ray pictures of the brain of the criminal; anyone can see, he argues, that the *cella turcica* was already calcified at the age of nineteen; it should be a flexible bone, growing, enabling the gland to grow. All the defendant's disorders might have resulted from this early calcification. Now, this particular explanation may be empirically false; but who can say that no such factors, far more complex, to be sure, exist?

When we know such things as these, we no longer feel so much tempted to say the criminal is responsible for his crime; and we tend also (do we not?) to excuse him—not legally (we still confine him to prison) but morally; we no longer call him a monster or hold him personally responsible for what he did. Moreover, we do this in general, not merely in the case of crime: "You must excuse Grandmother for being irritable; she's really quite ill and is suffering some pain all the time." Or: "The dog always bites children after she's had a litter of pups; you can't blame her for it: she's not feeling well, and besides she naturally wants to defend them." Or: "She's nervous and jumpy, but do excuse her: she has a severe glandular disturbance."

Let us note that the more *thoroughly* and in *detail* we know the causal factors leading a person to behave as he does, the more we tend to exempt him from responsibility. When we know nothing of the man except what we see him do, we say he is an ungrateful cad who expects much of other people and does nothing in return, and we are usually indignant. When we learn that his parents were the same way and, having no guilt feelings about this mode of behavior themselves, brought him up to be greedy and avaricious, we see that we could hardly expect him to have developed moral feelings in this direction. When we learn, in addition, that he is not aware of being ungrateful or selfish, but unconsciously represses the memory of events unfavorable to himself, we feel that the situation is unfortunate but "not really his fault." When we know that

this behavior of his, which makes others angry, occurs more constantly when he feels tense or insecure, and that he now feels tense and insecure, and that relief from pressure will diminish it, then we tend to "feel sorry for the poor guy" and say he's more to be pitied than censured. We no longer want to say that he is personally responsible; we might rather blame nature or his parents for having given him an unfortunate constitution or temperament.

In recent years a new form of punishment has been imposed on middle-aged and elderly parents. Their children, now in their twenties, thirties, or even forties, present them with a modern grievance: "My analysis proves that *you* are responsible for my neurosis." Overawed by these authoritative statements, the poor tired parents fall easily victims to the newest variations on the scapegoat theory.

In my opinion, this senseless cruelty —which disinters educational sins which have been buried for decades, and uses them as the basis for accusations which the victims cannot answer—is unjustified. Yes, "the truth loves to be centrally located" (Melville), and few parents— since they are human—have been perfect. But granting their mistakes, they acted as *their* neurotic difficulties forced them to act. To turn the tables and declare the children not guilty because of the *impersonal* nature of their own neuroses, while at the same time the parents are *personally* blamed, is worse than illogical; it is profoundly unjust.

And so, it would now appear, neither of the parties is responsible: "they acted as their neurotic difficulties forced them to act." The patients are not responsible for their neurotic manifestations, but then neither are the parents responsible for theirs; and so, of course, for their parents in turn, and theirs before them. It is the twentieth-century version of the family curse, the curse on the House of Atreus.

"But," a critic complains, "it's immoral to exonerate people indiscriminately in this way. I might have thought it fit to excuse somebody because he was born on the other side of the tracks, if I didn't know so many bank presidents who were also born on the other side of the tracks." Now, I submit that the most immoral thing in this situation is the critic's caricature of the conditions of the excuse. Nobody is excused merely because he was born on the other side of the tracks. But if he was born on the other side of the tracks *and* was a highly narcissistic infant to begin with *and* was repudiated or neglected by his parents *and* . . . (here we list a finite number of conditions), and if this complex of factors is *regularly* followed by certain behavior traits in adulthood, and moreover *unavoidably* so—that is, they occur no matter what he or anyone else tries to do—then we excuse him morally and say he is not responsible for his deed. If he is not responsible for A, a series of events occurring in his babyhood, then neither is he responsible for B, a series of things he does in adulthood, provided that B inevitably—that is, unavoidably—follows upon the occurrence of A. And according to psychiatrists and psychoanalysts, this often happens.

But one may still object that so far we have talked only about neurotic behavior. Isn't nonneurotic or normal or not unconsciously motivated (or whatever you want to call it) behavior still within the area of responsibility? There are reasons for answering "No" even here, for the normal person no more than the neurotic one has caused his own character, which makes him what he is. Granted that neurotics are not responsible for their behavior (that part of it which we call neurotic) because it stems from undigested infantile conflicts that they had no part in bringing about, and that are external to them just as surely as if their behavior had been forced on them by a malevolent deity (which is indeed one theory on the subject); but the so-called normal person is equally the product of causes in which his volition took no part. And if, unlike the neurotic's, his behavior is changeable by rational considerations, and if he has the will power to overcome the effects of an unfortunate early environment, this again is no credit to him; he is just lucky. If energy is available to him in a form in which it can be mobilized for constructive purposes, this is no credit to him, for this too is part of his psychic legacy. Those of us who can discipline ourselves and develop habits of concentration of purpose tend to blame those who cannot, and call them lazy and weak-willed; but what we fail to see is that they literally *cannot* do what we expect; if their psyches were structured like ours, they could, but as they are burdened with a tyrannical superego (to use psychoanalytic jargon for the moment), and a weak defenseless ego whose energies are constantly consumed in fighting endless charges of the superego, they simply cannot do it, and it is irrational to expect it of them. We cannot with justification blame them for their inability, any more than we can congratulate ourselves for our ability. This lesson is hard to learn, for we constantly and naively assume that other people are constructed as we ourselves are.

For example: A child raised under slum conditions, whose parents are socially ambitious and envy families with money, but who nevertheless squander the little they have on drink, may simply be unable in later life to mobilize a drive sufficient to overcome these early conditions. Common sense would expect that he would develop the virtue of thrift; he would make quite sure that he would never again endure the grinding poverty he had experienced as a child. But in fact it is not so: the exact conditions are too complex to be specified in detail here, but when certain conditions are fulfilled (concerning the subject's early life), he will always thereafter be a spendthrift, and no rational considerations will be able to change this. He will listen to the rational considerations and see the force of these, but they will not be able to change him, even if he tries; he cannot change his wasteful habits any more than he can lift the Empire State Building with bare hands. We moralize and plead with him to be thrifty, but we do not see how strong, how utterly overpowering, and how constantly with him, is the opposite drive, which is so easily manageable with us. But he is possessed by the all-consuming, all-encompassing urge to make the world see that he belongs, that he has arrived, that he is just as well off as anyone else, that the awful humiliations were not real, that they never actually occurred, for isn't he now able to spend and spend? The humiliation must be blotted out; and

conspicuous, flashy, expensive, and wasteful buying will do this; it shows the world what the world must know! True, it is only for the moment; true, it is in the end self-defeating, for wasteful consumption is the best way to bring poverty back again; but the person with an overpowering drive to mend a lesion to his narcissism cannot resist the avalanche of that drive with this puny rational consideration. A man with his back against the wall and a gun at his throat doesn't think of what may happen ten years hence. (Consciously, of course, he knows nothing of this drive; all that appears to consciousness is its shattering effects; he knows only that he must keep on spending—not why—and that he is unable to resist.) He hasn't in him the psychic capacity, the energy to stem the tide of a drive that at the moment is all-powerful. We, seated comfortably away from his flood, sit in judgment on him, and blame him and exhort him and criticize him; but he, carried along by the flood, cannot do otherwise than he does. He may fight with all the strength of which he is capable, but it is not enough. And we, who are rational enough at least to exonerate a man in a situation of "overpowering impulse" when we recognize it to be one, do not even recognize this as an example of it; and so, in addition to being swept away in the flood that childhood conditions rendered inevitable, he must also endure our lectures, our criticism, and our moral excoriation.

But, one will say, he could have overcome his spendthrift tendencies; some people do. Quite true: some people do. They are lucky. They have it in them to overcome early deficiencies by exerting great effort, and they are capable of exerting the effort. Some of us, luckier still, can overcome them with but little effort; and a few, the luckiest, haven't the deficiencies to overcome. It's all a matter of luck. The least lucky are those who can't overcome them, even with great effort, and those who haven't the ability to exert the effort.

But, one persists, it isn't a matter simply of luck; it *is* a matter of effort. Very well then, it's a matter of effort; without exerting the effort you may not overcome the deficiency. But whether or not you are the kind of person who has it in him to exert the effort is a matter of luck.

All this is well-known to psychoanalysis. They can predict, from minimal cues that most of us don't notice, whether a person is going to turn out to be lucky or not. "The analyst," they say, "must be able to use the residue of the patient's unconscious guilt so as to remove the symptom or character trait that creates the guilt. The guilt must not only be present, but *available* for use, *mobilizable*. If it is used up (absorbed) in criminal activity, or in an excessive amount of self-damaging tendencies, then it cannot be used for therapeutic purposes, and the prognosis is negative." Not all philosophers will relish the analyst's way of putting the matter, but at least as a physician he can soon detect whether the patient is lucky or unlucky—and he knows that whichever it is, it *isn't the patient's fault*. The patient's conscious volition cannot remedy the deficiency. Even whether he will cooperate with the analyst is really out of the patient's hands: if he continu-

ally projects the denying-mother fantasy on the analyst and unconsciously identifies him always with the cruel, harsh forbidder of the nursery, thus frustrating any attempt at impersonal observation, the sessions are useless; yet if it happens that way, he can't help that either. That fatal projection is not under his control; whether it occurs or not depends on how his unconscious identifications have developed since his infancy. He can try, yes—but the ability to try enough for the therapy to have effect is also beyond his control; the capacity to try more than just so much is either there or it isn't—and either way "it's in the lap of the gods."

The position, then, is this: if we *can* overcome the effects of early environment, the ability to do so is itself a product of the early environment. We do not give ourselves this ability; and if we lack it we cannot be blamed for not having it. Sometimes, to be sure, moral exhortation brings out an ability that is there but not being used, and in this lies its *occasional* utility; but very often its use is pointless because the ability is not there. The only thing that can overcome a desire, as Spinoza said, is a stronger contrary desire; and many times there simply is not wherewithal for producing a stronger contrary desire. Those of us who do have the wherewithal are lucky.

There is one possible practical advantage in remembering this. It may prevent us (unless we are compulsive blamers) from indulging in righteous indignation and committing the sin of spiritual pride, thanking God that we are not as this publican here. And it will protect from our useless moralizings those who are least equipped by nature for enduring them.

As with responsibility, so with deserts. Someone commits a crime and is punished by the state; "he deserved it," we say self-righteously— as if we were moral and he immoral, when in fact we are lucky and he is unlucky—forgetting that there, but for the grace of God and a fortunate early environment, go we. Or, as Clarence Darrow said in his speech for the defense in the Loeb-Leopold case:

I do not believe that people are in jail because they deserve to be. . . . I know what causes the emotional life. . . . I know it is practically left out of some. Without it they cannot act with the rest. They cannot feel the moral shocks which safeguard others. Is [this man] to blame that his machine is imperfect? Who is to blame? I do not know. I have never in my life been interested so much in fixing blame as I have in relieving people from blame. I am not wise enough to fix it.

I want to make it quite clear that I have not been arguing for determinism. Though I find it difficult to give any sense to the term "indeterminism," because I do not know what it would be like to come across an uncaused event, let us grant indeterminists everything they want, at least in words—influences that suggest but do not constrain, a measure of acausality in an otherwise rigidly causal order, and so on— whatever these phrases may mean. With all this granted, exactly the same situation faces the indeterminist and the determinist; all we have been saying would still hold true. "Are our powers innate or acquired?"

Suppose the powers are declared innate; then the villain may sensibly ask whether he is responsible for what he was born with. A negative reply is inevitable. Are they then acquired? Then the ability to acquire them—was *that* innate? or acquired? It is innate? Very well then. . . .

The same fact remains—that we did not cause our characters, that the influences that made us what we are are influences over which we had no control and of whose very existence we had no knowledge at the time. This fact remains for "determinism" and "indeterminism" alike. And it is this fact to which I would appeal, not the specific tenets of traditional forms of "determinism," which seem to me, when analyzed, empirically empty.

"But," it may be asked, "isn't it your view that nothing ultimately *could* be other than it is? And isn't this deterministic? And isn't it deterministic if you say that human beings could never act otherwise than they do, and that their desires and temperaments could not, when you consider their antecedent conditions, be other than they are?"

I reply that all these charges rest on confusions.

1. To say that nothing *could* be other than it is, is, taken literally, nonsense; and if taken as a way of saying something else, misleading and confusing. If you say, "I can't do it," this invites the question, "No? Not even if you want to?" "Can" and "could" are power words, used in the context of human action; when applied to nature they are merely anthropomorphic. "Could" has no application to nature—unless, of course, it is uttered in a theological context: one might say that God *could* have made things different. But with

regard to inanimate nature "could" has no meaning. Or perhaps it is intended to mean that the order of nature is in some sense *necessary*. But in that case the sense of "necessary" must be specified. I know what "necessary" means when we are talking about propositions, but not when we are talking about the sequence of events in nature.

2. What of the charge that we could never have acted otherwise than we did? This, I submit, is simply not true. Here the exponents of Hume-Mill-Schlick-Ayer "soft determinism" are quite right. I could have gone to the opera today instead of coming here; that is, if certain conditions had been different, I should have gone. I could have done many other things instead of what I did, if some condition or other had been different, specifically if my desire had been different. I repeat that "could" is a proper word, and "I could have done this" means approximately "I *should* have done this *if* I had wanted to." In this sense, all of us could often have done otherwise than we did. I would not want to say that I should have done differently even if *all* the conditions leading up to my action had been the same (this is generally not what we mean by "could" anyway); but to assert that I could have is empty, for if I *did* act differently from the time before, we would automatically say that one or more of the conditions were different, whether we had independent evidence for this or not, thus rendering the assertion immune to empirical refutation. (Once again, the vacuousness of "determinism.")

3. Well then, could we ever have, not acted, but *desired* otherwise than

we did desire? . . . Russell said, "We can do as we please but we can't please as we please." But I am persuaded that even this statement conceals a fatal mistake. Let us follow the same analysis through. "I could have done X" means "I should have done X if I had wanted to." "I could have wanted X" by the same analysis would mean "I should have wanted X if I had wanted to"—which seems to make no sense at all. (What does Russell want? To please as he doesn't please?)

What does this show? It shows, I think, that the only meaningful context of "can" and "could have" is that of *action*. "Could have acted differently" makes sense; "could have desired differently," as we have just seen, does not. Because a word or phrase makes good sense in one context, let us not assume that it does so in another.

I conclude, then, with the following suggestion: that we operate on two levels of moral discourse, which we shouldn't confuse; one (let's call it the upper level) is that of actions; the other (the lower, or deeper level) is that of the springs of action. Most moral talk occurs on the upper level. It is on this level that the Hume-Mill-Schlick-Ayer analysis of freedom fully applies. As we have just seen, "can" and "could" acquire their meaning on this level; so, I suspect, does "freedom." . . . All these distinctions are perfectly valid on this level (or in this dimension) of moral discourse; and it is, after all, the usual one—we are practical beings interested in changing the course of human behavior, so it is natural enough that 99 percent of our moral talk occurs here.

But when we descend to what I have called the lower level of moral discourse, as we occasionally do in thoughtful moments when there is no immediate need for action, then we must admit that we are ultimately the kind of persons we are because of conditions occurring outside us, over which we have had no control. But while this is true, we should beware of extending the moral terminology we used on the other level to this one also. "Could" and "can," as we have seen, no longer have meaning here. "Right" and "wrong," which apply only to actions, have no meaning here either. I suspect that the same is true of "responsibility," for now that we have recalled often forgotten facts about our being the product of outside forces, we must ask in all seriousness what would be added by saying that we are not *responsible* for our own characters and temperaments. What would it mean even? Has it a significant opposite? What would it be like to be responsible for one's own character? What possible situation is describable by this phrase? Instead of saying that it is *false* that we are responsible for our own characters, I should prefer to say that the utterance is meaningless—meaningless in the sense that it describes no possible situation, though it *seems* to because the word "responsible" is the same one we used on the upper level, where it marks a real distinction. If this is so, the result is that *moral* terms—at least the terms "could have" and "responsible"—simply drop out on the lower level. . . . whether or not we have personality disturbances, whether or not we have the ability to overcome deficiencies of early environment, is like the answer to the question whether or not we shall be struck down by a dread disease: "it's all a matter of luck." It is important to keep this in mind, for people almost always forget it, with consequences in human intolerance and unnecessary suffering that are incalculable.

4

SEX
of doing what comes naturally
EGOISM

Perhaps no people have changed as much as Americans in the past twenty-five years. Nowhere is the change more apparent than in our sexual ethics. It is hard to go anywhere today without hearing people talk of the "new morality," the "sexual revolution," the "permissive society," and the "erotic revolution."

In the midst of this seeming nose-thumbing at our puritanical past, people react in different ways. Some fully savor the newfound sexual freedom. Others remain on the sidelines, curious, perhaps envious, but still too inhibited to be anything else but rapt onlookers. Still others, ever mindful of past legendary downfalls, prophesy moral decay or worse.

One facet of the sexual revolution is the dramatic increase in premarital sex. *Sex* here is intended to mean sexual intercourse. By premarital sex, then, is meant sexual intercourse between a male and a female who are not or have not been married. Studies indicate that about half of the women and three-fourths of the men in America have sex before marriage.

The increasing incidence of and opportunities for premarital sex present a number of problems for today's young person. Dealing with peer pressure, reconciling the new morality with a more conventional upbringing, handling emotions that often accompany sexual intimacies, maintaining a healthful self-image, coping with the insecurities that the absence of marital bonding frequently causes, managing the fear or reality of venereal disease, dealing with the uncertainties of birth control devices—these are only some of the many concerns.

The changes in sexual morality have ushered in a whole host of related psychological and sociological problems. But even more important, the changes seem to have forced many single people to take a good long look at sexual values generally and to answer for themselves a question whose answer was often glibly given them by religion, parents, and society. That question is: how should I behave sexually? Is premarital sex always right? Specifically, is premarital sex ever an immoral thing to do? This is a real and pressing concern for many today, and it seems impossible to answer it adequately without considering its moral implications.

Many find an adequate answer in the "Ernest Hemingway ethic." Asked once what he thought was right, Hemingway replied: whatever you feel good about after doing. In other words, something is right if it is pleasurable, wrong if it is not. Clearly the assumption here is that the goodness of an action depends on its consequences. Because so many people bring this standard to their premarital sexual relations, the issue of sex seems appropriate for discussing this consequential approach to ethics.

For now, we shall focus on one consequential position—egoism, the doctrine that maintains that individuals should always act in their own best long-term interests.

CONSEQUENTIALISM*

Mark was dead set against it. But he didn't know how he could change Chuck's mind. After all, Chuck and Kathy had been dating for weeks. For Chuck that was reason enough for him and Kathy to sleep together.

But Mark didn't see it that way. He knew Kathy, liked and respected her. He also knew that Kathy's feelings for Chuck ran deeper than Chuck's for her. He figured that that was why she'd been resisting Chuck's advances. Now Chuck was proposing to give her an ultimatum: sleep with him or the whole thing was off. Mark didn't know how Kathy would react, but he thought she liked Chuck too much to risk losing him. One thing Mark was sure of: if they did get involved sexually, Kathy would view it as a total commitment. And that meant trouble.

Somehow he had to change Chuck's mind. He had to do something fast. Chuck trusted him. There was no question of that. Mark decided to capitalize on that trust. What he must do would hurt, perhaps even end, their friendship. But he had to risk that. Too much was at stake. He had to stop him before it was too late.

"So," Mark began, "the bait's set and now you're ready to spring the trap."

"You disapprove. I can tell."

Chuck was perceptive. Mark would have to be careful. He didn't want to appear self-righteous. Better to look a little archaic than self-righteous. No, self-righteousness was sure to fail. So Mark simply said, "Let's just say I'm skeptical."

"You don't think she'll do it?"

"No, it's not that. I think she will. I guess I'm just questioning the merit of the whole thing." As soon as he'd spoken, Mark knew that he'd said the wrong thing. "That part about merit," he thought, "what a dumb thing to say."

But then Chuck said something that left Mark believing that maybe his words

---

*Evidently Jacques Thiroux of Bakersfield College was the first to coin the convenient terms "consequentialism" and "nonconsequentialism" used throughout this text.

were well chosen after all. "What does merit have to do with getting Kathy to sleep with me?" It was really Chuck's tone, more than his words, that made Mark think he'd touched a nerve. Chuck was upset, but upset in the way people often get when someone reveals to them what they have tried so carefully to conceal from themselves.

Whether the nerve he'd touched indicated Chuck's own self-doubt and uncertainty, Mark didn't know. But maybe it did. Maybe that was why Chuck had opened up in the first place. In the past he had always been very tight-lipped about his relationship with Kathy. Now, suddenly, this reaction. Could it be that for all his bravado, deep down Chuck wasn't convinced that what he was doing was right? Although it was impossible to determine, Mark spoke as if that was the case.

"To tell you the truth," said Mark in a carefully controlled tone, "I don't think what you're doing is right."

The apparent difference in the attitudes of Mark and Chuck underscores a particularly nettlesome issue today—premarital sex. For a number of reasons that issue has grown troublesome. Attitudes toward marriage, emphasis on personal fulfillment, improved contraceptive devices, the weakening of traditional religious and institutional influences over human conduct, the impact of psychoanalytic theory—all have conspired in our time to leave individuals shouldering the burden of premarital sexual decisions alone.

Just what do you use as a basis for deciding whether to have premarital sex with someone? Evidently Chuck uses personal feeling. Others might suggest religious teaching. Still others would say love. In answer to the question of premarital sex, many would find a ready reply in an ethical theory with a long history. This theory contends that the morality of any action depends solely upon its consequences. Thus, if having premarital sex produces good consequences, then it is good. If it does not produce good consequences, then it is bad. Those who hold to this consequentialist view have been called *teleologists* or, more simply, *consequentialists*. Consequentialists generally divide into two main schools of ethical thought: *egoism*—the view that the consequences to self alone should be considered in deciding the morality of an action, and *utilitarianism*—the view that the consequences to everyone involved should be considered in deciding the morality of an action. Before focusing on the egoistic position, let us take a closer look at consequential theories in order to determine what role, if any, consequences should play in moral decisions.

CONSEQUENTIAL THEORIES

When we speak of consequential theories we mean those that maintain that the morality of an action depends upon the nonmoral consequences that the action brings about. Consequentialists determine the morality of an action by considering the ratio of good to evil that the action produces. The right act is the one that is intended to produce, will probably produce, or actually does produce at least as great a ratio of good to evil as any other course of action; the wrong act is the one that does not. We should perform right and only right actions.

Note that consequentialists insist that we evaluate the nonmoral value of an action. By *nonmoral* they mean what lies outside the realm of morality. Thus, whether you vacation in the mountains or at the beach, whether you sleep late in the morning, and whether you wear jeans or slacks generally are nonmoral issues. What is a nonmoral issue, however, can quickly become a moral one. If, for example, the bread-earner of a family suffers from skin cancer, whether that person vacations where the sun will worsen that condition could be a moral issue. Similarly, if by sleeping late some morning you fail to keep an appointment, or if by wearing jeans to your sister's wedding you hurt her and the family, then these nonmoral issues can easily take on moral overtones.

As an illustration of how consequentialists introduce nonmoral values into moral decisions, suppose that you're briskly driving down an almost deserted street one night, and, taking your eyes off the road for a second, you hit and dent the fender of a parked car. You stop and cautiously look around. There's no one in sight; not even a light on in any of the houses. You estimate that the damage to the parked car is about two hundred dollars. You'd like to leave a note on the windshield of the car, but you don't have insurance or the money to pay for the damage. Besides, the parked car is a brand new Cadillac Eldorado, and you presume that all Eldorado owners undoubtedly have full insurance coverage. If they don't, they're very unwise. Again, checking the neighborhood, you're positive that no one has seen or heard you and that the damage could not possibly be traced to you. What to do? Leave a note or vanish?

If you were a consequentialist, you would evaluate the nonmoral consequences of the two choices. Leaving the note would probably mean that you would pay the bill. If so, distinct inconveniences would follow, such as your having to work harder or longer to pay off the debt, your being less self-indulgent, and your having to economize. These are nonmoral values. On the other hand, should you depart without leaving the note, you will probably go unpenalized while the owner pays the bill for something that you directly caused. He will probably think that it was at least an inconsiderate reaction on your part; he may even decide that he will do the same thing, given the chance. You might even wonder what would happen if everyone acted this way—if everyone left the scene of an accident. And, of course, it would no doubt cross your mind that, unknown to you, someone might have seen you, in which case you might later be arrested and charged with leaving the scene of an accident.

Notice that the evaluation of each alternative involves an assessment of its nonmoral consequences. Consequentialists engage in this kind of analysis when determining the morality of an action.

At this point a question arises: what do consequentialists consider nonmorally good? It is difficult to pin consequentialists down on this question. Frequently, however, consequentialists are hedonists.

HEDONISM

Hedonism is the doctrine that the primary good in life is pleasure, that pleasure is the only entity that is good in itself. Some consequentialists have identified the good with what produces pleasure and evil with what produces pain. Thus, these consequentialists conclude that the moral action is the one that produces as great a ratio of pleasure to pain as any other alternative. This pleasure principle is an obvious factor in sex, where it can be identified with sensual gratification.

But hedonists include more than sensual gratification when they use the term *pleasure*. By *pleasure* they mean any kind of satisfaction, and not just the obvious pleasures that generally accompany the satisfying of sensual appetites, such as eating, drinking, and sex. Hedonism maintains that the more pleasure there is, the better off we all are, and that the life that contains the most intrinsic good is the one that contains the most pleasure and the least displeasure.

But don't get them wrong. Hedonists are not always conscious of seeking pleasure. On the contrary, they realize that consciously seeking pleasure may be as crippling to attaining it as being conscious of walking might be to walking itself. Nor do hedonists go to extreme measures to avoid pain. Frequently pain is necessary to achieve lasting pleasure. An obese person may painfully diet for months, motivated by the deferred pleasure the person will enjoy being thin. Chuck may ultimately decide not to force the issue in hopes that his temporary deprivation will yield a richer reward later. So, the key value for hedonists is achieving maximum pleasure in the long run, over a lifetime. As a result, they frequently forego short-term pleasure and tolerate short-term pain.

But not all consequentialists are hedonists. Some hold that knowledge as well as pleasure is worthwhile in itself. Even if knowledge does not add to happiness, they claim that it is good to have. For example, you may study philosophy or astronomy not necessarily to increase your own happiness or anyone else's, but simply to acquire knowledge about these fields.

Other consequentialists might add moral qualities to the list of values that are intrinsically good, as Mark does.

Mark: It seems to me that you should give a little more thought to being honest with Kathy.
Chuck: In my own way I have been.
Mark: In your own way. What about being as honest with her as you have been with me concerning your intentions?
Chuck: What, and ruin everything?

Mark suggests that honesty, in addition to pleasure, is good in itself. Other consequentialists might add charity, mercy, fidelity, generosity, and similar virtues. These, they claim, are in themselves worthwhile, even if they do not produce pleasure. In other words, it is important for Chuck to be honest with Kathy about his intentions, even if that means he will not have sex with her.

Still other consequentialists would argue that self-realization is good in and of itself. By *self-realization* they mean one's development of one's best capacities as a human being. For Aristotle, exercising one's best capacities meant developing and refining the uniquely human capacity to reason. A more recent view, as voiced by philosopher-novelist Ayn Rand, is one which maintains that the good is whatever promotes the survival of the human as a rational being. The human's survival as a human, she writes, means "the terms, methods, conditions and goals required for the survival of a rational being through the whole of his life-span—in all those aspects of existence which are open to his choice."*

We shall say more of self-realization shortly, for it plays an important part in contemporary egoism. Suffice it here to point out that consequentialists may be nonhedonists. What all consequentialists share with hedonists, however, are (1) some view about what is good and (2) the belief that what is right or obligatory is that which produces the greatest ratio of good to evil.

Returning to Chuck and Mark, it seems that Chuck is concerned with what will produce pleasure and happiness. So, he is hedonistic at least on this particular sexual issue. But Mark may be just as hedonistic. He would just want to introduce factors other than sensual pleasure. A fundamental question that now arises for the consequentialist is: for whom should you promote pleasure, for yourself alone or for everyone involved? This question marks a fundamental distinction between consequentialists. On the one hand there are egoists, those who believe that the good act is the one that produces, will probably produce, or is intended to produce at least as great a ratio of good to evil for the self alone as any alternative. On the other hand there are utilitarians, those who believe that the good act is the one that produces, will probably produce, or is intended to produce at least as great a ratio of good to evil for all concerned as any alternative would. We will spend the rest of this chapter examining egoism.

EGOISM

One consequential position is egoism. *Egoism is the normative theory that contends that the moral act is the one that promotes the individual's best long-term interests.* In debating the moral goodness or badness of an action, egoists use their own long-term advantage to measure the action's goodness. If an action produces, will probably produce, or is intended to produce at least as great a ratio of good to evil for the individual in the long run as any alternative, then the action is a good one; if not, then the action is bad.

It is convenient to distinguish between at least two kinds of egoists. *Personal egoists are those who claim that they should follow their own best long-term interests but do not say what other people should do. Impersonal egoists, on the other hand, argue that everyone should be egoistic.*

Not only may egoists vary in their beliefs about who should be egoistic, they may differ over which course of action will effect one's best long-term interests. But one thing is certain: all egoists agree that once those courses are known,

---

*Ayn Rand, *The Virtue of Selfishness* (New York: New American Library, 1964), p. 24.

they should be pursued. In short, all egoists say that people making a moral decision should consider their best long-term self-interests exclusively. But it is important not to misunderstand the phrase *best long-term self-interests*.

Mark: It seems to me that you're looking out primarily for yourself in this relationship.
Chuck: I think that's the only way to play it.
Mark: But why don't you *really* look out for yourself?
Chuck: What do you mean?
Mark: Why don't you maximize your chances for happiness by building a firmer basis for the relationship?
Chuck: I am. What could be a firmer basis than sex?
Mark: But don't you see that sex has to be rooted in something if it's going to be fulfilling over the long haul?
Chuck: Like what?
Mark: Like any number of things: mutual trust, honesty, affection, loyalty, interest.
Chuck: It sounds like you don't want me to go to bed with Kathy.
Mark: Look, all I'm suggesting is that your happiness with her might be all the more enriched if you delayed it.

There is a common misconception about egoism—that egoists are people who do what they want. Possibly what a person wants to do is stay in bed all day, eating, drinking, and making love. But likely this is incompatible with that person's best long-term interests, for the person is likely to sacrifice health, longevity, learning, and a source of income. So, rather than staying in bed, the person gets up, goes to school or work, and goes about the business of living in order to attain personal long-term goals. The point is that it is compatible with egoism to undergo unpleasant experiences, even painful ones, when these are viewed as contributing to long-term happiness. So, doing what you want is not the same as doing what you believe is in your best long-range interests. In this respect, Mark could easily be a more consistent egoist than Chuck.

It is risky to judge from appearances whether people are egoists. Honesty, charity, generosity, even altruism—all are compatible with egoism. Illustrative of this is an incident from Graham Greene's novel, *A Burnt-Out Case*. At one point the former English architect, then in Africa, informs a nun who has been working among the lepers for years that in England medical scientists are about to cure leprosy. Instead of being elated by the news, as the architect expects she will be, the nun shows quiet disappointment. Finally she confesses the reason for her misgivings: if leprosy is cured, she will not be able to go about the Lord's work. It appears the nun's altruistic motives actually have an egoistic basis. Whatever is compatible with one's own best long-term interests is compatible with egoism.

Another temptation in dealing with egoists is to assume that they are hedonists. It is true that many egoists are hedonistic, as was the ancient Greek philosopher Epicurus (341–270 B.C.), who argued that persons should live in such a way that they bring about as much pleasure for themselves as possible. But even Epicurus lived simply and moderately. It's said that he once wrote a friend, "Send me a cheese that I may fare sumptuously." Epicurus was not ordering a pizza, but was demonstrating the pleasure of simple tastes.

Other egoists identify the good with knowledge, power, rational self-interest, and what recently has become known as self-realization. As mentioned previously in the discussion of hedonism, the theory of self-realization views as right and good that which promotes all normal capacities of humans. Self-realization appears to be what thinkers have traditionally called the *doctrine of humanism,* a doctrine that historically has stressed distinctly human interests and ideals.

We see this humanism, or self-realization, doctrine in Plato's *Republic,* in which he discusses the three active principles within each person: Reason, Appetite, and Spirit. According to Plato, Reason is the rational part, the part that understands the nature of things and should control the body. Spirit is the passionate part of a person, the feeling part, the part consisting of sensations and virtues. Finally, Appetite is the desiring part, the part that craves food, drink, and other sensual pleasures. For Plato each part has its role to play, its function to serve. When these three elements work together, as they do when controlled by Reason, they result in personal harmony, order, and peace—self-realization. Similarly, in the first actual systematic presentation of morality, *Nichomachean Ethics,* Aristotle stresses the life of reason, which entails the harmonious development of all functions of the human organism. This, too, appears as a form of self-realization.

Today, self-realization as a goal of the good life gains impetus from what we will term *contemporary humanistic psychology,* as evidenced in the thought and writings of psychologists like Abraham Maslow. This humanistic psychology has spurred interest in expanding our awareness of self by increasing our creativity, improving our health, enhancing our learning and problem solving, and most importantly, by providing intrinsically satisfying "ecstatic" experiences. One result: a burgeoning of mind and brain investigation that attempts to see the human from all perspectives. Such study seems calculated to produce new concepts of self and self-fulfillment based on experiencing self and reality in nontraditional ways.

So, it is naive to assume an egoist is a hedonist. The fact is that ethical egoists may hold any theory of what is good and what is bad. Egoists, however, do appear to agree on *why* they are egoists. To understand their main argument we must introduce the doctrine of psychological egoism, which frequently serves as a basis for ethical egoism.

PSYCHOLOGICAL EGOISM

Egoism generally has flourished in the soil of contemporary psychology, specifically psychological egoism. Psychological egoism is not an ethical position but a doctrine concerning human behavior; it describes human behavior but it does not prescribe it. In other words, psychological egoists tell us what we do, not what we *should* do, just as cultural relativists inform us what societies are like, not what they *should* be like.

What is it that psychological egoists tell us? Simply that we always act or attempt to act in what is or what we believe to be our best interests. Some psychological egoists go further and insist that we cannot act in any other way. Proponents of psychological egoism have argued for the "pleasure principle," "ego satisfaction," or some other form of self-love as the goal of all human activity. Their argument leads them to conclude that humans must adopt ethical egoism as the only realistic ethical position.

But not all psychologists believe that psychological egoism is true. They point out that we can and do act in the interests of others. Thus Mark and Chuck can have concern for each other, Kathy, or anyone else. People do sometimes operate out of selfless, altruistic motives.

In a famous essay that questions psychological egoism, eighteenth-century bishop Joseph Butler speaks of "primary appetites," such as the desires for food, shelter, sex, and comfort. These, he says, underlie and are the objects of human behavior. According to Butler, one's own good is one of many objects of desire. But he also observes that often the objects of one's desire are for someone other than the self, as in the case of one's wanting somebody else to read a book or to take a healthful medicine. He also notes that primary appetites often war against self-love, as in the case of knowing it is not in one's best long-term interests. As an example, consider the ulcer victim who, despite realizing the long-range pain it will bring, eats a spicy pizza, washes it down with a quart of beer, tops that off with a hot fudge sundae, burps twice, and reaches for the Bisodol mints.

Psychological egoists would say that even the apparently altruistic action finds its motive in self-love, that we wish an ill person to take a medicine because it brings us pleasure. But simply because we derive pleasure from acting unselfishly doesn't mean that is *why* we so acted. If the other person chooses not to take the medicine, then we may be frustrated and left unhappy. And why? Seemingly because we wanted the person to get well. Even if the psychological egoists insist that in performing apparently altruistic actions people are always doing what they want to do, psychological egoists admit that humans are so constituted that they sometimes get satisfaction in behaving in someone else's interests.

In addition to the fact that psychologists themselves are divided on whether psychological egoism completely describes human motivation, there are a number of other objections to the doctrine. First, as dramatic defiance of the claim that all people act in their best long-term interests stand many lives that evidently avoid wealth, fame, power, physical well-being, and color television sets. What can the psychological egoist say of those who spend a lifetime in some remote corner of the world, administering to the ill, infirm, and needy? Of the fire fighter who loses his life to save another? Of the husband who is killed in defending his wife from a would-be rapist? It seems the psychological egoist may say that these people could not have behaved other than the way they did, that in the last analysis their behavior brought them a greater ratio of personal pleasure to pain than acting in any other way would have. But this claim, in turn, raises the problem of verification.

Perhaps the most telling objection to the egoistic description of human behavior is the impertinent "Prove it." It is one thing to say that a widow derived pleasure from putting her only child through college. But it is another thing to say that it was only to derive this pleasure that she swept the dusty corridors of large office buildings in the silent early morning hours for many years. The realm of human motivation is one only recently explored, and much mapping of the motivational territory is still needed. Thus, it is important to view almost all explanations of human behavior as just that, working hypotheses. This does not mean that psychological egoism could not completely account for human motivation. But to argue that psychological egoism is true because it cannot be disproved is to argue from ignorance.

But the real problem is that psychological egoism appears to defy verification procedures because it lacks a fundamental criterion of any sound hypothesis— testability. For example, to prove that an individual serves in a remote corner of the world at great personal sacrifice for self-interest requires an alternative possibility for greater personal pleasure or the elimination of all personal satisfaction from the existing situation, in which case the person should abandon it. But presumably no matter how pleasurable you make the alternative or how unpleasant you make the existing situation, if the person remains, then the psychological egoist would insist that the person was acting out of self-interest. If the person left, presumably the psychological egoist would still insist that the person was acting out of self-interest. Testing the truth of psychological egoism, then, evidently involves a double bind: "If the person stays, the person is egoistic. If the person leaves, the person is egoistic. The person must either stay or leave. Therefore, the person must be a psychological egoist." The argument clearly assumes that whatever the person does proves the person is an egoist. But why? This question is not answered. So, such an assumption is really begging the question.

We can conclude that psychological egoism, while serving as its basis, is not equivalent to ethical egoism. Psychological egoism describes human behavior; ethical egoism *prescribes* it. Psychological egoists tell us how we *do* behave; ethical egoists tell us how we *ought to* behave. Of course, if psychological egoism is a complete and accurate description of human behavior, then it is superfluous and inaccurate for ethical egoists to claim we ought to act in our own best interests, for we would not be able to act any other way. On the other hand, if psychological egoism is an incomplete or inaccurate doctrine, we cannot conclude that ethical egoism is therefore false. Indeed, perhaps ethical egoism should be the moral standard. If so, it must meet a number of objections.

OBJECTIONS TO ETHICAL EGOISM

1. *Personal egoism is inconsistent.* The first serious objection to egoism is directed against personal egoism, the position that contends that each individual should

act in terms of self-interest but does not say how others should act. To see the logical inconsistency of this position, let's rejoin Mark and Chuck.

Mark: Let me ask you something, Chuck. Do you think Kathy's being reasonable in refusing to sleep with you?
Chuck: No I don't.
Mark: What if she thinks it's wrong?
Chuck: She does.
Mark: And I suppose she thinks it's not in her best interests.
Chuck: The way she puts it is that she doesn't want to get hurt.
Mark: But you don't think the way she's treating you is right.
Chuck: You bet I don't.
Mark: But if you should act in a way that advances what you perceive as your best interests, why shouldn't she?
Chuck: I don't know. Maybe she should. All I know is that I should do what I think is best for me. I don't really know how anyone else should or shouldn't act.
Mark: Even though you say you don't know how she should act, you're reacting as if you do. You're saying her behavior's unreasonable.
Chuck: It's unreasonable because it's preventing me from getting what I want.

Chuck appears to be a personal egoist in the matter. When asked why they should always act in their own best long-term interests, it seems that personal egoists must reply that acting otherwise would cause them unnecessary pain. But if they inflict pain on themselves by acting against their own best long-term interests, wouldn't everyone acting against their own best interests inflict pain on themselves? It seems that they would. Then it seems that everyone should be egoistic.

When Mark asks why Kathy shouldn't act in her own best interests, he is naturally assuming that if Chuck can and should act in what he feels are his own interests, then Kathy or anyone else should do the same. If happiness is good in itself, evidently everyone should be ethically egoistic. By refusing to allow everyone else the same personal pursuit of happiness that they afford themselves, personal egoists seem logically inconsistent. Consequently, personal egoism is not a very popular egoistic position.

Many more egoists today are impersonal egoists—those maintaining that everyone should be egoistic. This was the egoism espoused historically by thinkers like Epicurus, Hobbes, and Nietzsche, and today by thinkers like Ayn Rand, John Hospers, and Jesse Kalin. All, not just the individual agent, should pursue their own best long-term interests, claim impersonal egoists. This position is more reasonable than personal egoism, but it still has problems.

2. *Whatever its variety, the egoistic standard cannot be verified.* Frequently antiegoists object that ethical egoism cannot be proved. In other words, there is no way of verifying that long-term self-interests should determine human behavior.

Mark: Chuck, do you ever think that maybe you should consider someone else's happiness occasionally?

Chuck: You mean Kathy.

Mark: Yes, I mean Kathy. But also I'm wondering how you can be so sure that considering your own happiness is the best way to decide anything, let alone this issue.

Chuck: Look, I've thought plenty about Kathy. And I know she'll be happy if she'd just get over her irrational fears.

Mark: Are they actually irrational? Or are they irrational because they don't square with your own idea of what will make you happy?

Chuck: Well, I don't know of any other way to be happy than to put yourself first. If you start worrying about what's going to make everybody else happy, then that's the best way to make sure you'll never be happy.

Although multifaceted, the jab of Mark's objection involves verification. He wants to know how Chuck can be sure that he should consider only his own interests. Those feeling like Chuck reply that they will be happier that way. But this is a doubtful claim, premised on an unknown fact. Although acting in our own best long-term interests may have produced happiness for us in the past, we do not really know for certain that it will continue that way. The ulcer patient who consumes a spicy pizza, beer, and a hot fudge sundae may not have felt a twinge of pain the last time he indulged. But he may the next time. So, the best the egoist can say is that acting out of self-interests will *probably* produce more happiness than not. But even this is debatable.

The more complex society becomes, the more interdependent individuals become and the less, it seems, we can act with only our best interests in mind. Perhaps, as impersonal egoists maintain, if all acted in their own best interests, then collectively there would be more happiness. But in maintaining this, egoists are no longer egoists; they are no longer acting out of self-interest but out of a universal happiness impulse. This moves them closer to a utilitarian ethic and results in another evident inconsistency.

But objections to egoism need not be restricted to personal and impersonal egoism. Egoism is open to attack on more general grounds.

3. *Egoism does not provide means for settling conflicts of interests.*

Chuck: Okay, I'll admit that Kathy or anybody else would be a fool not to look out for themselves first. And that includes me.

Mark: Let me ask you something. Who do you think has more to lose in this affair, you or Kathy?

Chuck: I don't see it in terms of losing anything. If you mean which of us is more in danger of getting hurt, in all honesty I'd say Kathy is.

Mark: Why?

Chuck: Because she feels more deeply about me than I do about her. To tell you the truth, I can't imagine ever feeling the way about her that she does about me.

Mark: So it's entirely possible that getting involved with you sexually may not be in her best interests, although it may be in yours.

Chuck: Sure, it's possible. But that's my point. If you go around wondering what's in everybody else's interest, you'll never get what you want. Besides, how's a guy supposed to know what's the right thing to do? On the one hand, let's say it's in my best interests to sleep with Kathy. And for the sake of argument let's say it's not in her best interests to sleep with me. How do you know what's the right thing to do?

Unwittingly, Chuck has raised an objection to his own egoism. Kathy's and his interests are opposed; which takes precedence? Antiegoists have charged that ethical egoism cannot resolve such problems.

To see the implications of this objection further, suppose that two men, Grey and Green, are prospects for a very important position with a company. Let's assume that it is in both their long-term interests to get the position, but that only one can get it. Obviously, should Grey get the job it would be in his best interests but not in Green's; similarly, if Green got the job it would be in his best long-term interests but not in Grey's. According to ethical egoism both should do whatever is necessary to promote their best long-term interests. Again, assuming that it was in his best long-term interests to secure the job, Grey ought to dispose of Green by whatever means, and Green ought to dispose of Grey by whatever means. Likewise, both must take steps to prevent the other from disposing of himself. In short, Grey ought to get rid of Green but Green ought to prevent Grey, and vice versa.

Apparently there are two opposing ethical obligations here. Are they both right? Of course, ethical egoists can reply, "We're not interested in deciding such disputes; ethical egoism isn't a moral court to resolve human disputes." They might go further and insist that such objections are only valid if we assume that ethical codes must arbitrate conflicts of interests. But surely an ethical code should at least help do that. After all, by definition a standard of moral behavior is prescriptive: it tells us how we ought to act. Yet, egoism seems unable to do this without appearing inconsistent and contradictory.

Related to this problem of conflicting egoistic interests are two other problems.

4. *Egoism introduces inconsistency into moral counsel.* Suppose that Grey goes to Brown for advice about how to handle the conflict that exists between his ambitions and Green's. Brown, an impersonal egoist, advises Grey to prevent Green's promotion by whatever means available. Shortly thereafter Green seeks out Brown's advice, whereupon Brown tells him to dispose of Grey by whatever means available. But this hardly seems to be a single, consistent attitude. The impersonal egoist would maintain that Brown is simply saying that both Grey and Green should try to dispose of the other and not that Brown hopes both will win. This may be. But, in fact, Brown is recommending as right conflicting courses of action.

But even though ethical egoists may escape the full impact of such objections, there's a related one that seems especially nettlesome.

5. *Egoism undermines the moral point of view.* Ethicists generally agree that the moral point of view is a necessary part of moral decision making. *By the moral point of view, ethicists mean the attitude of one who sees or attempts to see all sides of an issue without being committed to the interests of a particular individual or group.* So, the moral point of view is one that demands disinterest and impartiality. Most importantly, if we accept the legitimacy of the moral point of view, then we must look for it in any proposed ethical standard, including ethical egoism.

But ethical egoists cannot take the moral point of view, for they always are influenced by what is in their own best interests, regardless of the issue, principles, or circumstances involved. Consider in the preceding example the implications of moral counselor Brown's own egoism. Since he is an egoist, he must advise both Grey and Green in his own best long-term interests, not theirs. Suppose that in coming to Brown for advice, both Grey and Green ask Brown for a moral decision, that is, a decision about what is the right thing to do. According to egoism, Brown should not advise them according to their own best interests or anyone else's except his own. In other words, it's impossible for Brown to maintain a disinterested point of view, that is, an impartial one.*

The implications of this problem are serious, as we can observe by rejoining Mark and Chuck in the campus quad, where they have sat silently for some minutes. "For all his professed selfishness," Mark is thinking, "Chuck's really been moved by what I said. I can see it in the pain on his face. It's like the expression of someone who knows better than to do what he's been caught doing." This made Mark feel better. "At least," he thought, "Chuck might think it over. And that could make the difference. It would certainly delay things. And in the meantime I can work on him some more, get him to rethink his whole approach, show him how unwise it is."

"You know," began Chuck sheepishly, "I'm going to think this whole thing over. Maybe you're right." Mark said nothing. He thought it best to remain silent, to let the thoughts mixing around inside Chuck take hold.

"You know what bothers me the most?" Chuck asked. "Kathy thinks I love her—I don't, you know. But I said I did to make things easier. You know how guys can be." Mark nodded. They sat for awhile longer; there was nothing else to say. Then Chuck got up and limped off.

Mark remained behind. He felt good. He was convinced that he had done all he could to promote his own chances of winning Kathy. It seems he had desired her for some time.

---

*See Brian Medlin, "Ultimate Principles and Ethical Egoism," *Australian Journal of Philosophy*, XXXV, No. 2 (1957): 111–18.

SUMMARY

Consequential Position	Objections
Ethical Egoism: you should always act so that your actions produce what is in your own best long-term interests.	
a. *Personal Egoism:* the doctrine that an individual should always act in his or her best long-term interests but that does not say how others should act	**1.** If personal happiness is an ethical standard for one person, it should be for everyone; otherwise it is inconsistent.
b. *Impersonal Egoism:* the doctrine that all individuals should always act in their own best long-term interests	**1.** The standard cannot be verified. **2.** The standard does not resolve conflict of interests. **3.** The standard gives rise to inconsistencies in cases where moral counsel is given. **4.** The standard does not provide for a moral viewpoint, that is, for an impartial, disinterested approach to a moral problem.

CONCLUSIONS

Every day we are faced with ethical choices. An inherent part of these choices is the question: should I primarily seek my own best interests or should I give equal or greater weight to the interests of others? This is a choice between egoism and altruism. Egoists attempt to maximize their own happiness regardless of what occurs to others; altruists work for the welfare of all humankind.

The objections to egoism are serious. But critics are not suggesting that individuals should martyr themselves for the good of others. Understandably, critics suggest that egoists should distinguish between an interest *of* oneself and an interest *in* oneself. Granted that every human motive is an interest *of* a self, of a person. But it does not follow that every interest of a self is necessarily an interest *in* oneself. Whether one is an egoist or altruist, one pursues self-interest. But what each is interested in is quite different. The egoist is interested *in* his or her own happiness, the altruist is interested *in* the happiness of others, although, of course, not to the exclusion of self.

Failing to make this distinction, one invariably concludes, as egoists do, that although someone derived pleasure from an action overtly calculated to advance the welfare of others, the person's real motive or aim was his or her own pleasure. In other words, although people's conscious motives may be altruistic, their unconscious motives are egoistic. But there is hardly enough evidence to conclude this. If there were, the doctrine of ethical egoism would be at best redundant, for since people cannot but act in their own interests, why tell them that they *should?*

In the last analysis, the question that each of us must ask ourselves is: in my ethical code, should each individual count as one? In other words, we must take a stand on the principle of impartiality, which is the most prominent feature in the moral point of view. The principle of impartiality states that the good of every person is to count equally. Notice it does not enjoin us to leave ourselves out of the counting. But we are not to count ourselves as more than one. This principle of impartiality is an important one to mull over because of its ramifications. It figures to shape your attitudes in politics, education, foreign affairs, and, of course, in very personal areas such as premarital sex.

EXERCISES FOR ANALYSIS

EXERCISE 1

In the following passages, determine whether the reasons given justify the implied or stated conclusions. Look for fallacies.

1. "Premarital sex is wrong unless the people are in love. Then it's all right."

2. "Premarital sex is strictly the concern of the parties involved. If they don't see anything wrong with it, then there isn't. If they do, then they should avoid it. It's really impossible to generalize about premarital sex except to say that its morality depends exclusively on the feelings of the consenting parties."

3. She: Stop it.
   He: Why?

She: You know why.

He: But I love you.

She: That's what I mean.

He: That's a switch.

(Under what conditions, if any, could the presence of love make sex immoral?)

4. "Sex is good preparation for marriage. It provides a person with a lot of experiences and insights. And since I'm for anything that promotes a person's chances of having a successful marriage, I'm all for premarital sex."

5. "Sex is all right if the parties take birth control measures. If not, and they don't intend or desire a child, then it's wrong."

6. During her relationship with Rick, Laura realizes that all she's in it for is the sex. Clearly for Rick sex is part of a much deeper feeling he has for her. Laura is concerned. On the one hand, she does not want Rick to get involved any more than he already is. On the other, she does not want to jeopardize her own pleasure. She decides not to say anything to him, thus ensuring that the relationship will continue, at least for the time being. She feels she is morally justified in this decision. (Can Laura maintain the moral point of view here?)

EXERCISE 2

The following are condensed versions of some of the common arguments given against and for premarital sex.* Specifically, those arguing against premarital sex claim that it is always wrong. Those arguing for premarital sex claim that it is not always wrong, that it may sometimes be moral. Determine whether the justification in each argument is adequate. Would you add anything to any of the arguments? Are there additional arguments? As always, look for fallacies.

Arguments against Premarital Sex

1. Premarital sex is wrong because it violates a law of God. The Seventh Commandment reads, "Thou shalt not commit adultery." Historically, Biblical scholars have taken this to refer to all extramarital sex. Deuteronomy goes even so far as to prescribe death by stoning for any woman found to be nonvirgin when she marries. Clearly, therefore, premarital sex is forbidden by God's law.

2. An action that undermines marital fidelity is wrong. Premarital sex is such an action because it encourages a cavalier attitude toward marriage and marital fidelity, while predisposing persons toward marital infidelity.

3. The obvious natural end of sexual relations is propagation. It is true that there is frequently an indescribable pleasure in the sex act, but the primary purpose of sexual intercourse is clearly procreation. In premarital sex, individuals willfully

---

*See Wellman, *Morals & Ethics*, pp. 106–113.

frustrate this natural end. They subordinate the procreation principle to the pleasure principle. And even if they do not, even if they do intend procreation, since they are not married they have not established the most secure, advantageous, hospitable basis for childbearing and rearing. Thus, if an action frustrates the natural purpose of a thing, it is wrong. Premarital sex frustrates the natural purpose of sex. Therefore, premarital sex is immoral.

4. Most people just consider the fun and pleasure of premarital sex. Few ever realize until it is too late the incalculable emotional and psychological risks that they run when they get involved sexually. The emotional bonds, let alone the physical ones, that are forged are frequently more than an individual can manage. Since by its nature a premarital sexual relationship can end anytime, and most frequently does, the individuals involved are running enormous risks for themselves and others. Running such risks without the increased security that marriage brings and symbolizes is immoral.

Arguments for Premarital Sex

1. Surely premarital sex may be wrong when it involves rape, deceit, or selfishness. But many acts of premarital sex are performed out of loving concern for the other person. Such acts cannot be considered immoral. So, premarital sex is not always immoral.

2. When two individuals freely consent to have sex with each other, fully aware of each other's intentions, motives, and explanations, then it is strictly their own affair. For an outside party to declare such an act immoral is to violate the consenting parties' personal freedom and privacy. Thus, when an act of premarital sex affects only the participants, then it is private, and a private act is not blameworthy. Clearly, then, premarital sex is not always immoral.

3. It is unrealistic to expect people to remain celibate until they marry, especially in a society like ours that so greatly emphasizes sex while delaying marriage because of the demands for professional education. It is just as unfair to expect someone to ignore sex during what for many is the most sexually active period, between puberty and marriage. The fact that many people have premarital sex testifies to the almost irresistible sex drive that most normal humans feel. An act that is a response to what is almost an irresistible drive cannot always be immoral. Sex is such an act.

4. A mechanical act may be defined as one that is a mechanical reaction to a physiological need. Sex is such a natural act. It consists of performing mechanical operations in response to a physiological need. As a natural act, sex is no more moral or immoral than eating or sleeping. It is simply amoral. So, obviously premarital sex cannot always be immoral.

SELECTIONS FOR FURTHER READING

Egoism

Gauthier, David P., ed. *Morality and Rational Self-Interest.* Englewood Cliffs, N.J.: Prentice-Hall, 1970.

Kaufman, Walter. *Nietzsche: Philosopher, Psychologist, Antichrist.* New York: Random House, 1968.

MacIver, Robert Morrison, ed. *The Pursuit of Happiness.* New York: Simon & Schuster, 1955.

Maslow, Abraham. *Toward a Psychology of Being.* New York: Van Nostrand, 1962.

Olsen, Robert G. *The Morality of Self-Interest.* New York: Harcourt, Brace & World, 1965.

Rand, Ayn. *The Virtue of Selfishness.* New York: New American Library, 1964.

———. *Fountainhead.* New York: Bobbs-Merrill, 1943.

Randall, John H., Jr. *Aristotle.* New York: Columbia University Press, 1960.

Sex

Atkinson, Ronald R. *Sexual Morality.* New York: Harcourt Brace Jovanovich, 1966.

Duvall, Evelyn M. *Why Wait Until Marriage?* New York: Association Press, 1965.

Guyon, Rene. *Sexual Freedom.* Translated by Eden and Cedar Paul. New York: Knopf, 1950.

Reiss, Ira L. *Premarital Sexual Standards in America.* New York: Free Press, 1960.

Roy, R. *Honest Sex.* New York: New American Library, 1968.

Vinck, Jose De. *The Virtue of Sex.* New York: Hawthorn Books, 1966.

ELLIS/*Sex Without Guilt*

In the following selection from Sex Without Guilt, *psychotherapist Albert Ellis suggests that love is not necessary for sex. He contends that sex without love is a real possibility that should not only be personally acceptable, but socially as well. In short, for Ellis sex without love is possible and fulfilling, although admittedly sex with love is probably more fulfilling. Do you think that Ellis has demonstrated that his experience is broad enough for you to accept his conclusions as not hasty? Do your experiences corroborate Ellis's?*

A scientific colleague of mine, who holds a professorial post in the department of sociology and anthropology at one of our leading universities, recently asked me about my stand on the question of human beings having sex relations without love. Although I have taken something of a position on this issue in my book, *The American Sexual Tragedy*, I have never quite considered the problem in sufficient detail. So here goes.

In general, I feel that affectional, as against non-affectional, sex relations are *desirable* but not *necessary*. It is usually desirable that an association between coitus and affection exist—particularly in marriage, because it is often difficult for two individuals to keep finely tuned to each other over a period of years, and if there is not a good deal of love between them, one may tend to feel sexually imposed upon by the other.

The fact, however, that the co-existence of sex and love may be desirable does not, to my mind, make it necessary. My reasons for this view are several:

1. Many individuals—including, even, many married couples—*do* find great satisfaction in having sex relations without love. I do not consider it fair to label these individuals as criminal just because they may be in the minority.

Moreover, even if they are in the minority (as may well *not* be the case), I am sure that they number literally millions of men and women. If so, they constitute a sizeable subgroup of humans whose rights to sex satisfaction should be fully acknowledged and protected.

2. Even if we consider the supposed majority of individuals who find greater satisfaction in sex-love than in sex-sans-love relations, it is doubtful if all or most of them do so for *all* their lives. During much of their existence, especially their younger years, these people tend to find sex-without-love quite satisfying, and even to prefer it to affectional sex.

When they become older, and their sex drives tend to wane, they may well emphasize coitus with rather than without affection. But why should we condemn them *while* they still prefer sex to sex-love affairs?

3. Many individuals, especially females in our culture, who say that they only enjoy sex when it is accompanied by affection are actually being unthinkingly conformist and unconsciously hypocritical. If they were able to contemplate themselves objectively, and had the courage of their inner convictions, they would find sex without love eminently gratifying.

This is not to say that they would *only* enjoy non-affectual coitus, nor that they would always find it *more* satisfying than affectional sex. But, in the depths of their psyche and soma, they would deem sex without love pleasurable *too*.

And why should they not? And why should we, by our puritanical know-nothingness, force these individuals to drive a considerable portion of their sex feelings and potential satisfactions underground?

If, in other words, we view sexuoamative relations as desirable rather than necessary, we sanction the innermost thoughts and drives of many of our fellowmen and fellowwomen to have sex *and* sex-love relations. If we take the opposing view, we hardly destroy these innermost thoughts and drives, but frequently tend to intensify them while denying them open and honest outlet. This, as Freud pointed out, is one of the main (though by no means the only) source of rampant neurosis.

4. I firmly believe that sex is a biological, as well as a social, drive, and that in its biological phases it is essentially non-affectional. If this is so, then we can expect that, however we try to civilize the sex drives—and civilize them to *some* degree we certainly must—there will always be an underlying tendency for them to escape from our society-inculcated shackles and to be still partly felt in the raw.

When so felt, when our biosocial sex urges lead us to desire and enjoy sex without (as well as with), love, I do not see why we should make their experiences feel needlessly guilty.

5. Many individuals—many millions in our society, I am afraid—have little or no capacity for affection or love. The majority of these individuals, perhaps, are emotionally disturbed, and should preferably be helped to increase their affectional propensities. But a large number are not particularly disturbed, and instead are neurologically or cerebrally deficient.

Mentally deficient persons, for example, as well as many dull normals (who, together, include several million citizens of our nation) are notoriously shallow in their feelings, and probably intrinsically so. Since these kinds of individuals—like the neurotic and the organically deficient—are for the most part, in our day and age, *not* going to be properly treated and *not* going to overcome their deficiencies, and since most of them definitely *do* have sex desires, I again see no point in making them guilty when they have non-loving sex relations.

Surely these unfortunate individuals are sufficiently handicapped by their disturbances or impairments without our adding to their woes by anathematizing them when they manage to achieve some non-amative sexual release.

6. Under some circumstances—though these, I admit, may be rare—some people find more satisfaction in non-loving coitus even though, under other circumstances, these *same* people may find more satisfaction in sex-love affairs. Thus, the man who *normally* enjoys being with his girlfriend because he loves as well as is sexually attracted to her, may occasionally find immense satisfaction in being with another girl with whom he has distinctly non-loving relations.

Granting that this may be (or is it?) unusual, I do not see why it should be condemnable.

7. If many people get along excellently and most cooperatively with business partners, employees, professors, laboratory associates, acquaintances, and even spouses for whom they have little or no love or affection, but with whom they have certain specific things in common, I do not see why there cannot be individuals who get along excellently and most cooperatively with sex mates with whom they may have little else in common.

I personally can easily see the tragic plight of a man who spends much time with a girl with whom he has nothing in common but sex: since I believe that life is too short to be well consumed in relatively one-track or intellectually low-level pursuits, I would also think it rather unrewarding for a girl to spend much time with a male with whom she had mutually satisfying sex, friendship, and cultural interests but no love involvement. This is because I would like to see people, in their 70-odd years of life, have maximum rather than minimum satisfactions with individuals of the other sex with whom they spend considerable time.

I can easily see, however, even the most intelligent and highly cultured individuals spending a *little* time with members of the other sex with whom they have common sex and cultural but no real love interests. And I feel that, for the time expended in this manner, their lives may be immeasurably enriched.

Moreover, when I encounter friends or psychotherapy clients who become enamored and spend considerable time and effort thinking about and being with a member of the other sex with whom they are largely sexually obsessed, and for whom they have little or no love, I mainly view these sexual infatuations as one of the penalties of their being human. For humans are the kind of animals who are easily disposed to this type of behavior.

I believe that one of the distinct inconveniences or tragedies of human sexuality is that it endows us, and perhaps particularly the males among us, with a propensity to become exceptionally involved and infatuated with members of the other sex whom, had we no sex urges, we would hardly notice. That is too bad; and it might well be a better world if it were otherwise. But it is *not* otherwise, and I think it is silly and pernicious for us to condemn ourselves because we are the way that we are in this respect.

We had better *accept* our biosocial tendencies, or our fallible humanity—instead of constantly blaming ourselves and futilely trying to change certain of its relatively harmless, though still somewhat tragic, aspects.

For reasons such as these, I feel that although it is usually—if not always—*desirable* for human beings to have sex relations with those they love rather than with those they do not love, it is by no means *necessary* that they do so. When we teach that it *is* necessary, we only needlessly condemn millions of our citizens to self-blame and atonement.

The position which I take—that there are several good reasons why affectional, as against non-affectional, sex relations are desirable but not necessary—can be assailed on several counts. I shall now consider some of the objections to this position to see if they cannot be effectively answered.

It may be said that an individual who has non-loving instead of loving sex relations is not necessarily wicked but that he is self-defeating because, while going for immediate gratification, he will miss out on even greater enjoyments. But this would only be true if such an individual (whom we shall assume, for the sake of discussion, *would* get greater enjoyment from affectional sex relations than from non-affectional ones) were *usually or always* having non-affectionate coitus. If he were *occasionally* or *sometimes* having love with sex, and the rest of the time having sex without love, he would be missing out on very little, if any, enjoyment.

Under these circumstances, in fact, he would normally get *more* pleasure from *sometimes* having sex without love. For the fact remains, and must not be unrealistically ignored, that in our present-day society sex without love is *much more frequently* available than sex with love.

Consequently, to ignore non-affectional coitus when affectional coitus is not available would, from the standpoint of enlightened self-interest, be sheer folly. In relation both to immediate *and* greater enjoyment, the individual would thereby be losing out.

The claim can be made of course that if an individual sacrifices sex without love *now* he will experience more pleasure by having sex with love in the future. This is an interesting claim; but I find no empirical evidence to sustain it. In fact, on theoretical grounds it seems most unlikely that it will be sustained. It is akin to the claim that if an individual starves himself for several days in a row he will greatly enjoy eating a meal at the end of a week or a month. I am sure he will—provided that he is then not too sick or debilitated to enjoy anything! But, even assuming that such an individual derives enormous satisfaction from his one meal a week or a month, is his *total* satisfaction greater than it would have been had he enjoyed three good meals a day for that same period of time? I doubt it.

So with sex. Anyone who starves himself sexually for a long period of time—as virtually everyone who rigidly sticks to the sex with love doctrine must—will (perhaps) *ultimately* achieve greater satisfaction when he does find sex with love than he would have had, had he been sexually freer. But, even assuming that this is so, will his *total* satisfaction be greater?

It may be held that if both sex with and without love are permitted in any society, the non-affectional sex will drive out affectional sex, somewhat in accordance with Gresham's laws of currency. On the contrary, however, there is much reason to believe that just because an individual has sex relations, for quite a period, on a non-affectional basis, he will be more than eager to replace it, eventually, with sex with love.

From my clinical experience, I have often found that males who most want to settle down to having a single mistress or wife are those who have tried numerous lighter affairs and found them wanting. The view that sex without love eradicates the need for affectional sex relationships is somewhat akin to the ignorance is bliss theory. For it virtually says that if people never experienced sex with love they would never realize how good it was and therefore would never strive for it.

Or else the proponents of this theory seem to be saying that sex without love is so greatly satisfying, and sex with love so intrinsically difficult and disadvantageous to attain, that given the choice between the two, most people would pick the former. If this is so, then by all means let them pick the former: with which, in terms of their greater and total happiness, they would presumably be better off.

I doubt however, that this hypothesis *is* factually sustainable. From clinical experience, again, I can say that individuals who are capable of sex with love usually seek and find it; while those who remain non-affectional in their sex affairs generally are not particularly capable of sex with love and need psychotherapeutic help before they can become thus capable.

READING

MAY / Antidotes for the New Puritanism

The issue of sexual morality is inseparable from the value one places on sex. How do you see sex? What function does sex play in your life?

Today we regard ourselves as sexually enlightened. We allow ourselves to talk about it and "do it" perhaps more than any preceding age. Yet all this "enlightenment" has not solved the sexual problems in our culture. We make love, but frequently it isn't much good.

Let's concede for the sake of argument that the best way to approach sex is egoistically. Still we must ask ourselves: what actually is in our best long-term interests? Sadly, it is this question that many of us never ask. Thus, we indulge our sexual freedom, forgetful that our motives will be as much a factor in our sexual happiness or pleasure as orgasm. And our motives are inevitably tied up with the value we place on sex.

Many use sex as an opportunity to prove sexual power, to overcome solitariness, or to escape feelings of emptiness. Imposing these values on sex, it is not surprising that sexually the more we attempt to act in our own best interests, the less we seem to achieve them. In fact, the more impotent and solitary we feel, the emptier we feel. What value, then, should we place on sex? In "Antidotes for the New Puritanism," existential psychologist Rollo May suggests an answer that has implications for the egoist and nonegoist alike.

There are several strange and interesting dilemmas in which we find ourselves with respect to sex and love in our culture. When psychoanalysis was born in Victorian times half a century ago, repression of sexual impulses, feelings, and drives was the accepted mode. It was not nice to feel sexual, one would not talk about sex in polite company, and an aura of sanctifying repulsiveness surrounded the whole topic. Freud was right in pointing out the varied neurotic symptoms to which this repression of sex gave birth.

Then, in the 1920s, a radical change occurred almost overnight. The belief became a militant conviction in liberal circles that the opposite of repression—sex education, freedom of talking, feeling, and expression—would have healthy effects, and was obviously the only stand for the enlightened person. According to Max Lerner, our society shifted from acting as though sex did not exist to placing the most emphasis on sex of any society since the Roman.

Partly as a result of this radical change, we therapists rarely get nowadays in our offices patients who exhibit repression of sex in the pre-World War I Freudian sense. In fact we find just the opposite in the people who come for help: a great deal of talk about sex, a great deal of sexual

From Rollo May, "Antidotes for the New Puritanism," *Saturday Review,* Vol. 49, pp. 19–21 (March 26, 1966). Copyright © 1966 by *Saturday Review.* Reprinted by permission.

activity, practically no one complaining of any cultural prohibitions over his going to bed as often or with as many partners as he wishes.

But what our patients *do* complain of is lack of feeling and passion—so much sex and so little meaning or even fun in it! Whereas the Victorian person didn't want anyone to know that he or she had sexual feelings, now we are shamed if we do not. Before 1910 if you called a lady "sexy," you insulted her; nowadays the lady accepts the adjective as a prized compliment. Our patients often have problems of impotence or frigidity, but they struggle desperately not to let anyone know they *don't* feel sexually. The Victorian nice man or woman was guilty if he or she did perform sexually; now we are guilty if we *don't*.

One dilemma, therefore, is that enlightenment has not at all solved the sexual problems in our culture. To be sure, there are important positive results of the new enlightenment, chiefly in increased freedom for the individual. And some external problems are eased—sexual knowledge can be bought in any bookstore, contraception is available almost everywhere outside Boston, and external societal anxiety has lessened. *But internalized anxiety and guilt have increased.* And in some ways these are morbid, harder to handle, and impose a heavier burden upon the individual man and woman than external anxiety and guilt.

A second dilemma is that the new emphasis on technique in sex and love-making backfires. It often seems to me that there is an inverse relationship between the number of how-to-do-it books perused by a person, or rolling off the presses in a society, and the amount of sexual passion or even pleasure experienced by the persons involved. Nothing is wrong with technique as such, in playing golf or acting or making love. But the emphasis beyond a certain point on technique in sex makes for a mechanistic attitude toward love-making, and goes along with alienation, feelings of loneliness, and depersonalization.

The third dilemma I propose is that our highly vaunted sexual freedom has turned out to be a new form of puritanism. I define puritanism as a state of alienation from the body, separation of emotion from reason, and use of the body as a machine. These were the elements of moralistic puritanism in Victorian times; industrialism expressed these same characteristics of puritanism in economic guise. Our modern sexual attitudes have a new content, namely, full sexual expression, but in the same old puritan form—alienation from the body and feeling, and exploitation of the body as though it were a machine.

In our new puritanism bad health is equated with sin. Sin used to be "to give in to one's sexual desires"; now it is "not to have full sexual expression." A woman used to be guilty if she went to bed with a man; now she feels vaguely guilty if after a certain number of dates she still refrains. And her partner, who is always completely enlightened—or at least pretends to be—refuses to allay her guilt and does not get overtly angry at her sin of "morbid repression," her refusal to "give." This, of course, makes her "no" all the more guilt-producing for her.

All this means, of course, that

people have to learn to perform sexually but at the same time not to let themselves go in passion or unseemly commitment—which latter may be interpreted as exerting an unhealthy demand on the partner. *The Victorian person sought to have love without falling into sex; the modern person seeks to have sex without falling into love.*

Recently I amused myself by drawing an impressionistic picture of the attitude of the contemporary enlightened person toward sex and love. I call it the portrait of the new sophisticate:

The new sophisticate is not castrated by society but, like Origen, is self-castrated. Sex and the body are for him not something to be and live out, but tools to be cultivated like a TV announcer's voice. And like all genuine Puritans (very passionate men underneath) the new sophisticate does it by devoting himself passionately to the moral principle of dispersing all passion, loving everybody until love has no power left to scare anyone. He is deathly afraid of his passions unless they are kept under leash, and the theory of total expression is precisely his leash. His dogma of liberty is his repression; and his principle of full libidinal health, full sexual satisfaction, are his puritanism and amount to the same thing as his New England forefathers' denial of sex. The first Puritans repressed sex and were passionate; our new man represses passion and is sexual. Both have the purpose of holding back the body, both are ways of trying to make nature a slave. The modern man's rigid principle of full freedom is not freedom at all but a new straitjacket, in some ways as compulsive as the old. He does all this because he is afraid of his body and his compassionate roots in nature, afraid of the soil and his procreative power. He is our latter-day Baconian devoted to gaining power *over*

nature, gaining knowledge in order to get more power. And you gain power over sexuality (like working the slave until all zest for revolt is squeezed out of him) precisely by the role of full expression. Sex becomes our tool like the caveman's wheel, crowbar, or adz. Sex, the new machine, the *Machina Ultima.*

It is not surprising that, confronted by these dilemmas, people become more and more concerned about the technical, mechanical aspects of the sexual act. The questions typically asked about the act of lovemaking are not whether there was passion or meaning or even pleasure, but how well did one perform? Even the sexologists, whose attitude is generally the more the merrier, are raising their eyebrows these days about the anxious overemphasis on achieving the orgasm and the great importance attached to "satisfying" the partner. The man makes a point of asking the woman if she "made it," or is she "all right," or uses some other such euphemism for an experience for which obviously no euphemism is possible. We men are reminded by Simone de Beauvoir and other women who try to interpret the love act to us, that this is the last thing in the world a woman wants to be asked at that moment.

I often get the impression, amid the male flexing of sexual biceps, that men are in training to become sexual athletes. But what is the great prize of the game? Now it is well known in psychotherapeutic circles that the overconcern with potency is generally a compensation for feelings of impotence. Men and women both are struggling to prove their sexual power. Another motive of the game is to overcome their own solitariness. A third motive is often the desperate endeavor to escape feelings of emptiness and the threat of apathy: they pant and quiver to find an answering quiver in someone else's body to prove their own is not dead. Out of an ancient conceit we call this love.

The struggle to find an identity is also a central motive in acting out these sexual roles—a goal present in women as well as men, as Betty Friedan in *The Feminine Mystique* made clear. The point I wish to emphasize here is the connection between this dilemma about potency and the tendency in our society for us to become machines or ledger books even in bed. A psychiatrist colleague of mine tells me that one of his patients brought in the following dream. "I was in bed with my wife. Between us was my accountant. He was going to make love to my wife. Somehow it seemed all right."

Along with the overemphasis upon mechanism there goes, understandably enough, a lessening of passion and of feeling itself, which seems to take the form of a kind of anaesthesia in people who otherwise can perform the mechanical aspects of the sexual act very capably. This is one reason we therapists get a good number of patients these days with problems of impotence, frigidity, and simple lack of feeling in the sexual act. We psychiatrists often hear the disappointed refrain, "We made love, but it wasn't much good."

Sex is the "last frontier," David Riesman meaningfully wrote fifteen years ago in *The Lonely Crowd*. Gerald Sykes in the same vein spoke of sex as the "last green thing." It is surely true that the zest, adventure, the dis-covering of vast new areas of feeling and passion in one's self, the trying out of one's power to arouse feelings in others—these are indeed "frontier experiences." They are normally present as part of the psychosexual development of every individual, and the young person rightly gets a validation of himself from such experiences. Sex in our society did in fact have this power in the several recent decades since the 1920s, when almost every other activity was becoming "other-directed," jaded, emptied of zest and adventure.

But for various reasons—one of them being that sex had to carry by itself the weight for the validation of the personality on practically all other levels as well—the frontier freshness and newness and challenge of sex were more and more lost. We are now living in the post-Riesman age, and are experiencing the difficult implications of the "other-directed," radar behavior. The "last frontier" has become a teeming Las Vegas and no frontier at all.

Young people can no longer get a bootlegged feeling of personal identity out of the sexual revolt, since there is nothing left to revolt against. A study of drug addiction among young people, published recently in the *New York Times*, reports the young people are saying that the revolt against parents and society, the "kick" of feeling their own "oats" which they used to get from sex, they now have to get from drugs. It is not surprising that for many youngsters what used to be called love-making is now so often experienced as a futile "panting palm to palm," in Aldous Huxley's predictive phrase, and that they tell us that it is hard for them to understand what the poets were talking about.

Nothing to revolt against, did I say? Well, there is obviously one thing left to revolt against, and that is sex itself. The frontier, the establishing of identity, can be, and not infrequently is for the young people, a revolt against sexuality entirely. A modern Lysistrata in robot's dress is rumbling at the gates of our cities, or if not rumbling, at least hovering. As sex becomes more machine-like, with passion irrelevant and then even pleasure diminishing, the problem comes full circle, and we find, *mirabile dictu*, a progression from an *anaesthetic* attitude to an *antiseptic* one. Sexual contact itself then tends to be avoided. The sexual revolution comes finally back on itself not with a bang but a whimper.

This is another and surely least constructive aspect of the new puritanism: it returns, finally, to an ascetic attitude. This is said graphically in a charming limerick that seems to have sprung up on some sophisticated campus:

The word has come down from the Dean,
That with the aid of the teaching machine,
    King Oedipus Rex
    Could have learned about sex
Without ever touching the Queen.

What are the sources of these dilemmas? Perhaps if we can get some idea of what went wrong, we shall rediscover values in sex and love that will have genuine relevance for our age.

The essential element, I propose, in the dilemmas we have been discussing is the *banalization of sex and love*. Does not the tendency to make sex and love banal and vapid run through our whole culture? The plethora of books on the subject have one thing in common—they oversimplify sex and love, treating the topic like a combination of learning to play tennis and buying life insurance.

I have said above, describing the modern sophisticated man's dilemmas about sex, that he castrates himself "because he is afraid of his body, afraid of his compassionate roots in nature, afraid of the soil and his procreative powers." That is to say, something much more potent is going on in sexuality than one would gather from the oversimplified books on sex and love—something that still has the power to scare people. I believe banalization serves as a defense against this anxiety.

The widespread tendency among young people to "go steady"—premature monogamy, as it has been called—is an egregious illustration of our point. In my frequent visits to different college campuses for lectures, I have discussed this phenomenon with students, and something like the following seems to be going on. In our insecure age when all values are in flux, at least "the steady" is steady. Always having a date with the same fellow or girl on Saturday night, dancing with this same person through the entire party at college dances, always knowing this one is available, allays the anxiety of aloneness. But it also gets boring. This leads naturally enough to early sexuality: sex at least is something we can do when we run out of conversation—which happens often when the partners have not developed enough in their own right to be interesting very long to each other as persons. It is a strange fact in our society that what goes into building a relationship—the sharing of tastes, fantasies, dreams, hopes for the future and fears from the past—seems to make people more shy and vulnerable than going to bed with each other. They are more wary of the tenderness that goes with psychological and spiritual nakedness than they are of the physical nakedness in sexual intimacy.

Now substituting premature sexuality for meaningful intimate relationship relieves the young person's anxiety, but at the price of bypassing opportunity for further development. It seems that going steady, paradoxically, is related to promiscuity. I define "promiscuity" with Webster as the indiscriminate practice of sexuality whether with one person or a number: sex is indiscriminate when used in the service of security, or to fill up an emotional vacuum. But promiscuity is a lonely and alienating business. This loneliness becomes one of the pushes toward early marriage. Grasping each other in marriage gives a kind of security—a legal and social security at least—which temporarily allays loneliness, but at the price of the haunting dread of a boring marital future. *Each step in this pattern has within it the banalization of sex and love.*

Now the question rarely asked is, are not these young people—possibly wiser in their innocence than their culture in its sophistication—fleeing from some anxiety that is only too real? I propose that what scares them, like what scares our "new sophisticate," is an element in sex and love which is almost universally repressed in our culture, namely the *tragic, daimonic element.*

By "daimonic"—which I hasten to say does not refer to little "demons"—I mean the natural element within an individual, such as the erotic drive, which has the power to take over the whole person. The erotic urge pushes toward a general physiological aim, namely sexual release. But it can push the individual into all kinds of relationships without relation to the totality of his self.

But the potentially destructive effects of the daimonic are only the reverse side of the person's constructive vitality, his passion and other potentially creative activities. The Greeks used the term "daimon" to describe the inspired urges of the poet. Socrates, indeed, speaks of his "daimon" as his conscience. When this power goes awry—when one element takes over the total personality and drives the person into disintegrative behavior—it becomes "demon possession," the historical term for psychosis. The daimonic can be either creative or destructive, but either way it certainly is the opposite to banalization. The repression of the daimonic, tragic aspects of sex and love is directly related to their banalization in our culture.

The daimonic is present in all nature as blind, ambiguous power. But only in man does it become allied with the tragic. For tragedy is the self-conscious, personal realization of being in the power of one element; thus the Greeks defined tragedy as "inordinate desire," "pride," "reaching beyond just boundaries." We have only to call to mind Romeo and Juliet, Abelard and Héloise, Tristan and Isolde, Helen of Troy, to see the power of sexual love to seize a man and woman, lift them up into a whirlwind that defies rational control and may destroy not only themselves but others at the same time. These stories are told over and over again in Western classic literature, and passed down from generation to generation, for they come from a depth of human experience in sexual love that is profoundly significant. It is a level largely unmentioned in our day, much to the impoverishment of our talk and writing about sex and love.

If we are to overcome banalization, we must take sex and love on several different dimensions at once. Consider, as an analogy, Mozart's music. In some portions of his music Mozart is engaged in elegant play. In other portions his music comes to us as pure sensuous pleasure, giving us a sheer delight. But in other portions, like the death music at the end of *Don Giovanni*, Mozart is profoundly shaking: we are gripped by fate and the daimonic as the inescapable tragedy rises before us. If Mozart had only the first element, play, he would sooner or later be banal and boring. If he presented only pure sensuality, he would become cloying; or if only the fire and death music, his creations would be too heavy. He is great because he writes on all these dimensions; and he must be listened to on all these levels at once.

Sexuality and love similarly have these three dimensions. Sex not only can be play, but probably an element of sheer play should be fairly regularly present. By this token, casual relationships in sex may have their gratification or meaning in the sharing of pleasure, tenderness, and so on. But if one's whole pattern and attitude toward sex is only casual,

then sooner or later the playing itself becomes boring. The same is true about sensuality, obviously an element in any gratifying sex: if it has to carry the whole weight of the relationship, it becomes cloying. If sex is only sensuality, you sooner or later turn against sex itself. The third element, the daimonic and tragic, we emphasized here because that is the one almost wholly repressed in our culture, a fact that has much to do with the banalization of sex and love in our day. In a book like Erich Fromm's *Art of Loving,* for example, the daimonic, tragic element is completely missing.

An appreciation of the tragic and daimonic side of sex and love can help us not only to avoid oversimplification but to love better. Let me illustrate the constructive use of the daimonic. Every person, as a separate individual, experiences aloneness and strives to overcome his loneliness, this striving usually being some kind of love. Sexuality and love require self-assertion: if the person is not to some extent an individual in his own right, he will not only have nothing to give, nothing to relate with, but will be unable to assert himself and therefore unable to be genuinely part of the relationship. Both the man and woman need self-assertion in order to breach the separateness and make some kind of union with each other. Thus there is truth in the vernacular expressions about needing to "let oneself go" and "give oneself over" to the sexual act— or to any creative experience for that matter.

The psychotherapist Dr. Otto Rank once remarked in his latter years of practice that practically all the women who came to him had problems because their husbands were not assertive enough. Despite the oversimplified sound of this sentence, it contains a telling point: our effete cultivation of sex can make us so intellectual and detached about it that the simple power of the act evaporates, and we lose—and this loss is especially serious for women—the important elemental pleasure of "being taken," being "carried away." But the self-assertive power must be integrated with the other aspects of one's own personality, and with the total person of the mate; otherwise it becomes daimonic in the destructive sense.

Let us now summarize some values, potential and actual, in sexual love. There is, first, the overall value of enrichment and fulfilment of personality. This comes from expansion of one's awareness of one's self, one's feelings, one's experience of his capacity to give sexual pleasure and other feelings to the other person, and achieve thereby an expansion of meaning in interpersonal relationship. This fulfilment carries us beyond what we are at any given moment; I become in a literal sense more than I was. The most powerful symbol imaginable for this fulfilment is procreation—the possibility that a new being may be conceived and born. The "birth," however, can and does refer at the same time to the birth of new aspects of one's self.

Tenderness is a second value, a tenderness that is much more than indicated in that most unpoetic of all words, "togetherness." The experience of tenderness comes out of the fact that the two persons, longing as

all individuals do to overcome the separateness and isolation to which we are all heir because we are individuals, can participate in a relationship that for the moment is not two isolated selves but a union. In this kind of sexual intercourse, the lover often does not know whether a particular sensation of delight is felt by him or by his loved one—and it doesn't make any difference anyway. A sharing takes place which is a new gestalt, a new being, a new field of magnetic force. A gratifying sexual relationship thus has the gestalt of a painting—the various parts, the colors, feelings, forms, unite to become a new whole.

There is the third value which occurs ideally at the moment of climax in sexual intercourse. This is the point when the lovers are carried not only beyond their personal isolation, but when a shift in consciousness seems to occur that unites them also with nature. In Hemingway's novel, *For Whom the Bell Tolls,* the older woman, Pilar, waits for the hero, Robert Jordan, and the girl he loves when they have gone ahead into the mountain to make love; and when they return, she asks, "Did the earth move?" The shaking of the earth seems to be a normal part of the momentary loss of awareness of the self and the surging up of a sudden consciousness that includes the "earth" as well. There is an accelerating experience of touch, contact, union to the point where for a moment the awareness of separateness is lost, blotted out in a cosmic feeling of oneness with nature. I do not wish this to sound too "ideal," for I think it is a quality, however subtle, in all lovemaking except the most depersonalized sort. And I also do not wish it to sound simply "mystic," for despite limitations in our awareness, I think it is an inseparable part of actual experience in the love act.

This leads us immediately to the fourth value, sex and love as the affirmation of the self. Despite the fact that many people in our culture use sex to get a short-circuited, ersatz sense of identity, sexual love can and ought to provide a sound and meaningful way to the sense of personal identity. We emerge from love-making normally with renewed vitality, a vitality which comes not from triumph or proof of one's strength but from the expansion of awareness. Probably in love-making there is always some element of sadness—as, to use our previous analogy, there is in practically all music no matter how joyful—in the reminder that we have not succeeded absolutely in losing our separateness, nor is the infantile hope that we could recover the womb made into reality, and even our increased self-awareness can also be a poignant reminder that none of us ever overcomes his loneliness completely. But by one's replenished sense of one's own significance in the love act he can accept these unavoidable human limitations.

A final value inheres in the curious phenomenon in love-making:

that to be able to give to the other person is essential to one's own full pleasure in the act. This sounds like a banal moralism in our age of mechanization of sex and "release of tension" in sexual objects. But it is not sentimentality but a point which anyone can confirm in his own experience in the love act, that to give is essential to one's own pleasure. Many patients in psychotherapy find themselves discovering, generally with some surprise, that something is missing if they cannot "do something for," give something to the partner—the normal expression of which is the giving in the act of intercourse itself. Just as giving is essential to one's own full pleasure, the ability to receive is necessary in the love interrelationship also. If you cannot receive, your giving will be a domination of the partner. Conversely, if you cannot give, your receiving will leave you empty. The paradox is demonstrably true that the person who can only receive becomes empty, for he is unable actively to appropriate and make his own what he receives. I speak, thus, not of receiving as a passive phenomenon, but of *active receiving*: one knows he is receiving, feels it, absorbs it into his own experience whether he verbally acknowledges it or not, and is grateful for it.

5

SCIENTIFIC EXPERIMENTATION
*of lying to guinea pigs
on the road to utopia*
UTILITARIANISM

In 1961 psychologist Stanley Milgram of Yale University devised a useful experiment for studying obedience. In the experiment, an experimenter orders a naive subject to administer electric shocks to a victim. A simulated electric shock generator is used, clearly marked with thirty voltage levels, ranging from 15 to 450 volts. The generator also bears verbal labels that range from "Slight Shock" to "Danger: Severe Shock" to, finally, just "XXX." The victim, a confederate of the experimenter, is told how to respond beforehand. The naive subject is told that the shocks are being administered as part of a learning experiment designed to measure the effect of punishment on memory.

As the experiment unravels, the subject is ordered to give increasingly more powerful shocks to the victim. At some point the subject will presumably refuse to administer any more shocks, whereupon psychologists will learn to what degree and under what conditions humans will obey and cease to obey authority figures.

Just what did the Milgram studies indicate? Of the forty subjects involved, five refused to obey the experimental commands beyond the 300-volt level of "Intense Shock." Eight more subjects disobeyed the experimenter at various levels of "Extreme Intensity Shock," ranging from 315 to 360 volts. Now comes the stunning part. The remaining twenty-six subjects obeyed the orders of the experimenters to the end, willingly punishing the victim beyond the "Danger: Severe Shock" level of 420 volts into the "XXX" range of 450. At that point experimenters broke off the experiment. Conclusion: the individual who is commanded by a legitimate authority ordinarily obeys.

Since the Milgram studies were conducted, a number of ethicists have noted one obvious phenomenon that the experiment underscores: although subjects have learned from early childhood that it is morally wrong to hurt other persons against their will, subjects will do precisely that when they believe that they are legitimately ordered to do so. The implications of this fact are far-reaching. For one thing, it alerts us of the extent to which authority figures influence our thinking, values, and behavior. Specifically, it underscores a recurring moral fact of twentieth-century life—that most of us will conveniently excuse ourselves from making moral decisions when some "higher power" is around to decide for us.

Although we could profitably spend time discussing the implications of the Milgram studies, we are going to focus on another aspect, one that seems to have been overlooked. In order to conduct their research, the experimenters at Yale University *lied* to the subjects. This lying occurred at various stages of the experiment. For example, some subjects needed a reason for administering electric shock to the victims, so experimenters concocted a cover story. After experimenters introduced the subjects to the relation between punishment and learning, they told the subjects:

> In this study we are bringing together a number of adults of different occupations and ages. And we're asking some of them to be teachers and some of them to be learners. We want to find out just what effect different people have on each other as teachers and learners, and also what effect *punishment* will have on learning in this situation. Therefore, I'm going to ask one of you to be the teacher here tonight and the other one to be the learner. Does either of you have a preference?*

Not only did experimenters lie to subjects about the purpose of the experiment, but they deceived them into thinking that subjects could choose which role to play: teacher or learner. Subjects then drew slips of paper to determine who would be which. The drawing was rigged: all slips contained the word *teacher*. The confederate victims lied, saying that they had drawn *learner*.

After the drawing, "teacher" and "learner" were taken to a room where the lying continued. Administrators told the subjects that the victims were being strapped into an electric-chair apparatus, the straps being necessary to prevent excessive movement while the "learner" was being shocked. Administrators then attached electrodes to the victim's wrists, being scrupulous to inform subjects that electrode paste was being used in order to avoid blisters and burns. Finally, administrators lied to the subjects when they said that the electrodes were attached to the shock generator in the adjacent room, to which they escorted the subjects and began the experiment.

Quite obviously, in order to obtain valid test results, administrators couldn't inform subjects of the true nature of the experiment. Does this, then, justify the lying? Obviously many would argue that it does. Others would add that lying can be defended on grounds of beneficial social consequences. In other words, by lying, experimenters were able to determine information that was of great potential benefit to society, without injuring anyone or anything.

This justification would be supported by a great many consequential ethicists, who argue that the goodness of an action depends on the amount of happiness or pleasure that the action produces for everyone concerned. This ethical position is generally known as *utilitarianism*, an ethical view that has grown up in the last century with important ramifications. In this chapter we

---

*Paul G. Warga, *Personal Awareness: A Psychology of Adjustment* (Boston: Houghton Mifflin, 1974), p. 146.

will examine this ethic. We'll see how utilitarianism differs from egoism, consider roles that two English philosophers played in developing it, and examine two versions of utilitarianism—act and rule. The issue of questionable means to carry out scientific experimentation for apparently good ends will serve as a useful device to explore these aspects of utilitarianism.

UTILITARIANISM

Where egoism maintains that the promotion of one's own best long-term interests should be the standard of morality, utilitarianism insists that the promotion of the best long-term interests of everyone concerned should be the moral standard. Stated briefly, *the utilitarian doctrine asserts that we should always act so as to produce the greatest possible ratio of good to evil for everyone.* Again, as with all consequential positions, *good* and *evil* are taken to mean nonmoral good and evil.

As developed by John Stuart Mill (1806–1873), utilitarianism maintained that what is intrinsically good is pleasure or happiness. More recent utilitarians, however, view things other than happiness as having intrinsic worth (e.g., knowledge, power, beauty, and moral qualities). Their view is termed *pluralistic, or ideal, utilitarianism* and today attracts thinkers such as G. E. Moore* and Hastings Rashdall.† But since we will be primarily considering Mill's utilitarianism, we will be using *intrinsic good* to mean happiness. What we'll say about Mill's position, however, applies equally to pluralistic utilitarianism, if for *happiness* or *pleasure* the phrase *intrinsic good* is substituted.

Before evaluating the utilitarian doctrine, let's clear up some points about utilitarianism that frequently lead to its misapplication.

POINTS OF CLARIFICATION

First, in speaking of right and wrong acts, utilitarians are speaking about those over which we exercise control, those that are voluntary. This does not mean, however, that we must have premeditated the action. For example, suppose that as you're walking down a street you observe a child standing in a driveway as a car is backing up. The child will surely be struck. Without deliberation you rush to the scene and snatch the child away from the path of the car. Although

---

*G. E. Moore, *Principia Ethica* (London: Cambridge University Press, 1903).

†Hastings Rashdall, *A Theory of Good and Evil: A Treatise on Moral Philosophy*, 2 vols. (New York: Kraus Reprint, reprint of 1924 edition).

you didn't premeditate this action, you could have acted otherwise; you could have chosen not to save the child. This is a voluntary action.

Second, in referring to the "greatest possible ratio of good to evil," utilitarians do not indicate a preference for immediate or remote good. The emphasis is on *greatest*. If the long-term good will be greater than the short-term, we should prefer it, and vice versa. Frequently, however, the long-term good is less certain than the immediate good. In such cases we prefer the immediate good.

Third, in determining the "greatest possible ratio of good to evil for everyone," we must consider unhappiness or pain as well as happiness. For example, if it were possible to calculate pleasure and pain, then we should subtract from the total happiness our action would produce the total unhappiness it would produce. The result, in theory, will be an accurate measure of the action's worth. So, if an action produces eight units of happiness and four units of unhappiness, its net worth is four units. If a second action produces ten units of happiness and seven units of unhappiness, its net worth is three units. In such a case we should choose the first action over the second. In the event that both acts lead not to happiness but to unhappiness, we should do the one that leads to fewer units of unhappiness.

Fourth, when choosing between two actions, one that you prefer and one that you do not prefer, choose the one that produces the greatest net happiness. As Mill writes:

> The happiness which forms the utilitarian standard of what is right in conduct, is not the agent's own happiness, but that of all concerned. As between his own happiness and that of others, utilitarianism requires him to be as strictly impartial as a disinterested and benevolent spectator.*

Obviously you shouldn't disregard your own preferences, but you shouldn't give them added weight either. Count yourself as just one vote among the many. This does not mean that utilitarianism is a doctrine of unconditional self-sacrifice. Mill is clear on this:

> The utilitarian morality does recognize in human beings the power of sacrificing their own greatest good for the good of others. It only refuses to admit that the sacrifice is itself a good. A sacrifice which does not increase, or tend to increase, the sum total of happiness, it considers wasted. The only self-renunciation which it applauds, is devotion to the happiness, or to some of the means of happiness, of others; either of mankind collectively, or of individuals within the limits imposed by the collective interests of mankind.†

Notice that two of these utilitarian explanations seem to assume that we can calculate the goodness and badness of our actions in such a way that we can

---

*John Stuart Mill, *Utilitarianism*, 13th ed. (London: Longmans, Green, 1897), p. 19.
†Mill, p. 19.

choose one action over another. Is such mathematical calculation possible? Jeremy Bentham thought it was.

BENTHAM'S HEDONISTIC CALCULUS

In attempting to determine precisely how much pleasure and pain would result from a person's actions, British philosopher Jeremy Bentham (1748–1832) formulated his hedonistic calculus. In his calculus, Bentham set up six criteria for evaluating an action's pleasure value.

His first criterion was *intensity,* by which he meant the sensation of the pleasure experienced. The more intense the pleasure, the more desirable it is; the more intense the pain, the less desirable.

Bentham's second criterion was *duration,* by which he meant how long a pleasure lasted. In the case of two options, the action that leads to the longer pleasure is preferable.

His third criterion was *certainty.* In choosing between pleasures, we should choose the one that is more likely.

His fourth criterion was *propinquity,* by which he meant the nearness of the pleasure. Other things being equal, we should prefer the proximate pleasure to the remote one.

His fifth criterion was *fecundity,* by which he meant an option's likelihood to produce additional pleasures. Bentham argues that pleasure that produces even more pleasure is more desirable than one that doesn't.

Finally, Bentham listed *purity,* by which he meant how free of pain a pleasure is. Of two pleasures, we should prefer the one accompanied by the least pain.

Later, John Stuart Mill added *quality* to the list. By *quality* Mill meant the moral superiority that one pleasure holds over another. To illustrate, Mill asked whether a person would rather be a satisfied pig or Socrates dissatisfied. While many people were probably still mulling that one over, Mill answered his own question: Socrates. Thus, he concluded that some pleasures, in this case the pleasure of knowledge, are qualitatively more desirable than others, in this case a full stomach.

Does Bentham's hedonistic calculus allow us to calculate pleasure and pain mathematically? No, since the only criteria that can be empirically measured are duration and perhaps extent. This doesn't mean, of course, that we will never be able to calculate the other criteria. Perhaps someday we will be able to calculate pain intensity so accurately that we can determine how much pain a human incurs while watching a presidential news conference. Even so, we should still be faced with the problem of conflicting criteria.

Nevertheless, as general guidelines for evaluating moral decisions, Bentham's criteria are valuable. They provide us with measuring rods other than the one many of us use exclusively—immediate gratification.

In developing his calculus, Bentham seemed to have in mind a particular brand of utilitarianism, what is called *act utilitarianism*. This should be distinguished from the other main brand, *rule utilitarianism*.

ACT UTILITARIANISM

Act utilitarianism is the doctrine that maintains that the right act is the one that produces the greatest ratio of good to evil for all concerned. In performing an action we should ask ourselves, "What will be the consequences of this particular act in this particular situation?" If the consequences of an action effect more general good than the consequences of any other alternative, then the action is good.

To draw out this position, let's fictionalize the Milgram studies somewhat by imagining the experiment in its formative stage. Researchers and their assistants have met to be briefed about the particulars of the experiment. At the meeting are Dr. Jonas K. Prout and his research assistant, graduate student Diane Fabris. The meeting has excited everyone and has generated much discussion among the participants. Afterwards Dr. Prout and Ms. Fabris continue their discussion over a cup of coffee. During the conversation Ms. Fabris reveals some reservations about having to lie to the participants in order to obtain desired results. Prout understands her misgivings.

Prout: To be perfectly honest, Diane, there are a number of things in the field of experimental research that have troubled me from my earliest involvements. One is inflicting pain.

Fabris: Do you mean on animals?

Prout: Yes, nonhuman animals. In dealing with humans we invariably have their consent. But, you know, there's never been a consent form signed by the brightest of chimps or rodents.

Fabris: But you still experiment.

Prout: I do. Partially out of cowardice, I suppose. I choose not to incur the wrathful scorn of my scientifically minded colleagues. But I do it mostly, I prefer to think, for more noble reasons, the chief of which is to lessen the pain of my fellow humans and to increase their pleasure.

Fabris: But somehow it just smacks of doing the wrong thing for the right reason.

Prout: I suppose you're referring to the fact that a necessary component of our experiment is lying.

Fabris: Yes, that really bothers me. Call me a product of environmental conditioning if you want, but all my life I've been brought up to believe that the end does not justify the means. I can hear parents, teachers, religious leaders—everyone I'm supposed to respect and look to for some sort of moral direction—proclaiming that no matter how worthy the results, they do not justify wrongdoing. Why, just the other day in physiological psychology, Professor Reichenbach deplored medical experiments conducted on Jews during World War II. "No matter what the intended purpose, those actions constitute a moral abomination." His exact words.

Prout: I agree.

Fabris: So do I. And yet here we sit devising a way to intentionally mislead and deceive other humans for the purpose of some "noble" experiment.

Prout: But surely, Diane, you see that the situations are not analogous.

Fabris: In one important respect, I think they are. And that is that we're justifying what we consider wrongdoing by appealing to our lofty intentions and hoped-for results.

Prout: I think you're misunderstanding something crucial here. Simply because we must deceive, as you put it, to acquire our data, does not mean that we are condoning deception and duplicity as a general maxim of human behavior.

Fabris: Do you mean that we're condoning it just for this experiment?

Prout: I suppose that I do.

Fabris: Would you have condoned it in Watergate?

Prout: No, I would not have.

Fabris: Then I'm afraid I don't understand.

Prout: Let me try to explain. I prefer to examine each case as it arises and to restrict all considerations to that single case. We are not examining the moral proprieties of Hitler's Germany or Nixon's Watergate. We're examining a proposed experiment whose purpose it is to shed some empirical light on the process of obedience. It is true that in this case the experimental procedure calls for a certain amount of deception. However, I think such deception is justifiable, considering the potentially vast salutary dividend that society will reap through our efforts.

Dr. Prout clearly expresses an act utilitarian position. He is deciding this particular case within a specific context; he does not want what he is condoning in this instance to be universalized, to be automatically applied in all cases, or to be made into a rule of moral conduct. It is conceivable, he would admit, that at a different time, under other circumstances, he would not condone such deliberate deception. But in this instance he approves of lying because the probable results will produce the most happiness for the greatest number.

As you might imagine, there are a number of objections to act utilitarianism. Probably Ms. Fabris is feeling the pinch of some of these.

OBJECTIONS TO ACT UTILITARIANISM

1. *The consequences of actions are uncertain.*

> **Fabris:** You're assuming, Dr. Prout, that the consequences will be beneficial to society.
>
> **Prout:** Yes, I am. Because I believe that in all probability it is better for people to know how they are being influenced by authority figures than not to know.
>
> **Fabris:** I agree. But is it beneficial for people to know that scientists will lie in order to get what they want?

Prout: But we're not misrepresenting any of our findings. Whenever that has occurred, the scientific community has been among the first to deplore such activity, as it should be.

Fabris: No, we're not misrepresenting the results of our findings. But we are deliberately misrepresenting our procedure to the test subjects. And in reporting our results, we must publicize that deliberate misrepresentation, lying, was an integral part of how we conducted our business. It seems to me that such information could be tremendously harmful to the faith and trust that people have come to place in scientific method.

Prout: Are you saying that if the general public realizes that we have lied in this case, even at the procedural level of our experiment, that it will conclude that we could and might lie in other cases, at other levels?

Fabris: That's exactly what I'm saying. And I'm also saying that that would not be a good thing.

Prout: No, it would not be a good thing. But do you think that it is likely? Do you think that the average person will be as impressed with our methodological deception as he will be with our results, which, despite the deception, are valid?

Fabris: Obviously we won't know that until we conduct the experiment, then publicize it. But that's the point. We really don't know what the consequences of our lie are going to be.

Ms. Fabris has raised a common objection to act utilitarianism. Simply put, we can't ever be sure of the consequences of our actions. To evaluate the morality of those actions on a consequential basis is extremely problematic. Thus, a utilitarian stand is essentially a questionable claim springing from an unknown fact. Clearly the criticism applies generally to any consequential position—to egoism and both versions of utilitarianism. Dr. Prout would probably reply that it is not so much what the action produces as what the agent *intends* that it produce. But it is a safe bet that not one of the Watergate conspirators *intended* his action to lead to what it did. But does this make their actions right? If the intention of a parent is to discourage a child from stealing cookies from the cookie jar and to do this the parent cuts off the child's hands, we'd hardly call the action moral, although the intention may have been good. Ironically, in emphasizing intention here, the act utilitarian is not taking a consequential position at all but a nonconsequential one. This seems a glaring inconsistency.

But there are other objections to act utilitarianism that appear to be even more damaging. The chief one concerns the apparent immoral nature of certain actions, regardless of the consequences.

2. *Some actions are wrong, no matter how much good they produce.*

Prout: It seems to me that the speculative nature of consequences requires us to base our decision on grounds of likelihood. Would you accept the morality of our intentional deception if we could prove that in all likelihood the results would be more beneficial than not?

Fabris: I'm afraid I still wouldn't.

Prout: Why?

Fabris: Let me answer that by setting up a hypothetical situation. Suppose that a district attorney has apprehended a known felon for a particular crime. Let's suppose that this man has been guilty of countless other crimes and that he represents a direct and immediate threat to society. To put it bluntly: if he could be taken off the streets, in all likelihood everybody else would be the better for it.

Prout: I understand.

Fabris: One other point, a crucial one. In the course of his investigation, the D.A. discovers that the known felon did not commit the crime with which he's been charged. Nevertheless, the D.A. has enough circumstantial evidence to convict him, and most important, in all likelihood no one will ever find out that the D.A. has railroaded the known felon.

Prout: Your obvious question is: should the district attorney prosecute, accept a conviction, and preside over the felon's incarceration?

Fabris: Exactly.

Prout: And I hope my answer is obvious.

Fabris: It's not.

Prout: Then I'll express it: I believe it would be unjust to incarcerate the felon for something that he did not do. But before assuming that you've won your point on our ethical dilemma, I'd remind you, Diane, that you're scientist enough to realize that analogies prove nothing.

Dr. Prout is right: analogies don't *prove* anything. On the other hand, that does not mean Ms. Fabris is not right, for that would constitute an argument from ignorance. The fact is that Ms. Fabris's analogy presents a common objection to act utilitarianism.

The reason that Dr. Prout agrees that it would be wrong to imprison a man for something he did not do, even though he may have done other things at other times, is that the action appears patently unjust. In other words, there's at least something that is immoral in itself and that is imprisoning people for offenses that they did not commit. But in agreeing with Ms. Fabris, Dr. Prout is being inconsistent.

A thorough act utilitarian would weigh the probable consequences of such behavior. If in all likelihood imprisoning the known felon for something he did not do would produce the most happiness for the most number of people, then the act utilitarian would condone it. If upon evaluating the likely consequences the act utilitarian determined that imprisoning the felon would not produce the best consequences for the most people, then the act utilitarian would declare the action immoral. But under no circumstances would the act utilitarian agree that an action is in and of itself immoral. And it is on this point that objections are made. How, ask anti–act utilitarians, could anyone condone under any circumstances such seeming atrocities as genocide, the deliberate and wanton slaughter of infants, heinous muggings, rapes, plundering, and looting?

Consider further the situation of having to choose between two acts, both of which will produce the same ratio of good to evil. But the first act involves an injustice, putting a man in prison for something that he did not do. Because both acts produce an equal amount of good, it seems that the consistent act utilitarian must call both acts equally good. Yet, it is difficult to ignore that one act is unjust and that the other is not.

Or, suppose that the first act is calculated to produce a slightly greater ratio of good to evil than the second, but that the first act again involves an injustice. The consistent act utilitarian, it seems, must prefer the first act over the second. But, as before, it appears palpably wrong to ignore the injustice involved in the first act.

The point that Ms. Fabris is making, and one that anti–act utilitarians make, is that a particular act may be right or wrong regardless of its consequences. They say that the act may be wrong because it involves perpetrating an injustice, telling a lie, breaking a promise, or violating a rule. As a result, some ethicists, such as A. C. Ewing, conclude that "act utilitarian principles, logically carried out, would result in far more cheating, lying and unfair action than any good man would tolerate."[*]

Seeing the weaknesses in act utilitarianism but not willing to abandon utilitarianism altogether, many ethicists have sought a more defensible position in rule utilitarianism.

RULE UTILITARIANISM

According to rule utilitarianism we should not consider the consequences of a particular action but rather the rule under which the action falls. Ms. Fabris seems to be suggesting a rule utilitarian position.

Prout: You seem to be saying that we must consider cases other than the case of our proposed experiment in order to evaluate accurately the morality of our action.

Fabris: Yes, I think that's absolutely essential.

Prout: But it's hardly possible to consider or even imagine every conceivably similar case.

Fabris: I agree. But it is a relatively easy matter to examine what our action is condoning.

Prout: Deliberate deception?

Fabris: Yes.

Prout: But we're not condoning deliberate deception as a general rule of moral behavior. We're merely condoning it in this case, in which conditions are such that it is impossible to conduct our experiment in any other way.

---

[*]A. C. Ewing, *Ethics* (New York: Free Press, 1965), p. 41.

Fabris: Then you must be condoning it in all similar situations. You must at least be saying that under certain conditions it's all right to intentionally deceive people.

Prout: If by *certain conditions* you mean the conditions that prevail in the case of our proposed experiment, then I suppose I am.

Like Ms. Fabris, all rule utilitarians examine the consequences of the rule that a particular action seems to be implementing. Notice that they still appeal to the principle of utility, that is, the greatest good. But they appeal to it on a level of rules, not acts. Thus, for act utilitarians it might be perfectly moral to imprison a man for something that he did not do. For the rule utilitarians it would likely be immoral, because a rule that allows people to be imprisoned for something they didn't do would probably not produce a greater ratio of good to evil than its inverse: never imprison people for something they didn't do.

One strong argument for rule utilitarians was offered by English philosopher George Berkeley (1685–1753). Berkeley reasoned that if on each moral decision-making occasion a person must evaluate the consequences of a proposed action, enormous difficulties arise because of ignorance, prejudice, carelessness, lack of time, or indifference. The result would hardly be in the best interests of the general good. On the other hand, rules that everyone is aware of and attempts to implement simplify such problems, thereby advancing the common good. Just as we have traffic laws to promote the best interests of all drivers, and often small-town judges, so rules in the moral realm promote the general good.

To illustrate, rule utilitarians might argue that the rule which protects innocent people from being imprisoned is a good one. Therefore, to break it is immoral. Probably they believe that the rule is good because the consequences of breaking it are undesirable. Among those consequences they might list that people would not be convicted on evidence but on other criteria; that if this were the case then many people would lose faith in the law; that people, realizing that evidence could be manufactured against them to lead to their imprisonment, would become apprehensive, distrustful, and perhaps rebellious. Ultimately, there would be a likely chance that law and order would break down in society, thus producing general chaos, which is certainly not in everyone's best interests. Although rule utilitarianism seems to resolve some of the problems of act utilitarianism, and today is vigorously defended by philosophers such as R. B. Brandt,* it is not airtight.

OBJECTIONS TO RULE UTILITARIANISM

1. *It is extremely difficult to formulate a satisfactory rule.* One problem that arises in dealing with any rule theory is the formulation of the rule itself. For example,

---

*Richard B. Brandt, "In Search of a Credible Form of Rule-utilitarianism," in *Morality and the Language of Conduct*, ed. G. Nakhnikian and H. Castaneda (Detroit: Wayne State University Press, 1961).

is the rule "Never intentionally deceive anyone" a desirable one? One way to find out is to imagine a circumstance that will test its efficacy.

Suppose that someone was holding a pistol to your head and threatened to pull the trigger unless you told the next individual who entered the room that your name was something other than what it actually is. Should you in this circumstance deliberately deceive that person who enters the room? It certainly seems a healthy, if not moral, thing to do. So, maybe such a rule needs to be modified to read: "Never intentionally deceive someone *unless your life depends on it.*" But still, problems persist.

Suppose that you have been captured by an enemy who is trying to exact from you vital troop movement information. If you divulge the information, one hundred soldiers will most probably perish. If you don't, then you will undoubtedly die. Should you reveal the information? Here your own life may seem less worth preserving than the lives of a hundred soldiers. So, maybe the rule again should be amended to read: "Never intentionally deceive anyone *unless your own life or someone else's depends on it.*"

The point is that it is difficult to establish rules of moral behavior. True, we can qualify them, but frequently such qualifications so weaken and compromise the rule that we end up more with act utilitarianism than with rule. This might be the case with Dr. Prout and Ms. Fabris's proposed experiment. It is conceivable to formulate a rule that reads: "Never intentionally deceive anyone unless there is no other way to conduct a scientific experiment that promises great benefits for most of society." Here we seem to be tailoring a rule for a given situation. The result appears to be act utilitarianism in disguise.

There's another problem with rules. Frequently contradictory rules appear to provide equally desirable results.

2. *There is no way of deciding between contradictory rules that appear to produce equally desirable results.*

Prout: It seems to me that your argument hinges on the hypothetical question: what if everyone under similar circumstances acted as we intend to?
Fabris: Exactly.
Prout: And you conclude that the consequences would be harmful, not beneficial.
Fabris: That's right.
Prout: First of all, you can't draw such a conclusion with certainty.
Fabris: I agree. But it's as likely as the one you draw when you say that, if under similar conditions everyone acted as we intend to, then the results will be beneficial.
Prout: I don't believe that it is. But let's for the sake of argument say that they are equally probable. Then which would you choose?

Dr. Prout has a good point. Frequently contradictory rules may appear to provide equally desirable results. It seems that one can legitimately argue that the proposition "Never intentionally deceive someone unless the truth will deeply pain that person" will produce as great a ratio of good to evil as "Never intentionally deceive anyone even if telling the truth will deeply pain someone else." Which of two contradictory rules does the rule utilitarian choose?

If Diane is a thoroughgoing rule utilitarian, it seems that she cannot prefer one to the other. Since both produce equally beneficial results, one is not better than the other, even though one appears to be unjust. If she insists that we must prefer the one that does not allow the injustice, then she is being inconsistent in introducing nonconsequential factors into her evaluation. This leads to a further problem with rule utilitarianism.

3. *Rule utilitarianism ignores what appear to be blatant wrongs.*

> **Fabris:** In such a case as you describe, I'd say it was wrong to deliberately deceive.
> **Prout:** But the results are just as good as if we did deliberately deceive.
> **Fabris:** I know. But I guess I believe that deliberate deception under any circumstances is wrong.
> **Prout:** Even if the probable results of deliberately deceiving are beneficial?
> **Fabris:** I suppose so.

Diane ultimately assumes a nonconsequential position, suggesting that some things are wrong in themselves. This problem of blatantly wrong actions is perhaps the most difficult for rule utilitarians to resolve.

As an illustration, suppose doctors and scientists could guarantee that given a number of experimental patients on whom they could perform agonizingly painful and ultimately fatal operations, they could relieve the suffering of millions of other people. Would they be justified in performing these experiments on the "less desirable" and "less productive" members of society (e.g., convicted murderers, the permanently mentally ill, the terminally ill) without their consent? It seems that such experiments would produce the greatest good for the greatest number. Yet critics of utilitarianism, in this case both act and rule, argue for the intrinsic worth of the individual human and, consequently, consider any such scientific exploitation as immoral.

If Ms. Fabris maintains her belief that deliberate deception is inherently wrong, then she cannot be a utilitarian of any sort. In fact, it appears that she is a nonconsequentialist, someone who believes that criteria other than consequences must determine the morality of an action. The nonconsequentialist normative position is one that traditionally has had many adherents and one that we must devote several chapters to.

SUMMARY

<table>
<tr><td>Consequential Position</td><td>Objections</td></tr>
<tr><td>Utilitarianism: acting in such a way that your action produces the most happiness for the most number of people</td><td></td></tr>
<tr><td>a. Act: the doctrine that maintains that the right act is the one that produces the greatest balance of good over evil for all concerned</td><td>1. The consequences of actions cannot be predicted with accuracy.

2. Act utilitarianism ignores actions that appear to be wrong in themselves.</td></tr>
<tr><td>b. Rule: the doctrine that maintains that in evaluating the morality of an action we should evaluate the consequences of enacting the rule under which the act falls</td><td>1. It's difficult to formulate a rule.

2. Rule utilitarianism cannot resolve cases in which contradictory rules appear to provide equally desirable results.

3. Rule utilitarianism ignores actions that appear to be wrong in themselves.</td></tr>
</table>

CONCLUSIONS

It seems that any viable ethical system must consider the consequences of our actions, both for ourselves (egoism) and for others (utilitarianism). An ethical attitude that dismisses the consequences of actions seems too unrealistic and too rigid to serve as a useful guide in an increasingly complex society.

On the other hand, an ethical attitude that considers only the ends of actions appears to focus too much on the future at the expense of the past. The fact is that humans are creatures as much of the past as of the future. Each of us inherits a historical moral legacy as well as a biological and cultural one. To ignore this inheritance when making moral decisions severs the roots of the present and, ironically, the future. This does not mean that we should let traditional wisdom dictate how we should act ethically. It simply means that in ignoring, dismissing, or devaluing the past, consequential positions must disregard duties, obligations, and responsibilities that we have incurred from relationships that we have entered into. The result appears to be a narrow concept of what it means to be human and, ultimately, a limited view of human morality.

Nevertheless, such a view can easily creep into science. Because of science's increasing impact on our outlook, a strong contemporary tendency is to view the human as being subject to the same scientific laws as inanimate life. The result is frequently a full-blown view of the human as a computerlike mechanism, more thing than person, a means to an end but not an end in itself.

This tendency is particularly noticeable in the area of experimentation involving human subjects. In the case of the Milgram studies and of the experiment being conducted by Dr. Prout and Ms. Fabris, no injury to the human subjects was involved. But this is not always the case. The importance, funding, power, and breadth of biomedical research have so expanded in the past half century that a new social problem has arisen—the abuse of human subjects in medical experimentation. Specifically, some claim that human subjects are not always protected from undue risk and do not always have the opportunity to give willingly their informed consent to participate in experiments. *Informed consent* generally refers to the subject's acquiescence after being given a *complete* and *accurate* disclosure of the experiment, including its purpose, its procedure, its benefits, and, most important, its risks.

No one would seriously contend that experiments without informed consent are always moral. Some argue that any experiments conducted without the subject's consent are immoral. Others disagree; they claim that there are some instances—perhaps very few, but some—in which informed consent cannot or should not be part of the experiment. They might point to the Milgram studies as a case of an experiment that could not possibly be conducted within the parameters of informed consent, for it was logically impossible because of the nature of the experiment to provide subjects with complete and accurate information.

This question of informed consent is one that promises, or threatens, to become even thornier as medical and scientific experimentation advances. It's a safe bet that underlying its answer will be a judgment about the importance and relative priority of the social good.

EXERCISES FOR ANALYSIS

EXERCISE 1

In the following passages concerning the morality of experimentation without informed consent, determine whether the reasons given justify the stated or implied conclusions. As usual, watch for fallacies.

1. "Experimentation without informed consent will lead to what went on in Hitler's concentration camps. It should be resisted as an outrage to humanity."

2. "How can something be immoral if it doesn't injure anyone and has positive social consequences? The answer is that it can't. And that's why experimentation without informed consent is not always immoral."

3. "There's nothing wrong with experimenting on a prisoner without the person's informed consent, because prisoners owe society a debt, which society can exact however it chooses." (Do you think it's moral to get a prisoner to volunteer for experimentation by offering incentives, such as reduced time?)

4. "Experimentation without informed consent is clearly immoral, because, no matter what, humans should never be considered or treated as means to ends."

5. "Hardly anyone would say that the Milgram studies were immoral. That's pretty solid evidence that they weren't."

6. "I don't see anything inherently wrong with experimentation without informed consent. I certainly wouldn't mind participating, providing, of course, I didn't get hurt and the experiment would produce a lot of good."

7. "Who's to say that experimentation without informed consent will always be harmless and socially beneficial? No one. The fact is that once we approve that kind of procedure, we invite so-called authorities to 'volunteer' the services of those least capable to decide for themselves: children, the aged, the ill, prisoners."

8. "Researchers are inconsistent when they try to justify human experimentation without informed consent by arguing that the 'greater social good' is at stake. How can the greater social good be served when a basic human right is violated, the right to such knowledge that one needs in deciding questions of personal safety?"

EXERCISE 2

The following are condensed general arguments for and against the position that human experimentation without informed consent is always immoral. Evaluate the justification in each argument.

Arguments for Human Experimentation Without Informed Consent

1. Only if human experimentation without informed consent causes injury or is without great social benefit is it immoral. But there are instances when such experimentation does not cause injury and is not without great social benefit.

It's clear, therefore, that such experimentation is not always immoral. (In what sense is this argument strictly consequential? In what sense is the argument based on some principle that holds true regardless of consequences?)

2. Logic compels us to reject the idea that human experimentation without informed consent is always immoral. Why? Because by their nature some experiments must be conducted with subjects not fully informed. The Milgram studies are a good illustration. The obvious conclusion: such experimentation is not always immoral. (In what sense is the Milgram case atypical? Is this a consequential argument? In what sense? In what sense is it not? In considering the nonconsequential aspects, note the reliance on some principle of logic.)

3. Clearly every experiment on humans involves some risk to the subject. But calling the subject's attention to minimal risks unnecessarily alarms the subject and, worse, reduces the pool of potentially useful and constructive subjects. The result: a large pool of subjects is reduced, with the consequences that research is delayed and the healthful benefit of the research to those desperately in need is postponed, perhaps lost. One can only conclude that human experimentation without informed consent is not always immoral. (Is this argument primarily a consequential one? Is it primarily utilitarian? Is there enough information to determine whether it is act or rule?)

Arguments against Human Experimentation Without Informed Consent

1. A fundamental human right is the right we have to be informed when such information is available and would affect how we choose to dispose of ourselves. Because experimentation without informed consent violates this right, it is always immoral. (Is this a consequential argument? If not, why not?)

2. In the Western world we have traditionally recognized the inherent worth of the individual. Specifically, we believe that the human is not a means to an end but an end in itself. In condoning experimentation without informed consent, we do injury to this sacred concept and tradition. In effect, we proclaim that the individual is not really different from any other laboratory resource, that the human is as much a means to an end as a Bunsen burner or a test tube. Since such experimentation undermines our concept of human nature, it is immoral. (Is the third sentence a questionable claim? Could we still consider the human an end in itself and experiment without informed consent?)

3. Experimentation on humans without their informed consent makes the most defenseless members of society subject to exploitation and victimization. Minors, the senile, the gravely ill, the imprisoned, few of whom are in a position to fully understand and freely will their participation, become prey to scientific research. Thus, such experimentation is immoral. (Is this argument a utilitarian one? In what sense is it not, relying instead on some nonconsequential principle for its judgment?)

SELECTIONS FOR FURTHER READING

Utilitarianism

Bayles, M. D., ed. *Contemporary Utilitarianism*. Garden City, N.Y.: Anchor Books, 1968.

Brandt, R. B. *Ethical Theory*. Englewood Cliffs, N.J.: Prentice-Hall, 1959.

Hare, R. M. *Freedom and Reason*. London: Oxford University Press, 1963.

Hazlitt, Henry. *The Foundations of Morality*. Princeton, N.J.: Van Nostrand, 1964.

Lyons, D. *The Forms and Limits of Utilitarianism*. Oxford: Clarendon Press, 1965.

Narveson, Jan. *Morality and Utility*. Baltimore: Johns Hopkins Press, 1967.

Scientific Experimentation

Boulding, Kenneth. *The Meaning of the Twentieth Century*. New York: Harper & Row, 1964.

Burgess, Anthony. *A Clockwork Orange*. New York: Norton, 1963.

Engel, Leonard. *The New Genetics*. Garden City, N.Y.: Doubleday, 1967.

Glass, H. Bentley. *Science and Ethical Values*. Chapel Hill, N.C.: University of North Carolina Press, 1965.

Pappworth, M. H. *Human Guinea Pigs*. London: Routledge & Kegan Paul, 1966.

Rosenfeld, Albert. *The Second Genesis: The Coming Control of Life*. Englewood Cliffs, N.J.: Prentice-Hall, 1969.

Rostand, Jean. *Can Man Be Modified?* New York: Basic Books, 1959.

Skinner, B. F. *Walden Two*. New York: Macmillan, 1948.

Williams, Glanville. *The Sanctity of Life and the Criminal Law*. New York: Knopf, 1967.

SINGER/ *Animal Liberation*

Although this chapter has focused on the treatment of human subjects in scientific experimentation, a natural adjunct to this issue is the treatment of nonhuman subjects. We may have certain obligations with respect to treating human test subjects, but do we have any with respect to nonhuman animals? In "Animal Liberation," Peter Singer argues that we do.

In fact, Singer argues for the liberation movements to embrace nonhumans. No matter how much good we humans may accrue from making animals suffer, our obligation, argues Singer, is to prevent that suffering. Curiously, he uses as a basis for his argument Bentham's formula "Each to count for one and none for more than one." On the other hand, he roundly condemns the utility principle of the ends justifying the means, which has been the scientific rationale for experimenting with animals.

Throughout the essay you will hear Singer referring to a book entitled Animals, Men and Morals, *"a manifesto for an Animal Liberation movement." Singer's essay first appeared as a review of this book, which is edited by Stanley and Roslind Godlovitch and John Harris, published in London in 1972 by Taplinger. In reading the essay, consider whether Singer's position could be justified under rule utilitarianism.*

I

We are familiar with Black Liberation, Gay Liberation, and a variety of other movements. With Women's Liberation some thought we had come to the end of the road. Discrimination on the basis of sex, it has been said, is the last form of discrimination that is universally accepted and practiced without pretense, even in those liberal circles which have long prided themselves on their freedom from racial discrimination. But one should always be wary of talking of "the last remaining form of discrimination." If we have learned anything from the liberation movements, we should have learned how difficult it is to be aware of the ways in which we discriminate until they are forcefully pointed out to us. A liberation movement demands an expansion of our moral horizons, so that practices that were previously regarded as natural and inevitable are now seen as intolerable.

Animals, Men and Morals is a manifesto for an Animal Liberation movement. The contributors to the book may not all see the issue this way. They are a varied group. Philosophers, ranging from professors to graduate students, make up the largest contingent. There are five of them, including the three editors, and there is also an extract from the unjustly neglected German philosopher with

From the *New York Review of Books,* 5 April 1973. Reprinted by permission of the author. The "Postscript" was added later.

an English name, Leonard Nelson, who died in 1927. There are essays by two novelist/critics, Brigid Brophy and Maureen Duffy, and another by Muriel the Lady Dowding, widow of Dowding of Battle of Britain fame and the founder of "Beauty Without Cruelty," a movement that campaigns against the use of animals for furs and cosmetics. The other pieces are by a psychologist, a botanist, a sociologist, and Ruth Harrison, who is probably best described as a professional campaigner for animal welfare.

Whether or not these people, as individuals, would all agree that they are launching a liberation movement for animals, the book as a whole amounts to no less. It is a demand for a complete change in our attitudes to nonhumans. It is a demand that we cease to regard the exploitation of other species as natural and inevitable, and that, instead, we see it as a continuing moral outrage. Patrick Corbett, Professor of Philosophy at Sussex University, captures the spirit of the book in his closing words:

. . . We require now to extend the great principles of liberty, equality and fraternity over the lives of animals. Let animal slavery join human slavery in the graveyard of the past.

The reader is likely to be skeptical. "Animal Liberation" sounds more like a parody of liberation movements than a serious objective. The reader may think: We support the claims of blacks and women for equality because blacks and women really are equal to whites and males—equal in intelligence and in abilities, capacity for leadership, rationality, and so on. Humans and nonhumans obviously are not equal in these respects. Since justice demands only that we treat equals equally, unequal treatment of humans and nonhumans cannot be an injustice.

This is a tempting reply, but a dangerous one. It commits the non-racist and non-sexist to a dogmatic belief that blacks and women really are just as intelligent, able, etc., as whites and males—and no more. Quite possibly this happens to be the case. Certainly attempts to prove that racial or sexual differences in these respects have a genetic origin have not been conclusive. But do we really want to stake our demand for equality on the assumption that there are no genetic differences of this kind between the different races or sexes? Surely the appropriate response to those who claim to have found evidence for such genetic differences is not to stick to the belief that there are no differences, whatever the evidence to the contrary; rather one should be clear that the claim to equality does not depend on IQ. Moral equality is distinct from factual equality. Otherwise it would be nonsense to talk of the equality of human beings, since humans, as individuals, obviously differ in intelligence and almost any ability one cares to name. If possessing greater intelligence does not entitle one human to exploit another, why should it entitle humans to exploit nonhumans?

Jeremy Bentham expressed the essential basis of equality in his famous formula: "Each to count for one and none for more than one." In other words, the interests of every being that has interests are to be taken into account and treated equally with the like interests of any other being. Other moral philosophers, before and after Bentham, have made the same point in different ways. Our concern for others must not depend on whether they possess certain characteristics, though just what that concern involves may, of course, vary according to such characteristics.

Bentham, incidentally, was well aware that the logic of the demand for racial equality did not stop at the equality of humans. He wrote:

The day *may* come when the rest of the animal creation may acquire those rights which never could have been withholden from them but by the hand of tyranny. The French have already discovered that the blackness of the skin is no reason why a human being should be abandoned without redress to the caprice of a tormentor. It may one day come to be recognized that the number of the legs, the villosity of the skin, or the termination of the *os sacrum,* are reasons equally insufficient for abandoning a sensitive being to the same fate. What else is it that should trace the insuperable line? Is it the faculty of reason, or perhaps the faculty of discourse? But a full-grown horse or dog is beyond comparison a more rational, as well as a more conversable animal, than an infant of a day, or a week, or even a month, old. But suppose they were otherwise, what would it avail? The question is not, Can they *reason?* nor Can they *Talk?* but, Can they *suffer?**

Surely Bentham was right. If a being suffers, there can be no moral justification for refusing to take that suffering into consideration, and, indeed, to count it equally with the like suffer-

ing (if rough comparisons can be made) of another being.

So the only question is: Do animals other than man suffer? Most people agree unhesitatingly that animals like cats and dogs can and do suffer, and this seems also to be assumed by those laws that prohibit wanton cruelty to such animals. Personally, I have no doubt at all about this and find it hard to take seriously the doubts that a few people apparently do have. The editors and contributors of *Animals, Men and Morals* seem to feel the same way, for although the question is raised more than once, doubts are quickly dismissed each time. Nevertheless, because this is such a fundamental point, it is worth asking what grounds we have for attributing suffering to other animals.

It is best to begin by asking what grounds any individual human has for supposing that other humans feel pain. Since pain is a state of consciousness, a "mental event," it can never be directly observed. No observations, whether behavioral signs such as writhing or screaming or physiological or neurological recordings, are observations of pain itself. Pain is something one feels, and one can only infer that others are feeling it from various external indications. The fact that only philosophers are ever skeptical about whether other humans feel pain shows that we regard such inference as justifiable in the case of humans.

Is there any reason why the same inference should be unjustifiable for other animals? Nearly all the external signs which lead us to infer pain in other humans can be seen in other species, especially "higher" animals

The Principles of Morals and Legislation, ch. XVII, sec. 1, footnote to paragraph 4. (Italics in original.)

such as mammals and birds. Behavioral signs—writhing, yelping, or other forms of calling, attempts to avoid the source of pain, and many others—are present. We know, too, that these animals are biologically similar in the relevant respects, having nervous systems like ours which can be observed to function as ours do.

So the grounds for inferring that these animals can feel pain are nearly as good as the grounds for inferring other humans do. Only nearly, for there is one behavioral sign that humans have but nonhumans, with the exception of one or two specially raised chimpanzees, do not have. This, of course, is a developed language. As the quotation from Bentham indicates, this has long been regarded as an important distinction between man and other animals. Other animals may communicate with each other, but not in the way we do. Following Chomsky, many people now mark this distinction by saying that only humans communicate in a form that is governed by rules of syntax. (For the purposes of this argument, linguists allow those chimpanzees who have learned a syntactic sign language to rank as honorary humans.) Nevertheless, as Bentham pointed out, this distinction is not relevant to the question of how animals ought to be treated, unless it can be linked to the issue of whether animals suffer.

This link may be attempted in two ways. First, there is a hazy line of philosophical thought, stemming perhaps from some doctrines associated with Wittgenstein, which maintains that we cannot meaningfully attribute states of consciousness to beings without language. I have not seen this argument made explicit in print, though I have come across it in conversation. This position seems to me very implausible, and I doubt that it would be held at all if it were not thought to be a consequence of a broader view of the significance of language. It may be that the use of a public, rule-governed language is a precondition of conceptual thought. It may even be, although personally I doubt it, that we cannot meaningfully speak of a creature having an intention unless that creature can use a language. But states like pain, surely, are more primitive than either of these, and seem to have nothing to do with language.

Indeed, as Jane Goodall points out in her study of chimpanzees, when it comes to the expression of feelings and emotions, humans tend to fall back on non-linguistic modes of communication which are often found among apes, such as a cheering pat on the back, an exuberant embrace, a clasp of hands, and so on.* Michael Peters makes a similar point in his contribution to *Animals, Men and Morals* when he notes that the basic signals we use to convey pain, fear, sexual arousal, and so on are not specific to our species. So there seems to be no reason at all to believe that a creature without language cannot suffer.

The second, and more easily appreciated way of linking language and the existence of pain is to say that the best evidence that we can have that another creature is in pain is when he tells us that he is. This is a distinct line of argument, for it is not being denied

---

*Jane van Lawick-Goodall, *In the Shadow of Man* (Houghton Mifflin, 1971), p. 225.

that a non-language-user conceivably could suffer, but only that we could know that he is suffering. Still, this line of argument seems to me to fail, and for reasons similar to those just given. "I am in pain" is not the best possible evidence that the speaker is in pain (he might be lying) and it is certainly not the only possible evidence. Behavioral signs and knowledge of the animal's biological similarity to ourselves together provide adequate evidence that animals do suffer. After all, we would not accept linguistic evidence if it contradicted the rest of the evidence. If a man was severely burned, and behaved as if he were in pain, writhing, groaning, being very careful not to let his burned skin touch anything, and so on, but later said he had not been in pain at all, we would be more likely to conclude that he was lying or suffering from amnesia than that he had not been in pain.

Even if there were stronger grounds for refusing to attribute pain to those who do not have a language, the consequences of this refusal might lead us to examine these grounds unusually critically. Human infants, as well as some adults, are unable to use language. Are we to deny that a year-old infant can suffer? If not, how can language be crucial? Of course, most parents can understand the responses of even very young infants better than they understand the responses of other animals, and sometimes infant responses can be understood in the light of later development.

This, however, is just a fact about the relative knowledge we have of our own species and other species, and most of this knowledge is simply derived from closer contact. Those who have studied the behavior of other animals soon learn to understand their responses at least as well as we understand those of an infant. (I am not just referring to Jane Goodall's and other well-known studies of apes. Consider, for example, the degree of understanding achieved by Tinbergen from watching herring gulls.)* Just as we can understand infant human behavior in the light of adult human behavior, so we can understand the behavior of other species in the light of our own behavior (and sometimes we can understand our own behavior better in the light of the behavior of other species).

The grounds we have for believing that other mammals and birds suffer are, then, closely analogous to the grounds we have for believing that other humans suffer. It remains to consider how far down the evolutionary scale this analogy holds. Obviously it becomes poorer when we get further away from man. To be more precise would require a detailed examination of all that we know about other forms of life. With fish, reptiles, and other vertebrates the analogy still seems strong, with molluscs like oysters it is much weaker. Insects are more difficult, and it may be that in our present state of knowledge we must be agnostic about whether they are capable of suffering.

If there is no moral justification for ignoring suffering when it occurs, and it does occur in other species, what are we to say of our attitudes toward these other species? Richard Ryder, one of the contributors to

---

*N. Tinbergen, The Herring Gull's World (Basic Books, 1961).

Animals, Men and Morals, uses the term "speciesism" to describe the belief that we are entitled to treat members of other species in a way in which it would be wrong to treat members of our own species. The term is not euphonious, but it neatly makes the analogy with racism. The non-racist would do well to bear the analogy in mind when he is inclined to defend human behavior toward nonhumans. "Shouldn't we worry about improving the lot of our own species before we concern ourselves with other species?" he may ask. If we substitute "race" for "species" we shall see that the question is better not asked. "Is a vegetarian diet nutritionally adequate?" resembles the slaveowner's claim that he and the whole economy of the South would be ruined without slave labor. There is even a parallel with skeptical doubts about whether animals suffer, for some defenders of slavery professed to doubt whether blacks really suffer in the way that whites do.

I do not want to give the impression, however, that the case for Animal Liberation is based on the analogy with racism and no more. On the contrary, *Animals, Men and Morals* describes the various ways in which humans exploit nonhumans, and several contributors consider the defenses that have been offered, including the defense of meat-eating mentioned in the last paragraph. Sometimes the rebuttals are scornfully dismissive, rather than carefully designed to convince the detached critic. This may be a fault, but it is a fault that is inevitable, given the kind of book this is. The issue is not one on which one can remain detached. As the editors state in their Introduction:

Once the full force of moral assessment has been made explicit there can be no rational excuse left for killing animals, be they killed for food, science, or sheer personal indulgence. We have not assembled this book to provide the reader with yet another manual on how to make brutalities less brutal. Compromise, in the traditional sense of the term, is simple unthinking weakness when one considers the actual reasons for our crude relationships with the other animals.

The point is that on this issue there are few critics who are genuinely detached. People who eat pieces of slaughtered nonhumans every day find it hard to believe that they are doing wrong; and they also find it hard to imagine what else they could eat. So for those who do not place nonhumans beyond the pale of morality, there comes a stage when further argument seems pointless, a stage at which one can only accuse one's opponent of hypocrisy and reach for the sort of sociological account of our practices and the way we defend them that is attempted by David Wood in his contribution to this book. On the other hand, to those unconvinced by the arguments, and unable to accept that they are merely rationalizing their dietary preferences and their fear of being thought peculiar, such sociological explanations can only seem insultingly arrogant.

II

The logic of speciesism is most apparent in the practice of experimenting on nonhumans in order to benefit humans. This is because the issue is rarely obscured by allegations that nonhumans are so different from humans that we cannot know anything about whether they suffer. The defender of vivisection cannot use this argument because he needs to stress the similarities between man and other animals in order to justify the usefulness to the former of experiments on the latter. The researcher who makes rats choose between starvation and electric shocks to see if they develop ulcers (they do) does so because he knows that the rat has a nervous system very similar to man's, and presumably feels an electric shock in a similar way.

Richard Ryder's restrained account of experiments on animals made me angrier with my fellow men than anything else in this book. Ryder, a clinical psychologist by profession, himself experimented on animals before he came to hold the view he puts forward in his essay. Experimenting on animals is now a large industry, both academic and commercial. In 1969, more than 5 million experiments were performed in Britain, the vast majority without anesthetic (though how many of these involved pain is not known). There are no accurate U.S. figures, since there is no federal law on the subject, and in many cases no state law either. Estimates vary from 20 million to 200 million. Ryder suggests that 80 million may be the best guess. We tend to think that this is all for vital medical research, but of course it is not. Huge numbers of animals are used in university departments from Forestry to Psychology, and even more are used for commercial purposes, to test whether cosmetics can cause skin damage, or shampoos eye damage, or to test food additives or laxatives or sleeping pills or anything else.

A standard test for foodstuffs is the "LD50." The object of this test is to find the dosage level at which 50 percent of the test animals will die. This means that nearly all of them will become very sick before finally succumbing or surviving. When the substance is a harmless one, it may be necessary to force huge doses down the animals, until in some cases sheer volume or concentration causes death.

Ryder gives a selection of experiments, taken from recent scientific journals. I will quote two, not for the sake of indulging in gory details, but in order to give an idea of what normal researchers think they may legitimately do to other species. The point is not that the individual researchers are cruel men, but that they are behaving in a way that is allowed by our speciesist attitudes. As Ryder points out, even if only 1 percent of the experiments involve severe pain, that is 50,000 experiments in Britain each year, or nearly 150 every day (and about fifteen times as many in the United States, if Ryder's guess is right). Here then are two experiments:

O. S. Ray and R. J. Barrett of Pittsburg gave electric shocks to the feet of 1,042 mice. Then they caused convulsions by giving more intense shocks through cup-shaped electrodes applied to the animals' eyes or through pressure spring clips attached to their ears. Unfortunately some of the mice who "successfully completed Day One training were found sick or dead prior to testing on Day Two." [*Journal of Comparative and Physiological Psychology*, 1969, vol. 67, pp. 110–116]

At the National Institute for Medical Research, Mill Hill, London, W. Feldberg and S. L. Sherwood injected chemicals into the brains of cats—"with a number of widely different substances, recurrent patterns of reaction were obtained. Retching, vomiting, defaecation, increased salivation and greatly accelerated respiration leading to panting were common features." . . .

The injection into the brain of a large dose of Tubocuraine caused the cat to jump "from the table to the floor and then straight into its cage, where it started calling more and more noisily whilst moving about restlessly and jerkily . . . finally the cat fell with legs and neck flexed, jerking in rapid clonic movements, the condition being that of a major [epileptic] convulsion . . . within a few seconds the cat got up, ran for a few yards at high speed and fell in another fit. The whole process was repeated several times within the next ten minutes, during which the cat lost faeces and foamed at the mouth."

This animal finally died thirty-five minutes after the brain injection. [*Journal of Physiology*, 1954, vol. 123, pp. 148–167]

There is nothing secret about these experiments. One has only to open any recent volume of a learned journal, such as the *Journal of Comparative and Physiological Psychology*, to find full descriptions of experiments of this sort, together with the results obtained—results that are frequently trivial and obvious. The experiments are often supported by public funds.

It is a significant indication of the level of acceptability of these practices that, although these experiments are taking place at this moment on university campuses throughout the country, there has, so far as I know, not been the slightest protest from the student movement. Students have been rightly concerned that their uni-

versities should not discriminate on grounds of race or sex, and that they should not serve the purposes of the military or big business. Speciesism continues undisturbed, and many students participate in it. There may be a few qualms at first, but since everyone regards it as normal, and it may even be a required part of a course, the student soon becomes hardened and, dismissing his earlier feelings as "mere sentiment," comes to regard animals as statistics rather than sentient beings with interests that warrant consideration.

Argument about vivisection has often missed the point because it has been put in absolutist terms: Would the abolitionist be prepared to let thousands die if they could be saved by experimenting on a single animal? The way to reply to this purely hypothetical question is to pose another: Would the experimenter be prepared to experiment on a human orphan under six months old, if it were the only way to save many lives? (I say "orphan" to avoid the complication of parental feelings, although in doing so I am being overfair to the experimenter, since the nonhuman subjects of experiments are not orphans.) A negative answer to this question indicates that the experimenter's readiness to use nonhumans is simple discrimination, for adult apes, cats, mice, and other mammals are more conscious of what is happening to them, more self-directing, and, so far as we can tell, just as sensitive to pain as a human infant. There is no characteristic that human infants possess that the adult mammals do not have to the same or a higher degree.

(It might be possible to hold that what makes it wrong to experiment on a human infant is that the infant will in time develop into more than the nonhuman, but one would then, to be consistent, have to oppose abortion, and perhaps contraception, too, for the fetus and the egg and sperm have the same potential as the infant. Moreover, one would still have no reason for experimenting on a nonhuman rather than a human with brain damage severe enough to make it impossible for him to rise above infant level.)

The experimenter, then, shows a bias for his own species whenever he carries out an experiment on a nonhuman for a purpose that he would not think justified him in using a human being at an equal or lower level of sentience, awareness, ability to be self-directing, etc. No one familiar with the kind of results yielded by these experiments can have the slightest doubt that if this bias were eliminated the number of experiments performed would be zero or very close to it.

III

If it is vivisection that shows the logic of speciesism most clearly, it is the use of other species for food that is at the heart of our attitudes toward them. Most of *Animals, Men and Morals* is an attack on meat-eating—an attack which is based solely on concern for nonhumans, without reference to arguments derived from considerations of ecology, macrobiotics, health, or religion.

The idea that nonhumans are utilities, means to our ends, pervades our thought. Even conservationists who are concerned about the slaughter of wild fowl but not about the vastly greater slaughter of chickens for our tables are thinking in this way—they are worried about what we would lose if there were less wildlife. Stanley Godlovitch, pursuing the Marxist idea that our thinking is formed by the activities we undertake in satisfying our needs, suggests that man's first classification of his environment was into Edibles and Inedibles. Most animals came into the first category, and there they have remained.

Man may always have killed other species for food, but he has never exploited them so ruthlessly as he does today. Farming has succumbed to business methods, the objective being to get the highest possible ratio of output (meat, eggs, milk) to input (fodder, labor costs, etc.). Ruth Harrison's essay "On Factory Farming" gives an account of some aspects of modern methods, and of the unsuccessful British campaign for effective controls, a campaign which was sparked off by her *Animal Machines* (Stuart: London, 1964).

Her article is in no way a substitute for her earlier book. This is a pity since, as she says, "Farm produce is still associated with mental pictures of animals browsing in the fields, . . . of hens having a last forage before going to roost. . . ." Yet neither in her article nor elsewhere in *Animals, Men and Morals* is this false image replaced by a clear idea of the nature and extent of factory farming. We learn of this only indirectly, when we hear of the code of reform proposed by an advisory committee set up by the British government.

Among the proposals, which the government refused to implement on the grounds that they were too idealistic, were: *"Any animal should at least have room to turn around freely."*

Factory farm animals need liberation in the most literal sense. Veal calves are kept in stalls five feet by two feet. They are usually slaughtered when about four months old, and have been too big to turn in their stalls for at least a month. Intensive beef herds, kept in stalls only proportionately larger for much longer periods, account for a growing percentage of beef production. Sows are often similarly confined when pregnant, which, because of artificial methods of increasing fertility, can be most of the time. Animals confined in this way do not waste food by exercising, nor do they develop unpalatable muscle.

"A dry bedded area should be provided for all stock." Intensively kept animals usually have to stand and sleep on slatted floors without straw, because this makes cleaning easier.

"Palatable roughage must be readily available to all calves after one week of age." In order to produce the pale veal housewives are said to prefer, calves are fed on an all-liquid diet until slaughter, even though they are long past the age at which they would normally eat grass. They develop a craving for roughage, evidenced by attempts to gnaw wood from their stalls. (For the same reason, their diet is deficient in iron.)

"Battery cages for poultry should be large enough for a bird to be able to stretch one wing at a time." Under current British practice, a cage for four or five laying hens has a floor area of twenty inches by eighteen inches, scarcely larger than a double page of the *New*

York Review of Books. In this space, on a sloping wire floor (sloping so the eggs roll down, wire so the dung drops through) the birds live for a year or eighteen months while artificial lighting and temperature conditions combine with drugs in their food to squeeze the maximum number of eggs out of them. Table birds are also sometimes kept in cages. More often they are reared in sheds, no less crowded. Under these conditions all the birds' natural activities are frustrated, and they develop "vices" such as pecking each other to death. To prevent this, beaks are often cut off, and the sheds kept dark.

How many of those who support factory farming by buying its produce know anything about the way it is produced? How many have heard something about it, but are reluctant to check up for fear that it will make them uncomfortable? To non-speciesists, the typical consumer's mixture of ignorance, reluctance to find out the truth, and vague belief that nothing really bad could be allowed seems analogous to the attitudes of "decent Germans" to the death camps.

There are, of course, some defenders of factory farming. Their arguments are considered, though again rather sketchily, by John Harris. Among the most common: "Since they have never known anything else, they don't suffer." This argument will not be put by anyone who knows anything about animal behavior, since he will know that not all behavior has to be learned. Chickens attempt to stretch wings, walk around, scratch, and even dustbathe or build a nest, even though they have never lived under conditions that allowed these activities. Calves can suffer from maternal deprivation no matter at what age they were taken from their mothers. "We need these intensive methods to provide protein for a growing population." As ecologists and famine relief organizations know, we can produce far more protein per acre if we grow the right vegetable crop, soy beans for instance, than if we use the land to grow crops to be converted into protein by animals who use nearly 90 percent of the protein themselves, even when unable to exercise.

There will be many readers of this book who will agree that factory farming involves an unjustifiable degree of exploitation of sentient creatures, and yet will want to say that there is nothing wrong with rearing animals for food, provided it is done "humanely." These people are saying, in effect, that although we should not cause animals to suffer, there is nothing wrong with killing them.

There are two possible replies to this view. One is to attempt to show that this combination of attitudes is absurd. Roslind Godlovitch takes this course in her essay, which is an examination of some common attitudes to animals. She argues that from the combination of "animal suffering is to be avoided" and "there is nothing wrong with killing animals" it follows that all animal life ought to be exterminated (since all sentient creatures will suffer to some degree at some point in their lives). Euthanasia is a contentious issue only because we place some value on living. If we did not, the least amount of suffering would justify it. Accordingly, if we deny that we have a duty to exterminate all animal life, we must concede that we are placing some value on animal life.

This argument seems to me valid, although one could still reply that the value of animal life is to be derived from the pleasures that life can have for them, so that, provided their lives have a balance of pleasure over pain, we are justified in rearing them. But this would imply that we ought to produce animals and let them live as pleasantly as possible, without suffering.

At this point, one can make the second of the two possible replies to the view that rearing and killing animals for food is all right so long as it is done humanely. This second reply is that so long as we think that a nonhuman may be killed simply so that a human can satisfy his taste for meat, we are still thinking of nonhumans as means rather than as ends in themselves. The factory farm is nothing more than the application of technology to this concept. Even traditional methods involve castration, the separation of mothers and their young, the breaking up of herds, branding or ear-punching, and of course transportation to the abattoirs and the final moments of terror when the animal smells blood and senses danger. If we were to try rearing animals so that they lived and died without suffering, we should find that to do so on anything like the scale of today's meat industry would be a sheer impossibility. Meat would become the prerogative of the rich.

I have been able to discuss only some of the contributions to this book, saying nothing about, for instance, the essays on killing for furs and for sport. Nor have I considered all the detailed questions that need to be asked once we start thinking about other species in the radically different way presented by this book. What, for instance, are we to do about genuine conflicts of interest like rats biting slum children? I am not sure of the answer, but the essential point is just that we *do* see this as a conflict of interests, that we recognize that rats have interests too. Then we may begin to think about other ways of resolving the conflict—perhaps by leaving out rat baits that sterilize the rats instead of killing them.

I have not discussed such problems because they are side issues compared with the exploitation of other species for food and for experimental purposes. On these central matters, I hope that I have said enough to show that this book, despite its flaws, is a challenge to every human to recognize his attitudes to nonhumans as a form of prejudice no less objectionable than racism or sexism. It is a challenge that demands not just a change of attitudes, but a change in our way of life, for it requires us to become vegetarians.

Can a purely moral demand of this kind succeed? The odds are certainly against it. The book holds out no inducements. It does not tell us that we will become healthier, or enjoy life more, if we cease exploiting animals. Animal Liberation will require greater altruism on the part of mankind than any other liberation movement, since animals are incapable of demanding it for themselves, or of protesting against their exploitation by votes, demonstrations, or bombs. Is man capable of such genuine altruism? Who knows? If this book does have a significant effect, however, it will be a vindication of all those who have believed that man has within himself the potential for more than cruelty and selfishness.

POSTSCRIPT

Since this review is now appearing alongside philosophical discussions of rights and equality, it is worth noting that we can find indications of speciesism even amongst philosophers.

Richard Wasserstrom's "Rights, Human Rights, and Racial Discrimination" serves as an example. Wasserstrom defines "human rights" as those that humans have, and nonhumans do not have. He then argues that there are human rights, in this sense, to well-being and freedom. In defending the idea of a human right to well-being, Wasserstrom says that although we have no means of assessing the comparative worth of different people's enjoyment of, for instance, relief from acute physical pain, we know that denial of the opportunity to experience a good such as this makes it impossible to live a full or satisfying life. Wasserstrom then goes on to say: "In a real sense, the enjoyment of these goods differentiates human from nonhuman entities." But this statement is incredible—for when we look back to find what the expression "these goods" is supposed to refer to, we find that the *only* example we have been given is relief from acute physical pain—and this, surely, is something that nonhumans may appreciate as well as humans.

Later, too, Wasserstrom points out that the grounds for discrimination between blacks and whites that racists sometimes offer are not relevant to the question of capacity for bearing acute pain, and therefore should be disregarded. So again Wasserstrom is taking capacity for perceiving acute pain as crucial. I would want to say that if Wasserstrom's argument is valid against discrimination on the basis of race—and I think it is—then an exactly parallel argument applies against the grounds usually offered for discrimination on the basis of species, since these grounds are also not relevant to the question of ability to bear acute pain. When Ray and Barrett, in the experiment I described in the review, gave electric shocks to over a thousand mice, they must have assumed that the mice *do* feel acute physical pain, since the aim of the experiment was to find out where the mice were most sensitive; and nothing else, surely, is relevant to the question of whether it is legitimate to use mice for this purpose.

I should make it quite clear, of course, that I do not believe Richard Wasserstrom is deliberately endorsing a speciesist position, or in any way condoning the infliction of acute physical pain on nonhumans. I draw attention to the point only in order to show how easy it is, even for a philosopher, to accept unthinkingly a prevailing ideology that places other animals outside the sphere of equal consideration. I would guess that most of Wasserstrom's readers, with similar predispositions, will not have noticed on a first reading that the only basis he offers for "human rights" applies to nonhumans too.

HUXLEY/Brave New World

The theme of Aldous Huxley's futuristic novel Brave New World *is how the advancement of science affects human individuals. Specifically, the novel concerns a group of people who govern the Brave New World for the purpose of achieving social stability. To do this they carry out by scientific means a revolution of human control and conditioning. As Huxley himself pointed out,* Brave New World *stands as a warning that unless we choose to use applied science not as the end to which humans are made means but as the means for producing a race of free individuals, then we invite one or a series of totalitarian regimes to satisfy society's need for efficiency and stability.*

The selection that follows shows such a regime in operation. In this chapter we are introduced to the conditioning of eight-month-old babies. In reading the selection, be alert to the seemingly utilitarian justification for the conditioning. You should not conclude that John Stuart Mill would defend such a procedure. On the contrary, in his famous essay entitled "On Liberty," he argues ardently in favor of individual choice. Yet, at the same time, the principle of utility would seem to provide an ethical basis for a Brave New World.

Mr. Foster was left in the Decanting Room. The D.H.C. and his students stepped into the nearest lift and were carried up to the fifth floor.

INFANT NURSERIES. NEO-PAVLOVIAN CONDITIONING ROOMS, announced the notice board.

The Director opened a door. They were in a large bare room, very bright and sunny; for the whole of the southern wall was a single window. Half a dozen nurses, trousered and jacketed in the regulation white viscose-linen uniform, their hair aseptically hidden under white caps, were engaged in setting out bowls of roses in a long row across the floor. Big bowls, packed tight with blossom. Thousands of petals, ripe-blown and silkily smooth, like the cheeks of innumerable little cherubs, but of cherubs, in that bright light, not exclusively pink and Aryan, but also luminously Chinese, also Mexican, also apoplectic with too much blowing of celestial trumpets, also pale as death, pale with the posthumous whiteness of marble.

The nurses stiffened to attention as the D.H.C. came in.

"Set out the books," he said curtly.

In silence the nurses obeyed his command. Between the rose bowls the books were duly set out—a row of nursery quartos opened invitingly each at some gaily coloured image of beast or fish or bird.

"Now bring in the children."

They hurried out of the room and returned in a minute or two, each pushing a kind of tall dumbwaiter laden, on all its four wire-netted shelves, with eight-month-old babies, all exactly alike (a Bokanovsky Group, it was evident) and all (since their caste was Delta) dressed in khaki.

"Put them down on the floor."

The infants were unloaded.

"Now turn them so that they can see the flowers and books."

Turned, the babies at once fell silent, then began to crawl towards those clusters of sleek colours, those shapes so gay and brilliant on the white pages. As they approached, the sun came out of a momentary eclipse behind a cloud. The roses flamed up as though with a sudden passion from within; a new and profound significance seemed to suffuse the shining pages of the books. From the ranks of the crawling babies came little squeals of excitement, gurgles and twitterings of pleasure.

The Director rubbed his hands. "Excellent!" he said. "It might almost have been done on purpose."

The swiftest crawlers were already at their goal. Small hands reached out uncertainly, touched, grasped, unpetaling the transfigured roses, crumpling the illuminated pages of the books. The Director waited until all were happily busy. Then, "Watch carefully," he said. And, lifting his hand, he gave the signal.

The Head Nurse, who was standing by a switchboard at the other end of the room, pressed down a little lever.

There was a violent explosion. Shriller and ever shriller, a siren shrieked. Alarm bells maddeningly sounded.

The children started, screamed; their faces were distorted with terror.

"And now," the Director shouted (for the noise was deafening), "now we proceed to rub in the lesson with a mild electric shock."

He waved his hand again, and the Head Nurse pressed a second lever. The screaming of the babies suddenly changed its tone. There was something desperate, almost insane, about the sharp spasmodic yelps to which they now gave utterance. Their little bodies twitched and stiffened; their limbs moved jerkily as if to the tug of unseen wires.

"We can electrify that whole strip of floor," bawled the Director in explanation. "But that's enough," he signalled to the nurse.

The explosions ceased, the bells stopped ringing, the shriek of the siren died down from tone to tone into silence. The stiffly twitching bodies relaxed, and what had become the sob and yelp of infant maniacs broadened out once more into a normal howl of ordinary terror.

"Offer them the flowers and the books again."

The nurses obeyed; but at the approach of the roses, at the mere sight of those gaily-coloured images of pussy and cock-a-doodle-doo and baa-baa black sheep, the infants shrank away in horror; the volume of their howling suddenly increased.

"Observe," said the Director triumphantly, "observe."

Books and loud noises, flowers and electric shocks—already in the infant mind these couples were compromisingly linked; and after two hundred repetitions of the same or a similar lesson would be wedded indissolubly. What man has joined, nature is powerless to put asunder.

"They'll grow up with what the psychologists used to call an 'instinctive' hatred of books and flowers. Reflexes unalterably conditioned. They'll be safe from books and botany all their lives." The Director turned to his nurses. "Take them away again."

Still yelling, the khaki babies were loaded on to their dumb-waiters and wheeled out, leaving behind them the smell of sour milk and a most welcome silence.

One of the students held up his hand; and though he could see quite well why you couldn't have lower-caste people wasting the Community's time over books, and that there was always the risk of their reading something which might undesirably decondition one of their reflexes, yet . . . well, he couldn't understand about the flowers. Why go to the trouble of making it psychologically impossible for Deltas to like flowers?

Patiently the D.H.C. explained. If the children were made to scream at the sight of a rose, that was on grounds of high economic policy. Not so very long ago (a century or thereabouts), Gammas, Deltas, even Epsilons, had been conditioned to like flowers—flowers in particular and wild nature in general. The idea was to make them want to be going out into the country at every available opportunity, and so compel them to consume transport.

"And didn't they consume transport?" asked the student.

"Quite a lot," the D.H.C. replied. "But nothing else."

Primroses and landscapes, he pointed out, have one grave defect: they are gratuitous. A love of nature keeps no factories busy. It was decided to abolish the love of nature, at any rate among the lower classes; to abolish the love of nature, but *not* the tendency to consume transport. For of course it was essential that they should keep on going to the country, even though they hated it. The problem was to find an economically sounder reason for consuming transport than a mere affection for primroses and landscapes. It was duly found.

"We condition the masses to hate the country," concluded the Director. "But simultaneously we condition them to love all country sports. At the same time, we see to it that all country sports shall entail the use of elaborate apparatus. So that they consume manufactured articles as well as transport. Hence those electric shocks."

"I see," said the student, and was silent, lost in admiration.

There was a silence; then, clearing his throat, "Once upon a time," the Director began, "while our Ford was still on earth, there was a little boy called Reuben Rabinovitch. Reuben was the child of Polish-speaking parents." The Director interrupted himself. "You know what Polish is, I suppose?"

"A dead language."

"Like French and German," added another student, officiously showing off his learning.

"And 'parent'?" questioned the D.H.C.

There was an uneasy silence. Several of the boys blushed. They had not yet learned to draw the significant but often very fine distinction between smut and pure science. One, at last, had the courage to raise a hand.

"Human beings used to be . . ." he hesitated; the blood rushed to his cheeks. "Well, they used to be viviparous."

"Quite right." The Director nodded approvingly.

"And when the babies were decanted . . ."

"'Born'," came the correction.

"Well, then they were the parents—I mean, not the babies, of course; the other ones." The poor boy was overwhelmed with confusion.

"In brief," the Director summed up, "the parents were the father and the mother." The smut that was really science fell with a crash into the boys' eye-avoiding silence. "Mother," he repeated loudly rubbing in the science; and, leaning back in his chair, "These," he said gravely, "are unpleasant facts; I know it. But then most historical facts *are* unpleasant."

He returned to Little Reuben—to Little Reuben, in whose room, one evening, by an oversight, his father and mother (crash, crash!) happened to leave the radio turned on.

("For you must remember that in those days of gross viviparous reproduction, children were always brought up by their parents and not in State Conditioning Centres.")

While the child was asleep, a broadcast programme from London suddenly started to come through; and the next morning, to the astonishment of his crash and crash (the more daring of the boys ventured to grin at one another), Little Reuben woke up repeating word for word a long lecture by that curious old writer ("one of the very few whose works have been permitted to come down to us"), George Bernard Shaw, who was speaking, according to a well-authenticated tradition, about his own genius. To Little Reuben's wink and snigger, this lecture was, of course, perfectly incomprehensible and, imagining that their child had suddenly gone mad, they sent for a doctor. He, fortunately, understood English, recognized the discourse as that which Shaw had broadcasted the previous evening, realized the significance of what had happened, and sent a letter to the medical press about it.

"The principle of sleep-teaching, or hypnopaedia, had been discovered." The D.H.C. made an impressive pause.

The principle had been discovered; but many, many years were to elapse before that principle was usefully applied.

"The case of Little Reuben occurred only twenty-three years after Our Ford's first T-Model was put on the market." (Here the Director made a sign of the T on his stomach and all the students reverently followed suit.) "And yet . . ."

Furiously the students scribbled. *Hypnopaedia, first used officially in A.F. 214. Why not before? Two reasons. (a) . . .*

"These early experimenters," the D.H.C. was saying, "were on the wrong track. They thought that hypnopaedia could be made an instrument of intellectual education . . ."

(A small boy asleep on his right side, the right arm stuck out, the right hand hanging limp over the edge of the bed. Through a round grating in the side of a box a voice speaks softly.

"The Nile is the longest river in Africa and the second in length of all the rivers of the globe. Although falling short of the length of the Mississippi-Missouri, the Nile is at the head of all rivers as regards the length of its basin, which extends through 35 degrees of latitude . . ."

At breakfast the next morning, "Tommy," some one says, "do you know which is the longest river in Africa?" A shaking of the head. "But don't you remember something that begins: The Nile is the . . ."

"The-Nile-is-the-longest-river-in-Africa-and-the-second-in-length-of-all-the-rivers-of-the-globe . . ." The words come rushing out. "Although-falling-short-of . . ."

"Well now, which is the longest river in Africa?"

The eyes are blank. "I don't know."

"But the Nile, Tommy."

"The-Nile-is-the-longest-river-in-Africa-and-second . . ."

"Then which river is the longest, Tommy?"

Tommy bursts into tears. "I don't know," he howls.)

That howl, the Director made it plain, discouraged the earliest investigators. The experiments were abandoned. No further attempt was made to teach children the length of the Nile in their sleep. Quite rightly. You can't learn a science unless you know what it's all about.

"Whereas, if they'd only started on *moral* education," said the Director, leading the way towards the door. The students followed him, desperately scribbling as they walked and all the way up in the lift. "Moral education, which ought never, in any circumstances, to be rational."

"Silence, silence," whispered a loud speaker as they stepped out at the fourteenth floor, and "Silence, silence," the trumpet mouths indefatigably repeated at intervals down every corridor. The students and even the Director himself rose automatically to the tips of their toes. They were Alphas, of course; but even Alphas have been well conditioned. "Silence, silence." All the air of the fourteenth floor was sibilant with the categorical imperative.

Fifty yards of tiptoeing brought them to a door which the Director cautiously opened. They stepped over the threshold into the twilight of a shuttered dormitory. Eighty cots stood in a row against the wall. There was a sound of light regular breathing and a continuous murmur, as of very faint voices remotely whispering.

A nurse rose as they entered and came to attention before the Director.

"What's the lesson this afternoon?" he asked.

"We had Elementary Sex for the first forty minutes," she answered. "But now it's switched over to Elementary Class Consciousness."

The Director walked slowly down the long line of cots. Rosy and relaxed with sleep, eighty little boys and girls lay softly breathing. There was a whisper under every pillow. The D.H.C. halted and, bending over one of the little beds, listened attentively.

"Elementary Class Consciousness, did you say? Let's have it repeated a little louder by the trumpet."

At the end of the room a loud speaker projected from the wall. The Director walked up to it and pressed a switch.

". . . all wear green," said a soft but very distinct voice, beginning in the middle of a sentence, "and Delta Children wear khaki. Oh no, I don't want to play with Delta children. And Epsilons are still worse. They're too stupid to be able to read or write. Besides they wear black, which is such a beastly colour. I'm *so* glad I'm a Beta."

There was a pause; then the voice began again.

"Alpha children wear grey. They work much harder than we do, because they're so frightfully clever. I'm really awfully glad I'm a Beta, because I don't work so hard. And then we are much better than the Gammas and Deltas. Gammas are stupid. They all wear green, and Delta children wear khaki. Oh no, I *don't* want to play with Delta children. And Epsilons are still worse. They're too stupid to be able . . ."

The Director pushed back the switch. The voice was silent. Only its thin ghost continued to mutter from beneath the eighty pillows.

"They'll have that repeated forty or fifty times more before they wake; then again on Thursday, and again on Saturday. A hundred and twenty times three times a week for thirty months. After which they go on to a more advanced lesson."

Roses and electric shocks, the khaki of Deltas and a whiff of asafoetida—wedded indissolubly before the child can speak. But wordless conditioning is crude and wholesale; cannot bring home the finer distinctions, cannot inculcate the more complex courses of behaviour. For that there must be words, but words without reason. In brief, hypnopaedia.

"The greatest moralizing and socializing force of all time."

The students took it down in their little books. Straight from the horse's mouth.

Once more the Director touched the switch.

". . . so frightfully clever," the soft, insinuating, indefatigable voice was saying. "I'm really awfully glad I'm a Beta, because . . ."

Not so much like drops of water, though water, it is true, can wear holes in the hardest granite; rather, drops of liquid sealing-wax, drops that adhere, incrust, incorporate themselves with what they fall on, till finally the rock is all one scarlet blob.

"Till at last the child's mind *is* these suggestions, and the sum of the suggesions *is* the child's mind. And not the child's mind only. The adult's mind too—all his life long. The mind that judges and desires and decides—made up of these suggestions. But all these suggestions are *our* suggestions!" The Director almost shouted in his triumph. "Suggestions from the State." He banged the nearest table. "It therefore follows . . ."

A noise made him turn around.

"Oh, Ford!" he said in another tone, "I've gone and woken the children."

6

ABORTION
of living and loving and unwanted fetuses
SITUATION ETHICS

Jane Roe was an unmarried pregnant woman who wished to have an abortion, an intentional termination of a pregnancy by inducing the loss of the fetus. Unfortunately for Ms. Roe, she lived in Texas, where abortion statutes forbade abortion except to save the life of the mother. So, she went to court to prove that the statutes were unconstitutional.

The three-judge district court ruled that Jane Roe had reason to sue, that the Texas criminal abortion statutes were void on their face, and most importantly, that the right to choose whether to have children was protected by the Ninth through the Fourteenth Amendments. Since the district court had denied a number of other aspects of the suit, the case went to the United States Supreme Court. On 22 January 1973, in the now famous *Roe* v. *Wade* decision, the Supreme Court affirmed the district court's judgment.*

Expressing the views of seven members of the Court, Justice Blackmun pointed out that the right to privacy applies to a woman's decision of whether to terminate her pregnancy, but that her right to terminate is not absolute. Her right may be limited by the state's legitimate interests in safeguarding the woman's health, in maintaining proper medical standards, and in protecting human life. Blackmun went on to point out that the unborn are not included within the definition of *person* as used in the Fourteenth Amendment. Most importantly, he indicated that prior to the end of the first trimester of pregnancy, the state may not interfere with or regulate an attending physician's decision, reached in consultation with his patient, that the patient's pregnancy should be terminated. After the first trimester and until the fetus is viable, the state may regulate the abortion procedure only for the health of the mother. After the fetus becomes viable, the state may prohibit all abortions except those to preserve the health or life of the mother.

In dissenting, Justices White and Rehnquist said that nothing in the language or history of the Constitution supported the Court's judgment, that the

---

*See *U.S. Supreme Court Reports*, October Term 1972, lawyers' edition (Rochester, N.Y.: Lawyers' Cooperative Publishing, 1974), p. 147.

Court had simply manufactured a new constitutional right for pregnant women. The abortion issue, they said, should have been left with the people and the political processes they had devised to govern their affairs.

Thus, for the time being at least, the abortion question has been resolved legally. But the issue is hardly dead. A number of antiabortion movements have surfaced, which not only indicates that some people think abortion should be illegal, but that many believe it is wrong. Like euthanasia, abortion, whether legal or not, still remains a most personal moral concern for those who must confront it. Obviously its legality provides options that may not have been present before, but these can make the moral dilemma that much thornier; in the past one could always rationalize away the possibility of an abortion on the basis of its illegality.

Some say an abortion is right if (1) it is therapeutic, that is, when it is necessary to preserve the physical or mental health of the woman, (2) it prevents the birth of a severely handicapped child, or (3) it ends a pregnancy resulting from some criminal act of sexual intercourse. Others say that even therapeutic abortions are immoral. Still others argue that any restrictive abortion legislation is wrong and must be liberalized to allow a woman to have an abortion on demand, that is, at the request of her and her physician, regardless or even in the absence of reasons.

One approach to this problem and to moral questions generally is provided by situation ethicists, who are acutely sensitive to the problems inherent in blindly following legal prescriptions. Situation ethicists are exponents of an ethical system that has taken root in the twentieth century. Although there is a variety of situation ethics, in this chapter we will focus on the especially influential Christian situation ethics espoused by Joseph Fletcher.

Although Fletcher seems more a moralist than a philosophical thinker, his thought seems sufficiently widespread in one form or another for us to consider it. In general, *Fletcher's situation ethics is the normative position that we should act in such a way that our action produces the most Christian love, that is, the greatest possible amount of love fulfillment and benevolence.* It seems particularly appropriate to consider Christian situation ethics together with abortion because it has been a religious ethic that has provided and continues to provide the primary opposition to nonrestrictive abortion legislation. While placing himself squarely in the Christian tradition, Fletcher provides a view that justifies the morality of abortion, even abortion on demand. In this chapter we will see how he does this.

FLETCHER'S THREE APPROACHES TO ETHICAL DECISIONS

To help draw out Fletcher's thinking, let's introduce Ted and Joyce, two unmarried students living together away at college. Feeling secure in their use of birth control devices, they have never really discussed what they would do if Joyce became pregnant. For a while Joyce took birth control pills. But repeated blood clots in her legs made using pills very dangerous, so she substituted an intrauterine device. It is not uncommon for such devices to become dislodged, in which case impregnation can occur. This is precisely what happens to Joyce, who is nearly four months pregnant before she realizes it.

Although Ted and Joyce have discussed the abortion issue many times with friends, in class, and between themselves, somehow all that amounts to so much intellectualizing now that they are directly involved. Ted says that he is not ready for marriage, let alone child rearing. Besides, his education and career plans probably would not survive the responsibilities of parenthood. So he favors the abortion.

Had someone asked her six months earlier what she might do in such a case, Joyce admits that she would have preferred an abortion. Now that she is actually pregnant, however, she is not so sure. She feels that Ted's attitude is too cavalier; all his talk about personal inconvenience has made the problem sound so cold and clinical to her that she no longer is sure that an abortion is the right thing to do.

Ted and Joyce have a tough decision to make. On what basis will they make it? In his *Situation Ethics* Joseph Fletcher contends that there exist three primary avenues for making any moral decision: (1) the *legalistic*, which contends that moral rules are absolute laws that must always be obeyed, (2) the *antinomian* or *existentialist*, which contends that no guidelines exist, that each situation is unique and so requires a new decision, and (3) the *situational*, which falls somewhere between the other two, though more related to the antinomian. These approaches to ethical decisions play an important part in Ted and Joyce's dilemma.

Joyce: Do you remember how difficult it was for me to live with you?
Ted: Do I? Are you kidding? There were times when you made me feel that even proposing it was about the worst sin a person could commit.
Joyce: That's because I was practicing my religion.
Ted: Is that what's bothering you about the abortion—religion?
Joyce: Yes, a little bit.
Ted: But don't you see that this decision is similar to the one you had to make about us living together?
Joyce: How?
Ted: Well, at first you were dead set against it because of religion. But then I finally got you to see that you can't make blanket rules to cover every situation imaginable. To me it's as unrealistic to say that abortion is always wrong as it is to say that living together before marriage is always wrong. There are just too many variables, too many different cases.
Joyce: I don't know. Living together is one thing. But abortion—I don't know.

Joyce is feeling the pressure of her religious inheritance, what Fletcher calls the *legalistic* approach to ethics. At the very least her religion teaches that abortion not intended to preserve the life or health of the mother directly is always wrong. There are no exceptions, no allowances. One need not and should not consider unusual or even unique cases. The moral law still applies.

Understandably, Joyce felt the same legalistic bind when she was debating whether to live with Ted. Rules of her religion forbade premarital sex, which they would undoubtedly engage in. Evidently Ted convinced her that at least in their case such an injunction could not possibly be binding. He suggests a similar approach here, an antinomian one: each situation is unique; moral laws are not applicable; there are no substantive guidelines, directives, or principles for making moral decisions. This is essentially an act utilitarian position. Notice that he, like all act utilitarians, would not argue that abortion is always the right thing to do; each case must be considered individually. In their case, he feels that abortion is right.

Joyce: You're forgetting something very important. I could never have agreed to move in with you simply because it didn't matter one way or the other.
Ted: I didn't mean to suggest that you did.
Joyce: The point is that it *did* matter. It mattered more to me than anything else. And what mattered the most was love, the love I felt for you. And because of that love, I believed that it was the right thing to do, even though it went against everything I was brought up to believe was right.

One thing is clear. Joyce is providing act utilitarianism with a nuance, a subtlety that makes her approach significantly different from the pure act utilitarian's, while at the same time preserving many of its antinomian features. Joyce suggests that it was the presence of love that persuaded her to move in with Ted, rather than a mere totaling of the consequences of each option and deciding which produced the most good. Presumably in the absence of love she would not have lived with Ted; she would have thought it wrong. It is the introduction of love into ethical decisions that distinguishes Fletcher's situation approach. But it is hardly the love that makes the heart beat faster and the pulse race quicker.

THE SITUATIONAL APPROACH

According to Fletcher, the best approach for making moral decisions is Christian situation ethics. Although he recognizes that an individual approaches a moral decision "fully armed with the ethical maxims of his community and its heritage," he argues that in any particular situation it is better if the individual sets aside this moral legacy "if love seems better served by doing so."[*] In other words, for Fletcher rules and principles are valid only if they serve love in a specific situation; therefore, it is crucial that, in making a moral decision, individuals be fully acquainted with all the facts surrounding the case as well as the probable consequences that would attend each possible alternative. In these cautions

---

[*]Joseph Fletcher, *Situation Ethics: The New Morality* (Philadelphia: Westminster Press), 1966.

his thinking is clearly consequential. But he also argues that after all the calculation is completed, one must choose the act that will best serve love. Obviously the crucial element in Fletcher's situational approach is the meaning of love. To understand what Fletcher means, it is necessary to understand the Christian concept of *agape*.*

AGAPE: THE "LAW OF LOVE"

In the Christian tradition *agape* (pronounced AH-ga-pay) is unselfish love, epitomized by Jesus, who made the ultimate sacrifice for love of humankind. Agape is a principle expressing the type of actions that Christians are to regard as good. It is not something we are or have; it is something we do. It is a purpose, a preference, a disposition, an attitude, a way of relating to persons and of treating things. In a word, *agape is loving concern, a loving concern characterized by a love of God and neighbor.*

Fletcher contends that agape is the one unexceptionable principle in Christian ethics. Everything else is only valid if it serves love in any situation. What about the Ten Commandments? The Sermon on the Mount? According to Fletcher, even these should be viewed as cautious generalizations, not as absolutely binding moral principles. In this respect, he agrees with Martin Luther's statement.

> Therefore, when the law impels one against love, it ceases and should *no longer be a law.* But where no obstacle is in the way, the keeping of the law is a proof of love, which lies hidden in the heart. Therefore you have need of the law, that love may be manifested; but if it cannot be kept without injury to the neighbor, God wants us to suspend and ignore the law."†

In effect, Fletcher subordinates legalism to the principle of loving concern for one's neighbor. Traditional Christian moral laws are fine and even obligatory but *only* if they serve love. When they do not, they should be broken.

But don't misunderstand Fletcher. He is no romantic nurturing a hearts-and-flowers notion of love. *Prudence and careful evaluation, characterized by a willing of the neighbor's good, are the hallmarks of agape.* As such, justice is an integral part of Fletcher's agape, for justice involves giving to each person his or her due. When we truly love we must be practicing justice. If we separate justice from love, Fletcher claims that we make love sentimental. "Agape is what is due to all others," he writes, and "justice is nothing other than love working out its problems."‡

---

*For a succinct philosophical treatment of situational ethics, see Luther J. Binkley, *Conflict of Ideals* (New York: Van Nostrand Reinhold, 1969), pp. 225–276.
†Martin Luther, *Works*, ed. J. N. Linker (Luther House, 1905), 5: 175.
‡Fletcher, *Situation Ethics*, p. 95.

Fletcher believes that in formulating social policies, for example abortion laws, the Christian should join with the utilitarian in trying to produce the greatest good for the greatest number of people concerned, or as he calls it, "the greatest amount of neighbor welfare for the largest number of neighbors possible." Thus the hedonistic calculus of utilitarianism becomes for Fletcher "the agape calculus."*

Clearly Fletcher's concept of agape is not emotional or sentimental. It is not *liking*, but it is loving, that is, an attitude of good will and benevolence toward all people, even toward those that may not be likable.† This concept is most relevant to Ted and Joyce's discussion. Joyce contends that it was not merely questioning or rejecting legalistic ethics that impelled her into Ted's embrace. Rather it was something that transcended what she perceived as the constraints of legalism. Love. And evidently it is love that is the issue in their abortion dilemma.

Joyce: Ted, what you're not understanding is that I want to make this decision on the same basis that I decided to move in with you—on the basis of love.

Ted: So do I.

Joyce: I don't think so. I really don't. At least I don't think you mean love the way I do, and that's why we're not really understanding each other. I didn't realize how far apart we are in our concepts of love until I got pregnant and saw your reaction.

Ted: I don't know what you're talking about. You make it sound as if I don't love you.

Joyce: Let me ask you something. Why did you want me to live with you in the first place?

Ted: Because I wanted you. I needed you. I still do.

Joyce: But that's my point. You can just as easily want and need an object, a thing, but you wouldn't call that loving. No, I think you *like* me well enough, but love? I don't think so. There's too much "I" in what you say and not enough "you."

Ted: What's that supposed to mean?

Joyce: I don't think the loving person is self-centered. I don't think he's selfish and self-serving. And I don't think he is primarily interested in satisfying his own ends. I think the loving person is outer-directed, concerned with others, not self, wishing all that is good for others, even if it means personal discomfort and suffering.

Ted: You make it sound like loving is some kind of exercise in humanitarianism. Well, that's fine for someone like Albert Schweitzer but is hardly applicable to a man-woman relationship or to an abortion.

Joyce: Why isn't it applicable? I think it's most applicable. I think the true lover is one who puts the interest, well-being, and happiness of the beloved before his own. That's what I did when I moved in with you. I loved you so much that I was willing to put up with the hurtful disapproval of my parents,

---

*Binkley, *Conflict of Ideals*, p. 256.
†Ibid.

the censure of my church, the nagging guilt of self-doubts and self-judgment. And why? All because I believed that living with you meant loving you more completely, more fully than not living with you. And I believed that loving you completely would bring the most good into your life. Believing that was the only way that I could have done it.

It seems that Joyce's love is quite different from the emotional, erotic love that Fletcher prefers to call *liking* and that may characterize Ted's. Agape, similar to what Joyce describes, is not selfish; it is not looking for something in return. It gives freely, expecting no reciprocity. It does not spurn self-love, but requires us to love ourselves in the right way, that is, to love oneself for the sake of others. Ultimately agape is concerned about the neighbor for God's sake, and it is the only principle that makes an act right or wrong. As Fletcher writes, "Love could justify anything. There is no justification other than love's expedients. What else?"* It seems that Joyce would agree.

Let us summarize the main tenets of Fletcher's Christian ethics, derived from his concept of agape.†

1. Nothing is good in itself except love (taken to mean Christian love).

2. The prevailing standard of moral decision is love.

3. Love and justice are identical, justice being love distributed.

4. We love when we will the good of our neighbor, regardless of how we feel about that individual.

5. Nothing but the end justifies the means.

6. Love's decisions are determined by particular situations.

Fletcher's situation ethics, as you might imagine, is extremely controversial, particularly within the Christian community, which traditionally has been ethically legalistic.

OBJECTIONS TO SITUATION ETHICS

1. *Fletcher's distinction between loving and liking is not clear.* One objection to Fletcher's situation ethics involves his distinction between loving and liking. He defines *loving* as concern for others rooted in the love of God, as opposed to *liking*, which is characterized by emotionalism and sentimentality. But is the distinction that sharp? Or is it ambiguous and possibly a questionable claim?

Protestant theologian Paul Tillich, for one, makes no distinction between agape (God's unconditional love of all persons) and eros (human love expressed as desire). For Tillich, agape is the quality of depth in love, not a separate and

---

*Fletcher, *Situation Ethics*, p. 125.
†Binkley, *Conflict of Ideals*, p. 254.

unique kind. Even in the most spiritualized friendship and ascetic mysticism, claims Tillich, you will find some element of human desire, that is, Fletcher's "liking." As Tillich puts it, "A saint without libido would cease to be a creature."*

It does seem at least difficult to determine where eros ends and agape begins, especially in a relationship like Ted and Joyce's. In illustrating the difference between loving and liking, Fletcher contends that it would probably be wrong for a couple to have premarital sexual relations simply because they liked each other. On the other hand, Fletcher claims that they would be acting in accordance with agape if they had sex in order to force their parents into consenting to their proposed marriage. But even conceding this possibility, it is impossible to calculate which impulse moved them the most—loving each other or blackmailing their parents. One reason for this is the difficulty in determining people's motives.

2. *It is very difficult to determine one's own motives.*

> **Ted:** You know, all this is ancient history. I mean the whys behind our being here right now aren't really the issue. The real issue is what we're going to do about the abortion.
>
> **Joyce:** I want to be sure that whatever I do I follow love's lead. It's that simple.
>
> **Ted:** You seem to be saying that having the abortion or not having it isn't as important as your acting with love. Is that where you are?
>
> **Joyce:** That's exactly where I am. I'm trying to get you there, too.
>
> **Ted:** Well, all I know is that I don't want this baby. I didn't intend it. I'm not ready for it. If you want to know the truth, it scares me.
>
> **Joyce:** I'll remember that.
>
> **Ted:** What do you mean?
>
> **Joyce:** I mean the baby's effect on you is a factor I must consider.
>
> **Ted:** Well, I think it's a pretty important factor.
>
> **Joyce:** If you want to know the truth, I think personal inconvenience is the least important factor. In fact, to me it's the factor that taints any action.

Joyce's tone would chill an iceberg. It seems safe to say that she disapproves of Ted's apparent egoism. Evidently she believes that his intentions from the beginning were self-seeking. Perhaps they were. But who can say for sure? Human motivation is difficult to nail down. And where we attempt to assign motives, we run risks of expressing questionable claims based on unknown facts. For example, in his *Situation Ethics*, Fletcher cites the example of a young woman who is asked by an American intelligence agency to use sex to blackmail an enemy spy. The problem: should she value her chastity more than patriotism and service to her country? Fletcher's answer is no, which should put him right up there with Patrick Henry and Nathan Hale. He reasons that, in this case, acting out of patriotic motives would fulfill the command of agape more than acting selfishly and preserving her chastity.

---

*Paul Tillich, *Love, Power and Justice: Ontological Analyses and Ethical Applications* (New York: Oxford University Press, 1960), p. 33.

But couldn't she appeal to the same motives to preserve her chastity? She might reason that her country should not exploit a person sexually, whatever the reason. She might feel that it's high time to put intelligence agencies on notice that information gathering is not a blanket justification for demanding any kind of behavior. In other words, she might as easily interpret her refusal to use herself as sexual bait as being more patriotic and rendering a greater service to her country than her consent. In short, she might see her refusal as the most loving thing to do.

The fact that the same motives could produce different behavior suggests a problem with Fletcher's situation ethics: the ultimate moral decision rests with the individual and, most importantly, on the individual's perception of things. It is safe to say that it is impossible to determine precisely the reason for any human action. Obviously this does not mean that human motives do not exist. To argue that would be to argue from ignorance. But almost always there is a whole nexus of motives, some weighing more heavily than others. Just as often, it seems, the reasons and motives that we are most conscious of turn out to be rather superficial and insubstantial. Frequently residing beneath these conscious motives is a reservoir of unconscious and subconscious motivation.

When Joyce contemptuously disposes of Ted's personal inconvenience, she seems to overlook this. Although strictly egoistic concerns violate Fletcher's agape imperative, it is possible to imagine how they would be consistent with it. Ted reasons that he's not ready to be a father. He might argue that in not being ready to be a father, he is not in a financial position to support a child. This necessitates quitting school and sacrificing professional goals, probably having to take a job that he does not desire simply to make ends meet. He can imagine quickly coming to resent Joyce and the child, being haunted with feelings of entrapment, and finally abandoning the husband-father role altogether. So, he might conclude, "I am really being motivated by loving concern for all involved, not just for myself." Fletcher might applaud this. But no one is so psychologically naive as to attribute to Ted, without reservation, the motive of altruism rather than egoism. The point is, like eros and agape, egoism and altruism as sources of human motivation are difficult, if not impossible, to separate.

In short, it is very hard to be aware of your motives in a specific situation. To insist that you do know them invariably is to commit the fallacy of questionable claim. Because of this, critics of Fletcher's situation ethics argue for the necessity of some rules and principles that may act as guideposts to direct ethical choice. Without them, they claim, individuals are destined to flounder in a sea of ethical dilemmas, their only guide being the rather dim and uncertain lights of love and reason.

3. *There is a need for some rules or principles to serve as guideposts of ethical actions.*

Ted: So, you're going to have the baby, is that right?
Joyce: I never said that.
Ted: But you *want* to have the baby.
Joyce: No, as a matter of fact I do not want to have the baby.

Ted: Then I don't see what the problem is. If you don't want to have the baby and I don't want to have the baby, then let's get the abortion.

Joyce: It's not that simple.

Ted: I think it's just that simple.

Joyce: Look, I don't want to pay back the bank for my school loan, but I will.

Ted: That's an altogether different situation. You knew what you were getting into when you took out the loan. You intended to incur that debt. But you never intended to get pregnant.

Joyce: Well, I never intended to have an accident with my car, but I did. Remember? And I thought we both agreed that it was the right thing to leave a note on the windshield, even though we could have left with no problem.

Ted: What are you saying—that you have some obligation to have the baby?

Joyce: Not necessarily. I'm just trying to determine why I'm going to have the abortion or not.

Ted: Well, I think you have two good reasons for the abortion: one, you didn't intend to have the baby, and two, you don't want it.

Curiously enough, Fletcher agrees with Ted's conclusion. In his *Situation Ethics* he writes, "No unwanted and unintended baby should ever be born."* This general justification for abortion raises a couple of noteworthy points. On the one hand, Fletcher argues that no two situations are similar enough to allow for the formulation of general statements of morality. On the other hand, he states one: "No unwanted and unintended baby should ever be born." This seems an inconsistency.

Fletcher proposes rules elsewhere, as when he argues that the exploitation of persons is always wrong. It is true that he condemns exploitation because it is unloving, but whether the rule derives from his agapism seems irrelevant. It is still a general rule of human behavior.

Similarly, he condemns sexual intercourse without love. He writes:

The point is that, Christianly speaking, sex which does not have love as its partner, its *senior* partner, is wrong. If there is no responsible concern for the *other* one, for the partner as a subject rather than a mere object, as a person and not a *thing*, the act is immoral.†

So apparently even Fletcher's situational approach leads to at least some summary rules of conduct.

A summary rule is one which contends that following the practice advocated or avoiding the practice prohibited is generally the best way of acting. For example, a summary rule might be: "Telling the truth is *generally* love fulfilling" or "Paying your debts is *generally* love fulfilling." Summary rules should be contrasted with general

---

*Fletcher, *Situation Ethics*, p. 39.

†Fletcher, *Moral Responsibility: Situation Ethics at Work* (Philadelphia: The Westminster Press, 1967), p. 35.

rules, ones that do not allow exceptions. *A general rule is one which contends that you must always follow the practice advocated and avoid the one prohibited.* Thus, the general counterparts of the preceding summary rules might read: "Telling the truth is *always* love fulfilling" and "Paying your debts is *always* love fulfilling." Obviously general rules allow for no exceptions, whereas summary rules do. It seems that Fletcher must deny the existence of general rules, for they are legalistic. Yet it is difficult to interpret Fletcher's moral position on abortion as being anything but a general rule. If it is intended as a summary rule, as perhaps the ones on exploitation and sex without love are, then individuals again seem consigned to their own devices. They must determine when the interests of loving concern transcend the summary rule.

This is precisely what is occurring between Ted and Joyce. It may be true that an unwanted baby should never be born. But this is either a general rule, in which case Fletcher with his own situational approach is inconsistent, or a summary rule, in which case Joyce's reservations may be well founded.

Such problems have led many Christian thinkers, like Paul Ramsey, to argue that there are some principles of ethical conduct that would be more than summary. Ramsey suggests that investigating what love requires may reveal rules of general validity. His main criticism of Fletcher is that Fletcher has ended reasonable inquiry too soon. If individuals subscribe to Fletcher's situation ethics, says Ramsey, they will not inquire into whether love leads directly to general rules of human conduct.* Without such an inquiry, individuals are left to their own antinomian devices.

In effect, Ramsey and those like him are objecting to what they view as the completely consequential nature of Fletcher's situation ethics. Like rule utilitarians objecting to act utilitarians, they argue that although no two actions are precisely the same, any more than two individuals are, human behavior is often similar enough to allow the formulation of some guiding rules or principles. They could raise an additional objection that applies to any form of utilitarianism and thus refers to the consequences of actions.

4. *It is very difficult to determine who will be affected by an action and to what degree.* Ramsey argues that one of the most objectionable features of Fletcher's situational approach is that it attempts to restrict moral calculation to the consequences of an action. In other words, Fletcher constantly asks, "Is abortion the most loving thing to do?" The obvious follow-up question is, "For whom?" Fletcher answers, for those directly affected. But this is frequently difficult to determine, for our actions not only have direct effects but indirect ones as well that frequently have more far-reaching consequences.

> **Joyce:** Look, Ted, I know that there are good reasons to have an abortion and I may decide to do just that. But I have to admit that I'm troubled by what my reaction might be.
> **Ted:** You mean if you have the abortion?

---

*See Paul Ramsey, *Deeds and Rules in Christian Ethics* (New York: Scribner's, 1967).

Joyce: Yes. It's one thing to have an abortion, but it's another to live with it. To be perfectly honest, and you'll probably laugh at this, I don't know whether I'll feel terribly guilty about the whole thing and whether I can handle that kind of guilt.

Ted: I know that's a possibility, but how likely is it?

Joyce: I don't know. I've never had an abortion. All I know is that it's something that has to be accounted for and I intend to do just that.

As far as Joyce is concerned, there is no conclusive way for her to determine how she will react to the abortion. If she suffers mental damage that affects her the remainder of her life, that effect could well eclipse all the positive consequences of the abortion. How can she know for sure? Critics of situation ethics argue that anyone who pretends to know the consequences of complex moral decisions like this one is guilty of expressing a questionable claim.

An obviously related problem is the one involving conflicting interests, a major concern in the abortion issue. There is no question that having or not having the abortion will directly affect the lives of Joyce and Ted. But it also directly affects the fetus.

Joyce: And there's something else I'll have to consider, Ted. The baby I'm carrying.

Ted: It's not a baby. It's a fetus.

Joyce: You can call it what you like. All I know is that having an abortion will prevent that entity from being born, from being a person. And I think that's very serious.

Ted: Well, I do too, but it's not as if the fetus already was a person with rights and privileges the way that the born have.

Joyce: But it has the potential to. And an abortion directly interferes with that potential. That's pretty serious, I think. To me, it's certainly a consequence that's at least as important as your being able to continue your education. After all, we're literally talking here about allowing an entity to be born and to live or not to. It seems to me that this aspect must be considered out of loving concern.

As Ted suggests, according to the *Roe* v. *Wade* decision, the fetus is not to be considered a person as understood by the Fourteenth Amendment. Nevertheless, Joyce does have a point. The fetus is a potential person whose "personhood" probably would be realized without abortive intervention. Apparently the Court has made a value judgment: the existing privacy right of the pregnant woman supersedes consideration of fetal potentiality, including its potential to be a person. To Joyce, this judgment appears debatable morally, if not legally. Perhaps even more debatable is the ruling that pregnant women, in effect, can arbitrarily deal with the fetus in the first trimester of their pregnancy. This conclusion minimizes or ignores entirely the consequences for the fetus. Fletcher does the same when he argues that "no unwanted and unintended baby should ever be born."

The problem grows more difficult when we realize that cases have already been made for the moral treatment of nonhuman animals, even for vegetable and mineral "life." The obvious question: why not extend these to the nonviable fetus? Indeed, recently proposed policies of the Department of Health, Education, and Welfare regarding protection of human subjects include stringent prohibitions against fetal research. HEW's proposal prohibits any experiment that would prolong the life of an aborted fetus deemed to be nonviable and prohibits any experiment involving a woman who is about to have an abortion if such an experiment might harm the fetus. The result is a curious paradox: on the one hand we may legally kill the fetus; on the other we may not legally experiment on it.

So, situation ethicists must at some point reckon with the various aspects of their consequential approach. They must determine who will be affected by an action and to what degree. Then they must determine an even stickier problem: what priorities each affected entity will receive. And, of course, they must satisfactorily justify these calculations in the light of Christian love. It seems that these problems are particularly complex in the abortion area.

SUMMARY

Consequential Position

Situation Ethics: acting in such a way that your action produces the most Christian love, that is, the greatest possible amount of love fulfillment and benevolence

Objections

1. Fletcher's distinction between loving and liking is not clear.

2. It is very difficult to determine one's own motives.

3. There is a need for some rules or principles to serve as guideposts of ethical actions.

4. It is very difficult to determine who will be affected by an action and to what degree.

CONCLUSIONS

Apparently the problems inherent in any utilitarian position are evident in Fletcher's situation ethics. Especially troublesome is Fletcher's act utilitarian posture, which finds him unwilling to allow for rule formulation. As a result we must wonder how substantially different situation ethics is from antinomianism.

This problem may not be disturbingly apparent from a reading of Fletcher's work, until one realizes that most of the examples he provides are of extreme cases. Unusual cases are obviously not as common as typical ones. It seems that a more useful ethical code would be the one that provides for typical cases, not extreme ones. This suggests another conclusion: perhaps, Fletcher's agapeic calculus is best called upon in extreme cases, while a code with at least summary rules is best in more common situations.

But this conclusion should not be viewed as an indictment of the spirit of situation ethics. It seems that Fletcher has legitimate grounds for refusing to give general replies to questions like: Is abortion wrong? Can premarital sex be good? Is lying bad? He is probably right in insisting that a case must be sufficiently detailed before any realistic reply can be made. Although he does not provide enough detail in his own illustrations, his point is nonetheless a justifiable one: a legalistic approach to contemporary moral dilemmas is unrealistic and unworkable. Even worse, legalism seems to remove the burden of moral evaluation and decision making from the individual.

This legalistic weakness appears in the abortion problem. There was a time when most people, certainly those in the Christian tradition, regarded abortion as wrong for purposes other than to preserve the health and life of the mother. For many of these people some general rule such as "Thou shalt not kill" dictated their own position. But it is likely that many today who believe that such abortions are right are making a similarly legalistic decision, this time grounding it in the "law of the land," which allows abortion. Fletcher would caution Ted and Joyce about using legal prescriptions as the basis for a moral decision. It is in his emphasis on personal moral responsibility that Fletcher seems to make his most important contribution to the field of religious morality, which historically has been grounded in legalism.

At the same time, one is left wondering whether Fletcher himself has successfully avoided legalism. If Christian love is something one *does*, then *what* must one do? Perhaps love must be just. But, again, what must one do for an act to be just? Upon examining these questions, we may discover that Fletcher's situation ethics seems to be a form of legalism in disguise: one ought to or should so act as to bring love into the world.

EXERCISES FOR ANALYSIS

EXERCISE 1

Today the abortion debate centers primarily around the merits of restrictive versus nonrestrictive abortion legislation. By *restrictive* legislation is meant a law that prevents a pregnant woman from getting an abortion whenever she, on the advice of her doctor, requests one. Restrictive legislation can take any form from forbidding abortion on demand to forbidding even therapeutic abortions, although the latter kind of legislation is extremely rare. Nonrestrictive legislation proponents, therefore, range from those who argue that restrictive legislation is sometimes immoral to those who claim that it is always immoral.

The following are condensed verions of common arguments against restrictive abortion legislation and against nonrestrictive legislation.* Determine whether the justification provided in each case is adequate. As usual, look for fallacies.

Arguments against Restrictive Abortion Legislation

1. Clearly one of the functions of law is to protect the health of citizens as well as their lives. But restrictive abortion laws frequently endanger a woman's physical and psychological well-being. As a result, these laws are at least sometimes immoral.

2. Medical science has advanced to the point where doctors are often able to predict accurately the birth of a monstrously deformed baby. the chances that such a child will be happy are slim. Frequently children with severe physical handicaps later develop emotional and mental handicaps as a result. And, of course, such children are almost always a tremendous financial and emotional burden to a family. A law that requires the birth of such children is thus immoral. So, restrictive abortion legislation is at least sometimes immoral.

3. Frequently females are victims of criminal acts of sexual intercourse, as in cases of rape and incest. Often the result is an unwanted pregnancy. To require the woman to bear the child of such a criminal act is to compound her victimization by making her bear an unwanted child. This is patently unjust. Restrictive legislation, therefore, is at least sometimes immoral.

4. A law is only just if its effects fall equally on all members of society. Statistical research indicates that restrictive abortion legislation has the effect of discriminating against black, poor, and single persons. The reasons for this are complex, but a major factor is economic. Frequently a woman with money can travel to a state or country where abortion is permitted, whereas a poor woman cannot. Also, in many instances a married woman can more easily secure an abortion than a single woman. It appears that restrictive abortion legislation fosters these inequities and can therefore be immoral.

5. Women who really want abortions can get them, even though they may have to break the law to do it. The results are frequently disastrous. Strictly from a medical viewpoint, criminal abortions are dangerous, for the surgeon is frequently unskilled and the operation conditions often unhygienic. Where compli-

---

*See Wellman, *Morals & Ethics*, pp. 159–165.

cations arise, the woman's life may easily be lost; where postoperative complications set in, her health can be irreparably damaged. An even greater potential threat than the illegal abortion is the self-induced one. Since restrictive abortion laws can force women who really want and need abortions into direct and immediate threats to their health, they can be immoral.

6. Restrictive abortion laws encroach on the private relation that exists between a woman and her physician, and between a mother and father. They also violate the privacy proper to a most intimate personal choice: whether to bear a child. Since restrictive abortion legislation invades the individual's fundamental right to privacy, it is always immoral.

Arguments against Nonrestrictive Legislation

1. Murder is the intentional taking of an innocent human life. It is hard to imagine an act more heinous or immoral. Abortion, since it intentionally terminates the life of a fetus, is murder, and thus immoral. It follows that we should do all we can to prevent its occurring. But permitting abortion on demand would have the opposite effect. So, nonrestrictive abortion legislation, because it in effect encourages murder, is immoral.

2. The purpose of law is to protect citizens' rights. If a law invades a citizen's right, it is obviously unjust and immoral. Permitting abortion on demand is an invasion of the unborn's rights and is therefore immoral.

3. To permit abortion on demand is to injure the concept that life is sacred. It is on the sanctity of life principle that most moral codes are based. Even therapeutic abortions, performed to prevent the birth of severely handicapped children, suggest that we should exterminate the living who are severely handicapped, dysfunctional, senile, seriously injured, or incurably ill. Surely if therapeutic abortion sets such a dangerous precedent, then abortion on demand is even more inimical to the concept of human life. Therefore, nonrestrictive abortion legislation is immoral.

4. The relationship between a woman and the child she is bearing is the most intimate biological relationship that there is. It is also among the most intimate psychological and emotional relationships. By nature, a woman desires to bear the child that she is carrying. For her to do intentional damage to her fetus is to violate needs, impulses, and desires that exist at the deepest levels of the subconscious and unconscious mind. Because nonrestrictive abortion legislation encourages just this kind of harm to the woman, it is immoral.

EXERCISE 2

Compose three additional arguments against restrictive abortion legislation based on the following:

1. the undesirability of having unwanted children,

2. the right of a woman to control her own body,

3. abortion as a means of effective population control, particularly in third-world countries.

If you disagree with any of these positions, rather than defending it write an argument opposing it, demonstrating that it would be immoral to permit abortion for that reason.

SELECTIONS FOR FURTHER READING

Situation Ethics

Fletcher, John. *Moral Responsibility: Situation Ethics at Work.* Philadelphia: Westminster Press, 1967.
———. *Situation Ethics: The New Morality.* Westminster Press, 1966.

Ramsey, Paul. *Deeds and Rules in Christian Ethics.* New York: Scribner's, 1967.

Robinson, John. *Honest to God.* Philadelphia: Westminster Press, 1963.

Tillich, Paul. *Morality and Beyond.* New York: Harper & Row, 1963.

Abortion

Callahan, Daniel J. *Abortion: Law, Choice, and Morality.* New York: Macmillan, 1970.

Feinberg, Joel. *The Problem of Abortion.* Belmont, Calif.: Wadsworth, 1973.

Granfield, David. *The Abortion Decisions.* Garden City, N.Y.: Doubleday, 1969.

Lader, Lawrence. *Abortion.* Indianapolis: Bobbs-Merrill, 1966.

Noonan, John T. *The Morality of Abortion: Legal and Historical Perspectives.* Cambridge, Mass.: Harvard University Press, 1970.

St. John-Stevans, Norman. *The Right To Life.* New York: Holt, Rinehart and Winston, 1964.

THOMSON / A Defense of Abortion

In the essay that follows, author Judith Jarvis Thomson argues in favor of abortion, but not for abortion on demand. On the contrary, she posits a "Minimally Decent Samaritanism" principle that would prohibit abortion. The curious fact about her essay is that, unlike many in favor of abortion, she concedes for the sake of argument that the fetus is a person from the moment of conception. It is upon that concession that she builds her case.

Implied in Thomson's remarks is the belief that situations differ. In some cases an abortion may be warranted, in others not. Thus, there seems an antinomian bias in her approach. At the same time, by introducing the minimal Samaritan principle, she seems to provide some general guideline to judge the morality of abortion cases. Whether she has sufficiently spelled out that principle is something you can decide.

In reading this essay, compare and contrast Thomson's minimally decent Samaritan principle with Fletcher's agapism. Do you think that Thomson would agree with Fletcher when he writes, "An unwanted and unintended baby should never be born"?

Most opposition to abortion relies on the premise that the fetus is a human being, a person, from the moment of conception. The premise is argued for, but, as I think, not well. Take, for example, the most common argument. We are asked to notice that the development of a human being from conception through birth into childhood is continuous; then it is said that to draw a line, to choose a point in this development and say "before this point the thing is not a person, after this point it is a person" is to make an arbitrary choice, a choice for which in the nature of things no good reason can be given. It is concluded that the fetus is, or anyway that we had better say it is, a person from the moment of conception. But this conclusion does not follow. Similar things might be said about the development of an acorn into an oak tree, and it does not follow that acorns are oak trees, or that we had better say they are. Arguments of this form are sometimes called "slippery slope arguments"—the phrase is perhaps self-explanatory—and it is dismaying that opponents of abortion rely on them so heavily and uncritically.

I am inclined to agree, however, that the prospects for "drawing a line" in the development of the fetus looks dim. I am inclined to think also that we shall probably have to agree that the fetus has already become a human person well before birth. In-

From Judith Jarvis Thomson, "A Defense of Abortion," *Philosophy and Public Affairs* 1, no. 1: 47–66. Copyright © 1971 by Princeton University Press. Reprinted by permission. Ms. Thomson acknowledges her indebtedness to James Thomson for discussion, criticism, and many helpful suggestions.

deed, it comes as a surprise when one first learns how early in its life it begins to acquire human characteristics. By the tenth week, for example, it already has a face, arms and legs, fingers and toes; it has internal organs, and brain activity is detectable.* On the other hand, I think that the premise is false, that the fetus is not a person from the moment of conception. A newly fertilized ovum, a newly implanted clump of cells, is no more a person than an acorn is an oak tree. But I shall not discuss any of this. For it seems to me to be of great interest to ask what happens if, for the sake of argument, we allow the premise. How, precisely, are we supposed to get from there to the conclusion that abortion is morally impermissible? Opponents of abortion commonly spend most of their time establishing that the fetus is a person, and hardly any time explaining the step from there to the impermissibility of abortion. Perhaps they think the step too simple and obvious to require much comment. Or perhaps instead they are simply being economical in argument. Many of those who defend abortion rely on the premise that the fetus is not a person, but only a bit of tissue that will become a person at birth; and why pay out more arguments than you have to? Whatever the explanation, I suggest that the step they take is neither

easy nor obvious, that it calls for closer examination than it is commonly given, and that when we do give it this closer examination we shall feel inclined to reject it.

I propose, then, that we grant that the fetus is a person from the moment of conception. How does the argument go from here? Something like this, I take it. Every person has a right to life. So the fetus has a right to life. No doubt the mother has a right to decide what shall happen in and to her body; everyone would grant that. But surely a person's right to life is stronger and more stringent than the mother's right to decide what happens in and to her body, and so outweighs it. So the fetus may not be killed; an abortion may not be performed.

It sounds plausible. But now let me ask you to imagine this. You wake up in the morning and find yourself back to back in bed with an unconscious violinist. A famous unconscious violinist. He has been found to have a fatal kidney ailment, and the Society of Music Lovers has canvassed all the available medical records and found that you alone have the right blood type to help. They have therefore kidnapped you, and last night the violinist's circulatory system was plugged into yours, so that your kidneys can be used to extract poisons from his blood as well as your own. The director of the hospital now tells you, "Look, we're sorry the Society of Music Lovers did this to you—we would never have permitted it if we had known. But still, they did it, and the violinist now is plugged into you. To unplug you would be to kill him. But never mind, it's only for nine months. By then he

*Daniel Callahan, *Abortion: Law, Choice and Morality* (New York, 1970), p. 373. This book gives a fascinating survey of the available information on abortion. The Jewish tradition is surveyed in David M. Feldman, *Birth Control in Jewish Law* (New York, 1968), part 5, the Catholic tradition in John T. Noonan, Jr., "An Almost Absolute Value in History," in *The Morality of Abortion,* ed. John T. Noonan, Jr. (Cambridge, Mass., 1970).

will have recovered from his ailment, and can safely be unplugged from you." Is it morally incumbent on you to accede to this situation? No doubt it would be very nice of you if you did, a great kindness. But do you *have* to accede to it? What if it were not nine months, but nine years? Or longer still? What if the director of the hospital says, "Tough luck, I agree, but you've now got to stay in bed, with the violinist plugged into you, for the rest of your life. Because remember this. All persons have a right to life, and violinists are persons. Granted you have a right to decide what happens in and to your body, but a person's right to life outweighs your right to decide what happens in and to your body. So you cannot ever be unplugged from him." I imagine you would regard this as outrageous, which suggests that something really is wrong with that plausible-sounding argument I mentioned a moment ago.

In this case, of course, you were kidnapped; you didn't volunteer for the operation that plugged the violinist into your kidneys. Can those who oppose abortion on the ground I mentioned make an exception for a pregnancy due to rape? Certainly. They can say that persons have a right to life only if they didn't come into existence because of rape; or they can say that all persons have a right to life, but that some have less of a right to life than others, in particular, that those who came into existence because of rape have less. But these statements have a rather unpleasant sound. Surely the question of whether you have a right to life at all, or how much of it you have, shouldn't turn on the question of whether or not you

are the product of a rape. And in fact the people who oppose abortion on the ground I mentioned do not make this distinction, and hence do not make an exception in case of rape.

Nor do they make an exception for a case in which the mother has to spend the nine months of her pregnancy in bed. They would agree that would be a great pity, and hard on the mother; but all the same, all persons have a right to life, the fetus is a person, and so on. I suspect, in fact, that they would not make an exception for a case in which, miraculously enough, the pregnancy went on for nine years, or even the rest of the mother's life.

Some won't even make an exception for a case in which continuation of the pregnancy is likely to shorten the mother's life; they regard abortion as impermissible even to save the mother's life. Such cases are nowadays very rare, and many opponents of abortion do not accept this extreme view. All the same, it is a good place to begin: a number of points of interest come out in respect to it.

1. Let us call the view that abortion is impermissible even to save the mother's life "the extreme view." I want to suggest first that it does not issue from the argument I mentioned earlier without the addition of some fairly powerful premises. Suppose a woman has become pregnant, and now learns that she has a cardiac condition such that she will die if she carries the baby to term. What may be done for her? The fetus, being a person, has a right to life, but as the mother is a person too, so has she a right to life. Presumably they have an equal right to life. How is it supposed to come out that an abortion

may not be performed? If mother and child have an equal right to life, shouldn't we perhaps flip a coin? Or should we add to the mother's right to life her right to decide what happens in and to her body, which everybody seems to be ready to grant—the sum of her rights now outweighing the fetus' right to life?

The most familiar argument here is the following. We are told that performing the abortion would be directly killing* the child, whereas doing nothing would not be killing the mother, but only letting her die. Moreover, in killing the child, one would be killing an innocent person, for the child has committed no crime, and is not aiming at his mother's death. And then there are a variety of ways in which this might be continued. (1) But as directly killing an innocent person is always and absolutely impermissible, an abortion may not be performed. Or, (2) as directly killing an innocent person is murder, and murder is always and absolutely impermissible, an abortion may not be performed.† Or, (3) as

one's duty to refrain from directly killing an innocent person is more stringent than one's duty to keep a person from dying, an abortion may not be performed. Or, (4) if one's only options are directly killing an innocent person or letting a person die, one must prefer letting the person die, and thus an abortion may not be performed.‡

Some people seem to have thought that these are not further premises which must be added if the conclusion is to be reached, but that they follow from the very fact that an innocent person has a right to life.§ But this seems to me to be a mistake, and perhaps the simplest way to show this is to bring out that while we must certainly grant that innocent persons have a right to life, the theses in (1) through (4) are all false. Take (2), for example. If directly killing an innocent person is murder, and thus is impermissible, then the mother's directly killing the innocent person inside her is murder, and thus is

---

*The term "direct" in the arguments I refer to is a technical one. Roughly, what is meant by "direct killing" is either killing as an end in itself, or killing as a means to some end, for example, the end of saving someone else's life. See note § on this page, for an example of its use.

†Cf. *Encyclical Letter of Pope Pius XI on Christian Marriage,* St. Paul Editions (Boston, n.d.), p. 32: "however much we may pity the mother whose health and even life is gravely imperiled in the performance of the duty allotted to her by nature, nevertheless what could ever be a sufficient reason for excusing in any way the direct murder of the innocent? This is precisely what we are dealing with here." Noonan (*The Morality of Abortion,* p. 43) reads this as follows: "What cause can ever avail to excuse in any way the direct killing of the innocent? For it is a question of that."

‡The thesis in (4) is in an interesting way weaker than those in (1), (2), and (3): they rule out abortion even in cases in which both mother *and* child will die if the abortion is not performed. By contrast, one who held the view expressed in (4) could consistently say that one needn't prefer letting two persons die to killing one.

§Cf. the following passage from Pius XII, *Address to the Italian Catholic Society of Midwives:* "The baby in the maternal breast has the right to life immediately from God.—Hence there is no man, no human authority, no science, no medical, eugenic, social, economic or moral 'indication' which can establish or grant a valid juridical ground for a direct deliberate disposition of an innocent human life, that is a disposition which looks to its destruction either as an end or as a means to another end perhaps in itself not illicit.—The baby, still not born, is a man in the same degree and for the same reason as the mother" (quoted in Noonan, *The Morality of Abortion,* p. 45).

impermissible. But it cannot seriously be thought to be murder if the mother performs an abortion on herself to save her life. It cannot seriously be said that she *must* refrain, that she *must* sit passively by and wait for her death. Let us look again at the case of you and the violinist. There you are, in bed with the violinist, and the director of the hospital says to you, "It's all most distressing, and I deeply sympathize, but you see this is putting an additional strain on your kidneys, and you'll be dead within the month. But you *have* to stay where you are all the same. Because unplugging you would be directly killing an innocent violinist, and that's murder, and that's impermissible." If anything in the world is true, it is that you do not commit murder, you do not do what is impermissible, if you reach around to your back and unplug yourself from that violinist to save your life.

The main focus of attention in writings on abortion has been on what a third party may or may not do in answer to a request from a woman for an abortion. This is in a way understandable. Things being as they are, there isn't much a woman can safely do to abort herself. So the question asked is what a third party may do, and what the mother may do, if it is mentioned at all, is deduced, almost as an afterthought, from what it is concluded that third parties may do. But it seems to me that to treat the matter in this way is to refuse to grant to the mother that very status of person which is so firmly insisted on for the fetus. For we cannot simply read off what a person may do from what a third party may do. Suppose you find yourself trapped in a tiny

house with a growing child. I mean a very tiny house, and a rapidly growing child—you are already up against the wall of the house and in a few minutes you'll be crushed to death. The child on the other hand won't be crushed to death; if nothing is done to stop him from growing he'll be hurt, but in the end he'll simply burst open the house and walk out a free man. Now I could well understand it if a bystander were to say, "There's nothing we can do for you. We cannot choose between your life and his, we cannot be the ones to decide who is to live, we cannot intervene." But it cannot be concluded that you too can do nothing, that you cannot attack it to save your life. However innocent the child may be, you do not have to wait passively while it crushes you to death. Perhaps a pregnant woman is vaguely felt to have the status of house, to which we don't allow the right of self-defense. But if the woman houses the child, it should be remembered that she is a person who houses it.

I should perhaps stop to say explicitly that I am not claiming that people have a right to do anything whatever to save their lives. I think, rather, that there are drastic limits to the right of self-defense. If someone threatens you with death unless you torture someone else to death, I think you have not the right, even to save your life, to do so. But the case under consideration here is very different. In our case there are only two people involved, one whose life is threatened, and one who threatens it. Both are innocent: the one who is threatened is not threatened because of any fault, the one who threatens does not threaten because of any fault. For this reason we may feel that we bystanders cannot intervene. But the person threatened can.

In sum, a woman surely can defend her life against the threat to it posed by the unborn child, even if doing so involves its death. And this shows not merely that the theses in (1) through (4) are false; it shows also that the extreme view of abortion is false, and so we need not canvass any other possible ways of arriving at it from the argument I mentioned at the outset.

2. The extreme view could of course be weakened to say that while abortion is permissible to save the mother's life, it may not be performed by a third party, but only by the mother herself. But this cannot be right either. For what we have to keep in mind is that the mother and the unborn child are not like two tenants in a small house which has, by an unfortunate mistake, been rented to both: the mother *owns* the house. The fact that she does adds to the offensiveness of deducing that the mother can do nothing from the supposition that third parties can do nothing. But it does more than this: it casts a bright light on the supposition that third parties can do nothing. Certainly it lets us see that a third party who says "I cannot choose between you" is fooling himself if he thinks this is impartiality. If Jones has found and fastened on a certain coat, which he needs to keep him from freezing, but which Smith also needs to keep him from freezing, then it is not impartiality that says "I cannot choose between you" when Smith owns the coat. Women have said again and again "This body is *my* body!" and they have reason to feel angry, reason to

feel that it has been like shouting into the wind. Smith, after all, is hardly likely to bless us if we say to him, "Of course it's your coat, anybody would grant that it is. But no one may choose between you and Jones who is to have it."

We should really ask what it is that says "no one may choose" in the face of the fact that the body that houses the child is the mother's body. It may be simply a failure to appreciate this fact. But it may be something more interesting, namely the sense that one has a right to refuse to lay hands on people, even where it would be just and fair to do so, even where justice seems to require that somebody do so. Thus justice might call for somebody to get Smith's coat back from Jones, and yet you have a right to refuse to be the one to lay hands on Jones, a right to refuse to do physical violence to him. This, I think, must be granted. But then what should be said is not "no one may choose," but only "*I* cannot choose," and indeed not even this, but "'*I* will not *act*," leaving it open that somebody else can or should, and in particular that anyone in a position of authority, with the job of securing people's rights, both can and should. So this is no difficulty. I have not been arguing that any given third party must accede to the mother's request that he perform an abortion to save her life, but only that he may.

I suppose that in some views of human life the mother's body is only on loan to her, the loan not being one which gives her any prior claim to it. One who held this view might well think it impartiality to say "I cannot choose." But I shall simply ignore this possibility. My own view is that if a human being has any just, prior claim to anything at all, he has a just, prior claim to his own body. And perhaps this needn't be argued for here anyway, since, as I mentioned, the arguments against abortion we are looking at do grant that the woman has a right to decide what happens in and to her body.

But although they do grant it, I have tried to show that they do not take seriously what is done in granting it. I suggest the same thing will reappear even more clearly when we turn away from cases in which the mother's life is at stake, and attend, as I propose we now do, to the vastly more common cases in which a woman wants an abortion for some less weighty reason than preserving her own life.

3. Where the mother's life is not at stake, the argument I mentioned at the outset seems to have a much stronger pull. "Everyone has a right to life, so the unborn person has a right to life." And isn't the child's right to life weightier than anything other than the mother's own right to life, which she might put forward as ground for an abortion?

This argument treats the right to life as if it were unproblematic. It is not, and this seems to me to be precisely the source of the mistake.

For we should now, at long last, ask what it comes to, to have a right to life. In some views having a right to life includes having a right to be given at least the bare minimum one needs for continued life. But suppose that what in fact *is* the bare minimum a man needs for continued life is something he has no right at all to be given? If I am sick unto death, and the only thing that will save my life is the touch of Henry Fonda's cool hand on my fevered brow, then all the same, I have no right to be given the touch of Henry Fonda's cool hand on my fevered brow. It would be frightfully nice of him to fly in from the West Coast to provide it. It would be less nice, though no doubt well meant, if my friends flew out to the West Coast and carried Henry Fonda back with them. But I have no right at all against anybody that he should do this for me. Or again, to return to the story I told earlier, the fact that for continued life that violinist needs the continued use of your kidneys does not establish that he has a right to be given the continued use of your kidneys. He certainly has no right against you that *you* should give him continued use of your kidneys. For nobody has any right to use your kidneys unless you give him such a right; and nobody has the right against you that you shall give him this right— if you do allow him to go on using your kidneys, this is a kindness on your part, and not something he can claim from you as his due. Nor has he any right against anybody else that *they* should give him continued use of your kidneys. Certainly he had no right against the Society of Music Lovers that they should plug him into you in the first place. And if you now start to unplug yourself, having learned that you will otherwise have to spend nine years in bed with him, there is nobody in the world who must try to prevent you, in order to see to it that he is given something he has a right to be given.

Some people are rather stricter about the right to life. In their view, it does not include the right to be given anything, but amounts to, and only to, the right not to be killed by anybody. But here a related difficulty arises. If everybody is to refrain from killing that violinist, then everybody must refrain from doing a great many different sorts of things. Everybody must refrain from slitting his throat, everybody must refrain from shooting him—and everybody must refrain from unplugging you from him. But does he have a right against everybody that they shall refrain from unplugging you from him? To refrain from doing this is to allow him to continue to use your kidneys. It could be argued that he has a right against us that *we* should allow him to continue to use your kidneys. That is, while he had no right against us that we should give him the use of your kidneys, it might be argued that he anyway has a right against us that we shall not now intervene and deprive him of the use of your kidneys. I shall come back to third-party interventions later. But certainly the violinist has no right against you that *you* shall allow him to continue to use your kidneys. As I said, if you do allow him to use them, it is a kindness on your part, and not something you owe him.

The difficulty I point to here is not peculiar to the right of life. It reappears in connection with all the other natural rights; and it is something which an adequate account of rights must deal with. For present purposes it is enough just to draw attention to it. But I would stress that I am not arguing that people do not have a right to life—quite to the contrary, it seems to me that the primary

control we must place on the acceptability of an account of rights is that it should turn out in that account to be a truth that all persons have a right to life. I am arguing only that having a right to life does not guarantee having either a right to be given the use of or a right to be allowed continued use of another person's body—even if one needs it for life itself. So the right to life will not serve the opponents of abortion in the very simple and clear way in which they seem to have thought it would.

4. There is another way to bring out the difficulty. In the most ordinary sort of case, to deprive someone of what he has a right to is to treat him unjustly. Suppose a boy and his small brother are jointly given a box of chocolates for Christmas. If the older boy takes the box and refuses to give his brother any of the chocolates, he is unjust to him, for the brother has been given a right to half of them. But suppose that, having learned that otherwise it means nine years in bed with that violinist, you unplug yourself from him. You surely are not being unjust to him, for you gave him no right to use your kidneys, and no one else can have given him any such right. But we have to notice that in unplugging yourself, you are killing him; and violinists, like everybody else, have a right to life, and thus in the view we were considering just now, the right not to be killed. So here you do what he supposedly has a right you shall not do, but you do not act unjustly to him in doing it.

The emendation which may be made at this point is this: the right to life consists not in the right not to be killed, but rather in the right not to be killed unjustly. This runs a risk of circularity, but never mind: it would enable us to square the fact that the violinist has a right to life with the fact that you do not act unjustly toward him in unplugging yourself, thereby killing him. For if you do not kill him unjustly, you do not violate his right to life, and so it is no wonder you do him no injustice.

But if this emendation is accepted, the gap in the argument against abortion stares us plainly in the face: it is by no means enough to show that the fetus is a person, and to remind us that all persons have a right to life— we need to be shown also that killing the fetus violates its right to life, i.e., that abortion is unjust killing. And is it?

I suppose we may take it as a datum that in a case of pregnancy due to rape the mother has not given the unborn person a right to the use of her body for food and shelter. Indeed, in what pregnancy should it be supposed that the mother has given the unborn person such a right? It is not as if there were unborn persons drifting about the world, to whom a woman who wants a child says "I invite you in."

But it might be argued that there are other ways one can have acquired a right to the use of another person's body than by having been invited to use it by that person. Suppose a woman voluntarily indulges in intercourse, knowing of the chance it will issue in pregnancy, and then she does become pregnant; is she not in part responsible for the presence, in fact the very existence, of the unborn person inside? No doubt she did not invite it in. But doesn't her partial responsibility for its being there itself

give it a right to the use of her body?*
If so, then her aborting it would be more like the boy's taking away the chocolates, and less like your unplugging yourself from the violinist— doing so would be depriving it of what it does have a right to, and thus would be doing it an injustice.

And then, too, it might be asked whether or not she can kill it even to save her own life: If she voluntarily called it into existence, how can she now kill it, even in self-defense?

The first thing to be said about this is that it is something new. Opponents of abortion have been so concerned to make out the independence of the fetus, in order to establish that it has a right to life, just as its mother does, that they have tended to overlook the possible support they might gain from making out that the fetus is *dependent* on the mother, in order to establish that she has a special kind of responsibility for it, a responsibility that gives it rights against her which are not possessed by any independent person—such as an ailing violinist who is a stranger to her.

On the other hand, this argument would give the unborn person a right to its mother's body only if her pregnancy resulted from a voluntary act, undertaken in full knowledge of the chance a pregnancy might result from it. It would leave out entirely the unborn person whose existence is due to rape. Pending the availability of some further argument, then, we would be left with the conclusion that unborn persons whose existence is due to rape have no right to the use

*The need for a discussion of this argument was brought home to me by members of the Society for Ethical and Legal Philosophy, to whom this paper was originally presented.

of their mothers' bodies, and thus that aborting them is not depriving them of anything they have a right to and hence is not unjust killing.

And we should also notice that it is not at all plain that this argument really does go even as far as it purports to. For there are cases and cases, and the details make a difference. If the room is stuffy, and I therefore open a window to air it, and a burglar climbs in, it would be absurd to say, "Ah, now he can stay, she's given him a right to the use of her house—for she is partially responsible for his presence there, having voluntarily done what enabled him to get in, in full knowledge that there are such things as burglars, and that burglars burgle." It would be still more absurd to say this if I had had bars installed outside my windows, precisely to prevent burglars from getting in, and a burglar got in only because of a defect in the bars. It remains equally absurd if we imagine it is not a burglar who climbs in, but an innocent person who blunders or falls in. Again, suppose it were like this: people-seeds drift about in the air like pollen, and if you open your windows, one may drift in and take root in your carpets or upholstery. You don't want children, so you fix up your windows with fine mesh screens, the very best you can buy. As can happen, however, and on very, very rare occasions does happen, one of the screens is defective; and a seed drifts in and takes root. Does the personplant who now develops have a right to the use of your house? Surely not—despite the fact that you voluntarily opened your windows, you knowingly kept carpets and upholstered furniture, and you knew that screens were some-

times defective. Someone may argue that you are responsible for its rooting, that it does have a right to your house, because after all you *could* have lived out your life with bare floors and furniture, or with sealed windows and doors. But this won't do—for by the same token anyone can avoid a pregnancy due to rape by having a hysterectomy, or anyway by never leaving home without a (reliable!) army.

It seems to me that the argument we are looking at can establish at most that there are *some* cases in which the unborn person has a right to the use of its mother's body, and therefore *some* cases in which abortion is unjust killing. There is room for much discussion and argument as to precisely which, if any. But I think we should sidestep this issue and leave it open, for at any rate the argument certainly does not establish that all abortion is unjust killing.

5. There is room for yet another argument here, however. We surely must all grant that there may be cases in which it would be morally indecent to detach a person from your body at the cost of his life. Suppose you learn that what the violinist needs is not nine years of your life, but only one hour: all you need do to save his life is spend one hour in that bed with him. Suppose also that letting him use your kidneys for that one hour would not affect your health in the slightest. Admittedly you were kidnapped. Admittedly you did not give anyone permission to plug him into you. Nevertheless it seems to me plain you *ought* to allow him to use your kidneys for that hour—it would be indecent to refuse.

Again, suppose pregnancy lasted

only an hour, and constituted no threat to life or death. And suppose that a woman becomes pregnant as a result of rape. Admittedly she did not voluntarily do anything to bring about the existence of a child. Admittedly she did nothing at all which would give the unborn person a right to the use of her body. All the same it might well be said, as in the newly emended violinist story, that she *ought* to allow it to remain for that hour—that it would be indecent in her to refuse.

Now some people are inclined to use the term "right" in such a way that it follows from the fact that you ought to allow a person to use your body for the hour he needs, that he has a right to use your body for the hour that he needs, even though he has not been given that right by any person or act. They may say that it follows also that if you refuse, you act unjustly toward him. This use of the term is perhaps so common that it cannot be called wrong; nevertheless it seems to me to be an unfortunate loosening of what we would do better to keep a tight rein on. Suppose that box of chocolates I mentioned earlier had not been given to both boys jointly, but was given only to the older boy. There he sits, stolidly eating his way through the box, his small brother watching enviously. Here we are likely to say "You ought not to be so mean. You ought to give your brother some of those chocolates." My own view is that it just does not follow from the truth of this that the brother has any right to any of the chocolates. If the boy refuses to give his brother any, he is greedy, stingy, callous—but not unjust. I suppose that the people I have in mind will say

it does follow that the brother has a right to some of the chocolates, and thus that the boy does act unjustly if he refuses to give his brother any. But the effect of saying this is to obscure what we should keep distinct, namely the difference between the boy's refusal in this case and the boy's refusal in the earlier case, in which the box was given to both boys jointly, and in which the small brother thus had what was from any point of view clear title to half.

A further objection to so using the term "right" that from the fact that A ought to do a thing for B, it follows that B has a right against A that A do it for him, is that it is going to make the question of whether or not a man has a right to a thing turn on how easy it is to provide him with it; and this seems not merely unfortunate, but morally unacceptable. Take the case of Henry Fonda again. I said earlier that I had no right to the touch of his cool hand on my fevered brow, even though I needed it to save my life. I said it would be frightfully nice of him to fly in from the West Coast to provide me with it, but that I had no right against him that he should do so. But suppose he isn't on the West Coast. Suppose he has only to walk across the room, place a hand briefly on my brow—and lo, my life is saved. Then surely he ought to do it, it would be indecent to refuse. Is it to be said, "Ah, well, it follows that in this case she has a right to the touch of his hand on her brow, and so it would be an unjustice in him to refuse"? So that I have a right to it when it is easy for him to provide it, though no right when it's hard? It's rather a shocking idea that anyone's rights should fade away and disappear as it gets harder and harder to accord them to him.

So my own view is that even though you ought to let the violinist use your kidneys for the one hour he needs, we should not conclude that he has a right to do so—we should say that if you refuse, you are, like the boy who owns all the chocolates and will give none away, self-centered and callous, indecent in fact, but not unjust. And similarly, that even supposing a case in which a woman pregnant due to rape ought to allow the unborn person to use her body for the hour he needs, we should not conclude that he has a right to do so; we should conclude that she is self-centered, callous, indecent, but not unjust, if she refuses. The complaints are no less grave; they are just different. However, there is no need to insist on this point. If anyone does wish to deduce "he has a right" from "you ought," then all the same he must surely grant that there are cases in which it is not morally required of you that you allow that violinist to use your kidneys, and in which he does not have a right to use them, and in which you do not do him an injustice if you refuse. And so also for mother and unborn child. Except in such cases as the unborn person has a right to demand it—and we were leaving open the possibility that there may be such cases—nobody is morally *required* to make large sacrifices, of health, of all other interests and concerns, of all other duties and commitments, for nine years, or even for nine months, in order to keep another person alive.

6. We have in fact to distinguish between two kinds of Samaritan: the Good Samaritan and what we might call the Minimally Decent Samaritan.

The story of the Good Samaritan, you will remember, goes like this:

A certain man went down from Jerusalem to Jericho, and fell among thieves, which stripped him of his raiment, and wounded him, and departed, leaving him half dead.

And by chance there came down a certain priest that way; and when he saw him, he passed by on the other side.

And likewise a Levite, when he was at the place, came and looked on him, and passed by on the other side.

But a certain Samaritan, as he journeyed, came where he was; and when he saw him he had compassion on him.

And went to him, and bound up his wounds, pouring in oil and wine, and set him on his own beast, and brought him to an inn, and took care of him.

And on the morrow, when he departed, he took out two pence, and gave them to the host, and said unto him, "Take care of him; and whatsoever thou spendest more, when I come again, I will repay thee."   (Luke 10:30–35)

The Good Samaritan went out of his way, at some cost to himself, to help one in need of it. We are not told what the options were, that is, whether or not the priest and the Levite could have helped by doing less than the Good Samaritan did, but assuming they could have, then the fact they did nothing at all shows they were not even Minimally Decent Samaritans, not because they were not Samaritans, but because they were not even minimally decent.

These things are a matter of degree, of course, but there is a difference, and it comes out perhaps most clearly in the story of Kitty Genovese, who, as you will remember, was murdered while thirty-eight people watched or listened, and did nothing at all to help her. A Good Samaritan would have rushed out to give direct assistance against the murderer. Or perhaps we had better allow that it would have been a Splendid Samaritan who did this, on the ground that it would have involved a risk of death for himself. But the thirty-eight not only did not do this, they did not even trouble to pick up a phone to call the police. Minimally Decent Samaritanism would call for doing at least that, and their not having done it was monstrous.

After telling the story of the Good Samaritan, Jesus said, "Go, and do thou likewise." Perhaps he meant that we are morally required to act as the Good Samaritan did. Perhaps he was urging people to do more than is morally required of them. At all events it seems plain that it was not morally required of any of the thirty-eight that he rush out to give direct assistance at the risk of his own life, and that it is not morally required of anyone that he give long stretches of his life—nine years or nine months—to sustaining the life of a person who has no special right (we were leaving open the possibility of this) to demand it.

Indeed, with one rather striking class of exceptions, no one in any country in the world is *legally* required to do anywhere near as much as this for anyone else. The class of exceptions is obvious. My main concern here is not the state of the law in respect to abortion, but it is worth drawing attention to the fact that in no state in this country is any man compelled by law to be even a Minimally Decent Samaritan to any person; there is no law under which charges could be brought against the thirty-eight who stood by while Kitty Genovese died. By contrast, in most states in this country women are compelled by law to be not merely Minimally Decent Samaritans, but Good Samaritans to unborn persons inside them. This doesn't by itself settle anything one way or the other, because it may well be argued that there should be laws in this country—as there·are in many European countries—compelling at least Minimally Decent Samaritanism.* But it does show that there is a gross injustice in the existing state of the law. And it shows also that the groups currently working against liberalization of abortion laws, in fact working toward having it declared unconstitutional for a state to permit abortion, had better start working for the adoption of Good Samaritan laws generally, or earn the charge that they are acting in bad faith.

I should think, myself, that Minimally Decent Samaritan laws would be one thing, Good Samaritan laws quite another, and in fact highly improper. But we are not here concerned with the law. What we should ask is not whether anybody should be compelled by law to be a Good Samaritan, but whether we must accede to a situation in which somebody is being compelled—by nature, perhaps—to be a Good Samaritan. We have, in other words, to look now at third-party interventions. I have been arguing that no person is morally required to make large sacrifices

---

*For a discussion of the difficulties involved, and a survey of the European experience with such laws, see *The Good Samaritan and the Law,* ed. James M. Ratcliffe (New York, 1966).

to sustain the life of another who has no right to demand them, and this even where the sacrifices do not include life itself; we are not morally required to be Good Samaritans or anyway Very Good Samaritans to one another. But what if a man cannot extricate himself from such a situation? What if he appeals to us to extricate him? It seems to me plain that there are cases in which we can, cases in which a Good Samaritan would extricate him. There you are, you were kidnapped, and nine years in bed with that violinist lie ahead of you. You have your own life to lead. You are sorry, but you simply cannot see giving up so much of your life to the sustaining of his. You cannot extricate yourself, and ask us to do so. I should have thought that—in light of his having no right to the use of your body—it was obvious that we do not have to accede to your being forced to give up so much. We can do what you ask. There is no injustice to the violinist in our doing so.

7. Following the lead of the opponents of abortion, I have throughout been speaking of the fetus merely as a person, and what I have been asking is whether or not the argument we began with, which proceeds only from the fetus' being a person, really does establish its conclusion. I have argued that it does not.

But of course there are arguments and arguments, and it may be said that I have simply fastened on the wrong one. It may be said that what is important is not merely the fact that the fetus is a person, but that it is a person for whom the woman has a special kind of responsibility issuing from the fact that she is its mother. And it might be argued that all my analogies are therefore irrelevant— for you do not have that special kind of responsibility for that violinist, Henry Fonda does not have that special kind of responsibility for me. And our attention might be drawn to the fact that men and women both *are* compelled by law to provide support for their children.

I have in effect dealt (briefly) with this argument in section 4 above; but a (still briefer) recapitulation now may be in order. Surely we do not have any such "special responsibility" for a person unless we have assumed it, explicitly or implicitly. If a set of parents do not try to prevent pregnancy, do not obtain an abortion, but rather take it home with them, then they have assumed responsibility for it, they have given it rights, and they cannot *now* withdraw support from it at the cost of its life because they now find it difficult to go on providing for it. But if they have taken all reasonable precautions against having a child, they do not simply by virtue of their biological relationship to the child who comes into existence have a special responsibility for it. They may wish to assume responsibility for it, or they may not wish to. And I am suggesting that if assuming responsibility for it would require large sacrifices, then they may refuse. A Good Samaritan would not refuse—or anyway, a Splendid Samaritan, if the sacrifices that had to be made were enormous. But then so would a Good Samaritan assume responsibility for that violinist; so would Henry Fonda, if he is a Good Samaritan, fly in from the West Coast and assume responsibility for me.

8. My argument will be found unsatisfactory on two counts by many

of those who want to regard abortion as morally permissible. First, while I do argue that abortion is not impermissible, I do not argue that it is always permissible. There may well be cases in which carrying the child to term requires only Minimally Decent Samaritanism of the mother, and this is a standard we must not fall below. I am inclined to think it a merit of my account precisely that it does *not* give a general yes or a general no. It allows for and supports our sense that, for example, a sick and desperately frightened fourteen-year-old schoolgirl, pregnant due to rape, may of *course* choose abortion, and that any law which rules this out is an insane law. And it also allows for and supports our sense that in other cases resort to abortion is even positively indecent. It would be indecent in the woman to request an abortion, and indecent in a doctor to perform it, if she is in her seventh month, and wants the abortion just to avoid the nuisance of postponing a trip abroad. The very fact that the arguments I have been drawing attention to treat all cases of abortion, or even all cases of abortion in which the mother's life is not at stake, as morally on a par ought to have made them suspect at the outset.

Secondly, while I am arguing for the permissibility of abortion in some cases, I am not arguing for the right to secure the death of the unborn child. It is easy to confuse these two things in that up to a certain point in the life of the fetus it is not able to survive outside the mother's body; hence removing it from her body guarantees its death. But they are importantly different. I have argued that you are not morally required to spend nine months in bed, sustaining the life of that violinist; but to say this is by no means to say that if, when you unplug yourself, there is a miracle and he survives, you then have a right to turn around and slit his throat. You may detach yourself even if this costs him his life; you have no right to be guaranteed his death, by some other means, if unplugging yourself does not kill him. There are some people who will feel dissatisfied by this feature of my argument. A woman may be utterly devastated by the thought of a child, a bit of herself, put out for adoption and never seen or heard of again. She may therefore want not merely that the child be detached from her, but more, that it die. Some opponents of abortion are inclined to regard this as beneath contempt—thereby showing insensitivity to what is surely a powerful source of despair. All the same, I agree that the desire for the child's death is not one which anybody may gratify, should it turn out to be possible to detach the child alive.

At this place, however, it should be remembered that we have only been pretending throughout that the fetus is a human being from the moment of conception. A very early abortion is surely not the killing of a person, and so is not dealt with by anything I have said here.

READING

ZAHN/ A Religious Pacifist Looks at Abortion

Although author Gordon C. Zahn is sympathetic with many of the objectives of the women's liberation movement, he strongly opposes abortion on demand. He takes his stand by applying the concept of human rights to the fetus. Zahn insists that the fetus has a right to life at the moment of conception. To willingly and directly violate this right is immoral.

Do you think that Zahn has adequately refuted Thomson's insistence that a woman's right to privacy can supersede the fetus's right to life? Do you see any points on which Thomson and Zahn agree? Could Fletcher's situational approach be used to justify Zahn's position?

Prudence, if nothing else, would seem to dictate that a celibate male, especially one committed to pacifism, should avoid getting embroiled in controversy with the women's liberation crowd. Ordinarily I would be all set to go along with this and not only for reasons of such prudential restraint. I am in general agreement with the movement's objectives and principles and more than ready to give it the benefit of almost every doubt—even though I do wish at times that its principal spokesmen (?) could be a little more, if not "lady-like," at least gentlemanly in their rhetoric and tone. But these are minor reservations.

There is one point of substance, however, on which I must register strong disagreement, and that is the increasing emphasis being placed on "free abortion on demand" as a principal plank in the liberationists' platform. From my perspective as a religious pacifist, I find this proposal thoroughly abhorrent, and I am disturbed by the willingness of so many who share my political and theological approach in most respects to go along with or condone a practice which so clearly contradicts the values upon which that approach is based.

In the past I have criticized "establishment" Christians, in particular official Catholic ecclesiastical and theological spokesmen, for their hypersensitivity to the evil of killing the unborn and their almost total disregard of the evil of "post-natal" abortion in the form of the wholesale destruction of human life in war. The argument works both ways and with equal force: those of us who oppose war cannot be any less concerned about the destruction of human life in the womb.

From Gordon C. Zahn, "A Religious Pacifist Looks at Abortion," *Commonweal,* 28 May 1971. Reprinted by permission of Commonweal Publishing Co., Inc.

In discussing this issue from a pacifist standpoint I do not intend to enter upon two controversies which, though clearly related to the problem of abortion, are somewhat peripheral to my essential concern for life and the reverence for life. Thus, the whole question of the morality of contraception, obviously one of the alternatives to abortion as a means of population control, involves moral principles of an altogether different order. More closely related but also excluded from consideration here is the legal question, that is whether or not anti-abortion legislation now on the statute books should be repealed, modified, or retained. One can argue, as I shall here, that abortion is immoral and still recognize compelling practical and theoretical reasons for not using state authority to impose a moral judgment that falls so far short of universal acceptance within the political community. On the other hand, there are equally compelling arguments upholding legal prohibition of what has long been considered by many to be a form of murder; and this takes on added force to the extent that repeal of laws already in effect will be interpreted as official authorization of the hitherto forbidden practice. Since the intention here is to discuss the objections to abortion itself, this very important legal question will be left for others to debate and resolve.

Nor will I comment upon what I consider the tactical blunder on the part of the liberationists to "borrow trouble" by making so touchy an issue—on emotional as well as moral grounds—a central part of their program. I must, however, reject the rationale that is usually advanced to support their demands, the "property rights" line which holds that because a woman's body is "her own," she and she alone must be left free to decide what is to be done about the developing fetus. Leaving aside the obvious fact that the presence of the fetus suggests a decision that could have been made earlier, this line of argument represents a crude reversion to the model of *laissez-faire* economics Catholics of a liberal or radical persuasion have long since repudiated. Even if one were to accept the characterization of a woman's body as "property" (is it not one of the liberationists' complaints that men and man-made laws have reduced her to that status?), the claim to absolute rights of use and disposal of that property could not be taken seriously. The owner of a badly needed residential building is not, or at least *should not be,* free to evict his tenants to suit a selfish whim or to convert his property to some frivolous or non-essential use. In such a case we would insist upon the traditional distinction which describes property as private in ownership but social in use.

To use another example, the moral evil associated with prostitution does not lie solely, perhaps not even primarily, in the illicit sex relationship but, rather, in the degradation of a person to precisely this status of a "property" available for "use" on a rental or purchase basis. It is a tragic irony that the advocates of true and full personhood for women have chosen to provide ideological justification for attitudes which have interfered with recognition of that personhood in the past.

This is not to say, of course, that a woman does not have prior rights over her own body but only that the exercise of those rights must take into account the rights of others. In monogamous marriage this would preclude a wife's "freedom" to commit adultery (a principle, it should be unnecessary to add, which applies to the husband as well). Similarly, in the case of a pregnancy in wedlock, the husband's rights concerning the unborn child must be respected too; indeed, even in pregnancy out of wedlock, the putative father retains parental rights to the extent that he is ready to assume his share of responsibility for the child's future needs. In both cases, and this is the crux of the argument, of course, the rights of the unborn child, perhaps the most important claimant of all, must be respected and protected.

HUMAN RIGHTS

These categories of rights, I insist, are not to be put in any "property rights" or similar economic frame of reference. They represent elementary human rights arising out of an intimacy of union between responsible persons which transcends purely utilitarian or proprietary considerations. The governing consideration as far as the unborn child is concerned is simply this: when do these rights come into existence? The answer offered here, and I think it is the only answer compatible with a pacifist commitment, is that they exist at the moment of conception marking the beginning of the individual's life process.

This has nothing to do with the old theological arguments over whether or not the soul can be said to be present at conception; it rests completely upon the determination of whether or not there is now something "living" in the sense that, given no induced or spontaneous interferences, it will develop into a human person. We know for certain that this fertilized ovum is not going to develop into a dog or cat or anything else: whatever its present or intervening states, it will at the end emerge as a human child. One need only consider the usual reaction to a spontaneous or accidental termination of a *wanted* pregnancy. The sorrow of the prospective parents, a sorrow shared by friends and relatives alike, testifies not only to the fact that something has "died" but, also, that this "something" was human.

So, too, with the medical arguments over when the fetus becomes "viable" and, therefore, eligible for birth. It is the life that is present, not the organism, which should concern us most. Once we agree that society's origin and purpose lie in the fulfillment of human capacities and needs, we have established the basis for a reverence for life which goes far beyond such purely technical determination. Should a life once begun be terminated (whether before or after the point of viability) because the prospective mother did not have adequate food and care or because she was forced by the demands of her social or economic condition to undergo excessive physical or psychological strain, we would have no problem about charging society with a failure to meet its responsibility. There is no reason to change this judgment when the termination is brought about by deliberate act, either to avoid some personal inconvenience or to serve what may be rationalized into the "greater good" of the family unit or, as the eugenicist might put it, society as a whole. Just as rights begin with the beginning of the life process, so does society's obligation to protect them.

Recently a new and somewhat terrifying "viability" test has been proposed in arguments supporting abortion. No longer is it to be the stage of physiological development which determines whether or not life is to be terminated but rather the degree to which "personhood" has emerged or developed. Although strict logic might suggest that personhood can be established only after the fetus has entered upon its extra-uterine existence (that is, after the child has been born), advocates of this new test are apparently willing to extend it back into the later weeks of pre-natal development as well.

Two objections to this test should be immediately obvious. In the first place (and the "generous allowance" of pre-natal personhood serves as a good illustration of this point), we are caught up with the same old problems of judgment that plagued the older viability standards: if the fetus is to be considered viable at x-weeks, what about the day before that period is completed? If personhood can be manifested in the pre-natal period when, let us say, fetuses can be compared in terms of differential activity, what about the hour before such differences can be noticed? Is more activity a sign that personhood is advanced, or might the absence of much activity be a sign of equal, though different, emergence of personhood?

The second objection is even more troubling. Under the old notion of physiological viability, the child once born was unquestionably viable. The same may not be true—or may not remain so in the face of changing social definitions—once the emergence or development of personhood is the measure. My experience as a conscientious objector in World War II doing alternate service in a home for mental deficients introduced me to literally hundreds of individuals whose state of retardation was such that they could be described as "animals" or even "vegetables" by members of the institutional staff. Later, working in a hospital for mental diseases, I attended paretic and senile patients who had reached the state of regression and psychological deterioration at which the same terms could be applied to them and their behavior. However ardent and sincere the disclaimers may be, applying the test of personhood to the unborn is certain to open the way to pressures to apply that same test to the already born. In this sense, then, abortion and euthanasia are ideological twins.

In the old theological formulations of the problem, the condemnation of abortion was justified in terms of the "sanctity" or the "intrinsic worth" of human life. Today much of the argument supporting abortion rests upon similar abstractions applied now to the intrinsic worth of the prospective mother's life or of siblings whose living standards and life-chances might be threatened by the additional pregnancy. These are valid concerns and deserve serious and sympathetic understanding, and society does have a responsibility to find answers to these problems that do not involve the sacrifice of the human life that has begun. Pacifism and opposition to abortion converge here, for both find their ultimate justification in the Christian obligation to revere human life and its potential and to respect all of the rights associated with it.

The developmental model used by those who propose emergence of personhood as the test is basically sound, but as used by the advocates of abortion it becomes a logical enormity arguing for a development from an undefined or unstipulated beginning. A more consistent approach would see human life as a continuity from the point of clinically determined conception to the point of clinically determined death. This physiological lifespan is then convertible to an existential framework as a developmental pattern of dependence relationships: at the earliest stages of a pregnancy the dependence is total; as the fetus develops, it takes on some of its own functions; at birth, its bodily functions are physiologically independent, but existential dependency is still the child's dominant condition. The rest of the pattern is obvious enough. As the individual matures and achieves the fullness of personhood, both functional and behavioral independence become dominant (though never total; culture and its demands must be taken into account). Finally, advanced age and physical decline returns him to a state of dependency which may, at the end, approximate that of his earliest childhood.

Society's responsibilities to the individual stand in inverse relationship to the growth and decline of his independence and autonomy. It would follow, then, that the immorality of abortion (and euthanasia as well) lies precisely in the fact that they propose to terminate the life process when the dependency is most total, that it would do so with the approval or authorization of society, that it would seek to justify this betrayal of society's responsibility on purely pragmatic grounds. The various claims made for the social utility of abortion (reducing the threat of over-population and now pollution; sparing the already disadvantaged family the strain of providing for yet another mouth, etc.) or the even less impressive justifications in terms of personal and all too often selfish benefits to the prospective parent(s) have to be put in this context; and once they are, they lose much of their force.

The earlier reference to the sorrow caused by the loss through miscarriage of a wanted child does not obscure the fact that most abortion proposals are concerned with preventing the birth of unwanted children. No one will deny that being regarded as an unwanted intruder in the family circle will be psychologically if not always physically harmful, but there should be other solutions to this problem than "sparing" the intruder this unpleasantness by denying him life in the first place. If a child is "unwanted" before conception, science has provided sufficient means for avoiding the beginning of the life process.

Since the sexual enlightenment burst upon us a generation or so ago, we have replaced the old Victorian notions about "the mystery of sex" with a kind of mechanistic assumption that man is the helpless victim of his chemistry and unconscious impulses, an assumption which reduces sexual intercourse to a direct, natural, and almost compulsive response to stimuli and situations. The other side of this particular coin is the not so hidden danger that man himself will be redefined in strictly biological terms, a largely accidental event brought into being by the union of two adult organisms acting in response to that irresistible urge. This is reflected in many of the statements made by advocates of abortion in their references to the conceived child as a "fertilized ovum." The term is perfectly accurate in the strictly physiological sense; in the Christian perspective, however, it leaves something to be desired.

The act of intercourse, like any other human act, is and must remain subject to human responsibility. This means that those who enter upon it should consider the possible consequences of the act and acknowledge responsibility for those consequences if and when they come to pass. Ideally this would mean that unwanted children would not be conceived; where the ideal is not achieved—or where the participants change their minds after the child is conceived—it will be society's obligations to assume the responsibility for the new life that has been brought into being.

Unwanted pregnancies resulting from a freely willed and voluntary act of sexual intercourse are one thing; those resulting from rape require special consideration. Even here, I would hold, the reverence for life which forms the basis of this pac-ifist rejection of abortion would preclude the intentional termination of the life process begun under such tragic circumstances. The apparent harshness of this position may be mitigated somewhat by reflecting that pregnancies attributable to true rape (or incest) represent a small proportion of the unwanted. Certainly they do not constitute a large enough proportion to justify the emphasis placed upon them by proponents of abortion. This provides small consolation to the victim who has already undergone the physically and psychologically traumatic experience of the assault itself and must still suffer the consequences of an act for which she bears no active responsibility. Nevertheless, the life that has begun is a human life and must be accorded the same rights and protection associated with the life resulting from normal and legitimate conceptions. Here again society must do what it can to provide all possible assistance to the victim including compensation (if one can speak of "compensation" in this context) for the sacrifice she has been called upon to make. In most cases we must assume the mother will not want to keep the child after birth, at which point society's responsibility for its future development will become complete. If a mother does decide to keep the child, society will still have the obligation to make some continuing provision for adequate care and support.

The position I have outlined here has been described as unrealistic and even irresponsible in that it absolutizes the right of every "fertilized ovum" to develop, as one critic put it, "in a planet which can no longer support that kind of reproduction and where it threatens the possibility of realizing the lives which exist." The adjectives unrealistic and irresponsible do not trouble me; they are fairly standard descriptions of the pacifist approach, and this is a pacifist case against abortion. What does trouble me is the rest of the criticism. The ability or inability of the planet to support present and projected population totals is still a contested issue, and even if the prospects were as desperate as the statement suggests, the question would still remain as to whether the termination of unborn life is a desirable or acceptable solution. And as for the "realization" of the life which exists, it is essential to face the prior question of who is to determine what that involves and by what standards. How long, we must ask, before the quotas now being set in terms of "zero population growth" and similar *quantitative* formulae are refined by eugenic selectionists into *qualitative* quotas instead? This is not an idle fear, and one would think that a movement dedicated to the elimination of long-standing inequalities based on the qualitative distinction of sex should be particularly sensitive to the possibility.

Beyond this there is that matter of "absolutizing" the right to life, and to this I am ready to plead guilty. At a time when moral absolutes of any kind are suspect and the fashions in theological and ethical discourse seem to have moved from situationalism to relativism and now to something approximating indifferentism, it strikes me as not only proper but imperative that we proclaim the value of every human life as well as the obligation to respect that life wherever it exists—if not for what it is at any given moment (a newly fertilized ovum; a convicted criminal; the habitual sinner) at least for what it may yet, with God's grace, become.

It is not just a matter of consistency; in a very real sense it is the choice between integrity and hypocrisy. No one who publicly mourns the senseless burning of a napalmed child should be indifferent to the intentional killing of a living fetus in the womb. By the same token, the Catholic, be he bishop or layman, who somehow finds it possible to maintain an olympian silence in the face of government policies which contemplate the destruction of human life on a massive scale, has no right to issue indignant protests when the same basic disregard for human life is given expression in government policies permitting or encouraging abortion.

7

PRIVACY
of sealed lips and court orders
ACT AND SINGLE RULE
NONCONSEQUENTIALISM

During the Charles Manson murder trial in 1971, authorities obtained a written statement from a potential witness, Virginia Graham, that was a confession by defendant Susan Atkins implicating Manson and revealing plans of the so-called Manson family to murder several show business figures in bizarre ways. Transcripts of the confession went to each attorney and to the judge, Charles Older. No other transcripts were released. Yet a few days later a reporter for the *Los Angeles Herald Examiner*, William Farr, reported sources as saying that members of the Manson family had compiled a list of show business personalities who were marked for murder.

Judge Older said that the story violated the gag rule on trial participants, and he demanded the sources of Farr's story. Reporter Farr said that his sources were two attorneys, but he refused to divulge their names. Older thereupon gave Farr an open-ended jail sentence, forty-six days of which Farr served in 1973 before being freed by U.S. Supreme Court Justice William O. Douglas pending appeal. In August 1975 a U.S. court of appeals upheld Older's ruling but not his open-ended sentence. In its decision, the court said that a newsperson's right to disclose sources was secondary to a defendant's right to a fair trial. The case now seems destined for a Supreme Court ruling.

Farr's is a provocative legal case. The question of constitutional rights, privileges, and their relative priorities is a gummy one. But the Farr case also raises a curious moral question involving duties and obligations. Did Farr have a moral obligation not to disclose the names of his informants if a guaranteed anonymity led them to divulge the information? If he did, just how far did this obligation extend? Did it end short of his going to jail? If in keeping the promise of anonymity to his informants he was unable to meet other obligations, did his promise-keeping obligation cease? You might also wonder whether any promise of secrecy to Farr's informants was nullified when Farr was informed by Judge Older that he was not privileged by the First Amendment to keep such a promise. Perhaps Farr could reason that the conditions under which he made the promise were actually not operative, and therefore he had no obligation to keep it.

Obviously there is a cluster of questions we could raise. But one point is clear: no matter how much good he could produce for himself or everyone else concerned, Farr at least partially believed that he had an overriding duty to keep his sources secret. Clearly, then, Farr's stand in part appears based on a non-consequential attitude toward morality.

In ethics, nonconsequentialism is often termed *deontology*. *Deontology is the ethical doctrine that denies that an action or rule's consequences are the only criterion for determining the morality of an action.* Deontologists insist that some things are right or wrong, not because they produce a certain ratio of good to evil but because of the nature of the action itself.

For example, some nonconsequentialists might argue that lying, breaking promises, or killing is wrong in itself and not only because it may produce undesirable consequences. Just why are these actions or any other actions wrong? That's what this chapter is about.

We shall see that in answering this question, nonconsequentialists generally divide into act and rule positions. Under rule nonconsequentialism we shall restrict the discussion to two theories that propose single rules as standards of moral behavior: the divine command theory and Immanuel Kant's categorical imperative. At the end of the chapter we will expand the discussion to show how cases like Bill Farr's foreshadow an issue of growing importance in today's society—personal privacy.

NONCONSEQUENTIAL THEORIES

Whereas consequential normative positions argue that we should consider only consequences in evaluating an action, nonconsequential theories maintain that we should consider other factors as well. In some cases nonconsequentialists even contend that we should not consider the consequences at all.

For example, some nonconsequentialists may insist that adultery is wrong because the law of God forbids it. Others may argue that cheating on your income tax is wrong because a federal law forbids it. The point is that nonconsequentialists deny that the rightness or wrongness of an action depends solely on the comparative ratio of good to evil that the action produces. Thus, nonconsequentialists could believe that telling the truth is always right, no matter how undesirable the consequences. Like consequentialism, nonconsequentialism generally takes two forms—act and rule.

ACT NONCONSEQUENTIAL THEORIES

Act nonconsequential theories usually maintain that there are no rules or guidelines to govern ethical behavior, that we must evaluate each act as it comes along and determine its rightness or wrongness. Thus, in one context lying may be bad, but in another it may be good; it all depends on the situation. Act nonconsequentialists insist that blanket statements about acts are impossible.

In its extreme form, act nonconsequentialism contends that we can never formulate any rules or guidelines at all, that each situation is fundamentally different from any other; therefore, each situation must be evaluated as a unique ethical dilemma. Of course, extreme act nonconsequentialism would not introduce an action's consequences in determining its morality.

In ancient times Aristotle seems to have espoused this view, and in the eighteenth century Joseph Butler did. Butler advocated that persons about to embark on an ethical course should ask themselves whether the proposed action will be right or wrong. He concluded that the decisions they make would be the right ones, providing they are "fair minded."*

A more moderate act nonconsequential position maintains that general principles or rules of thumb can develop from particular situations and then be used as a basis for making subsequent decisions. This presumes, of course, that recurring situations are sufficiently similar to a prior one to allow application of a rule. For example, let's say that you have determined that the last time you lied to a trusted friend you did the wrong thing. The next time a sufficiently similar situation arises, you have grounds to suspect that it is wrong to lie again. In no case, however, do even moderate act nonconsequentialists claim that a rule would or should override a particular judgment regarding what a person ought to do. In other words, not even a moderate act nonconsequentialist would say never lie. As you might expect, there are a number of weaknesses in the act nonconsequential position.

OBJECTIONS TO ACT NONCONSEQUENTIAL THEORIES

1. *Act nonconsequentialism provides no ethical direction.* To help us draw out some of the weaknesses in the act nonconsequential position, let's meet Rita Swan, television journalist, wife, and mother of two children under five years of age.

Like Bill Farr, Rita Swan faces the dilemma of whether to reveal to a court the source she used for exposing corruption in the public works department of her city, a source to whom she promised anonymity, or to remain silent and thus jeopardize her own and her family's welfare. Complicating her problem is a promise that she and her husband Al made to each other that whenever either of them is faced with a professional decision that directly affects the well-being of the family, the other partner's view shall prevail. In this case Al believes that Rita should reveal her source; Rita disagrees.

Rita Swan must make a decision. In choosing she must break one of her promises. What should she do?

---

*Joseph Butler, *Five Sermons* (New York: Liberal Arts Press, 1949), p. 45.

Let's consider what help extreme act nonconsequentialism can provide. By definition it can provide none. Rita must consider this situation unique and resolve it accordingly. Extreme act nonconsequentialism, it seems, can't even provide general principles, such as "Always keep a promise" or "There's no obligation to keep a promise that was made in the absence of circumstances that you could not reasonably be expected to anticipate and which void the promise." In such cases we're left to rely on our intuition, feelings, and inclinations to determine the right thing to do. In short, extreme act nonconsequentialism seems to leave us in a state of ethical limbo, not unlike being in Bakersfield, California, on a Saturday night. Act nonconsequentialism extremists argue that the situation should guide the ethical choice. But this appears to be begging the question, for the situation can only provide data and facts which crystallize the choices. The problem nevertheless persists: which option to choose?

2. *Act nonconsequentialism makes feelings the guide to moral decisions.* Unfortunately, modified act nonconsequentialism does not provide much more help. Granted the Swan case is not unique, but it is uncommon enough to make rule-of-thumb formulation difficult. Even if Rita has some general rules to apply, according to act nonconsequentialists she arrived at them on the basis of intuition or decisions she had made in the past. However, the way you feel about a certain situation seems insufficient reason for claiming that what you do is moral, unless what you feel is right is actually right. If you maintain that feelings determine moral standards, then you could reasonably argue that Adolf Hitler acted morally in executing six million Jews because he *felt* that it was the right thing to do. But surely this is a questionable claim.

The problem, it seems, can be summed up in this way: where consequentialists wish to consider consequences exclusively, act nonconsequentialists apparently wish to ignore them entirely and at the same time provide no direction for moral behavior. Both positions seem to be untenable and limited pictures of moral action.

3. *Act nonconsequentialism precludes the formulation of necessary general ethical rules.* Finally, act nonconsequentialists' claim that no two situations are the same and that it is therefore impossible to generalize moral behavior deserves examination, for it seems like a questionable claim. True, no two actions may be the same, but the issue is whether they are sufficiently similar to allow moral generalization.

For example, suppose Rita Swan asks you what to do and you tell her to protect her source. Five minutes later she asks you again, and this time you tell her to reveal her source. Assuming that nothing more than the ticking of a clock has occurred during the intervening minutes, should you not respond as you did the first time since the situations are sufficiently similar to warrant the same response? When Rita asks you why you changed your mind and you reply that the decision you just made bears no connection to the one you made five minutes earlier, it seems she will rightly consider your logic as well as your ethics strange, or certainly inconsistent.

In short, when act nonconsequentialism chooses to ignore similarities between past and present, it relinquishes a most potent tool in inductive reasoning, the analogy. Thus, when someone reasons, "I won't buy another car from Honest Sam the used car man because the last one I bought was a lemon," the person reasons analogically. If there are enough similarities between the instances and few significant differences, then the analogy is sound. Analogical reasoning is one of the most useful methods we have for maintaining some measure of control over our lives. In ethics, surely when we attribute goodness or badness to an action, we should attribute it to another action that is similar in all relevant respects.

These objections to act nonconsequentialism have led many to adopt a rule nonconsequential position. Let's consider it.

RULE NONCONSEQUENTIAL THEORIES

According to rule nonconsequentialism there exists one or more rules to serve as moral standards. For example, some might hold that you should always tell the truth. No matter how good the consequences might be that result from lying, some rule nonconsequentialists might say that to violate the rule of truth-telling is always wrong. Unlike moderate act nonconsequentialism, though, rule nonconsequentialism would maintain that these rules are not derived from particular examples or actions but from the nature of the actions themselves.

Like their consequentialist counterpart, rule nonconsequentialists divide into two groups: those that espouse one rule and those that espouse more than one. For the time being we will consider just single rules, namely the divine command theory and Immanuel Kant's categorical imperative.

Divine Command Theory

An example of a single rule nonconsequential theory is the rule that says we should always do the will of God. This theory has been termed the *divine command theory,* or *theological voluntarism.* Whatever the situation, the theory goes, if we do what God wills, then we do the right thing; if we do not do what God wills, then no matter what the consequences, we do wrong.

To understand the divine command theory better, it is helpful to see what kinds of thinkers the theory excludes. First, the theory would exclude those who believe that we should obey God's law because by so doing we will promote our own or the general good, or be faithful to some virtuous principles. Perhaps by being obedient to God's law we do accomplish these ends, but those espousing the divine command theory do not justify their actions on any other basis than that God wills a particular action.

Second, the divine command theory excludes those who defend the morality of an action on the basis of some supernatural reward promised to the faithful and denied others. True, maybe the faithful will be rewarded and behaving righteously is in their best long-term interests. But theological voluntarists would not justify moral actions on these egoistic grounds. Having defined divine command theory and seen two groups of thinkers it excludes, we will now raise some objections to it.

Objections to the Divine Command Theory

1. *We do not know what God has commanded.* One obvious question that arises with theological voluntarism is how we know what God has commanded. Frequently voluntarists point to a holy book or scripture as evidence. The Ten Commandments is the likely source for Jews and Christians. Yet we are still left wondering how we know that scriptures represent the inspired word of God. Some would say because it says so in the scriptures. But this is circular reasoning. After all, how do we know that there is a God at all? And if there is, can we be sure that he or she expressed himself or herself in one source and not in another? So, the claim that we know what God has commanded appears questionable.

2. *The divine command theory cannot satisfactorily explain why God commands something.* An even stickier objection is whether God commands something because it is right or whether something is right because God commands it. If God commands something because it is right, then the divine command theory collapses because it contends that something is right *because* God commands it. If something is right because God commands it, then anything God commands must be right. Should God command cruelty, then it seems it would be right—a difficult proposition to accept. Voluntarists often argue that it would contradict God's benevolent nature to do what is patently evil. But this raises other problems. One of them was raised long ago by the ancient Greek philosopher Epicurus: "Is God willing to prevent evil, but not able? Then is he impotent. Is he able, but not willing? Then is he malevolent. Is he both able and willing? Whence then is evil?"

3. *Divine laws are difficult to apply.* There is, finally, the practical problem of applying divine laws. Take, for example, the Swan case. What divine law should Rita Swan follow? Perhaps the most relevant one here is the one that enjoins us not to bear false witness. Presumably if we promise to do something and then break that promise, we have in effect borne false witness. But even assuming that this law applies and not some other, perhaps from another divine scripture, how do we know which promissory obligation takes precedence for Swan? Some would answer with one popular expression of the divine command—the golden rule.

The golden rule commands us to treat others the way we would want to be treated. If you want to be treated fairly, treat others fairly; if you want to be loved, love others. The core of this principle is impartiality, the doctrine that you should never make an exception of yourself. Do not do to others what you are unwilling to have them do to you. Given our Judeo-Christian background, this ethical rule is perhaps the one that is most familiar to us. Let's see if the golden rule eases Rita Swan's dilemma.

> **Rita:** Look, Al, for a minute put yourself in my informant's shoes. What if I had promised you that no matter what happened—*no matter what*—your identity would remain anonymous.

Al: So?

Rita: So, would you want me to break my promise?

Al: Are you saying that because I wouldn't want to be treated that way, that I shouldn't want your informant treated that way?

Rita: Exactly.

Al: But how do you know he feels the same way?

Rita: What difference does that make?

Al: Plenty of difference. What if he reasons, "I don't mind if somebody lies to me, so I guess it's all right for me to lie to them."

One problem with the golden rule, which Al suggests, is that it does not seem specific enough. It does not account for different desires. As George Bernard Shaw put it, "Don't do unto others as you would have them do to you—their tastes might be different."

To illustrate, suppose a car thief reasons, "I can steal as many cars as I want, since I allow anyone who wants to, to steal my beat-up car." Surely the golden rule cannot sanction such behavior; perhaps this is too narrow an application of it. More accurately, the golden rule prescribes that if we have something of value that we would not want taken, then we should not take something that someone else values, whatever it is. Still problems persist.

Suppose the same thief is perfectly willing to do as he would be done by. In other words, because he has no reservations about stealing, he is perfectly willing to help others steal in return. Certainly the golden rule cannot condone that conduct; yet by itself it seems powerless to discriminate the good action from the bad. The golden rule seems to say that if something is good for you to do, it is good for everyone else to do; if bad for you, then it is bad for everyone else. But it is not telling what is good or bad.

Another problem with the golden rule is that what is good or bad for someone else is not always good or bad for you. Suppose that you decide that it is wrong for the couple next door to get divorced. Are you then committed to believe that it is wrong for you to get divorced? It is possible that your circumstances are different. Perhaps the other couple have children, but you do not; perhaps they have had a trial separation, but you have not; perhaps they are involved in extramarital affairs, but you are not. It seems, then, that to be useful the golden rule must imply that what is wrong for others is wrong for us, providing the circumstances are sufficiently similar. But then we must decide when circumstances are sufficiently similar.

Philosophers have not been indifferent to these objections to the golden rule and to the divine command theory generally. In the eighteenth century philosopher Immanuel Kant (1724–1804) attempted to remedy these weaknesses by formulating another single rule nonconsequential position called the *categorical imperative*.

Kant's Categorical Imperative

To understand Kant's thought it helps to note the emphasis he placed on the idea of a good will. Kant believed that nothing was good in itself except a good will.

Intelligence, judgment, sensitivity, all facets of the human personality are, perhaps, good and desirable, but only if the will is good that makes use of them. *By will, Kant meant the uniquely human capacity to act according to the concept of laws, that is, principles.* Kant saw these laws or principles operating in nature. A good will, therefore, is one that acts in accordance with nature's laws.

In estimating the total worth of our actions, Kant believed that a good will takes precedence over all else. Contained in a good will is the concept of duty. Only when we act from duty does our action have moral worth. When we act only out of feelings or inclinations, our actions, though otherwise identical with the ones that spring from a sense of duty, have no true moral worth.

To illustrate, merchants have a duty not to shortchange their customers. But simply because they do not shortchange their customers does not mean that they are acting from a good will. They may be acting from an inclination to promote business or to avoid legal entanglement; thus, they are acting in accordance with a duty but not *from* duty. In other words, their actions may be in keeping with duty, but they have not willed the action from a sense of duty to be fair and honest. So, for Kant, actions have true moral worth only when they spring from a recognition of a duty and a choice to implement it.

For example, suppose that you were deeply troubled, your mind so clouded with sorrow that you in no way felt like being kind or loving to anyone. If you owned a dog, you'd snap at it. In the midst of this misery, suppose you came across a beggar in the street. Without any inclination, but only from a sense of duty to help the less fortunate, you give the beggar a quarter. This action, it seems, would have true moral worth, for it sprang from a sense of duty. When you so act, said Kant, you act out of love: "The beneficence from duty, when no inclination impels it and even when it is opposed by a natural and unconquerable aversion, is practical love." This love resides in the will.

When we act from duty we act in accordance with reason. Humans, noted Kant, are rational creatures, and the moral law—whatever it may be—will be applicable to all rational creatures. Kant believed that reason must be universal, that is, if we all followed reason correctly, we would arrive at the same conclusion; he required this element of universality in a moral theory.

But still we are left wondering what duties we should follow and how we know them. Kant believed that through reason alone we could arrive at a moral law not based on any divine command or empirical evidence relating to similar situations or consequences. Just as we know seemingly through reason alone that a square has four sides and that no square is a circle, so by the same kind of reasoning we can come to absolute moral truths.

For Kant, an absolute moral truth had to be logically consistent; it had to be free of internal contradiction. To say, for example, that a square has three sides or that a square is circular is to state a logical contradiction. Kant aimed to ensure that his absolute moral law would be free of such contradictions. If he could formulate such a rule, he reasoned, it would oblige everyone without exception to follow it. Kant believed that he formulated such a logically consistent rule in his categorical imperative.

The Categorical Imperative Kant believed that there was just one command or imperative that was categorical, that is, one which presented an action as of itself necessary, without regard to any other end. He believed that from this one categorical imperative, this universalizable command, we could derive all commands of duty. Simply stated, *Kant's categorical imperative says that we should act in such a way that we could wish the maxim of our action to become a universal law.*

By *maxim* Kant seems to mean the subjective principle of action, the principle that people formulate in determining their conduct. For example, suppose you make a promise but are willing to break it if it suits your purposes. Your maxim can be expressed, "I'll make promises that I'll break whenever keeping them no longer suits my purposes." This is the subjective principle that directs your action. Kant insisted that we could wish the maxim of our action to become a universal law. Could your maxim about promises be universally acted upon?

The maxim "I'll make promises that I'll break whenever keeping them no longer suits my purposes" could not be universally acted upon because it involves a contradiction of will. You are willing that it be possible to make promises and have them honored. But if everyone intended to break promises when they desired to, then promises could not be honored in the first place. In other words, part of the nature of a promise is that it be believed; a law that allowed promise breaking would contradict the very nature of a promise.

Note that Kant is not a consequentialist. He is not arguing that the consequences of a universal law condoning promise breaking would be bad and therefore the rule is bad. Instead he is claiming that the rule is self-contradictory, that it is self-defeating, that the institution of promise making would necessarily dissolve upon universalizing such a maxim. A closer look at the promise-keeping example and Kant's categorical imperative reveals the three conditions that Kant considered necessary for a rule of conduct to be a moral rule.

Kant's Three Conditions for a Moral Rule To be a moral rule, the rule of conduct must first be consistently universalizable, for Kant's moral rule prescribes categorically, not hypothetically. A hypothetical prescription tells us what we should do *if* we desire certain consequences. Thus: "*If* we wish people to think well of us, we should keep promises." The goodness of promise keeping in these hypothetical prescriptions depends on consequences. But Kant's imperative is *categorical,* that is, *it commands regardless of consequences.* A categorical imperative takes the form "Do this" or "Don't do that," no ifs, ands, or buts. Such a command must be universalizable, for if it were not, then its worth would be determined on empirical grounds, that is, hypothetical ones. Put another way, if a person did not follow a moral rule simply because it could become a universal law of moral conduct, the person would allow empirical conditions to determine whether to follow a rule. The rule would thereby lose its inherent necessity and universality.

Second, Kant also believed that for a rule of conduct to be a moral rule, humans would treat each other as ends in themselves and not just means to ends if they followed it. Here we see shades of the golden rule. Kant believed that humans as rational beings would be inconsistent if they did not treat everyone else the way that they wanted to be treated. And since, according to Kant, rational beings recognize their own inner worth, they would never wish to be used as entities possessing relative worth, as means to ends.

Finally, Kant argues that for a rule of conduct to be a moral rule it must allow persons who are universally legislating it to impose it upon themselves. Thus, in the case of racist legislation, where the lawmakers do not bind themselves by the rules that they legislate, then the rule has no moral import.

It is true that in making his case for promise keeping and related moral issues, Immanuel Kant is logically persuasive. But his categorical imperative doctrine is not without flaws. There are a number of objections to it, but two are major ones.

Objections to Kant's Categorical Imperative

1. *Duties frequently conflict.* Unquestionably, logical difficulty arises with Kant's prescriptions when rules conflict. If it is wrong to break a promise, then what do we do when promises conflict? Rita Swan must make such a decision.

> **Al:** You know, Rita, I'm sure you don't intend this, but it seems to me that you're thinking only about your duty to your informant.
> **Rita:** And not about you and the children?
> **Al:** Yes.
> **Rita:** You know better than to think that, Al. Why do you think this is such a terrible decision to make? If I weren't thinking about you so much, I could decide much more easily.
> **Al:** Well, obviously there's a conflict between two obligations: one to your family and one to your informant.
> **Rita:** The problem is which takes precedence?
> **Al:** For me, it's clearly your family. And for you?

How helpful is Kant's categorical imperative in settling conflicts like these? Rita would perform either action from a sense of duty, so she would have a good will in either case. In cases of promise keeping, Kant apparently believed that we should never break a promise. But in this case such an obligation is impossible to meet, for no matter how she acts Rita will break a promise.

It is possible to argue that she should never have made the promise to her informant. But at the same time she probably thought she could keep her promise, as Bill Farr apparently did. It is possible to argue that she made the promise to the informant under the rule "You must always keep your promises except when by keeping them you will seriously hurt, injure, or be unable to help someone else." But Kant does not argue this way. He insists that there are no circumstances under which you can break a promise. But if this is so, then how does Rita handle the promise that she has made to her family? This problem raises another objection.

2. *There is no compelling reason that the prohibition against certain actions should hold without exception.* Frequently critics of Kant seriously question or indeed reject his principle of universalizability. They wonder why the prohibition against actions like lying, promise breaking, killing, and similar actions must function without exception. They charge that Kant failed to distinguish between saying that *a person should make no exceptions to a rule* and that *the rule itself has no exceptions.*

The statement that a person should make no exceptions to a rule simply means that one should never exclude oneself from a rule's application. Thus, if killing is wrong, it is wrong for me as well as for you. To say that "Killing is wrong, except when I do it" would not be universalizable, for then killing would be right for all to do. But because no one may make of oneself an exception to a rule, it does not follow that the rule itself has no exceptions.

Suppose, for example, we decide that killing is sometimes right, perhaps in self-defense. Thus, the rule becomes "Never kill except in self-defense." Perhaps this rule could be refined, but the point remains: this rule is just as universalizable as "Don't kill." The phrase *except in self-defense* can be viewed not as an exception to the rule but as a qualification of it. Thus, critics of Kant ask why a qualified rule isn't just as good as an unqualified one. Recognizing this, we no longer need state rules in the simple, direct, unqualified manner that Kant did.

So, the apparent problem with Kant's system is the rigidity of the rules that he deduces. There just are no exceptions to them once they have qualified under the categorical imperative. A more realistic approach, it seems, would be to replace absolute rules (ones that allow no exceptions) with a series of rules, duty to which depends on their relative importance in relation to other relevant rules. This, of course, would entail a rule nonconsequentialism based on more than a single rule. Just such an approach has been taken in the twentieth century by English philosopher David Ross. We leave Ross and his thinking for the next chapter.

SUMMARY

Nonconsequential Rule

Act: There are no rules or guidelines to govern ethical behavior; we must evaluate each act as it comes along and determine its rightness or wrongness.

Rule: There exists one or more rules to serve as moral standards.

Objections

1. Act nonconsequentialism provides no ethical direction.

2. Act nonconsequentialism makes feelings the guide to moral decisions.

3. Act nonconsequentialism precludes the formulation of necessary general ethical rules.

a. *Divine command theory:* acting in such a way that your action squares with the laws of God	**1.** We do not know what God has commanded.
	2. The divine command cannot satisfactorily explain why God commands something.
	3. Divine laws are difficult to apply.
b. *Kant's categorical imperative:* acting in such a way that you could wish the maxim of your action to become a universal law	**1.** Duties frequently conflict.
	2. There is no compelling reason that the prohibition against certain actions should hold without exception.

CONCLUSIONS

Nonconsequential normative positions, in recognizing the problems with consequentialism, make a needed contribution to ethical thought. Especially noteworthy is Immanuel Kant's emphasis on good will, the intention behind the action.

Whereas consequentialists ignore will and intention entirely in evaluating the morality of an action, Kant rightly introduces it. We say "rightly" because it seems extremely reasonable to introduce one's intention in determining the morality of an action, because morality deals with what one ought to do. What one ought to do implies that one has a choice, and choice is inseparable from intention.

Introducing will into moral evaluation also seems reasonable because of the historical consensus that underpins this attitude. In evaluating each other's actions, humans have invariably weighed one another's motives. Thus, we say of people, "Well, their heart was in the right place," or "They meant well anyway." In effect we seem naturally inclined to introduce one's intentions when evaluating the moral worth of persons and their behavior. Yet nonconsequential theory is far from unassailable.

First we must wonder if all nonconsequential positions have not thrown out the proverbial baby with the bath water. Although the morality of an action may depend on more than its consequences, it nevertheless seems that the consequences must be considered. Entirely disregarding them seems as indefensibly extremist as considering them exclusively.

This criticism seems particularly applicable to act nonconsequentialism, which allows for no rules or only vague rules of thumb. Without introducing consequences and having no rules to go by, it is difficult to imagine on what bases other than feelings and intuition we can determine a moral act, which are indeed vague standards.

Single rule nonconsequentialism, on the other hand, does provide a norm, as with the divine command theory or Kant's categorical imperative. But particular application of either of these presents problems, especially in ranking the relative importance of conflicting rules. But by far the biggest problem with nonconsequential positions is that they ignore the consequences of actions.

Ignoring consequences of actions can make for a very rigid and inflexible moral system, especially as it is proposed in single rule deontology. It is one thing to say always do unto others as you would have them do unto you, or always act so that the maxim of your action could become a universal law. But it is quite another thing to live with the consequences of actions based on those rules.

For Rita Swan or Bill Farr, or for you or me, it may be little consolation to know that we have been true to our principles if by so doing we have produced much pain, heartache, and suffering for ourselves and others. This does not mean, of course, that we are not right in "sticking to our guns." It simply means that in sticking to our guns, our guns necessarily stick to us. We still must live with the consequences of what we do.

In the last analysis what ought Rita do? It's hard to say. What she will do, though, will greatly depend on how much she emphasizes the principle of privacy, for this is essential to the issue here. By the principle of privacy we mean the right not to be watched, listened to, or reported upon without permission, and not to have public attention focused upon one uninvited. Central to Rita's belief that she must not break her promise is the conviction that there exists between her as a journalist and her informant a unique relationship that can only survive in a context of confidentiality and privacy, without which a free press is logically impossible. And without a free press there can be no free society. Her justification, curiously, seems to carry distinct Kantian overtones in its reliance on logical consistency.

We should note also that the privacy issue is hardly confined to situations like the Farr or Swan cases. Today we are faced not only with governmental intrusions into our professional lives but into our personal lives as well. The profusion of electronic gadgetry has spawned a great number of snooping devices and techniques that can literally make true the adage "The walls have ears." In many cases where these devices have been used to obtain incriminating evidence, the courts have clearly ruled whether they were used legally. But whether legal or not, their use raises moral questions.

Are you and I, simply because we are human beings, entitled to privacy? If you say yes, you will probably regard an invasion of privacy as not only illegal but immoral, because it undermines the dignity of the human being. Whatever your position, it is clear from recent events that the issue of individual privacy versus governmental intrusion will intensify.

EXERCISES FOR ANALYSIS

EXERCISE 1

Below are four cases that demand some kind of moral resolution. How would you resolve them? Make sure you compose adequate justification for your position. Also note the consequential and nonconsequential factors in each case and in your resolution.

1. One day Father Dreiser, a Catholic priest, listens to the confession of a man who confesses to committing the recent rash of murders in the parish. Dreiser recognizes the man's voice as that of the church custodian. After the man leaves, Dreiser agonizes over a decision. Should he report what he's learned to the authorities and thus prevent other murders? Or is he bound by a holy oath not to reveal what he has heard in a confessional?

2. Mr. and Mrs. Fredericks have an understanding with their son, Mitch. In essence, Mitch's room is his castle. It is off limits to any uninvited guests, especially his parents. In return, Mitch promises to keep his room neat and clean. Recently, though, Mr. and Mrs. Fredericks have become concerned about the widespread use of drugs at Mitch's school. In fact, some of his best friends are rumored to be using drugs. One Friday night while Mitch is out, Mr. Fredericks suggests that in the interest of their son, he and his wife take a look at Mitch's room. Mrs. Fredericks objects, saying that such behavior would be a breach of their agreement.

3. A U.S. president considers having the White House fitted with listening and recording devices. The purpose is strictly to keep a historical record, since it is important for future generations to have records of presidential decisions that are as accurate as possible. Because the president doesn't want to inhibit free expression, the people will not be told that they're being recorded. The president wonders whether installing these devices is entirely moral.

(Would the law have a material bearing on the president's decision?)

4. Sylvia Potter is a college librarian. One day a police official comes to the library wanting some information relating to a car theft. It seems that the night before authorities discovered an abandoned stolen vehicle, on the back seat of which they found a college library book. The owner of the car denies any knowledge of how the book got there. The police official asks Ms. Potter the name of the person who last withdrew the book from the college library. On the one hand, she wishes to help the authorities; she even feels a duty to. On the other hand, she regards such information as confidential. "After all," she tells the police official, "if you were having domestic problems and withdrew a book on that subject, would you want that information made public?" The police official informs Potter that if he must he can obtain a court order to force her to comply. What should she do?

EXERCISE 2

Concerning the privacy issue, one scholar has written:

> Is there a principle of privacy that extends immunity to inquiry to all human activities, to be overridden only by special considerations? . . . Or is it rather that there is a general freedom to inquire, observe, and report on human affairs, as on other things, unless a special case can be made for denying it with respect to certain activities that are *specifically* private?*

The following are condensed general arguments for the principle of privacy and for the general freedom of inquiry. Determine whether the justification in each argument is adequate. Look for Kantian elements in the arguments.

Arguments for the Principle of Privacy

1. An integral part of being a human being is entering into relationships with other humans. The existence of these relationships depends not only on satisfying the mechanics of role expectancy, but on the personal understanding between the people involved, on how they care about one another. The only way that this necessarily qualitative element in some relationships can be established is through privacy. This is so because some relationships can only survive with care and attention, necessitating continuous adjustment as the personalities involved change. None of this can be accomplished in the light of public exposure. So, since privacy is necessary to the concept and function of personal relationships, then the principle of privacy must be respected.

2. Certainly in any society, because an individual has social responsibilities, there are times when the public good must take precedence over individual rights. But at the same time, the doctine of public good, however it is defined, is not absolute in the sense that it should never be subordinate to other considerations. On the contrary, we must recognize that only where the requirements of their social lives leave them great breadth for individual expression, creativity, and development can human beings function in an atmosphere compatible with their nature. Because privacy is necessary to allow individuals a wide variety of choice in the way they live, the principle of privacy must be respected.

3. Surely an intrinsic part of being a human is to be self-governing, in the sense that we can make the fateful decisions that affect our lives. In other words, all other things being equal, an individual would rather choose what to think, do, and say than to be coerced. This personal autonomy is something we are inclined to by nature and should aim for in social institutions. But this individual right and social ideal cannot flourish in an atmosphere in which individuals must be guarded for fear of being monitored and observed. Thus, because privacy is

---

*Stanley I. Benn, "Privacy," in *Nomos*, ed. J. Roland Pennock and John W. Chapman (New York: Atherton Press, 1971), 13:4.

necessary to the concept and functioning of personal autonomy, the principle of privacy must be respected.

Arguments for the General Freedom of Inquiry

1. Individuals must face what is perhaps a harsh fact of life: no man is an island. Today perhaps more than at any other time, we have become painfully aware that, for better or worse, all our lives are interdependent. As a result, we have become impressed with a fact of human nature: everything a human is and does has significance for society at large. Clearly, then, the social significance of our actions and reactions overrides any other concern. The only way to ensure that individuals meet their social responsibilities is to emphasize and respect the general freedom of inquiry.

2. Too great an emphasis on personal privacy invariably becomes a defense mechanism for the protection of antisocial behavior. This is so because enthusiasm for personal privacy rests on an individualistic conception of society. But this conception is opposed to what society is by nature: a union of persons with similar ethnic, racial, cultural, religious, and political interests. Undue stress on personal privacy, rooted as it is in an individualistic conception of society, gravely damages the nature of society by fostering an "every man for himself" attitude. So, because it is necessary for the proper functioning of society to check antisocial behavior, the general freedom of inquiry must be respected.

SELECTIONS FOR FURTHER READING

Single Rule Nonconsequentialism

Brunner, E. *The Divine Imperative*. London: Hutchinson, 1950.

Kant, Immanuel. *Critique of Practical Reason and Other Writings in Moral Philosophy*. Edited and translated by Lewis W. Beck. Chicago: University of Chicago Press, 1949.

Korner, S. *Kant*. Baltimore: Penguin, 1950.

Niebuhr, Reinhold. *An Interpretation of Christian Ethics*. New York: Harper, 1935.

Prichard, H. A. *Moral Obligations*. Oxford: Clarendon Press, 1949.

Ramsey, Paul. *Basis Christian Ethics*. New York: Scribner's, 1950.

Singer, Marcus G. *Generalization in Ethics: An Essay in the Logic of Ethics with the Rudiments of a System of Moral Philosophy*. New York: Atheneum, 1961.

Privacy

Halmos, Paul. *Solitude and Privacy*. Westport, Conn.: Greenwood, 1953.

Laing, R. D. *The Divided Self*. New York: Pantheon, 1969.

Naismith, Grace. *Private and Personal.* New York: McKay, 1966.

Pennock, J. Roland, and Chapman, John W., eds. *Privacy.* New York: Lieber-Atherton, 1971.

Wasserstrom, Richard. *Morality and Law.* Belmont, Calif.: Wadsworth, 1970.

Westin, Alan. *Privacy and Freedom.* New York: Atheneum, 1967.

THE CALDWELL DECISION/*Opinion of the Court by Mr. Justice White*

On 29 June 1972, the U.S. Supreme Court ruled that a grand jury could compel
newspersons to reveal their sources of information. The closeness of the decision, five
to four, indicates its controversial nature.

The case was prompted by three newspersons, Earl Caldwell, Paul Branzburg,
and Paul Pappas, each of whom contended that in order to gather news it was necessary
to agree not to identify sources of information, or to be selective in publishing facts,
or both. Caldwell and Branzburg, on investigative assignments, had won the
confidence of leaders in the black activist organization known as the Black Panthers,
about which they later wrote. When officials asked the reporters to identify Black
Panther members, they refused on grounds of confidential privilege. Similarly,
Branzburg refused to identify two young men who, believing they would remain
unidentified, agreed to be filmed making hashish from marijuana.

In the portions of the Court's opinion that follow, authored by Justice White,
note that the confidentiality privilege is viewed strictly in the context of public safety.
In other words, the purpose of the privilege is the furtherance of protection of public
interest. When it does not serve that purpose, it cannot and should not be honored.
White's position, then, seems utilitarian in the sense that the applicability of the
privilege depends exclusively on its advancing the public good and not on its necessity
to the existence of a free, unfettered press.

Do you think White justifies his opinion? Does he successfully refute the objection
that confidentiality is necessary for the press to collect and disseminate news freely?

The issue in these cases is whether requiring newsmen to appear and testify before state or federal grand juries abridges the freedom of speech and press guaranteed by the First Amendment. We hold that it does not. . . .

Petitioners Branzburg and Pappas and respondent Caldwell press First Amendment claims that may be simply put: that to gather news it is often necessary to agree either not to identify the source of information published or to publish only part of the facts revealed, or both; that if the reporter is nevertheless forced to reveal these confidences to a grand jury, the source so identified and other confidential sources of other reporters will be measurably deterred from furnishing publishable information, all to the detriment of the free flow of information protected by the First Amendment. Although petitioners do not claim an absolute privilege

Abridged from Branzburg v. Hayes, 408 U.S. 665.

against official interrogation in all circumstances, they assert that the reporter should not be forced either to appear or to testify before a grand jury or at trial until and unless sufficient grounds are shown for believing that the reporter possesses information relevant to a crime the grand jury is investigating, that the information the reporter has is unavailable from other sources, and that the need for the information is sufficiently compelling to override the claimed invasion of First Amendment interests occasioned by the disclosure. Principally relied upon are prior cases emphasizing the importance of the First Amendment guarantees to individual development and to our system of representative government, decisions requiring that official action with adverse impact on First Amendment rights be justified by a public interest that is "compelling" or "paramount," and those precedents establishing the principle that justifiable governmental goals may not be achieved by unduly broad means having an unnecessary impact on protected rights of speech, press, or association. The heart of the claim is that the burden on newsgathering resulting from compelling reporters to disclose confidential information outweighs any public interest in obtaining the information. . . .

A number of states have provided newsmen a statutory privilege of varying breadth, but the majority have not done so, and none has been provided by federal statute. Until now the only testimonial privilege for unofficial witnesses that is rooted in the federal Constitution is the Fifth Amendment privilege against compelled self-incrimination. We are asked to create another by interpreting the First Amendment to grant newsmen a testimonial privilege that other citizens do not enjoy. This we decline to do. Fair and effective law enforcement aimed at providing security for the person and property of the individual is a fundamental function of government, and the grand jury plays an important, constitutionally mandated role in this process. On the records now before us, we perceive no basis for holding that the public interest in law enforcement and in ensuring effective grand jury proceedings is insufficient to override the consequential, but uncertain, burden on newsgathering which is said to result from insisting that reporters, like other citizens, respond to relevant questions put to them in the course of a valid grand jury investigation or criminal trial. . . .

The preference for anonymity of those confidential informants involved in actual criminal conduct is presumably a product of their desire to escape criminal prosecution, and this preference, while understandable, is hardly deserving of constitutional protection. It would be frivolous to assert—and no one does in these cases—that the First Amendment, in the interest of securing news or otherwise, confers a license on either the reporter or his news sources to violate otherwise valid criminal laws. Although stealing documents or private wiretapping could provide newsworthy information, neither reporter nor source is immune from conviction for such conduct, whatever the impact on the flow of news. Neither is immune, on First Amendment grounds, from testifying against the other, before the grand jury or at a criminal trial. The Amendment does not reach so far as to override the interest of the public in ensuring that neither reporter nor source is invading the rights of other citizens through reprehensible conduct forbidden to all other persons. To assert the contrary proposition

is to answer it, since it involves in its very statement the contention that the freedom of the press is a freedom to do wrong with impunity, and implies the right to frustrate and defeat the discharge of those governmental duties upon the performance of which the freedom of all, including that of the press, depends. . . . It suffices to say that, however complete is the right of the press to state public things and discuss them, that right, as every other right enjoyed in human society, is subject to the restraints which separate right from wrong-doing. *Toledo Newspaper Co.* v. *United States*, 1918.

Thus, we cannot seriously entertain the notion that the First Amendment protects a newsman's agreement to conceal the criminal conduct of his source, or evidence thereof, on the theory that it is better to write about crime than to do something about it. Insofar as any reporter in these cases undertook not to reveal or testify about the crime he witnessed, his claim of privilege under the First Amendment presents no substantial question. The crimes of news sources are no less reprehensible and threatening to the public interest when witnessed by a reporter than when they are not.

There remain those situations where a source is not engaged in criminal conduct but has information suggesting illegal conduct by others. Newsmen frequently receive infor-

mation from such sources pursuant to a tacit or express agreement to withhold the source's name and suppress any information that the source wishes not published. Such informants presumably desire anonymity in order to avoid being entangled as a witness in a criminal trial or grand jury investigation. They may fear that disclosure will threaten their job security or personal safety or that it will simply result in dishonor or embarrassment.

The argument that the flow of news will be diminished by compelling reporters to aid the grand jury in a criminal investigation is not irrational, nor are the records before us silent on the matter. But we remain unclear how often and to what extent informers are actually deterred from furnishing information when newsmen are forced to testify before a grand jury. The available data indicate that some newsmen rely a great deal on confidential sources and that some informants are particularly sensitive to the threat of exposure and may be silenced if it is held by this Court that, ordinarily, newsmen must testify pursuant to subpoenas, but the evidence fails to demonstrate that there would be significant constriction of the flow of news to the public if this Court reaffirms the prior common law and constitutional rule regarding the testimonial obligations of newsmen. Estimates of the inhibiting effect of such subpoenas on the willingness of informants to make disclosures to newsmen are widely divergent and to a great extent speculative. It would be difficult to canvass the views of the informants themselves; surveys of reporters on this topic are chiefly opinions of predicted informant behavior and must be viewed in the light of the professional self-interest of the interviewees.

Reliance by the press on confidential informants does not mean that all such sources will in fact dry up because of the later possible appearance of the newsman before a grand jury. The reporter may never be called and if he objects to testifying, the prosecution may not insist. Also, the relationship of many informants to the press is a symbiotic one which is unlikely to be greatly inhibited by the threat of subpoena: quite often, such informants are members of a minority political or cultural group which relies heavily on the media to propagate its views, publicize its aims, and magnify its exposure to the public. Moreover, grand juries characteristically conduct secret proceedings, and law enforcement officers are themselves experienced in dealing with informers and have their own methods for protecting them without interference with the effective administration of justice. There is little before us indicating that informants whose interest in avoiding exposure is that it may threaten job security, personal safety, or peace of mind, would in fact be in a worse position, or would think they would be, if they risked placing their trust in public officials as well as reporters. We doubt if the informer who prefers anonymity but is sincerely interested in furnishing evidence of crime will always or very often be deterred by the prospect of dealing with those public authorities characteristically charged with the duty to protect the public interest as well as his.

Accepting the fact, however, that an undetermined number of infor-

mants not themselves implicated in crime will nevertheless, for whatever reason, refuse to talk to newsmen if they fear identification by a reporter in an official investigation, we cannot accept the argument that the public interest in possible future news about crime from undisclosed, unverified sources must take precedence over the public interest in pursuing and prosecuting those crimes reported to the press by informants and in thus deterring the commission of such crimes in the future.

We note first that the privilege claimed is that of the reporter, not the informant, and that if the authorities independently identify the informant, neither his own reluctance to testify nor the objection of the newsman would shield him from grand jury inquiry, whatever the impact on the flow of news or on his future usefulness as a secret source of information. More important, it is obvious that agreements to conceal information relevant to commission of crime have very little to recommend them from the standpoint of public policy. Historically, the common law recognized a duty to raise the "hue and cry" and report felonies to the authorities. Misprision of a felony—that is, the concealment of a felony "which a man knows but never assented to . . . [so as to become] either principal or accessory" [4 Blackstone, *Commentaries*] was often said to be a common law crime. The first Congress passed a statute which is still in effect, defining a federal crime of misprision:

Whoever, having knowledge of the actual commission of a felony cognizable by a court of the United States, conceals and does not as soon as possible make known the same to some judge or other person in civil or military authority under the United States shall be [guilty of misprision]. . . .

Neither are we now convinced that a virtually impenetrable constitutional shield, beyond legislative or judicial control, should be forged to protect a private system of informers operated by the press to report on criminal conduct, a system that would be unaccountable to the public, would pose a threat to the citizen's justifiable expectations of privacy, and would equally protect well-intentioned informants and those who for pay or otherwise betray their trust to their employer or associates. The public through its elected and appointed law enforcement officers regularly utilizes informers, and in proper circumstances may assert a privilege against disclosing the identity of these informers. But

The purpose of the privilege is the furtherance and protection of the public interest in effective law enforcement. The privilege recognizes the obligation of citizens to communicate their knowledge of the commission of crimes to law-enforcement officials and, by preserving their anonymity, encourages them to perform that obligation. [*Roviaro* v. *United States*, 1957.] . . .

We are admonished that refusal to provide a First Amendment reporter's privilege will undermine the freedom of the press to collect and disseminate news. But this is not the lesson history teaches us. As noted previously, the common law recognized no such privilege, and the constitutional argument was not even asserted until 1958. From the begin-

ning of our country the press has operated without constitutional protection for press informants, and the press has flourished. The existing constitutional rules have not been a serious obstacle to either the development or retention of confidential news sources by the press.

It is said that currently press subpoenas have multiplied, that mutual distrust and tension between press and officialdom have increased, that reporting styles have changed, and that there is now more need for confidential sources, particularly where the press seeks news about minority cultural and political groups or dissident organizations suspicious of the law and public officials. These developments, even if true, are treacherous grounds for a far-reaching interpretation of the First Amendment fastening a nationwide rule on courts, grand juries, and prosecuting officials everywhere. The obligation to testify in response to grand jury subpoenas will not threaten these sources not involved with criminal conduct and without information relevant to grand jury investigations, and we cannot hold that the Constitution places the sources in these two categories either above the law or beyond its reach. . . .

The requirements of those cases, which hold that a state's interest must be "compelling" or "paramount" to justify even an indirect burden on First Amendment rights, are also met here. As we have indicated, the investigation of crime by the grand jury implements a fundamental governmental role of securing the safety of the person and property of the citizen, and it appears to us that calling reporters to give testimony in the matter and for the reasons that other citizens are called "bears a reasonable relationship to the achievement of the governmental purpose asserted as its justification." If the test is that the Government "convincingly show a substantial relation between the information sought and a subject of overriding and compelling state interest," it is quite apparent 1) that the state has the necessary interest in extirpating the traffic in illegal drugs, in forestalling assassination attempts on the President, and in preventing the community from being disrupted by violent disorders endangering both people and property; and 2) that, based on the stories Branzburg and Caldwell wrote and Pappas' admitted conduct, the grand jury called these reporters as they would others—because it was likely that they could supply information to help the Government determine whether illegal conduct had occurred and, if it had, whether there was sufficient evidence to return an indictment. . . .

READING

THE CALDWELL DECISION/ *Mr. Justice Douglas, dissenting*

In contrast to White, Justice Douglas in his dissenting opinion focuses on what he believes to be an inviolable right of a newsperson—the right not to appear before a grand jury unless implicated in a crime. Douglas sees two principles at stake here: (1) "the people . . . must have absolute freedom of and therefore privacy of their individual opinions and beliefs regardless of how suspect or strange they may appear to others," and (2) "an individual must also have absolute privacy over whatever information he may generate in the course of testing his opinions and beliefs." Why does Douglas think that forcing Caldwell to divulge his sources violates these privacy rights?

Most important, to Douglas, forcing reporters to testify before grand juries undermines the freedom of the press and, at the same time, does violence to the First Amendment. In effect, Douglas seems to argue, as a legal Kantian might, no matter how much good might come from forcing newspersons to divulge their sources to a grand jury, such an action is unconstitutional. Do you agree? Do you detect any fallacies in Douglas's appeal?

My view is close to that of the late Alexander Meiklejohn:

For the understanding of these principles it is essential to keep clear the crucial difference between "the rights" of the governed and "the powers" of the governors. And at this point, the title "Bill of Rights" is lamentably inaccurate as a designation of the first ten amendments. They are not a "Bill of Rights" but a "Bill of Powers and Rights." The Second through the Ninth Amendments limit the powers of the subordinate agencies in order that due regard shall be paid to the private "rights of the governed." The First and Tenth Amendments protect the governing "powers" of the people from abridgment by the agencies which are established as their servants.

In the field of our "rights," each one of us can claim "due process of law." In the field of our governing "powers," the notion of "due process is irrelevant." [*The First Amendment Is Absolute*, 1961.]

He also believed that "Self-government can exist only insofar as the voters acquire the intelligence, integrity, sensitivity, and generous devotion to the general welfare that, in theory, casting a ballot is assumed to express," and that "[p]ublic discussions of public issues, together with the spreading of information and opinion bearing on those issues, must have a freedom unabridged by our agents. Though they govern us, we, in a deeper sense, govern them. Over

---

Abridged from U.S. v. Caldwell, 408 U.S. 714.

256 The Caldwell Decision

our governing, they have no power. Over their governing we have sovereign power."

Two principles which follow from this understanding of the First Amendment are at stake here. One is that the people, the ultimate governors, must have absolute freedom of and therefore privacy of their individual opinions and beliefs regardless of how suspect or strange they may appear to others. Ancillary to that principle is the conclusion that an individual must also have absolute privacy over whatever information he may generate in the course of testing his opinions and beliefs. In this regard, Caldwell's status as a reporter is less relevant than is his status as a student who affirmatively pursued empirical research to enlarge his own intellectual viewpoint. The second principle is that effective self-government cannot succeed unless the people are immersed in a steady, robust, unimpeded, and uncensored flow of opinion and reporting which are continuously subjected to critique, rebuttal, and re-examination. In this respect, Caldwell's status as a news-gatherer and an intregral part of that process becomes critical.

I

Government has many interests that compete with the First Amendment. Congressional investigations to determine how existing laws actually operate or whether new laws are needed. While congressional committees have broad powers, they are subject to the restraints of the First Amendment. As we said in *Watkins* v.

United States: "Clearly, an investigation is subject to the command that the Congress shall make no law abridging freedom of speech or press or assembly. While it is true that there is no statute to be reviewed, and that an investigation is not a law, nevertheless an investigation is part of lawmaking. It is justified solely as an adjunct to the legislative process. The First Amendment may be invoked against infringement of the protected freedoms by law or by lawmaking."

Hence matters of belief, ideology, religious practices, social philosophy, and the like are beyond the pale and of no rightful concern of government, unless the belief or the speech or other expression has been translated into action.

Also at stake here is Caldwell's privacy of association. We have held that "[I]nviolability of privacy in group association may in many circumstances be indispensable to preservation of freedom of association, particularly where a group espouses dissident beliefs." [*NAACP* v. *Alabama; NAACP* v. *Button.*]

As I said in *Gibson* v. *Florida Legislative Committee,* ". . . the associational rights protected by the First Amendment . . . cover the entire spectrum in political ideology as well as in art, in journalism, in teaching, and in religion. [G]overnment is . . . precluded from probing the intimacies of spiritual and intellectual relationships in the myriad of such societies and groups that exist in this country, *regardless of the legislative purpose to be served. . . .* If that is not true, I see no barrier to investigation of newspapers, churches, political parties, clubs, societies, unions, and any other associations for their political, economic, social, philosophical, or religious views." (Emphasis added.)

The Court has not always been consistent in its protection of these First Amendment rights and has sometimes allowed a government interest to override the absolutes of the First Amendment. For example, under the banner of the "clear and present danger" test, and later under the influence of the "balancing" formula, the Court has permitted men to be penalized not for any harmful conduct but solely for holding unpopular beliefs.

In recent years we have said over and again that where First Amendment rights are concerned any regulation "narrowly drawn," must be "compelling" and not merely "rational" as is the case where other activities are concerned. But the "compelling" interest in regulation neither includes paring down or diluting the right, nor embraces penalizing one solely for his intellectual viewpoint; it concerns the State's interest, for example, in regulating the time and place or perhaps manner of exercising First Amendment rights. Thus one has an undoubted right to read and proclaim the First Amendment in the classroom or in a park. But he would not have the right to blare it forth from a sound truck rolling through the village or city at 2 a.m. The distinction drawn in *Cantwell* v. *Connecticut* should still stand: "[T]he Amendment embraces two concepts—freedom to believe and freedom to act. The first is absolute but, in the nature of things, the second cannot be."

Under these precedents there is no doubt that Caldwell could not be brought before the grand jury for the sole purpose of exposing his political belief. Yet today the Court effectively permits that result under the guise of allowing an attempt to elicit from him "factual information." To be sure, the inquiry will be couched only in terms of extracting Caldwell's recollection of what was said to him during the interviews, but the fact remains that his questions to the Panthers and therefore the respective answers were guided by Caldwell's own preconceptions and views about the Black Panthers. His entire experience was shaped by his intellectual viewpoint. Unlike the random bystander, those who affirmatively set out to test an hypothesis, as here, have no tidy means of segregating subjective opinion from objective facts. . . .

II

Today's decision will impede the wide-open and robust dissemination of ideas and counterthought which a free press both fosters and protects and which is essential to the success of intelligent self-government. Forcing a reporter before a grand jury will have two retarding effects upon the ear and the pen of the press. Fear of exposure will cause dissidents to communicate less openly to trusted reporters. And, fear of accountability will cause editors and critics to write with more restrained pens.

I see no way of making mandatory the disclosure of a reporter's confidential source of the information on which he bases his news story.

The press has a preferred position in our constitutional scheme not to enable it to make money, not to set newsmen apart as a favored class, but to bring fulfillment to the public's right to know. The right to know is crucial to the governing powers of the people, to paraphrase Alexander Meiklejohn. Knowledge is essential to informed decisions.

As Mr. Justice Black said in *New York Times Co.* v. *United States,* "The press was to serve the governed, not the governors. . . . The press was protected so that it could bare the secrets of government and inform the people."

Government has an interest in law and order; and history shows that the trend of rulers—the bureaucracy and the police—is to suppress the radical and his ideas and to arrest him rather than the hostile audience. Yet as held in *Terminiello* v. *Chicago,* one "function of free speech under our system of government is to invite dispute." We went on to say, "It may indeed best serve its high purpose when it induces a condition of unrest, creates dissatisfaction with conditions as they are, or even stirs people to anger. Speech is often provocative and challenging. It may strike at prejudices and preconceptions and have profound unsettling effects as it presses for acceptance of an idea."

The people who govern are often far removed from the cabals that threaten the regime; the people are often remote from the sources of truth even though they live in the city where the forces that would undermine society operate. The function of the press is to explore and investigate events, inform the people what is go-

ing on, and to expose the harmful as well as the good influences at work. There is no higher function performed under our constitutional regime. Its performance means that the press is often engaged in projects that bring anxiety or even fear to the bureaucracies or departments or officials of government. The whole weight of government is therefore often brought to bear against a paper or a reporter.

A reporter is no better than his source of information. Unless he has a privilege to withhold the identity of his source, he will be the victim of governmental intrigue or aggression. If he can be summoned to testify in secret before a grand jury, his sources will dry up and the attempted exposure, the effort to enlighten the public, will be ended. If what the Court sanctions today becomes settled law, then the reporter's main function in American society will be to pass on to the public the press releases which the various departments of government issue.

It is no answer to reply that the risk that a newsman will divulge one's secrets to the grand jury is no greater than the threat that he will in any event inform to the police. Even the most trustworthy reporter may not be able to withstand relentless badgering before a grand jury.

The record in this case is replete with weighty affidavits from responsible newsmen, telling how important are the sanctity of their sources of information. When we deny newsmen that protection, we deprive the people of the information needed to run the affairs of the nation in an intelligent way. Madison said:

A popular Government, without popular information, or the means of acquiring it, is but a Prologue to a Farce or a Tragedy; or, perhaps both. Knowledge will forever govern ignorance; And a people who mean to be their own Governors, must arm themselves with the power which knowledge gives (to W. T. Barry, August 4, 1822). [*The Complete Madison*, 1953.]

Today's decision is more than a clog upon newsgathering. It is a signal to publishers and editors that they should exercise caution in how they use whatever information they can obtain. Without immunity they may be summoned to account for their criticism. Entrenched officers have been quick to crash their powers down upon unfriendly commentators.

The intrusion of government into this domain is symptomatic of the disease of this society. As the years pass the power of government becomes more and more pervasive. It is a power to suffocate both people and causes. Those in power, whatever their politics, want only to perpetuate it. Now that the fences of the law and the tradition that has protected the press are broken down, the people are the victims. The First Amendment, as I read it, was designed precisely to prevent that tragedy.

8

WAR
of following orders to hell and back
PRIMA FACIE DUTIES

One of the most tragic pages in the history of the Vietnam war involved Lt. William L. Calley, Jr. Calley was tried and convicted of the premeditated murder of 22 My Lai villagers on March 16, 1968. During his trial Calley admitted to firing at a handful of Vietnamese civilians in My Lai and decreeing the mass execution of others, but he insisted that he had done nothing wrong. "I never sat down and analyzed whether they were men, women and children," Calley told the court-martial jury. "I was ordered to go in there and destroy the enemy. That was my job that day. That was my mission."*

For Calley, following the orders of his superiors was his paramount moral obligation. It overrode any other consideration, even those concerning killing. As Calley put it, "I felt then and still do that I acted as I was directed and that I carried out orders I was given. And I do not feel I was wrong in doing so."†

In finding Calley guilty of murder, the jury obviously thought that in this case Calley had an obligation that transcended obedience, an obligation to preserve the lives of those 22 peasant civilians. Many people agreed, but probably as many disagreed. How are such conflicts of moral obligations to be resolved?

In 1930 English philosopher William David Ross published *The Right and the Good*, in which he proposed a solution to the conflict-of-duties problem apparent in nonconsequential positions. In this chapter we will discuss Ross's view, which is generally classified under the heading of prima facie duties. We choose to examine Ross's thought in the context of war because by its nature war dramatically tests the moral code and fiber of societies and individuals. War thrusts moral beliefs into conflict, especially those concerning individual duties and obligations. What should the soldier do who has been ordered to kill civilians? Should the pilot be morally concerned about the faceless thousands his bombs kill and displace? Should prisoners of war be killed when they endanger the well-being of their captors?

---

*See Robert Baum and James Randell, *Ethical Arguments for Analysis* (New York: Holt, Rinehart and Winston, 1973), p. 48. Later comments by Calley implied that he no longer believed that what he did was not morally wrong.
†Ibid.

Many answer these questions by pointing to the formal agreements, conventions, and treaties among nations that prescribe how armies are to behave during war. All of these agreements taken together constitute a substantial body of laws of war. The Hague Convention of Land Warfare, the Geneva Conventions on the Law of War, the Nuremberg directives—all attempt to mitigate the ravages of war by prohibiting needless cruelties and atrocities. For the most part these laws deal with how certain persons, like civilians and prisoners, are to be treated and what sorts of weapons and military tactics are impermissible. But, at the same time, what these laws of war define as war crimes are only acts that cannot be justified by military necessity. In effect, all these so-called laws of war permit cruelties committed out of military necessity, whatever that is. As one commentator has noted, the laws of war function

> as a general justification for the violation of most, if not all, of even the specific prohibitions which constitute a portion of the laws of war. Thus, according to one exposition of the laws of war, the flat prohibition against the killing of enemy combatants who have surrendered is to be understood to permit the killing of such persons where that is required by "military necessity."[*]

Apparently, then, the soldier who faces an order to kill prisoners or civilians is in a bind. On the one hand, the soldier can appeal to the moral directives of numerous national treaties; on the other, he can appeal to the order of a superior officer who insists that such wanton killing is necessary. Which duty is morally binding?

The unforgiving fact of war is that it does not allow us the luxury of moral assumptions, the undisturbed sleep of the self-righteous. Rather, it casts duties into mutually antagonistic roles, compelling us to order duty priorities as does perhaps no other human activity.

ROSS'S THEORY OF PRIMA FACIE DUTIES

Ross begins his attempt to provide methodology for resolving conflicts of duties by dismissing the consequentialist belief that what makes an act right is whether it produces the most good. Frequently, Ross notes, consequences of conflicting behaviors counterbalance each other. Instead of a consequentialism, Ross argues that when deciding among ethical alternatives we must weigh the options to determine what duties we fulfill in performing or refraining from performing each option. Then we must decide which duty among the alternatives is the most obligatory.

---

[*]Richard Wasserstrom, "The Laws of War," in *Today's Moral Problems*, ed. Richard Wasserstrom (New York: Macmillan, 1975), p. 483.

Notice at least two characteristics of his thinking that clearly place Ross in the nonconsequential camp. First, judgment of action's morality is not solely dependent on its consequences. Second, there are duties or obligations which bind us morally; these, presumably, can be stated in rules.

As Ross explains, an act may fall under a number of rules at once. For example, the rule to keep a promise may in a given circumstance conflict with the rule not to do anyone harm. To illustrate, suppose a political candidate promises a wealthy builder that if the builder funds his campaign and he gets elected, he will deliver an attractive government contract to the builder. The politician is subsequently elected and makes good his promise. The fact is that the contractor does good work and his prices are competitive. But, of course, the politician does not even consider any other bids.

On the one hand the politician has certainly fulfilled his promise, which he may have viewed as binding. On the other hand he has violated his duty to society, which trusts that he will not collude with private concerns to advance his own or their own interests, but will always act strictly in the interests of the public good. As a result, we would probably believe that the politician has acted immorally, but not because the consequences of his action were wrong. He acted immorally because he would probably consider the reasons against what he did to count more than the reasons for what he did. In other words, we would have evaluated the conflicting duties and decided in favor of the one we felt to be more morally compelling.

Calley's case is not entirely dissimilar. On the one hand, Calley is obligated by oath to obey his superiors. On the other, he appears obligated by the laws of war not to harm innocent civilians. When the court-martial jury found him guilty, they apparently decided that his obligation not to harm civilians outweighed his duty to obey orders.

In both these cases, as in most others, each act is accompanied by a number of motivational reasons. Each reason in turn appeals to a moral duty—to keep a promise, to be faithful to the people who trust you, to be fair, to be honest. Each of these moral duties provides grounds for doing a particular action, and yet no single one provides sufficient grounds. In other words, simply because the politician has a duty to keep his promise is not grounds enough for delivering the government contract to his supporter. Simply because Calley has an obligation to obey his superiors is not grounds for his murdering civilians. In each case other reasons appear that impose other duties. Ross terms these duties *prima facie duties*.

PRIMA FACIE DUTIES

To help understand what Ross means by *prima facie* duties, let's introduce a character, Lieutenant Marcus. Lieutenant Marcus is serving with the U.S. Army during war time. His current mission is to wrest from the enemy strategic villages and hamlets.

Recently the combat has turned particularly bloody and vicious, with children and other civilians being used by the enemy to destroy U.S. troops. The enemy has also adopted the policy of taking no prisoners. Just the week before Marcus and his comrades came upon an open grave containing the bodies of eighteen American soldiers. All had their hands tied behind their backs and had been shot in the back of the head. Among the dead were several friends of Marcus's. In addition, Marcus's company, having been in the field a long time, is in critical need of supplies. In fact, there is a real question whether they have enough supplies to return to their base of operations.

As a result of these events and conditions, Lieutenant Marcus's captain has ordered the company to take no prisoners until further notice. Upon entering a village, the men are to destroy "anything that moves." In answer to the question of whether that order includes women, children, and other civilians, the captain simply replies, "'Anything that moves' means anything!" A number of things about the captain's order are bothering Marcus. Above all else he does not like the idea of killing civilians; he expresses his reservations to his friend, Lieutenant Lattimere.

Marcus: I don't know if I can do it. I don't know whether I can obey the captain's order.
Lattimere: It's an order, isn't it?
Marcus: Sure it's an order. And under ordinary circumstances I wouldn't even question it.
Lattimere: As a military officer, you have sworn not to question it.
Marcus: I know what I've sworn. But I don't know about this.

Marcus and Lattimere are agreed that breaking an oath that they have taken is wrong. They clearly believe that soldiers are generally obliged to follow orders of superior officers.

In speaking of duties that generally oblige us, William Ross uses the term *prima facie,* which is a Latin phrase meaning "on first appearance." By a *prima facie duty,* then, Ross means one that on first appearance carries with it a moral obligation, but actually does not because of additional circumstances. Specifically, he considers a prima facie duty the characteristic an act has in virtue of being of a certain kind, for example, keeping a promise. In other words, a prima facie duty is one that we recognize on face value as one that we should be obliged to discharge if all other things were equal, if there did not exist any conflicting duties.

For example, the politician we spoke of earlier ordinarily ought to keep his promise because promise keeping, according to Ross, is a prima facie duty. But ought he actually keep it? No, because of other more pressing duties. By *actual duty* Ross means what we actually ought to do in a situation, that is, what we are morally obliged to do after we have weighed and considered all the prima facie duties involved. In this case, the actual duty of the politician appears to be to break his promise to the contractor, at least insofar as opening the contract to a fair bidding procedure. There are prima facie duties evident in Marcus's case.

Lattimere: Look, you know better than to think you pick and choose which orders to follow.

Marcus: When they break laws of war I do.

Lattimere: Laws of war don't tell you to sacrifice yourself for the enemy, Marcus. You heard the captain. We're hurting. We don't have enough supplies for ourselves, let alone any prisoners. Besides, the enemy tore up the law book when they started using civilians in combat and slaughtering our prisoners. No, the captain's right; we've got no obligations to treat them humanely, not any more.

To use Ross's terminology, there exist here two tokens of at least one prima facie duty—to keep promises. On the one hand is the duty to be faithful to the orders of superior officers; on the other is the duty to remain faithful to the laws of war that bind every combatant, certainly every officer.

Lattimere: Don't get me wrong. I don't like killing civilians any more than you do. And under ordinary circumstances I'd be the first to condemn it. But these aren't ordinary circumstances.

Marcus: A civilian's a civilian no matter what the circumstances.

Lattimere: Well, how do you know they're civies?

Marcus: A five-year-old's a civilian, believe me.

Lattimere: Is he? Not with three sticks of dynamite strapped around his back he's not.

Marcus: So turn him around. Strip him. Examine him. Don't just blow his brains out.

Lattimere: You're missing the whole point.

Marcus: Which is?

Lattimere: The enemy is committed to that kind of warfare. You know it yourself. Today that kid or lady or old man may be a civilian, but who knows about tomorrow? The truth of it is that where the enemy is concerned there are no civilians. And that's not our doing, Marcus, it's theirs. But all this is irrelevant. The captain's given the order. Our obligation is to obey it, not debate it.

Lattimere would argue that ordinarily military personnel do have a duty to abide by the laws of war. Certainly that would preclude killing defenseless civilians and prisoners. But he argues that neither he nor Marcus ought to be bound by this duty because of the unusual circumstances. In effect Lattimere sees his obligation to be faithful to the laws of war as a prima facie duty in this instance. His actual duty? Obeying the captain's order. Curiously, Marcus views the captain's order as the prima facie one and his actual duty to be allegiance to the laws of war, which he sees as forbidding what he has been ordered to do.

At this point a number of questions arise with respect to Ross's prima facie duties. Perhaps the most basic is, How do we know what our prima facie duties are to begin with? Ross answers this by citing six categories of prima facie duties.

1. Duties of Fidelity

The horns of Marcus and Lattimere's dilemma stem from previous acts of their own, from promises that they have explicitly or implicitly made. *Ross calls these duties of fidelity, that is, duties that rest on prior acts of our own.*

Included under duties of fidelity would be the duty not to lie, "which seems to be implied in the act of entering into conversation," the conversation of politicians notwithstanding. Under duties of fidelity Ross would also include faithfulness to contracts that we have entered into, including oaths that we have sworn. Ross would also include obligations to repair wrongful acts, that is, duties of reparation. In war, for example, a nation that has acted immorally would be duty-bound to repair the damages that its action caused. In recent years in the United States, a number of racial and ethnic groups, the American Indian among them, have used this justification for demanding compensation from the government for allegedly wanton treatment.

2. Duties of Gratitude

By prima facie duties of gratitude Ross means duties that rest on acts of other people toward the agent. Ross argues that we are bound by obligations arising from relationships that exist between people, such as those between friends or relatives.

For example, suppose that you annually contribute one hundred dollars to your favorite charity. The week before you're about to make your yearly contribution, a good friend whom you have not seen in years calls you up. You are delighted to hear your friend's voice and fondly recall the many times the person stood by you in times of crisis. Now your friend is in need of one hundred dollars. In this case a duty of gratitude would probably oblige you to give the money to your friend rather than to the charity. Could a duty of gratitude possibly enter into Marcus's case?

Lattimere: You know, there's something you should think about here besides the laws of war.
Marcus: What's that?
Lattimere: Your buddies. You're so worried about what you owe the enemy. Well, what about what you owe the guys who are helping to keep you alive?
Marcus: You're not telling me that I've an obligation to murder people out of gratitude to my buddies, are you?
Lattimere: I'm saying that if you don't give the enemy notice that their atrocities will be met with atrocities, then you are indirectly encouraging the wanton slaughter of your own kind. And I don't think that's right.
Marcus: Well, I think that wholesale killing of civilians is heinous.

Lattimere clearly sees an obligation of gratitude here, stemming from the unique relationship that exists between a soldier and a comrade in arms. Marcus, on the other hand, cannot see how that obligation measures up with what he views as the criminal nature of killing civilians and prisoners. By so doing Marcus anticipates Ross's third category of prima facie duties.

3. Duties of Justice

By duties of justice Ross means those duties that rest on the fact or possibility of a distribution of pleasure or happiness that is not in accordance with the merits of the people concerned.

Imagine the case of imprisoning a man for something that he did not do, although he is obviously guilty of other crimes for which he has never been brought to justice. Although removing him from society would appear to be in everyone's best interests (except his own, maybe), a duty of justice would oblige us not to imprison him; for he does not deserve to be imprisoned for something that he did not do, no matter how beneficial the consequences. Marcus senses a comparable duty of justice in his situation.

Marcus: Look, Lattimere, don't you remember how outraged we all were when we looked into that open grave last week?
Lattimere: And still are.
Marcus: Right. And why?
Lattimere: Because it was a cruel, savage slaughter, that's why.
Marcus: And needless. Those GIs were no longer a real threat to anybody.
Lattimere: A threat? Are you kidding? They were tied up!
Marcus: Exactly. Think about that. Those guys were no longer in the war. They were captives, prisoners. They were bound up! You don't go around killing defenseless people, people who are no longer a threat to you.
Lattimere: They deserved better than that.
Marcus: Of course they did; that's the point. They didn't deserve to be lined up and shot at all, any more than the ones we're going to kill tomorrow or the day after. That kind of behavior just isn't consistent with what we stand for, Lattimere, either as individuals or as a nation.

Marcus has introduced into his argument the element of justice and fairness. In general he sees such wartime atrocities as murdering civilians and prisoners as not giving to individuals what they deserve. Because they aren't part of the war, these persons do not deserve the treatment that is directed at combatants. Therefore, such an act is inherently unjust and wrong. Moreover, in alluding to what he and his nation stand for, Marcus foreshadows Ross's prima facie duties of beneficence.

4. Duties of Beneficence

By duties of beneficence Ross means duties that rely on the fact that there are other people in the world whose virtue, intelligence, or happiness we can improve. Suppose, for example, you are shopping in a large shopping center. Suddenly you hear the banshee wail of a little girl who has lost her mother. You are in a position to help the child find her mother and thus still the child's anxiety, and also to restore peace to the premises. Out of beneficence you ought to help the child. Similarly, Marcus feels a duty of beneficence.

Lattimere: What do you mean by that kind of behavior isn't consistent with what we stand for?

Marcus: As a nation, a world power, we pride ourselves on fair play, don't we? On being a country with a conscience? On having some concept of right and wrong?

Lattimere: Sure we do. That's one of the reasons we're here in the first place.

Marcus: Well, I think that we have an obligation to the rest of the world to demonstrate that no matter what our feelings or personal suffering we will not resort to the inhuman and immoral conduct of the enemy. To me this is a great opportunity to dramatize to the world that not even war justifies atrocity, that even the heinous behavior of one side does not permit the other such license. We have a chance here, Lattimere, to render this weary planet a great service by raising its standard of virtue. And who knows, perhaps even diminishing the chances of another war.

Marcus argues that the United States as a world leader has certain obligations. Among these is the duty to improve the virtues or moral standards of all peoples. To shirk this obligation presumably would leave people worse off. Marcus could also argue that in addition to this duty of beneficence, the country also has an obligation to itself, a duty of self-improvement, and that as individuals he and Lattimere have a similar duty.

5. Duties of Self-improvement

By duties of self-improvement Ross means those that rest on the fact that we can improve our own condition with respect to virtue, intelligence, or happiness. To understand Ross's duties of self-improvement, suppose that you are an exceptionally talented person. You play many musical instruments, paint very well, seem to have a natural language-learning ability, and exhibit high scientific acumen.

While you are in the midst of determining your life's goals, a rich relative dies, leaving you so much money that you need not work another day in your life. If you decided to use this inheritance so that you could live luxuriously for the rest of your life, making no attempt to cultivate your talents, then you would have violated a duty to improve yourself. Duties of self-improvement seem applicable also to Marcus's case.

Lattimere: Still, Marcus, you're a U.S. Army officer.

Marcus: I know. And I'm bound by an oath I've sworn. Well, I'm not using that oath to hide behind and do something I believe is wrong.

Lattimere: But what if every military officer thought that way?

Marcus: Then maybe we wouldn't get such orders.

Lattimere: And maybe we wouldn't have any army at all. Look, no one can hold you responsible in war for doing what you're told to do. But they sure can if you don't.

Marcus: Sorry, Lattimere, I just don't buy that Bormann defense any more.

Lattimere: Bormann defense?

Marcus: Martin Ludwig Bormann, third deputy of the Nazi party. You remember. Like Bormann, we're just following orders, so we're not responsible. Sorry, but that doesn't cut it for me.

Lattimere: What we're being asked to do isn't genocide.

Marcus: No, not exactly. But we're using the same defense, the same moral justification for our behavior. And I just can't live with that. A second ago you asked who could hold me responsible for following orders. I can.

Marcus is feeling the pinch of Ross's duty to self-improvement, in this case a duty to improve his condition with respect to virtue. He is suggesting that he did not lose his conscience the day he donned a military uniform and officer's bars. He still feels an obligation that transcends the moral perceptions and military orders of his superiors. To ignore those personal obligations is to be untrue to himself, to retard his own moral sense and growth. In short, to deny his own moral instincts is to be less than what he could be.

Despite the dutiful reasons that Marcus has provided for his position, there is probably one duty that he feels that overrides any of the others. This is the duty not to injure someone unnecessarily.

6. Duties of Nonmaleficence

By duties of nonmaleficence Ross means duties of not injuring others. Ross includes this obligation to contrast with duties of beneficence. Although not injuring others incidentally means not doing them good, Ross interprets the avoidance of injuring others as a more pressing duty than beneficence.

To contrast the duties of beneficence and nonmaleficence, consider this example. Suppose a friend of yours is in desperate need of an ethics text for a course she's taking. In two weeks she will have the money to buy a copy, but a big exam is scheduled for next week. One afternoon while you are eating in the school cafeteria, you spot an unattended ethics text on the table a few feet from you. Your friend surely needs the book, and she wouldn't have to know where you got it. You do have an obligation to help her if you can. In this case, however, your duty not to injure the owner of the book would override your duty to help advance the virtuous development of your friend. It is precisely this duty of nonmaleficence that Marcus feels most bound to oblige.

Lattimere: So you think you've an obligation that takes precedence over your military oath.

Marcus: I do. I can't justify senseless killing, not even on the order of the president of the United States.

Lattimere: Not even if it means endangering your own and your comrades' lives.

Marcus: Not even that would justify it.

No matter what the circumstances, Marcus evidently views his paramount obligation as not wantonly injuring others. True, to destroy everything that moves in the village they will soon occupy would violate laws of war, retard the moral perception of humankind, and set back Marcus's own moral development. But ultimately it is from a duty of noninjury that Marcus refuses to obey his captain's orders.

Yet, Lattimere is not convinced. Part of his skepticism centers around his own perception of duties in this case. Another part involves the emphasis that he gives to certain duties, an emphasis that Marcus does not share. These differences are symptomatic of two apparently major weaknesses in Ross's concept of prima facie duties.

OBJECTIONS TO ROSS'S PRIMA FACIE DUTIES

1. *It is difficult, if not impossible, to determine the relative weight and merit of conflicting duties.* Even a superficial examination of Marcus's dilemma reveals a number of conflicting duties. First and most obvious is the conflict between duties of fidelity. On the one hand Marcus is obligated to uphold his military oath; on the other he seems bound by laws of war. Had Ross addressed himself to this problem, he probably would have argued that Marcus's primary obligation was one of noninjury, and therefore he should disobey the order. Undoubtedly Ross could make a strong case for this position, but it is questionable whether the case would be absolutely irrefutable.

The fact is that Ross's duties of nonmaleficence are vague. Certainly he never intended it to rule out cases of self-defense. Indeed, in this case Marcus himself sees nothing wrong with killing the enemy who is actively engaged in trying to destroy him, his comrades, and his nation. In effect, then, both he and Ross must admit that injuring others is sometimes justifiable. The question is when.

By conceding that injuring others is sometimes justifiable, Marcus at least exposes his position to the subjective interpretation that a thoroughgoing pacifist position does not. Logically, by admitting that injuring others is sometimes moral, Marcus must admit that Lattimere and the captain may be right in this instance. True, Marcus does not think that they are; but he logically must admit that they could be. Intensifying Marcus's dilemma is the fact that Lattimere and the captain are at least partially defending their behavior on grounds of self-defense. Presumably they consider what they are about to do as a kind of preventive strike whose effect will be to remove from war a real threat to themselves and deter similar threats.

The point is that even in this case the noninjury duty is vague. Its vagueness is aggravated when additional, conflicting duties are present, as in the case here. The result can be real confusion about what one's actual duty is. Further complicating this problem is an even more basic one that involves prima facie, rather than actual, duties. Critics wonder how we know what our prima facie duties are to begin with.

2. *It is impossible to verify what our prima facie duties are.* How does Marcus know that he has a moral obligation to honor his oath? To refrain from injuring others?

To develop his own and others' views? Ross answers that these acts constitute self-evident duties to anyone of sufficient mental maturity who has given them enough attention.

But what if people disagree with Ross's list of prima facie duties? Certainly people disagree about the weight they deserve. Clearly Lattimere stresses his obligation to the oath and to protecting the interests of his own kind. But suppose people did not think, for example, that a person bears an obligation to keep a promise. It seems that Ross must say that such people lacked "sufficient mental maturity" or that they did not give the proposition "sufficient attention."

But then question arises as to the nature of "sufficient mental maturity." Also, individuals must wonder when they have given "sufficient attention" to a moral statement. In Ross's view people have attended sufficiently to a moral proposition when they recognize his list as prima facie duties. But this appears to involve circular reasoning, begging the question.

Suppose, for example, that you told someone, "Study the violin long enough and you'll become a virtuoso." Forty years later the person returns still only capable of making the violin squeak. Understandably the person wants to know why, having studied five hours a day for forty years, he is not a virtuoso. You reply, "You haven't studied long enough." Besides inviting a punch in the nose, you are in effect saying to the person, "Play the violin until you become a virtuoso and you will become a virtuoso!" Similarly, Ross seems to be saying, "When you recognize a duty as prima facie right, then you'll recognize a duty as prima facie right."

SUMMARY

Rule Nonconsequential Position

Ross's prima facie duties: In making a moral decision, we must obey our actual duty as calculated by weighing alternatives involved on the basis of the various prima facie duties that they impose.

Objections

1. Ross's scheme does not resolve duty conflicts.

2. Ross does not satisfactorily explain how we know that we are duty-bound or what those duties are.

CONCLUSIONS

Like all nonconsequential positions, Ross's prima facie duties make a worthwhile contribution to ethical thought by recognizing the problems inherent in consequentialism and trying to deal with them. In addition, by isolating areas of general moral obligation, Ross has attempted to give a useful guide to moral decisions. Finally, Ross's multirule approach precludes the inflexibility of single rule nonconsequential systems like Kant's categorical imperative and the divine command theory.

But the Marcus-Lattimere debate reveals a number of weaknesses in Ross's prima facie system. First, there is the apparent ambiguity in the duties themselves. Too often, just what beneficence, gratitude, noninjury, and the other duties precisely mean is left to the moral agent's interpretation. This introduces an element of antinomianism that hardly seems compatible with rule nonconsequentialism. Related to this is another shortcoming: Ross's ethic assumes that there are obligations, but does not explain what makes particular actions obligatory.

In addition, there is the seemingly ever-present problem of assigning relative weight to duties. Which takes precedence and under what conditions? Finally, despite Ross's healthful respect for the past, one must wonder whether consequences can be disregarded so casually.

Perhaps the best way to look at Ross's prima facie system is as a general guide to help people in moral conflict make their own decisions, just as a judge renders a verdict given the principles of the law, despite the fact that the principles are never specific. This lack of specificity, although it may be inconsistent with Ross's thinking, is not altogether undesirable. On the contrary, it introduces what appears to be a needed recognition and respect for the fact that ultimately individuals must interpret, weigh, order, and act on duties. The inclusion of this autonomous principle, if it does not undermine Ross's system, leaves it less bloodless than it may otherwise be.

EXERCISES FOR ANALYSIS

EXERCISE 1

The following passages may contain errors in reasoning. What are these fallacies? Also, note aspects of Ross's prima facie duties where present.

1. "Of course the U.S. atomic bombing of Hiroshima and Nagasaki in August 1945 was morally justifiable, even though it killed, maimed, and permanently scarred thousands of civilians. Just think how many American lives would have been lost if we hadn't dropped the bombs."

2. A citizen of a nondemocratic, highly totalitarian, totally oppressive government joins an underground organization in order to fight for freedom. Soon the organization resorts to terrorist activities: bombing theaters, churches, and

other places where primarily civilians gather; kidnapping governmental officials and sometimes civilians; skyjacking commercial flights. The citizen feels
that there is something inherently wrong with these tactics. When he protests,
he finds that his loyalty to the cause is questioned. He is told that the underground organization is not doing anything that the government has not been
doing for years. Besides, he is reminded, the tactics work.

3. "The best standard for determining what is morally right in war is the behavior of the enemy. Give them what they dish out—only more of it!"

4. "If we continue to allow the Arabs to dictate how much fuel we'll have, we're
going to find ourselves stranded on freeways in crippled cars. Surely such an
eventuality justifies measures, even war, to prevent that from happening."

5. "Since war is the worst evil imaginable, we should avoid it at all costs." (Is
there an inconsistency here?)

6. "All people are morally obliged to do what they personally see as right and
to avoid what they personally see as wrong. So, it's really immoral of a government to prosecute someone for refusing to be part of a war that the person sees
as immoral."

7. Soldier: Okay, so you think war is immoral. So why not serve in a noncom-
batant capacity?
Pacifist: Because I'd still be supporting the war.
Soldier: No you wouldn't. You'd be supporting the lives of fellow country-
men.
Pacifist: Sure, by helping them risk their own lives and mobilizing the effort
to kill others.

EXERCISE 2

There are many war-related issues that involve morality—the morality of
particular wartime actions, the morality of particular wars, the morality of
particular persons during war, the morality of particular countries during war.
But the fundamental issue concerns the morality of war as a human institution.
No thoughtful person would insist that all war is justifiable in the sense that they
are all moral. But many claim that at least some wars are justifiable. Others insist
no war is ever justifiable. Following are condensed common arguments for and
against war. Determine whether the justification for each is adequate. Also,
note which are consequentialist and which are nonconsequentialist. Are any of
the arguments compatible with Ross's prima facie system?

Arguments for War

1. There is no better place to observe the moral justification for war than in the
expected consequences of that war. Many wars are fought to liberate peoples

from the yoke of tyranny and totalitarianism; others are fought to prevent further holocausts; still others for self-defense. How can anyone seriously argue that such wars are immoral? The point is that justification for war lies in the intended consequences of the fighting. If those consequences are consistent with generally accepted principles of human life and dignity, then that war can be just.

2. One of the most natural forms of human behavior is what is commonly known as self-defense. Self-defense is the action that individuals take to prevent immediate and imminent harm to themselves. Because individuals are entitled to the security and integrity of life and limb, they are certainly justified in reacting in a self-defensive manner. Now, all that applies to individuals with respect to self-defense also applies to nations, which are composed of individuals. Thus, since some wars are taken as self-defense measures, at least some wars are justifiable.

3. History records that one of the most frequent causes of a war is the unwarranted aggression of one country upon another. It is understandable why wars result from such behavior, for everyone recognizes the inherent wrongness of such an action. To stand by and allow such behavior would not only encourage more of the same but also constitute inexcusable dereliction of duty. After all, we are obliged as individuals and nations to do all that we can to correct wrongdoing and prevent it from occurring. So, when war is an action taken in response to aggression, it is justifiable.

Arguments against War

1. It is unwise and unjustifiable to rationalize a war on the basis of some future dividend the war may produce. If we have learned anything from history, it is that we cannot be certain of the future. The so-called war to end all wars actually became the first of several wars in which millions of lives were lost. The just-one-more-bombing-mission mentality of the Vietnam war perpetuated a tragedy that eventually led to the deaths of thousands. Invariably, the just cause of one nation is the infernal mania of another; the righteous defenders of liberty and equality are at the same time the godless purveyors of enslavement and totalitarianism. The fact is that war is an activity whose consequences cannot be predicted; for that reason not even some wars, those rationalized by appeal to good consequences, are justifiable.

2. Justification of war on the grounds of self-defense seems to hinge on the analogy between persons and nations, a questionable one indeed. After all, nations do not suffer and die the same way that individuals do. Nations do not have the reflexive systems that humans do. Neither do nations necessarily suffer the same fate that individuals do who do not defend themselves from attack. In all probability, a nation that refuses to defend itself will be occupied and subjected to enemy rule, whereas an individual would probably suffer serious bodily harm, even death. But this weak analogy aside, consider that an inherent part of the self-defense concept is that an agent will use only as much force as is necessary to rebuff a threat. Now, when has a nation waged such a war? Indeed, history is replete with the deaths of billions of people, a large number of whom died in alleged defense of their nation. The fact is that self-defense invariably becomes a justification for total war, and thus cannot, for all practical purposes, be considered a legitimate moral defense for war. It's clear that even a war that springs from self-defense is not moral.

3. Justifying war on the basis of a response to aggression is illogical. In defending the righteousness of war, many contend that a war is in answer to the aggression of a people or nation. In saying this they assume that aggression is inherently evil, that it can never be justified. But some acts of aggression—for example, acts taken to free or liberate a people—are different from other acts, that is, those intended to dominate and enslave. If aggression is wrong, isn't it inconsistent for people to approve of aggression when it takes the form of retaliation? The point is that war justified as a response to aggression is logically inconsistent, and no war can be defended on this ground.

4. The preceding arguments are commendable in revealing the inadequacies of the most common moral justifications for war. In doing that, they go a long way toward showing that war cannot be justified. But they fail to make the most obvious point—that war produces needless suffering. Just imagine the countless millions of military and civilian lives lost in war. Think about the suffering of those who are not fortunate enough to die, but must live maimed, deformed, and permanently scarred. Consider the millions of displaced, disoriented, and orphaned. Try to feel the emotional pain that war causes, the anxiety, worry, and breakdown. Now, defend war. Is it possible? No matter how righteous the cause or noble the end, war is never justifiable, for it causes needless human suffering.

SELECTIONS FOR FURTHER READING

Duties

Prichard, H. A. *Moral Obligation.* New York: Oxford University Press, 1949.

Raphael, David Daiches. *Moral Judgments.* New York: Macmillan, 1955.

Ross, William David. *Foundation of Ethics.* New York: Oxford University Press, 1937.

———. *The Right and the Good.* Oxford: Clarendon Press, 1930.

Saint-Exupery, Antoine de. *Night Flight.* New York: Harcourt Brace Jovanovich, 1974.

War

Clausewitz, Karl von. *On War*. Baltimore: Penguin, 1971.

Falk, Richard A. *Morality and War in the Contemporary World*. New York: Praeger, 1963.

Ginsberg, Robert, ed. *The Critique of War: Contemporary Philosophical Explorations*. Chicago: Regnery, 1969.

Mayer, Peter, ed. *The Pacifist Conscience*. New York: Holt, Rinehart and Winston, 1966.

Merleau-Ponty, Maurice. *Humanism and Terror*. Boston: Beacon Press, 1969.

Ramsey, Paul. *The Just War: Force and Political Responsibility*. New York: Scribner's, 1968.

Tucker, Robert. *The Just War: A Study in Contemporary American Doctrine*. Baltimore: Johns Hopkins University Press, 1960.

Wasserstrom, Richard, ed. *War and Morality*. Belmont, Calif.: Wadsworth, 1970.

Zahn, Gordon C. *War, Conscience and Dissent*. New York: Hawthorn, 1967.

NARVESON/ *Pacifism: A Philosophical Analysis*

In the following essay Jan Narveson argues that pacifism is a self-contradictory doctrine. Narveson concedes that pacifism is a prima facie duty but not an absolute one. An absolute duty is one that is always binding, no matter what the circumstances. To call something absolutely wrong means that there are no circumstances that would justify that action or in any way mitigate its immorality. The pacifist would contend that war is not prima facie wrong but absolutely wrong. It is this contention and what it implies that Narveson objects to.

Several different doctrines have been called "pacifism," and it is impossible to say anything cogent about it without saying which of them one has in mind. I must begin by making it clear, then, that I am limiting the discussion of pacifism to a rather narrow band of doctrines, further distinctions among which will be brought out below. By "pacifism," I do *not* mean the theory that violence is evil. With appropriate restrictions, this is a view that every person with any pretensions to morality doubtless holds: Nobody thinks that we have a right to inflict pain wantonly on other people. The pacifist goes a very long step further. *His* belief is not only that violence is evil but also that it is morally wrong to use force to resist, punish, or prevent violence. This further step makes pacifism a radical moral doctrine. What I shall try to establish below is that it is in fact, more than merely radical—it is actually incoherent because self-contradictory in

its fundamental intent. I shall also suggest that several moral attitudes and psychological views which have tended to be associated with pacifism as I have defined it do not have any necessary connection with that doctrine. Most proponents of pacifism, I shall argue, have tended to confuse these different doctrines, and that confusion is probably what accounts for such popularity as pacifism has had.

It is next in order to point out that the pacifistic attitude is a matter of degree, and this in two respects. In the first place, there is the question: How much violence should not be resisted, and what degree of force is one entitled to use in resisting, punishing, or preventing it? Answers to this question will make a lot of difference. For example, everyone would agree that there are limits to the kind and degree of force with which a particular degree of violence is to be met: we do not have a right to kill someone for rapping us on the ribs, for example, and yet there is no tendency toward pacifism in this. We might go further and maintain, for example, that capital punishment, even for the crime of murder, is unjustified without doing so on pacifist grounds. Again, the pacifist should say just what sort of a reaction constitutes a forcible or violent one. If somebody attacks me with his fists and I pin his arms to his body with wrestling holds which restrict him but cause him no pain, is that all right in the pacifist's book? And again, many non-pacifists could consistently maintain that we should avoid, to the extent that it is possible, inflicting a like pain on those who attempt to inflict pain on us. It is unnecessary to be a pacifist merely in order to deny the moral soundness of the principle, "an eye for an eye and a tooth for a tooth." We need a clarification, then, from the pacifist as to just how far he is and is not willing to go. But this need should already make us pause, for surely the pacifist cannot draw these lines in a merely arbitrary manner. It is his reasons for drawing the ones he does that count, and these are what I propose to discuss below.

The second matter of degree in respect of which the pacifist must specify his doctrine concerns the question: Who ought not to resist violence with force? For example, there are pacifists who would only claim that they themselves ought not to. Others would say that only pacifists ought not to, or that all persons of a certain type, where the type is not specified in terms of belief or non-belief in pacifism, ought not to resist violence with force. And, finally, there are those who hold that everyone ought not to do so. We shall see that consid-erations about this second variable doom some forms of pacifism to contradiction.

My general program will be to show that (1) only the doctrine that everyone ought not to resist violence with force is of philosophical interest among those doctrines known as "pacifism"; (2) that doctrine, if advanced as a moral doctrine, is logically untenable; and (3) the reasons for the popularity of pacifism rest on failure to see exactly what the doctrine is. The things which pacifism wishes to accomplish, insofar as they are worth accomplishing, can be managed on the basis of quite ordinary and con-servative moral principles.

Let us begin by being precise about the kind of moral force the principle of pacifism is intended to have. One good way to do this is to consider what it is intended to deny. What would non-pacifists, which I sup-pose includes most people, say of a man who followed Christ's sug-gestion and, when unaccountably slapped, simply turned the other cheek? They might say that such a man is either a fool or a saint. Or they might say, "It's all very well for him to do that, but it's not for me"; or they might simply shrug their shoulders and say, "Well, it takes all kinds, doesn't it?" But they would not say that a man who did that ought to be punished in some way; they would not even say that he had done any-thing wrong. In fact, as I have men-tioned, they would more likely than not find something admirable about it. The point, then, is this: The non-pacifist does not say that it is your duty to resist violence with force. The non-pacifist is merely saying that there's nothing wrong with doing so, that one has every right to do so if he is so inclined. Whether we wish to add that a person would be foolish or silly to do so is quite another question, one on which the non-pacifist does not *need* to take any particular position.

Consequently, a genuine pacifist cannot merely say that we may, if we wish, prefer not to resist violence with force. Nor can he merely say that there is something admirable or saintly about not doing so, for, as pointed out above, the non-pacifist could perfectly well agree with that. He must say, instead, that, for whatever class of people he thinks it applies to, there is something positively wrong about meeting violence with force. He must say that, insofar as the people to whom his principle applies resort to force, they are committing a breach of moral duty—a very serious thing to say. Just how serious, we shall ere long see.

Next, we must understand what the implications of holding pacifism as a moral principle are, and the first such implication requiring our attention concerns the matter of the size of the class of people to which it is supposed to apply. It will be of interest to discuss two of the four possibilities previously listed, I think. The first is that in which the pacifist says that only pacifists have the duty of pacifism. Let us see what this amounts to.

If we say that the principle of pacifism is the principle that all and only pacifists have a duty of not opposing violence with force, we get into a very odd situation. For suppose we ask ourselves, "Very well, which people are the pacifists then?" The answer will have to be "All those people who believe that pacifists have the duty

not to meet violence with force." But surely one could believe that a certain class of people, whom we shall call "pacifists," have the duty not to meet violence with force without believing that one ought not, oneself, to meet violence with force. That is to say, the "principle" that pacifists ought to avoid meeting violence with force, is circular: It presupposes that one already knows who the pacifists are. Yet this is precisely what that statement of the principle is supposed to answer! We are supposed to be able to say that anybody who believes that principle is a pacifist; yet, as we have seen, a person could very well believe that a certain class of people called "pacifists" ought not to meet violence with force without believing that he himself ought not to meet violence with force. Thus everyone could be a "pacifist" in the sense of believing that statement and yet no one believe that he *himself* (or anyone in particular) ought to avoid meeting violence with force. Consequently, pacifism cannot be specified in that way. A pacifist must be a person who believes either that he himself (at least) ought not to meet force with force or that some larger class of persons, perhaps everyone, ought not to meet force with force. He would then be believing something definite, and we are then in a position to ask why.

Incidentally, it is worth mentioning that when people say things such as "Only pacifists have the duty of pacifism," "Only Catholics have the duties of Catholicism," and, in general, "Only X-ists have the duties of X-ism" they probably are falling into a trap which catches a good many people. It is, namely, the mistake of supposing that what it *is* to have a certain duty is to *believe* that you have a certain duty. The untenability of this is parallel to the untenability of the previously mentioned attempt to say what pacifism is. For, if having a duty is believing that you have a certain duty, the question arises, "*What* does such a person believe?" The answer that must be given if we follow this analysis would then be, "He believes that he believes that he has a certain duty"; and so on, ad infinitum.

On the other hand, one might believe that having a duty does not consist in believing that one has and yet believe that only those people really have the duty who believe that they have it. But in that case, we would, being conscientious, perhaps want to ask the question, "Well, *ought* I to believe that I have that duty, or oughtn't I?" If you say that the answer is "Yes," the reason cannot be that you already do believe it, for you are asking whether you *should*. On the other hand, the answer "No" or "It doesn't make any difference—it's up to you," implies that there is really no reason for doing the thing in question at all. In short, asking whether I ought to believe that I have a duty to do *x*, is equivalent to asking whether I should *do x*. A person might very well believe that he ought to do *x* but be wrong. It might be the case that he really ought *not* to do *x;* in that case the fact that he believes he ought to do *x*, far from being a reason why he ought to do it, is a reason for us to point out his error. It also, of course, presupposes that he has some reason other than his belief for thinking it is his duty to do *x*.

Having cleared this red herring out of the way, we must consider the view of those who believe that they themselves have a duty of pacifism and ask ourselves the question: What general kind of reason must a person have for supposing a certain type of act to be *his* duty, in a moral sense? Now, one answer he might give is that pacifism as such is a duty, that is, that meeting violence with force is, as such, wrong. In that case, however, what he thinks is not merely that *he* has this duty, but that *everyone* has this duty.

Now he might object, "Well, but no; I don't mean that everyone has it. For instance, if a man is defending, not himself, but *other* people, such as his wife and children, then he has a right to meet violence with force." Now this, of course, would be a very important qualification to his principle and one of a kind which we will be discussing in a moment. Meanwhile, however, we may point out that he evidently still thinks that, if it weren't for certain more important duties, everyone would have a duty to avoid meeting violence with force. In other words, he then believes that, other things being equal, one ought not to meet violence with force. He believes, to put it yet another way, that if one does meet violence with force, one must have a special excuse or justification of a moral kind; then he may want to give some account of just which excuses and justifications would do. Nevertheless, he is now holding a general principle.

Suppose, however, he holds that no one *else* has this duty of pacifism, that only he himself ought not to meet force with force, although it is quite all right for others to do so. Now if this is what our man feels, we may continue to call him a "pacifist," in a somewhat attenuated sense, but he is then no longer holding pacifism as a *moral* principle or, indeed, as a principle at all.* For now his disinclination for violence is essentially just a matter of taste. I like pistachio ice cream, but I wouldn't dream of saying that other people have a duty to eat it; similarly, this man just doesn't *like* to meet force with force, although he wouldn't dream of insisting that others act as he does. And this is a secondary sense of "pacifism," first, because pacifism has always been advocated on moral grounds and, second, because non-pacifists can easily have this same feeling. A person might very well feel squeamish, for example, about using force, even in self-defense, or he might not be able to bring himself to use it even if he wants to. But none of these has anything to do with asserting pacifism to be a duty. Moreover, a mere attitude could hardly license a man to refuse military service if it were required of him, or to join ban-the-bomb crusades, and so forth. (I fear, however, that such attitudes have sometimes caused people to do those things.)

And, in turn, it is similarly impossible to claim that your support of pacifism is a moral one if your position is that a certain selection of people, but no one else, ought not to meet force with force, even though you are unprepared to offer any reason whatever for this selection. Suppose, for example, that you hold that only the Arapahoes, or only the Chinese, or only people more than six feet high have this "duty." If such were the case, and no reasons offered at all, we could only conclude that you had a very peculiar attitude toward the Arapahoes, or whatever, but we would hardly want to say that you had a moral principle. Your "principle" amounts to saying that these particular individuals happen to have the duty of pacifism just because they are the individuals they are, and this, as Bentham would say, is the "negation of all principles." Of course, if you meant that somehow the property of being over six feet tall *makes* it your duty not to use violence, then you have a principle, all right, but a very queer one indeed unless you can give some further reasons. Again, it would not be possible to distinguish this from a sheer attitude.

Pacifism, then, must be the principle that the use of force to meet force is wrong *as such*, that is, that nobody may do so unless he has a special justification.

There is another way in which one might advocate a sort of "pacifism," however, which we must also dispose of before getting to the main point. One might argue that pacifism is desirable as a tactic: that, as a matter of fact, some good end, such as the reduction of violence itself, is to be achieved by "turning the other cheek." For example, if it were the case that turning the other cheek caused the offender to break down and repent, then that would be a very good reason for behaving "pacifistically." If unilateral disarmament causes the other side to disarm, then certainly unilateral disarmament would be a desirable policy. But note that its desirability, if this is the argument, is due to the fact that peace is desirable, a moral position which anybody can take, pacifist or no, plus

---

*Compare, for example, K. Baier, *The Moral Point of View* (Cornell, 1958), p. 191.

the purely contingent fact that this policy causes the other side to disarm, that is, it brings about peace.

And, of course, that's the catch. If one attempts to support pacifism because of its probable effects, then one's position depends on what the effects are. Determining what they are is a purely empirical matter, and, consequently, one could not possibly be a pacifist as a matter of pure principle if his reasons for supporting pacifism are merely tactical. One must, in this case, submit one's opinions to the governance of fact.

It is not part of my intention to discuss matters of fact, as such, but it is worthwhile to point out that the general history of the human race certainly offers no support for the supposition that turning the other cheek always produces good effects on the aggressor. Some aggressors, such as the Nazis, were apparently just "egged on" by the "pacifist" attitude of their victims. Some of the S.S. men apparently became curious to see just how much torture the victim would put up with before he began to resist. Furthermore, there is the possibility that, while pacifism might work against some people (one might cite the British, against whom pacifism in India was apparently rather successful—but the British are comparatively nice people), it might fail against others (e.g., the Nazis).

A further point about holding pacifism to be desirable as a tactic is that this could not easily support the position that pacifism is a *duty*. The question whether we have no *right* to fight back can hardly be settled by noting that not to fight back might cause the aggressor to stop fighting. To prove that a policy is a desirable one because it works is not to prove that it is *obligatory* to follow it. We surely need considerations a good deal less tenuous than this to prove such a momentous contention as that we have no *right* to resist.

It appears, then, that to hold the pacifist position as a genuine, full-blooded moral principle is to hold that nobody has a right to fight back when attacked, that fighting back is inherently evil, as such. It means that we are all mistaken in supposing that we have a right of self-protection. And, of course, this is an extreme and extraordinary position in any case. It appears to mean, for instance, that we have no right to punish criminals, that all of our machinery of criminal justice is, in fact, unjust. Robbers, murderers, rapists, and miscellaneous delinquents ought, on this theory, to be let loose.

Now, the pacifist's first move, upon hearing this, will be to claim that he has been misrepresented. He might say that it is only one's *self* that one has no right to defend, and that one may legitimately fight in order to defend other people. This qualification cannot be made by those pacifists who qualify as conscientious objectors, however, for the latter are refusing to defend their fellow citizens and not merely themselves. But this is comparatively trivial when we contemplate the next objection to this amended version of the theory. Let us now ask ourselves what it is about attacks on *other* people which could possibly justify *us* in defending them, while we are not justified in defending ourselves? It cannot be the mere fact that they are other people than ourselves, for, of course, everyone is a different person from everyone else, and if such a consideration could ever of itself justify anything at all it could also justify anything whatever. That mere difference of person, as such, is of no moral importance, is a presupposition of anything that can possibly pretend to be a moral theory.

Instead of such idle nonsense, then, the pacifist would have to mention some specific characteristic which every *other* person has which we lack and which justifies us in defending them. But this, alas, is impossible, for, while there may be some interesting difference between *me*, on the one hand, and everyone else, on the other, the pacifist is not merely addressing himself to me. On the contrary, as we have seen, he has to address himself to everyone. He is claiming that each person has no right to defend himself, although he does have a right to defend other people. And, therefore, what is needed is a characteristic which distinguishes *each* person from everyone else, and not just *me* from everyone else—which is plainly self-contradictory.

If the reader does not yet see why the "characteristic" of being identical with oneself cannot be used to support a moral theory, let him reflect that the proposition "Everyone is identical with himself" is a trivial truth—as clear an example of an analytic proposition as there could possibly be. But a statement of moral principle is not a trivial truth; it is a substantive moral assertion. But non-tautologous statements, as everyone knows, cannot logically be derived from tautologies, and, consequently, the fact that everyone is identical with himself cannot possibly be used to prove a moral position.

Again, then, the pacifist must re-treat in order to avoid talking idle nonsense. His next move, now, might be to say that we have a right to defend all those who are not able to defend themselves. Big, grown-up men who are able to defend themselves ought not to do so, but they ought to defend mere helpless children who are unable to defend themselves.

This last, very queer theory could give rise to some amusing logical gymnastics. For instance, what about groups of people? If a group of people who cannot defend themselves singly can defend themselves together, then when it has grown to that size ought it to stop defending itself? If so, then every time a person *can* defend someone else, he would form with the person being defended a "defensive unit" which was able to defend itself, and thus would by his very presence debar himself from making the defense. At this rate, no one will ever get defended, it seems: The defenseless people by definition cannot defend themselves, while those who can defend them would enable the group consisting of the defenders and the defended to defend themselves, and hence they would be obliged not to do so.

Such reflections, however, are merely curious shadows of a much more fundamental and serious logical problem. This arises when we begin to ask: But why should even defenseless people be defended? If resisting violence is inherently evil, then how can it suddenly become permissible when we use it on behalf of other people? The fact that they are defenseless cannot possibly account for this, for it follows from the theory in question, that everyone ought to put himself in the position of people who are defenseless by refusing to defend himself. This type of pacifist, in short, is using the very characteristic (namely, being in a state of not defending oneself) which he wishes to encourage in others as a reason for denying it in the case of those who already have it (namely, the defenseless). This is indeed self-contradictory.

To attempt to be consistent, at least, the pacifist is forced to accept the characterization of him at which we tentatively arrived. He must indeed say that no one ought ever to be defended against attack. The right of self-defense can be denied coherently only if the right of defense, in general, is denied. This in itself is an important conclusion.

It must be borne in mind, by the way, that I have not said anything to take exception to the man who simply does not wish to defend himself. So long as he does not attempt to make his pacifism into a principle, one cannot accuse him of any inconsistency, however much one might wish to say that he is foolish or eccentric. It is solely with moral principles that I am concerned here.

We now come to the last and most fundamental problem of all. If we ask ourselves what the point of pacifism is, what gets it going, so to speak, the answer is, of course, obvious enough: opposition to violence. The pacifist is generally thought of as a man who is so much opposed to violence that he will not even use it to defend himself or anyone else. And it is precisely this characterization which I wish to show is far from being plausible, morally inconsistent.

To begin with, we may note something which at first glance may seem merely to be a matter of fact, albeit one which should worry the pacifist, in our latest characterization of him. I refer to the commonplace observation that, generally speaking, we measure a man's degree of opposition to something by the amount of effort he is willing to put forth against it. A man could hardly be said to be dead set against something if he is not willing to lift a finger to keep it from going on. A person who claims to be completely opposed to something yet does nothing to prevent it would ordinarily be said to be a hypocrite.

As facts, however, we cannot make too much of these. The pacifist could claim to be willing to go to any length, short of violence, to prevent violence. He might, for instance, stand out in the cold all day long handing out leaflets (as I have known some to do), and this would surely argue for the sincerity of his beliefs.

But would it really?

Let us ask ourselves, one final time, what we are claiming when we claim that violence is morally wrong and unjust. We are, in the first place, claiming that a person *has no right* to indulge in it, as such (meaning that he has no right to indulge in it, *unless* he has an overriding justification). But what do we mean when we say that he has no right to indulge in it? Violence, of the type we are considering, is a two-termed affair: one does violence *to* somebody, one cannot simply "do violence." It might be oneself, of course, but we are not primarily interested in those cases, for what makes it wrong to commit violence is that it harms the people to whom it is done. To say that it is wrong is to say that those to whom it is done have a right *not* to have it done to them. (This must again be qualified by pointing out that this is so only if they have done nothing to merit having that right abridged.)

Yet what could that right to their own security, which people have, possibly consist in, if not a right at least to defend themselves from whatever violence might be offered them? But lest the reader think that this is a gratuitous assumption, note carefully the reason why having a right involves having a right to be defended from breaches of that right. It is because the prevention of infractions of that right is precisely what one has a right to when one has a right at all. A right just *is* a status justifying preventive action. To say that you have a right to X but that no one has any justification whatever for preventing people from depriving you of it, is self-contradictory. If you claim a right to X, then to describe some action as an act of depriving you of X, is logically to imply that its absence is one of the things that you have a right to.

Thus far it does not follow logically that we have a right to use force in our own or anyone's defense. What does follow logically is that one has a right to whatever may be necessary to prevent infringements of his right. One might at first suppose that the universe *could* be so constructed that it is never necessary to use force to prevent people who are bent on getting something from getting it.

Yet even this is not so, for when we speak of "force" in the sense in which pacifism is concerned with it, we do not mean merely physical "force." To call an action a use of force is not merely to make a reference to the laws of mechanics. On the contrary, it is to describe whatever is being done as being a means to the infliction on somebody of something (ordinarily physical) which he does not want done to him; and the same is true for "force" in the sense in which it applies to war, assault and battery, and the like.

The proper contrary of "force" in this connection is "rational persuasion." Naturally, one way there *might* be of getting somebody not to do something he has no right to do is to convince him he ought not to do it or that it is not in his interest to do it. But it is inconsistent, I suggest, to argue that rational persuasion is the only morally permissible method of preventing violence. A pragmatic reason for this is easy enough to point to: Violent people are too busy being violent to be reasonable. We cannot engage in rational persuasion unless the enemy is willing to sit down and talk; but what if he isn't? One cannot contend that every human being can be persuaded to sit down and talk before he strikes, for this is not something we can determine just by reasoning: it is a question of observation, certainly. But these points are not strictly relevant anyway, for our question is not the empirical question of whether there is some handy way which can always be used to get a person to sit down and discuss moral philosophy when he is about to murder you. Our question is: *If* force is the only way to prevent violence in a given case, is its use justified *in that case?* This is a purely moral question which we can discuss without any special reference to matters of fact. And, moreover, it is precisely this question which we should have to discuss with the would-be violator. The point is that if a person can be rationally persuaded that he ought not to engage in violence, then precisely what he would be rationally persuaded of if we were to succeed would be the proposition that the use of force is justifiable to prevent him from doing so. For note that if we were to argue that only rational persuasion is permissible as a means of preventing him, we would have to face the question: Do we mean *attempted* rational persuasion, or *successful* rational persuasion, that is, rational persuasion which really does succeed in preventing him from acting? Attempted rational persuasion might fail (if only because the opponent is unreasonable), and then what? To argue that we have a right to use rational persuasion which also succeeds (i.e., we have a right to its success as well as to its use) is to imply that we have a right to prevent him from performing the act. But this, in turn, means that, if attempts at rational persuasion fail, we have a right to the use of force. Thus what we have a right to, if we ever have a *right* to anything, is not merely the use of rational persuasion to keep people from depriving you of the thing to which you have the right. We do indeed have a right to that, but we also have a right to anything else that might be necessary (other things being equal) to prevent the deprivation from occurring. And it is a logical truth, not merely a contingent one, that what *might* be necessary is *force*. (If merely saying something could miraculously deprive someone of the ability to carry through a course of action, then those speech-acts would be called a type of force, if a very

mysterious one. And we could properly begin to oppose their use for precisely the same reasons as we now oppose violence.)

What this all adds up to, then, is that *if* we have any rights at all, we have a right to use force to prevent the deprivation of the thing to which we are said to have a right. But the pacifist, of *all* people, is the one most concerned to insist that we do have some rights, namely, the right not to have violence done to us. This is logically implied in asserting it to be a duty on everyone's part to avoid violence. And this is why the pacifist's position is self-contradictory. In saying that violence is wrong, one is at the same time saying that people have a right to its prevention, by force if necessary. Whether and to what extent it may be necessary is a question of fact, but, since it is a question of fact only, the *moral* right to use force on some possible occasions is established.

We now have an answer to the question. How much force does a given threat of violence justify for preventive purposes? The answer, in a word, is "Enough." That the answer is this simple may at first sight seem implausible. One might suppose that some elaborate equation between the aggressive and the preventive force is needed: the punishment be proportionate to the crime. But this is a misunderstanding. In the first place, prevention and punishment are not the same, even if punishment is thought to be directed mainly toward prevention. The punishment of a particular crime logically cannot prevent *that* instance of the crime, since it presupposes that it has already been performed; and punishment need not involve the use of any violence at all, although law-enforcement officers in some places have a nasty tendency to assume the contrary. But preventive force is another matter. If a man threatens to kill me, it is desirable, of course, for me to try to prevent this by the use of the least amount of force sufficient to do the job. But I am justified even in killing him *if* necessary. This much, I suppose, is obvious to most people. But suppose his threat is much smaller: suppose that he is merely pestering me, which is a very mild form of aggression indeed. Would I be justified in killing him to prevent this, under any circumstances whatever?

Suppose that I call the police and they take out a warrant against him, and suppose that when the police come, he puts up a struggle. He pulls a knife or a gun, let us say, and the police shoot him in the ensuing battle. Has my right to the prevention of his annoying me extended to killing him? Well, not exactly, since the immediate threat in response to which he is killed is a threat to the lives of the policemen. Yet my annoyer may never have contemplated real violence. It is an unfortunate case of unpremeditated escalation. But this is precisely what makes the contention that one is justified in using enough force to do the job, whatever amount that may be, to prevent action which violates a right less alarming than at first sight it seems. For it is difficult to envisage a reason why extreme force is needed to prevent mild threats from realization except by way of escalation, and escalation automatically justifies increased use of preventive force.

The existence of laws, police, courts, and more or less civilized modes of behavior on the part of most of the populace naturally affects the answer to the question of how much force is necessary. One of the purposes of a legal system of justice is surely to make the use of force by individuals very much less necessary than it would otherwise be. If we try to think back to a "state of nature" situation, we shall have much less difficulty envisaging the need for large amounts of force to prevent small threats of violence. Here Hobbes's contention that in such a state every man has a right to the life of every other becomes understandable. He was, I suggest, relying on the same principle as I have argued for here: that one has a right to use as much force as necessary to defend one's rights, which include the right of safety of person.

I have said that the duty to avoid violence is only a duty, other things being equal. We might arrive at the same conclusion as we have above by asking the question: Which "other things" might count as being *un-*equal? The answer to this is that whatever else they may be, the purpose of preventing violence from being done is necessarily one of these justifying conditions. That the use of force is never justified to prevent initial violence being done to one logically implies that there is nothing wrong with initial violence. We cannot characterize it as being wrong if preventive violence is not simultaneously being characterized as justifiable.

We often think of pacifists as being gentle and idealistic souls, which in its way is true enough. What I have been concerned to show is that they are also confused. If they attempt to formulate their position using our standard concepts of rights, their position involves a contradiction: Violence is wrong, *and* it is wrong to resist it. But the right to resist is precisely what having a right of safety of person is, if it is anything at all.

Could the position be reformulated with a less "committal" concept of rights? I do not think so. It has been suggested* that the pacifist need not talk in terms of this "kind" of rights. He can affirm, according to this suggestion, simply that neither the aggressors nor the defenders "have" rights to what they do, that to affirm their not having them is simply to be against the use of force, without this entailing the readiness to use force if necessary to protect the said rights. But this will not do, I believe. For I have not maintained that having a right, or believing that one has a right, entails a *readiness* to defend that right. One has a perfect right not to resist violence to oneself if one is so inclined. But our question has been whether self-defense is justifiable, and not whether one's belief that violence is wrong entails a willingness or readiness to use it. My contention has been that such a belief does entail the justifiability of using it. If one came upon a community in which no sort of violence was ever resisted and it was claimed in that community that the non-resistance was a matter of conscience, we should have to conclude, I think, not that this was a community of saints, but rather that this community lacked the con-

cept of justice—or perhaps that their nervous systems were oddly different from ours.

The true test of the pacifist comes, of course, when he is called upon to assist in the protection of the safety of other persons and not just of himself. For while he is, as I have said, surely entitled to be pacific about his own person if he is so inclined, he is not entitled to be so about the safety of others. It is here that the test of principles comes out. People have a tendency to brand conscientious objectors as cowards or traitors, but this is not quite fair. They are acting as if they were cowards or traitors, but claiming to do so on principle. It is not surprising if a community should fail to understand such "principles," for the test of adherence to a principle is willingness to act on it, and the appropriate action, if one believes a certain thing to be grossly wrong, is to take steps to prevent or resist it. Thus people who assess conscientious objection as cowardice or worse are taking an understandable step: from an intuitive feeling that the pacifist does not really believe what he is saying they infer that his actions (or inaction) must be due to cowardice. What I am suggesting is that this is not correct: The actions are due, not to cowardice, but to confusion.

I have not addressed myself specifically to the question whether, for instance, conscription is morally justifiable, given that the war effort on behalf of which it is invoked is genuinely justifiable. Now, war efforts very often aren't justifiable (indeed, since at least one of the parties to each war must be an aggressor, a minimum of 50 per cent of war efforts must be

---

*I owe this suggestion to my colleague, Leslie Armour.

unjustifiable); but if they ever are, is it then justifiable to conscript soldiers? In closing, I would suggest an answer which may seem surprising in view of my arguments a few pages back. My answer is that it is, but that in the case of conscientious objectors, the only justifiable means of getting them to comply is rational persuasion.

The reason is that, in showing that self-defense is morally justifiable, one has not simultaneously shown that the defense of other people is morally *obligatory*. The kinds of arguments needed to show that an act is obligatory are quite different from those which merely show that it is justified. And, since what has been shown is that self-defense is justifiable and not obligatory, the only conclusion that can be immediately inferred from this is that defense of others is also justifiable and not obligatory. Would it be possible to show that the defense of others (at least in some circumstances) is obligatory and not merely justifiable, without at the same time showing that self-defense is obligatory and not merely justifiable?

The only thing I can suggest here is that the answer requires us to speculate about the obligations of living in a community. If a community expects its members to assist in the common defense when necessary, it can make this clear to people and give them their choice either to be prepared to meet this obligation or to live somewhere else. But a community of pacifists would also be quite conceivable, a community in which no citizen could expect the others to defend him as a part of their community responsibilities. One might not care to live in such a community, but then,

a pacifist might not care to live in our sort. When the community is a whole nation of present-day size, it is much more difficult to put the issue clearly to each citizen in advance. But the upshot of it is that (1) the issue depends upon what sort of community we conceive ourselves to have; (2) we do not have clearly formed views on this point; (3) there is no basic moral duty to defend others; (4) we therefore have no direct right to force people to become soldiers in time of justified wars; (5) but we do have a right to deny many basic community services to people who will not assist us in time of need by contributing the force of their arms; and so (6) the only thing to do is to try to argue conscientious objectors into assistance, pointing to all of the above factors and leaving them their choice.

Too much can easily be made of the issue of conscription *versus* voluntary service in time of war. (In time of peace, we have another issue altogether; my arguments here apply only when there is clear justification for defensive measures.) It must be remembered that there is a limit to what law can do in "requiring" compliance, and the pacifist is precisely the person who cannot be reached by the ordinary methods of the law, since he has made up his mind not to be moved by force. The philosophical difference lies, not in the question of whether compliance is ultimately voluntary, since with all laws it to some extent must be, but in the moral status which military service is presumed to have. The draft is morally justifiable if the defense of persons is considered a basic obligation of the citizen. In contemporary communities, it seems to me that there is good reason for giving it that status.

Many questions remain to be discussed, but I hope to have exposed the most fundamental issues surrounding this question and to have shown that the pacifist's central position is untenable.

TRUMBO/*Johnny Got His Gun*

World War I began like a Fourth of July parade—billowing flags, marching bands, smartly outfitted troops, patriotic speeches. Nine million corpses later it ended.

In 1938 Dalton Trumbo wrote about that war in what has become a classic antiwar novel, Johnny Got His Gun. *The story concerns young Joe Bonham, who, like so many of his age, marches off to tunes of glory to fight "the war to end all wars." But unlike many who went with him, Joe is not lucky enough to die. Instead he returns, little more than a mass of protoplasm. Worst of all, although having only a tactual sense, Joe is acutely aware of his predicament, as well as his past and inevitable future.*

By tapping his head against the wall, Joe is finally able to effect a Morse code and to communicate to the hospital staff. His request: that he be allowed to leave, even if that only means to be taken "down to the places where people are having fun where they are on the lookout for freakish things."

In the selection that follows Joe receives an answer to his request. His reaction is about as strong an antiwar statement as one is likely to find in literature.

Note that Trumbo's assessment is that war is absolutely immoral. Do you agree? What justification does Trumbo provide for his thesis?

He felt the vibrations of heavy feet leaving the room. The man who had come in and tapped the question and who had stood listening to his reply for how long he couldn't imagine had gone. He was alone with the nurse again. He was left alone to wonder.

He began to have misgivings. Just as he had always suspected himself of some mistake in his count of time so now he felt wild little ripples of fear shudder through his flesh. He had been so eager to tap that perhaps his message hadn't made sense. Perhaps he had made a mistake in remembering the code so that his words came out as a jumble of letters with no meaning. His thoughts had rushed through his head so tumultuously that perhaps he hadn't got them down in order clearly and sanely. Perhaps ten thousand other possibilities had come between him and the message he was bleeding inside to give them. Or perhaps the man had just gone away to talk to his superior and would soon return with an answer.

That was it. Oh please god that must be it he was sure of it. The man would return soon with an answer. All he had to do was lie back and rest he was so tired. It seemed to him that he was lying in some kind of dream coma like a man who has spent all his emotions in one wild drunk and afterward is simply sick and disgusted and sure of the worst. He had

From Dalton Trumbo, *Johnny Got His Gun*, Bantam Books, 1970. Reprinted by permission.

been tapping now for weeks months maybe years he couldn't tell because the tapping had taken the place of time for him and all his energies had gone into it all his energies and all his hopes and all his life.

He stiffened.

The vibrations were coming toward him again. The man was returning with an answer. Great merciful god thank you here it is here it is my answer. Here is my triumph here is my return from the dead here is life vibrating against the floor singing in my bedsprings singing like all the angels in heaven.

A finger began to tap against his forehead.

·—— ···· ·— —
W H A T

···· ·· ·——
Y O U

·— ··· —·—
A S K

·· ···
I S

·— ——· ·— ·· —· ··· —
A G A I N S T

·—· · ——· ··— ·—·· ·— — ·—— ——· ···
R E G U L A T I O N S

·—— ···· ———
W H O

·— ·—· ·
A R E

···· ·· ·——
Y O U

The tapping went on against his forehead but he paid no more attention to it. Everything in his mind went suddenly blank hollow completely quiet. A moment of this and then he began to think about the message to make certain there was no mistake that it meant exactly what it said. And he knew it did.

He could almost hear the wail of pain that went up from his heart. It was a sharp terrible personal pain the kind of pain that comes only when someone to whom you have never done any harm turns on you and says goodbye goodbye forever without any reason for doing it. Without any reason at all.

He had done nothing to them. He wasn't to blame for the trouble he was causing yet they were drawing the curtain around him stuffing him back into the womb back into the grave saying to him goodbye don't bother us don't come back to life the dead should stay dead and we are done with you.

But why?

He had hurt no one. He had tried to give them as little trouble as possible. He was a great care that was true but he hadn't intentionally become so. He wasn't a thief or a drunkard or a liar or a murderer. He was a man a guy no worse no better than anybody else. He was just a guy who'd had to go to war who'd been bad hurt and now was trying to get out from his prison to feel fresh cool air on his skin to sense the color and movement of people around him. That was all he wanted. And to him who had harmed nobody they were saying goodnight goodbye stay where you are don't give us any trouble you are beyond life you are beyond death you are even beyond hope you are gone and you are finished forever goodnight and goodbye.

In one terrible moment he saw the whole thing. They wanted only to forget him. He was upon their conscience so they had abandoned him they had forsaken him. They were the only people in the world who could help him. They were his last court of appeal. He might rage and storm and howl against their verdict but it would do him no good. They had decided. Nothing could change them. He was completely at their mercy and they had no mercy. For him there was no hope. He might just as well come face to face with the truth.

Every moment of his life since he had awakened into the darkness and dumbness and terror every moment of it had been concentrated upon the time some day some year when he would break through to them. Now he had done it. He had broken through and they had refused him. Before even in his most terrible moments there had been a vague hope that kept him going. It had prevented him from going stark raving crazy it had shined like a glow in the distance toward which he never stopped moving. Now the glow was gone and there was nothing left. There was no reason for him to fool himself about it any longer. These people didn't want him. Darkness desertion loneliness silence horror unending horror—these were his life from now on without a single ray of hope to lighten his sufferings. They were his whole future. It was for them that his mother had borne him. Curse her curse the world curse the sunlight curse god curse every decent thing on earth. God damn them god damn them and torture them as he was being tortured. God give them darkness and silence and dumbness and helplessness and horror and fear the great towering terrible fear that was with him now the desolation and the loneliness that would be with him forever.

No.

No no no.

He wouldn't let them do it.

It was impossible for one human being to do this to another. No one could be so cruel. They didn't understand that was all he hadn't made it plain enough to them. He couldn't give up now he must go on and on until they understood because they were good people they were good kindly people and they needed only to understand.

He began to tap again.

He began to tap again and to tell them pleadingly haltingly humbly that please he wanted out. He wanted to feel air against him the fresh clean air outside a hospital. Please understand. He wanted the feel of people of his own kind free and happy. There really wasn't any good reason except that. The thing about showing him in a case forget that it was just a way to raise money and make it easier on them. Only that. He was lonesome. That was all just lonesome. There were no more reasons he could give them. There was nothing he could do except to try to let them know that inside the skin that covered his body there was so much terror so much loneliness that it was only right they should permit him such a small thing as the freedom he could pay for.

As he tapped he felt the nurse's hand against his forehead stroking him soothing him. He thought to himself I wish I could see her face. It must be a beautiful face she has such beautiful hands. Then against the stump of his left arm he felt a sudden wet coolness. The man who had tapped his answer was applying an alcoholic swab. Oh god he thought I know what that means don't do it please don't. Then he felt the sharp deadly prick of the needle. They were giving him dope again.

Oh god he thought they won't even let me talk. They won't even listen to me any more. All they want is to make a madman out of me so that whenever I tap my messages to them they can say he's only crazy don't pay any attention to him poor fellow he's nuts. That's what they're trying to do god they're trying to drive me crazy and I've fought so hard I've been so strong that the only way they can do it is by giving me dope.

He felt himself sinking back back into the place where they wanted to thrust him. He felt the tingle of his own flesh and he began to see the vision. He saw the yellow sand and he saw the heat waves coming up from it. Above the heat waves he saw Christ in his flowing robes and his crown of thorns with the blood dripping from them. He saw Christ quivering in the desert heat coming up from Tucson. And far off in the distance he heard a woman's voice crying my son my little boy my son . . .

In sheer terrible desperation he shut out the voice he pushed the vision away. Not yet. Not yet. He wasn't through. He would talk to them he would keep on tapping. The muscles of his body were turning to water but he would keep on tapping. He would not let them lower the lid to his coffin. He would scream and claw and fight as any man should do when they are burying him alive. In his last moment of consciousness in his last moment of life he would still fight he would still tap. He would keep on and on and on tapping all the while tapping when he was asleep tapping when he was doped tapping when he was in pain tapping forever. They might not answer him they might ignore him but at least they would never be able to forget that as long as he lived here was a man who was talking to them talking to them all the time.

His taps came slower and slower and the vision swam toward him and he pushed it away and it swam toward him again. The woman's voice faded in and out like something that is carried on the wind. But still he tapped.

He was tapping why? why? why?

Why didn't they want him? Why were they shutting the lid of the coffin against him? Why didn't they want him to speak? Why didn't they want him to be seen? Why didn't they want him to be free? It was five maybe six years now since he had been blown out of the world. The war must be over by now. No war could last that long killing so many people there weren't enough people to kill. If the war was over then all the dead had been buried and all the prisoners had been released. Why shouldn't he be released too? Why not unless they figured him as one of the dead and if that was true why didn't they kill him why didn't they put a stop to his suffering? Why should he be a prisoner? He had committed no crime. What right had they to keep him? What possible reason could they have to be so inhuman to him?

Why? why? why?

And then suddenly he saw. He had a vision of himself as a new kind of Christ as a man who carries within himself all the seeds of a new order of things. He was the new messiah of the battlefields saying to people as I am so shall you be. For he had seen the future he had tasted it and now he was living it. He had seen the airplanes flying in the sky he had seen the skies of the future filled with them black with them and now he saw the horror beneath. He saw a world of lovers forever parted of dreams never consummated of plans that never turned into reality. He saw a world of dead fathers and crippled brothers and crazy screaming sons. He saw a world of armless mothers clasping headless babies to their breasts trying to scream out their grief from throats that were cancerous with gas. He saw starved cities black and cold and motionless and the only things in this whole dead terrible world that made a move or a sound were the airplanes that blackened the sky and far off against the horizon the thunder of the big guns and the puffs that rose from barren tortured earth when their shells exploded.

That was it he had it he understood it now he had told them his secret and in denying him they had told him theirs.

He was the future he was a perfect picture of the future and they were afraid to let anyone see what the future was like. Already they were looking ahead they were figuring the future and somewhere in the future they saw war. To fight that war they would need men and if men saw the future they wouldn't fight. So they were masking the future they were keeping the future a soft quiet deadly secret. They knew that if all the little people all the little guys saw the future they would begin to ask questions. They would ask questions and they would find answers and they would say to the guys who wanted them to fight they would say you are lying thieving sons-of-bitches we won't fight we won't be dead we

will live we are the world we are the future and we will not let you butcher us no matter what you say no matter what speeches you make no matter what slogans you write. Remember it well we we we are the world we are what makes it go round we make bread and cloth and guns we are the hub of the wheel and the spokes and the wheel itself without us you would be hungry naked worms and we will not die. We are immortal we are the sources of life we are the lowly despicable ugly people we are the great wonderful beautiful people of the world and we are sick of it we are utterly weary we are done with it forever and ever because we are the living and we will not be destroyed.

If you make a war if there are guns to be aimed if there are bullets to be fired if there are men to be killed they will not be us. They will not be us the guys who grow wheat and turn it into food the guys who make clothes and paper and houses and tiles the guys who build dams and power plants and string the long moaning high tension wires the guys who crack crude oil down into a dozen different parts who make light globes and sewing machines and shovels and automobiles and airplanes and tanks and guns oh no it will not be us who die. It will be you.

It will be you—you who urge us on to battle you who incite us against ourselves you who would have one cobbler kill another cobbler you who would have one man who works kill another man who works you who would have one human being who wants only to live kill another human being who wants only to live. Remember this. Remember this well you people who plan for war. Remember this you patriots you fierce ones you spawners of hate you inventors of slogans. Remember this as you have never remembered anything else in your lives.

We are men of peace we are men who work and we want no quarrel. But if you destroy our peace if you take away our work if you try to range us one against the other we will know what to do. If you tell us to make the world safe for democracy we will take you seriously and by god and by Christ we will make it so. We will use the guns you force upon us we will use them to defend our very lives and the menace to our lives does not lie on the other side of a nomansland that was set apart without our consent it lies within our own boundaries here and now we have seen it and we know it.

Put the guns into our hands and we will use them. Give us the slogans and we will turn them into realities. Sing the battle hymns and we will take them up where you left off. Not one not ten not ten thousand not a million not ten millions not a hundred millions but a billion two billions of us all the people of the world we will have the slogans and we will have the hymns and we will have the guns and we will use them and we will live. Make no mistake of it we will live. We will be alive and we will walk and talk and eat and sing and laugh and feel and love and bear our children in tranquillity in security in decency in peace. You plan the wars you masters of men plan the wars and point the way and we will point the gun.

9

REVERSE DISCRIMINATION
of righting sexism and fighting fire with fire
SOCIAL JUSTICE

In recent years laws have been passed and programs formulated to ensure fair and equal treatment of all persons in employment practices. Nevertheless, unequal practices still exist. To help remedy these, the federal government in the early 1970s instituted an affirmative action program.

Before affirmative action, many institutions already followed nondiscriminatory as well as merit-hiring employment practices to equalize employment opportunities. In proposing the affirmative action program, the government recognized the worth of such endeavors, but said that it didn't think that they were enough. Affirmative action, therefore, refers to positive measures beyond neutral nondiscriminatory and merit-hiring employment practices. It is an aggressive program intended to identify and remedy discrimination practiced against many people who are qualified for jobs.

One of the most controversial aspects of affirmative action are its preferential and quota-hiring systems. *Preferential hiring* is an employment practice designed to give special consideration to persons from groups that traditionally have been victimized by racism, sexism, or other forms of discrimination. *Quota hiring* is the policy of hiring and employing people in direct proportion to their numbers in society or in the community. According to affirmative action guidelines, preferential and quota hiring go hand in glove; thus, for simplicity, we will refer to both by the phrase *quota hiring*. Courts are increasingly requiring companies and unions to provide apprentice and reapprentice training to hire, promote, and train minorities and women in specified numerical ratios, in specified job categories, until specified remedial goals are reached.

To illustrate how a quota-hiring system might work, suppose that an equally qualified man and woman are applying for a single job. The employer, conscious of affirmative action guidelines, realizes that the company historically has discriminated against women. So, the employer plugs in a quota-hiring factor that clearly serves the female's interests. She gets the job. Problem: is the employer's action moral? Has the male applicant been treated unfairly? Would it have been fairer had their names been thrown into a hat from which one was drawn? Obviously a quota-hiring system raises questions of social justice.

301

Undoubtedly some will wonder: why not focus directly on the morality of sexism? By *sexism* is meant the unequal treatment of a person exclusively on the basis of sex. Perhaps we should focus on it, but consider that in all our discussions so far we have made reasonable cases for at least two sides of an issue. True, perhaps one side was more flawed than another, but in all cases reasonable people could disagree. But the fact is that no one seriously argues any more that sexism, as defined, is moral. So, if we focused on sexism we would be inviting a most lopsided discussion. This would be unfortunate in the light of so many aspects of sexism that genuinely deserve moral debate. One of these aspects involves such proposed remedies as quota hiring.

Another reason for not considering sexism exclusively is that this chapter concerns social justice. Many discussions of social justice founder because they remain abstract, content to theorize while scrupulously avoiding practice. For example, it is easy and safe to argue that a government must remedy racial injustice. It's far more controversial to argue that a government must implement forced busing to do so. The same applies to sexism. Most would agree that the government has an obligation to correct the social injustice of sexism, but how?

It is one thing to recognize, deplore, and want to correct any injustice. It is another thing entirely to remedy the injustice fairly. Sadly, too many discussions of social justice ignore means entirely, often offering the defense that the means vary from situation to situation. Undoubtedly. But the debate that flies around so many social justice questions today concerns proposed means. We should learn to examine every situation's means and also the common but agonizing predicament of applauding the intention and even the probable consequences of an action, but deploring the action itself. For many people, quota hiring is just such a problem.

So, in this chapter we consider the concept of social justice, especially as it relates to quota hiring to correct sexism. Specifically we will air one contemporary view of social justice that already has received widespread attention—John Rawls's maximin principle of justice. Central to Rawls's thinking is the concept of contract theory, a political idea concerning the proper relationship between the state and the individual. To understand this contract theory it will be helpful to begin with some general remarks about a concept that we have already referred to—justice.

JUSTICE

One undeniable fact about human beings is that we are social animals. We work with, depend on, and relate to each other for our survival and prosperity. The totality of the relationships among people is known as society. A specific society consists of a group of human beings broadly distinguished from other groups by similar interests, shared institutions, and a common culture. The relationships that exist between an individual and society are often ill defined and fraught with moral conflict.

One element of this relationship is justice. Social and political philosophers since Plato have spoken of the need for a just society and have offered their concepts of it. Our political and social structures seek to attain justice through a contract between the individual and the state, by which is meant municipal, state, and federal governments in general. In evaluating a state we invariably wonder how fairly it treats its citizens. We probably think that the just state is the one that tries to treat its citizens fairly; the unjust one the one that does not. But what are justice and fair play?

This question plays a prominent role in women's fight for equality. Historically women have been one of the most oppressed and exploited social groups. This has been particularly true in the area of employment and in too many instances remains true. Too often, only because of their sex, women are denied jobs that they can easily perform. Even more often they receive lower pay than men who perform the same work. And when promotion time comes around, females are frequently passed over.

A quota-hiring system as previously defined is a direct effort to remedy this unequal treatment. But whether a government has the right to tell persons whom they must hire is a question that is hotly debated. Some say that the government has no right to invade what is clearly the realm of individual privacy. Others say that the government not only has the right but the obligation to redress blatant inequality when it directly violates the rights of its citizens, in this case women. What is at issue is the proper line of demarcation between individual and society; and this line, wherever it lies, involves the question of justice. It also directly affects our lives and personal morality.

To plumb this question more deeply, let's introduce two young people, Fred and Laura. Like many recent college graduates, they are looking for work. By chance they meet in the reception room of a large engineering firm, where they are both applying for the same job.

Fred: I don't mind admitting that I wish my competition for this job was exclusively male.

Laura: Now don't tell me that you don't think women can make good engineers, because I've been hearing that for four years.

Fred: No, it's not that. In fact, the top graduate from my class was a female. It's just that I think I'd have a better chance to get this job if a female weren't applying.

Laura: Are you kidding? How many women engineers do you know of? If they hire anyone here, it'll be a male.

Fred: I don't think so. With all the federal regulations around today, companies like this one are just dying to hire a qualified female.

Laura: So what's wrong with that? If you ask me it's about time we got an even deal.

Fred: I agree. I'm just saying that my own job prospects are that much less.

Laura: If you're better qualified, you'll get the job, don't worry.

Fred: I'm not so sure. Yesterday a personnel guy told me that the choice for the position I was applying for came down to me and a woman. As far as he was concerned, I was the more qualified, at least on paper. Don't get me wrong, she met the job specs. It was just that I looked better.

Laura: But she got the job. Is that what happened?

Fred: He said that he didn't really have any choice, but that he wanted me to know so I wouldn't think it was anything personal or that I was unqualified.

Laura: Well, I can understand how you must feel. But on the other hand you must remember all the job opportunities that women have missed out on because of sexism.

Fred: I keep telling myself that. But I still can't help thinking that I wasn't responsible for that.

Laura: Of course you weren't. But unless the government intervenes aggressively, sexism in employment is going to continue.

Fred: I don't see why you just can't hire someone on their merits.

Laura: Ideally that's how it should be done. But the point is that it is not being done that way. And simply to say to the employer, "Start doing it," will not right the inequality at all.

Fred: But if fair employment practices were enforced, the problem would eventually right itself.

Laura: *Eventually,* sure. But we have an obligation to right it as soon as we can. And the only way we can is to take positive steps to make sure that fairness prevails in the job market. And one way is to make employers hire a certain number of women.

Fred: Even if they are not as qualified as some men?

Laura: As long as they meet job requirements.

Obviously Fred feels that affirmative action guidelines have the effect of treating him unjustly. When we speak of someone being treated unjustly, we usually mean that the person's rights are being violated. The meaning and nature of rights are difficult to establish precisely. For our purposes let's define *a right as an area of decision that other persons do or should respect and that the law does or should protect.** Fred feels that he has the right to be considered for a job solely on the criteria that apply directly to it, what are commonly called job specifications. Since his sex is not directly related to the performance on the job for which he is applying, he feels that he is being treated unfairly; ironically, this is essentially the rationale for quota hiring. Fred might argue that the state has invaded the rights of the employer, as well as his own in formulating the doctrine of quota hiring. So, in Fred's mind, the state would not be at all just in this instance.

When we speak of the "just state," we usually mean the one that ensures a person's rights, whereas the unjust state violates them. Almost all would agree that the just state must ensure the individual's general rights, such as the freedom of expression rights, which include freedom of speech, religion, press, and assembly. Similarly, there is little dispute that the state must ensure certain human or natural rights, such as the right to life, as well as respect for and

---

*Wellman, *Morals & Ethics*, p. 252.

guarantee of the individual's right to be treated equally with other citizens, regardless of religion, race, and sex. But in order to ensure these individual rights, the state must have certain rights or powers of its own.

We tend to think that the state derives these rights as a kind of regulatory agency, with which individuals have entered into a contract whereby they forsake certain individual freedoms in return for the protection of certain rights. The theory behind this contractual relationship is complex, but it is necessary to understand it in order to perceive the dimensions of the justice issue.

CONTRACT THEORY

The so-called contract theory does not refer to a Mafia-sponsored method of erasing certain social problems. Rather, contract theory is an explanation of the origin of the state and a defense of its authority. We see evidence of this contract theory as far back as Plato, but its most noteworthy proponents were Thomas Hobbes (1588–1679) and John Locke (1632–1704). Jean Jacques Rousseau (1712–1778) further advanced the theory.

Hobbes based his political philosophy on the principles of the scientific materialism of the seventeenth century. According to scientific materialism, the world is a mechanical system that can be explained by laws of motion. Even the behavior of humans or complex societies, it was argued, were subject to geometric and physical explanations. Hobbes accepted this view of reality and from it deduced how things must necessarily occur.

In his most famous work, *Leviathan*, Hobbes portrays humans as selfish, unsocial creatures driven by two needs, survival and personal pleasure—a view undoubtedly shared today by the advertising moguls of Madison Avenue. This state is characterized by constant struggle, strife, and war, in which individual is pitted against individual in a battle of self-preservation and gain. As Hobbes writes in *Leviathan*:

> To this, war of every man against every man, this also is consequent: that nothing can be unjust. . . . It is consequent also to the same conditions, that there be no propriety, no dominion, no mine and thine distinct; but only that to be every man's, that he can get; and for so long, as he can keep it.

Granting that the instinct for self-preservation was the basic drive behind human behavior, Hobbes also believed that humans had the capacity to reason.

Although Hobbes never viewed reason to be as energizing a force as self-preservation, he believed that reason could regulate human actions and anticipate their results. So, Hobbes pictures humans as self-centered but rational. This rationality enables them to evaluate the long-term results of behavior originally motivated by self-interest.

Rational concern for their own survival and best long-term interests impel humans to enter into a contract with each other that creates society. Because they recognize that they are destined to be "solitary, poor, nasty, brutish," humans agree to accept an authority outside themselves that has the power to force all to act in the best interests of the majority. For Hobbes this authority is irrevocable. Once set up, the political body with this power exercises complete authority over its subjects and remains in power as long as it's able to compel them to do what they otherwise would not.

So, although individuals contract for society, the society is superior to the individuals, who owe complete allegiance to it. For Hobbes, the state cannot bear any resistance to its rule; however, if such resistance becomes effective, then the state proves itself unable to govern, in which case the established officials no longer rule and the people are no longer subjects. At that point the people revert to their natural state of self-preservation and gain, where they remain until they form another contract.

In contrast with Hobbes's rather pessimistic view of humans, John Locke viewed them as essentially moral beings who ought to obey natural moral rules. Where Hobbes saw the human's natural state characterized by warfare, Locke saw it characterized, at least partially, by a system of natural moral laws. As a result, Locke viewed humans as inherently free and equal, regardless of the existence of any government. It is not, he argued, a government that decrees mutual respect for the freedom and liberties of all, but nature itself.

Nevertheless, like Hobbes, Locke saw a need for a contract. Although he maintained that humans are by nature free, rational, and social creatures, he said that they establish governments because three things are missing in the state of nature: (1) a firm, clearly understood interpretation of natural law, (2) unbiased judges to resolve disputes, and (3) personal recourse in the face of injustices. So, to maintain their *natural rights*, individuals enter into a social contract, whereby they create a political entity capable of preserving the inherent rights of "life, liberty and estate." This contract is based on the consent of the majority, and all willingly agree to obey the decisions of the majority. The state's authority, according to Locke, is limited by the terms of the contract, which is continuously reviewed by the citizenry. So, unlike Hobbes's absolutist state, Locke's is specific and limited. Most important, one of the fundamental moral rights that humans retain in the political state is the right to resist and to challenge authority. While Hobbes believed that resistance to authority was never justified, Locke regarded rebellion as an inherent human right.

Although the contrast between Hobbes and Locke is sharp, they do agree that humans are rational and that this rationality enables them to perceive the necessity of forming a social contract. This contract theory, especially as enunciated by Locke, has heavily influenced our own concept of government, as these lines from the Declaration of Independence suggest:

> To secure these rights (life, liberty and the pursuit of happiness), governments are instituted among Men, deriving their just powers from the consent of the governed. That whenever any Form of Government becomes destructive of these

ends, it is the Right of the People to alter or to abolish it, and to institute a new Government, laying its foundation on such principles and organizing its powers in such form, as to them shall seem most likely to effect their safety and Happiness.

The Declaration and the contract theory agree that when a government "becomes destructive of" the individual rights of life, liberty, and the pursuit of happiness ("estate" for Locke), the people have the right to dismiss it. Problems of social justice arise, however, in interpreting and applying the contract.

INTERPRETING THE CONTRACT

Precisely when is a government destroying individual rights? Perhaps it wouldn't be hard to define when it is depriving us of our lives, but what about liberty and the pursuit of happiness? It could be argued that the liberties referred to are political and civil in nature and thus can be spelled out constitutionally. Still, it's one thing for a constitution to guarantee the right of assembly, it's quite another for the mayor of a city to interpret an assembly as a mob, and for a court to uphold the forceful action the mayor took to disperse that mob. In other words, the U.S. Constitution, like the contract theory on which it is based, provides a general framework to ensure liberties but rightly leaves great latitude for the interpretation and possible restriction of those liberties.

However, it is difficult to determine when a government has become destructive of the pursuit of happiness. For example, some might argue that a graduated income tax destroys the pursuit of happiness. When affluent persons' earnings and holdings are taxed considerably more than lower-income earning persons, some contend that the government is violating the wealthy's pursuit of happiness. In our example, Fred might argue that his pursuit of happiness has been lessened by the affirmative action program. His job possibilities are diminished, and worse, his pride of academic achievement, sense of self-worth, and concept of fair play have been damaged. Laura, on the other hand, would defend not only the right of the government to intervene, but its duty as well.

Under the social contract, then, we give up certain rights to get others. Specifically, under our political system we are guaranteed the rights of life, liberty, and the pursuit of happiness. The problem with such remedies for inequality as quota hiring is whether the government is actually securing these rights. Put another way: is the government acting in such a way that it is actually depriving us of these rights?

There is no simple answer to this question. Obviously, what makes it especially nettlesome is that the issue involves a conflict of rights. On the one hand, there is the right of all job applicants to be treated equally insofar as they will be evaluated only on criteria directly related to their ability to perform the job. On the other hand, it seems that the only way to ensure that persons are not discriminated against on sexual grounds and to remedy this existent problem as quickly as possible is to compel employers to hire a certain number of females. At issue is when, if at all, a government may violate individual rights in order to redress a social problem that apparently involves inequity. In this one issue are evident problems of liberty, equality, and justice, all subjects that social philosophers have traditionally debated.

Already receiving widespread attention is one important contribution to this debate, the maximin principle of justice, which was developed by Harvard University professor John Rawls in the 1970s. Although directly addressing economic questions, as a broad theory of social justice the maximin principle can, and perhaps should, address the problems of sexism in employment and quota hiring. Make no mistake, Rawls's theory is complex. As a result, its discussion in an introductory text like this one must be incomplete and oversimplified. Yet, because Rawls's theory stands as a contemporary alternative to utilitarianism and Marxism, even a superficial presentation of it seems preferable to none at all.

RAWLS'S MAXIMIN PRINCIPLE

For a long time there were basically two views on the question of whether there are individual rights that no person or state can morally violate. One was the utilitarian view, according to which principles of justice are rules that work for the common good. In effect, utilitarianism contends that there are no individual rights that are inviolable. If by violating an individual right we bring about more general good than individual suffering, we may violate that right.

The other view, associated with John Locke and Immanuel Kant, prohibits the use of one person to advance another's end. We have previously seen evidence of this tradition in the fabric of American political theory, which holds that there are some "unalienable rights" that, no matter how much collective good will result, may never be violated.

In 1971 John Rawls's *A Theory of Justice* presented a modern alternative to utilitarianism, that, at the same time, he hoped would be compatible with his belief that justice requires us to improve the lives of the poorest members of society. He calls the alternative the *maximin principle of justice* because by it Rawls intends to maximize the welfare of the minimal social level.

To begin with, Rawls believes that the basis of society is a set of tacit agreements. The problem: to identify the conditions that these agreements should satisfy. Before doing this Rawls points to some unsatisfactory historical explanations of these conditions.

One of these is Hobbes's social contract theory, which Rawls claims is inconsistent. If we agree to subordinate ourselves to an absolute sovereign only because we desire to foster our own security, it would follow that once our security was gained we would have no reason to remain bound by the agreement.

Yet Hobbes obliges us to the rule of sovereign power. Thus, the inconsistency.

In attacking Hobbes this way, Rawls argues that basic social agreements must be acceptable in perpetuity. In other words, social agreements must not depend on one's relative position in a society at a given time. If they do, says Rawls, then they are inconsistent with the nature of a social contract.

According to Rawls, Plato presented another unsatisfactory explanation of the basic conditions on which social agreements are made. In Plato's ideal state, leaders have the right to deceive and manipulate the citizenry intentionally in order to preserve order. Rawls contends that such a condition is incompatible with human nature. In brief, most people in a society would not willingly agree to a social principle that makes them means to ends. Thus, Rawls is suggesting another condition necessary for social agreements: agreements must be able to withstand public exposure, that is, if they were publicized, society would support them.

So, Rawls has isolated two conditions that he considers essential for social agreements: (1) the agreement is made in perpetuity, that is, it does not depend on individual circumstances or whim; and (2) the publicity of the agreement would increase one's commitment to it, that is, its efficacy does not depend on public ignorance.

Rawls then introduces the attitude of the ideal observer. By *attitude of the ideal observer* Rawls simply means the viewpoint of impartiality and disinterest, the attitude that we must maintain in order to determine principles of social justice. The role of the ideal observer is consistent with the two conditions that Rawls has laid down for social agreements, for it categorically ignores our particular characteristics, including personal skills, talents, inclinations, social positions, and political beliefs. When assuming this role, we operate under what Rawls calls a "veil of ignorance." By *veil of ignorance* Rawls means the attitude of a free and rational person who has eliminated all factors of inequality. Having donned this veil of ignorance, we have arrived at the "original position," the position from which we can derive principles of social justice.*

THE ORIGINAL POSITION

Like all contract theorists, Rawls asks us to imagine a "natural state," a hypothetical state of nature in which people are ignorant of their talents and socioeconomic conditions. This is what he means by the *original position.* In this natural state, says Rawls, we find that people are mutually self-interested, rational, and similar in their needs, interests, and capacities.

By saying that people are *mutually self-interested,* Rawls means that in situations involving questions of justice in which people commonly participate, each

---

*This overview is drawn from Ethel M. Albert, Theodore C. Denise, and Sheldon P. Peterfreund, *Great Traditions in Ethics,* 3rd ed. (New York: Van Nostrand, 1975), pp. 416–419.

person is interested in his or her own advantage. By *rational* Rawls means that persons know their interests more or less accurately. Because they are rational, when they are asked in this original position to choose a fundamental principle of justice to be followed, individuals would agree that the *liberty* and *difference principles* are fair. By the *liberty principle* Rawls means that each person participating in a practice or affected by it has an equal right to the greatest amount of liberty that is compatible with a like liberty for all. By the *difference principle* Rawls means that inequality is allowable only insofar as it serves everyone's advantage and arises under conditions of equal opportunity.

Before proceeding, we should mention that by *person* Rawls means not only particular human beings but also collective agencies, and by *practice* he means any form of activity that a system of rules specifies, such as offices, roles, rights, and duties. Now, let's take a closer look at the heart of Rawls's theory of justice— the principles of equal liberty and difference. First, the equal liberty principle.

THE EQUAL LIBERTY PRINCIPLE

In developing the equal liberty principle, Rawls admits that there is nothing new about it or his principle of justice for that matter. On the contrary, it is a point on which all social philosophers and ethicists agree. Certainly Fred and Laura can agree on it.

Laura: Don't get me wrong. Ideally I believe that everyone should have the same job opportunities.
Fred: You mean that job opportunities should be open to everyone.
Laura: That's right. And I also believe that any job should be won as a result of fair competition.
Fred: By *fair competition* I presume you mean an evaluative process by which the applicants are judged on their merits.
Laura: On their merits and only on their merits, as those merits bear directly on job performance.

The notion of equality that Laura introduces here is an integral part of Rawls's equal liberty principle. *Equality* means that all are to be treated the same. Stated more technically, by *equality* Rawls means the impartial and equitable administration and application of the rules which define a practice. The equal liberty principle expresses this concept. *Impartiality* means a spirit of disinterestedness should color the distribution of goods and evils, that no person should receive preferred consideration. By *equitable administration* Rawls seems to mean that the distribution must be fair and just to begin with.

An example might help to clarify this equal liberty principle. Suppose the government decided that every family of four should have an income of at least $5000 per year. Any family with an income below that would be subsidized the difference. The equal liberty principle demands that this rule be administered to all families of four in the sub-$5000 category; the rule would not be impartially administered if a family of four making less than $5000 was excluded. Neither would it be equitably administered if it failed to distinguish income reduced by factors outside the family's control from income that was not so reduced. To illustrate, suppose two families each earned $4000 a year. But the first family incurred medical bills totaling $1700; the second family did not. An equitable distribution, it seems, would involve a $2700 subsidy to the first family and $1000 to the second. Of course, any other family in circumstances like the first family's has the right to expect the same treatment. Keep in mind that Rawls is defining liberty with reference to the pattern of rights, duties, powers, and liabilities established by a practice. In this case, families making less than $5000 a year have the *right* to expect equal treatment insofar as governmental subsidies go.

But Rawls's equal liberty principle expresses the idea of equality in a second, more important way. Laura is aware of this.

Laura: As I said, *ideally* everyone should have the same opportunity to compete for a job.

Fred: But in practice they don't.

Laura: In practice there are all kinds of prerequisites, regulations, and conditions that must be met before a person can realistically compete.

Fred: You mean even if a person can do a job.

Laura: Sure. For example, an uncle of mine was recently let go from his job because he didn't have the college education the job requires.

Fred: So what's wrong with that?

Laura: He's been doing the job efficiently for seventeen years. The company simply updated its job specifications, and he no longer met the education requirements.

Fred: But he could have returned to school.

Laura: Sure he could have, but he didn't want to. But that's really irrelevant. The point is that he had already proved himself capable of doing the job, and everyone admitted that further education was not necessary or relevant for his continuing to perform the job. But nevertheless the company decided that further education was necessary to hold the job. So, practically speaking, he does not have the same opportunity to compete for a job because he is no longer being evaluated by criteria that are directly related to job performance.

Laura's point is that an intrinsic part of all regulations is that they infringe on personal liberty. Without the education required, her uncle is no longer able to hold or even compete for the job that he has performed efficiently for seventeen years. In his equal liberty principle Rawls recognizes this inherent characteristic of all laws and other practices: by nature they encroach on the equal liberty of those subject to them.

Thus, a law that requires motorists to drive on the right-hand side of the road is an infringement on their freedom to drive on either side whenever they wish. Some would argue that justice only requires an *equal* liberty, that is, as long as every motorist is required to drive on the right-hand side of the road, justice is being served. Or, in Laura's example, as long as college education is required of everyone applying for the job, then such a requirement is just. On this point, however, Rawls seems more philosophically perceptive than his opponents, for he notes that if a more extensive liberty were possible for all without loss, damage, or conflict, then it would be irrational to settle upon a lesser liberty. In the case of driving, as motorists continually prove, more extensive liberty is not possible without great loss and injury. But in the case of Laura's uncle, an argument could be made for a more extensive liberty than the college-education job specification.

Crucial to any theory of social justice, therefore, is determining when inequality is permissible. Rawls discusses this problem with his difference principle.

THE DIFFERENCE PRINCIPLE

Rawls's difference principle defines what kinds of inequalities are permissible. It specifies under what conditions the equal liberty principle may be violated. Before illuminating it, let's return to Fred and Laura.

Fred: It seems to me that you'd agree that if a company hires a female over a more qualified male simply because she's a female, then they are acting unfairly and that he has been treated unfairly.

Laura: Why?

Fred: Because they have not treated the two equally.

Laura: I agree they have not been treated equally. But you must consider why they haven't been. They haven't been in order to right a serious social evil, sexual discrimination.

Fred: But you're using sexual discrimination to fight sexual discrimination. One wrong doesn't justify another, you know.

Laura: But there's a difference. I may be using sexual discrimination, but I'm using it in order to redress a serious social ill that is already injuring a vast proportion of the population and threatens to get worse. In the past, where sexism has operated in employment practices, it was functioning only as a social poison, not as an antidote to a problem.

Fred: You seem to be saying that equality is all right, providing it serves certain social ends.

Laura: What do you mean?

Fred: Is racial equality right and desirable only because it benefits society? Would you say that blacks should be treated as equals with whites because and only as long as the benefits to society outweigh the disadvantages? To me equality is not dependent on consequences.

It is clear that Laura's concept of equality is contingent, Fred's is not. This means that Laura's idea of equality depends on something else for its justification, rather than being justified in and of itself, as Fred suggests. Laura believes that equality is contingent on social improvement. In other words, inequality is permissible as long as it produces the most good for the most number. Clearly this is a utilitarian doctrine. And just as clearly this is *not* what Rawls means.

For Rawls equality is not contingent. This alone casts him in a nonconsequential role. With his difference principle, Rawls would allow inequality only if in all likelihood the practice involving inequality works to the advantage of *every* individual affected. In other words, *all* persons concerned must find their conditions to be better with the inequality than without it. Observe that the difference principle, therefore, disallows inequalities generally justified on utilitarian grounds, that is, on the grounds that the disadvantages of persons in one position are outweighed by the advantages of those in another.

So, although Rawls's difference principle resembles the utilitarian doctrine of promoting the greatest happiness, it is significantly different. Consider, as an illustration, the issue of slavery. Classical utilitarianism would permit one to argue that slavery is unjust because the advantages to the slaveholder do not counterbalance the disadvantages to the slave and the society burdened with a comparatively inefficient system of labor. Although Rawls would agree that slavery was immoral, he could not agree for this reason. If he did he would be making the difference principle superior to the equal liberty principle. But Rawls contends that the equal liberty principle is logically prior to the difference principle. This means that when an action violates the equal liberty principle, that action is always unjust and immoral.

Although classical utilitarianism never condoned slavery, the utilitarian ethic could theoretically condone it under conditions that produced the most good for the most number of people. In other words, in utilitarianism the concept of justice invariably derives from some notion of efficiency. But Rawls's justice is best described as reciprocity. *Reciprocity is the principle that requires that a practice be such that all members could and would accept it and be bound by it.* It is the requirement of the possibility of mutual acknowledgment of principles by free people having no authority over one another that makes the idea of reciprocity fundamental to justice and fairness. Without this acknowledgment, Rawls claims that there can be no basis for a true community. Certainly slaveholders would not accept their own servitude; more importantly, slaves, since they are by definition unfree and unequal, are not in any position to acknowledge the practice freely to begin with. So, because slavery violates a fundamental aspect of the equal liberty principle it is wrong.

In effect, then, where there is conflict between his two principles, Rawls relies on his first principle of justice, the equal liberty principle. He insists that the equal liberty principle is logically prior to the difference principle. In contrast, the utilitarian sees liberty as contingent on social productivity, as Laura seems to in defending quota hiring. In other words, liberty is desirable insofar as it produces the most happiness for the most number of people.

Obviously the utilitarian position does not allow the objection to the loss of liberty as long as the greatest number of people benefit. Rawls would argue that any position that even allows the possibility of the loss of equal liberty is unacceptable. "Each person possesses an inviolability founded on justice that even the welfare of society as a whole cannot override. . . . Therefore . . . the rights secured by justice are not subject to political bargaining or to the calculus of social interests."* On the question of quota hiring, Fred would probably sympathize with this statement.

Fred: What you're saying is that equality is desirable only as long as the majority benefits.
Laura: A more appropriate way to put it would be to say that inequality is acceptable as long as it produces the most good for the most number of people concerned.
Fred: I just can't see how you can justify inequalities on such a utilitarian basis.

There is no question that Rawls escapes what Fred intimates is a most repugnant element in classical utilitarianism—treating the individual as a means to an end. Undoubtedly Rawls has breathed new and needed life into the nearly defunct social contract theory. His proponents would argue further that Rawls has provided a new and realistic basis for redistributing position and wealth. Yet, despite what appear to be positive features in Rawls's maximin principle theory of justice, there are serious problems. Let's consider them.

OBJECTIONS TO THE MAXIMIN PRINCIPLE

1. *Rawls makes unsupportable assumptions—questionable claims.* These assumptions are evident at different levels of his maximin principle scheme, as we will see in returning to Laura and Fred.

> **Fred:** As far as I'm concerned, you could only justify sexual discrimination if you could be reasonably sure that in an ideal situation most reasonable people, even those who would be discriminated against, would allow it in order to improve the total condition of society.
> **Laura:** What do you mean by the *ideal situation?*
> **Fred:** I mean a situation in which there is no pressure, in which nobody has a hold over anyone else, in which nobody is coerced into thinking one way or another.
> **Laura:** I think that under those conditions reasonable people would allow the kind of sexual discrimination that may be evident in quota hiring.
> **Fred:** Even if they knew it could be directed at them?
> **Laura:** Yes. Because if they were reasonable they'd understand that if they didn't allow it, at least for a time, things would be considerably worse for them.

---

*John Rawls, *A Theory of Justice* (Cambridge: Harvard University Press, 1971), p. 4.

Fred: I don't see it that way at all. To me no one would agree to allow sexual biases to creep into society except those who would directly benefit from them. They would see such a practice as a violation of their fundamental right to be treated like everyone else in matters where sex was not directly related.

Laura: I disagree. Even if they did see it as a violation of their fundamental rights, they would also see that if they do not temporarily allow this violation, they are inviting more grave violations.

We can call the ideal state to which Fred refers Rawls's state of veiled ignorance. Rawls assumes that when we wear the veil of ignorance, we are mutually self-interested, rational, and possessing similar needs, interests, and capacities. Again, by *mutual self-interests* Rawls means that people establish practices normally on the basis of their own advantage. But this is so only because Rawls assumes that humans would be rational.

When Rawls describes persons as rational, he implies a great many things that seem questionable. Among them are that persons more or less know their own interests, can trace the likely consequences of one course over another and resist temptations of personal gain, and are not greatly bothered by the perceptible difference between their condition and someone else's. So, the assumption that humans are rational carries with it a heavy freight of questionable claims. It is one thing to hypothesize that people exhibit this highly sophisticated rationality; it is another to posit a theory of social justice upon it.

But even conceding this kind of rationality, problems arise. Fred argues that under ideal conditions, let's say the ones that Rawls describes as part of his definition of rationality, no one would agree to introduce the practice of sexual discrimination because they would be unwilling to be discriminated against.

But this appears to be true only if we assume a kind of germ-free, vacuumlike decision-making context, only if we assume that there is no sexual discrimination to begin with. But Laura does not assume this, and this underscores the problem. What would occur if you asked the same rational, self-interested, uncoerced people how they would redress *already existing* sexually discriminatory employment practices? Perhaps they would maintain, as Fred does, that such an action violates the equal liberty principle. But perhaps they might not. Perhaps they might emphasize the need to redress this injustice as quickly as possible and thus invoke Rawls's difference principle. In answer to critics like Fred, they could argue that once job opportunities are correctly balanced, then society will have attained the state that all people in the veil of ignorance would perceive as most fair and in keeping with their own self-interests. So, they might say to Fred that this inequality would work to his advantage, too.

The fact is that assumptions are invariably bound up with interpretations. Ironically, in providing a flexibility that neither utilitarianism nor rule nonconsequentialism does, Rawls seems to have built into his system a measure of whim that allows one sometimes to underscore the equal liberty principle and other times the difference principle, depending on points of emphases. This despite his claim that the equal liberty principle is logically prior to the principle of difference.

A similar objection turns up again when we note that in his third assumption Rawls assumes that persons have roughly similar needs, interests, and capacities, so that fruitful cooperation among them is possible. In the case of job discrimination by sex, however, the needs seem to conflict. One party, the female, needs redress. Presumably the speediest way to provide it is to injure another party, the male. The question is, Does Rawls's difference principle allow this injury? Or does his equal liberty principle forbid it? Unless we have badly misinterpreted Rawls, it seems that one could argue either way, depending on how one rationalized the situation. This problem is evident despite Rawls's claim that people should be judged on their merits.

This strongly, but not conclusively, suggests that in Rawls's theory of social justice, quota hiring would be immoral. After all, qualified males do have the opportunity to compete with females for jobs, to attain the fruits and benefits of position. Under no circumstances is anyone arguing that it is moral to hire the unqualified male or female. The issue reduces to a statistical factor: should the qualified female be provided with a favorable hiring ratio reflecting the current ratio of sexual discrimination in employment, or in the free market competition with males should she be provided a fifty-fifty chance of gaining employment? It seems that Rawls's maximin principle is loose enough to allow reasonable proponents of his theory to differ in their replies.

This apparent looseness in Rawls's theory shows up in a second objection, and it concerns another assumption.

2. *Rawls assumes that people would agree with the principle of difference only because he takes the view of the worst off in society.* In his principle of difference Rawls claims that inequalities are permissible as long as everyone benefits from them. (This, incidentally, seems inconsistent with the sentiment of the prior statement: "If some offices were not open, those excluded would normally be justified in feeling unjustly treated, *even if they benefited from the greater efforts of those who were allowed to compete for them* [italics added].") This, of course, is an assumption. Whether it's questionable depends on its basis.

> **Fred:** You're saying that inequalities are all right as long as they benefit society.
>
> **Laura:** As it happens in quota hiring I think that they'll benefit everyone, even men.
>
> **Fred:** But not to the same degree. I grant you that men traditionally have held a preferred position on the job market, as unfair as that might have been. So, even though quota hiring may have the effect of bringing the country closer to the ideal of equality and fair play, it diminishes us personally by destroying our preferred position.
>
> **Laura:** Which you should never have had anyway.
>
> **Fred:** Maybe not. But the fact is that we do. And now you're not only asking us to relinquish that preferred status but also to assume the role of

victim, to accept the injustice that we are supposed to strike down.

Laura: I'm asking that only as a temporary measure in order to correct the imbalance.

Fred: But this temporary measure is a permanent measure for me personally. It is dramatically altering my whole life.

Laura: Only because you fail to see that in the long run you will actually benefit, too.

It seems that as long as Rawls talks of slavery he does not have to face the problem inherent in something as complex and controversial as quota hiring. To declare slavery inherently unjust and to pass legislation prohibiting it does not at the same time enslave the slaveholder, although it might temporarily diminish his or her preferred economic status. In quota hiring, it appears that the victimizer is turned into the victim; in effect, the slaveholder has become the slave, at least in terms of employment. Yet, to solve the problem as quickly as possible this seems inevitable.

Let's return to Rawls's veil of ignorance state for a minute. Suppose that the practice people are trying to resolve in this state is sexual discrimination in employment. If this were not already an established practice, then rational, self-interested persons would no doubt say that sexual discrimination in employment was immoral. But it is a practice, and they must deal with the complaints of those who are being victimized by it. How would they react?

If the view of the worst off in the group is taken, in this case the females, then probably these people would agree on the morality of quota hiring. But why assume this view? This is what Rawls's critics ask. It does not seem a justifiable claim that the better off, in this case the males, would automatically agree to the morality of quota hiring. So, if we take the view of the better off, we would probably conclude that the morality of quota hiring is at least doubtful.

Rawls's apparent tendency to see things through the eyes of the worst off, and by so doing to ignore the moral viewpoint of impartiality and disinterestedness, suggests a third objection, which concerns the utilitarian tendency to view people as means to ends.

3. *Rawls is inconsistent, for the difference principle, contrary to Rawls's claim, actually has the effect of regarding humans as means to others' ends.* Rawls makes it clear that he wishes to rule out what he considers a pernicious element in utilitarianism— the tendency to regard individuals as the means to other individuals' welfare. But Rawls's critics say that he does the very thing that he tries to avoid. A good example is the graduated income tax system.

Suppose that by putting a 75 percent tax on any income over $100,000 we can improve the lot of the worst off in society by $1.00.* Ought we do it? The answer seems to depend on whose viewpoint you take. In fact, our graduated income tax system works like this; the better off are more heavily taxed than the less

---

*See Robert Nozick, *Anarchy, State and Utopia* (New York: Basic Books, 1975).

well off. In defending this practice, one may fall back on the equal liberty principle, arguing that in the original position, when all wealth is distributed evenly, people would agree to maintain the equal distribution of wealth. But in so doing, one must necessarily view things through the eyes of the majority, who realize that by definition an uneven distribution of wealth means that most of them will have less than the few of them.

Critics of Rawls ask, But why this viewpoint? Why this appeal to popularity? They charge that if one took the view of the minority, those who would stand to profit by an uneven distribution of wealth, one would probably not agree to the graduated income tax practice. It seems that in taking the view of the majority, one is necessarily forced to provide a strictly utilitarian defense. But this seems inconsistent with Rawls's expressed contempt for considering humans as means to others' ends. Now let's see how this criticism applies to quota hiring.

> **Fred:** Personally, I don't like the idea of being victimized so that someone else won't be.
>
> **Laura:** I know what you're saying. But it seems to me that you're focusing on just one small corner of the total picture.
>
> **Fred:** Maybe I am. But aren't you doing the same in order to advance your own cause?
>
> **Laura:** Perhaps, but I don't think so. As I said before, I see this quota hiring as a temporary measure, as unfortunate and maybe as unfair as it is, it is justified in order to right an imbalance in job distribution. Once that imbalance is corrected, then by definition there will no longer be a need for quota hiring.

Fred contends that he is being used as a means to a social end, in this case the end of equal job distribution. He resents it. Is his resentment justified? Indeed, is the quota-hiring system violating the equal liberty principle? You can decide.

> **Fred:** Well, I still think it's wrong. But I do hope for something.
>
> **Laura:** What's that?
>
> **Fred:** I hope this company has two positions available.
>
> **Laura:** Me, too.

SUMMARY

Nonconsequential Theory	Objections
Rawls's Maximin Principle of Justice: The moral act is the one that produces	1. Rawls makes unsupportable assumptions, including ones that claim

for the individual the greatest amount of liberty that is compatible with a like liberty for all; an inequality is permissible only insofar as it serves everyone's advantage and arises under conditions of equal opportunity.

all humans are self-interested, rational, and possessed of common needs and desires.

2. Rawls assumes that persons would agree with the difference principle only because he takes the view of the worst off in society.

3. The difference principle shares the utilitarian principle of regarding individuals as means to other individuals' ends.

CONCLUSIONS

It seems that from time immemorial men and women have valued personal freedom and liberties, specifically political and moral freedom—the right to do something without having to abridge or break a law to do it. There is also apparent agreement that the state bears the responsibilities for protecting its citizens from ills against which they are helpless as individuals and for fostering an atmosphere in which citizens can enrich their own lives within a social context. Disagreement arises, however, when we try to spell out precisely which freedoms, liberties, and rights the individual and state shall possess.

In drawing the line of demarcation between individual and society, John Rawls has made important contributions. First, he has rejuvenated the basis of our constitutional government—the social contract. In recognizing that some human rights are inviolable, he places himself squarely in the socioreligious tradition of the West. This is not intended as an appeal to provincialism, but as an acknowledgment of Rawls's sensitivity to the usefulness of historical tradition in proposing a contemporary theory of social justice.

Second, Rawls is to be applauded for at least attempting to roll back the utilitarian trend to treat humans as means to ends. Again, in recognizing the inherent worth and dignity of the individual, Rawls roots himself deeply in the soil of his political and religious traditions.

Finally, and this is perhaps his most important contribution, Rawls has taken on what is a candidate for today's major social problem—the growing gap between the haves and the have-nots. This problem is manifest on many levels: the economic, between the well-off and poor; the racial, between the whites and nonwhites; the sexual, between the male and female. Although directly addressing the economic problem of redistributing goods, Rawls's theory, as we saw, applies to other problems of social justice as well. If nothing else, Rawls has brought serious philosophical and moral debate to problems that have previously been topics primarily of sociological interest.

It is true that Rawls's theory shows weaknesses. The presence of questionable claims and inconsistencies weakens its theoretical superstructure; evidence of the traditional utilitarian tendency of justifying the means by the ends shows up in its practical application. In addition, Rawls's theory has invited some serious philosophical criticism.* It is probably still too soon to make substantial conclusions about Rawls's theory of justice except to note that it has provoked desperately needed thinking about our social problems, for how we ultimately redress problems such as Laura and Fred's depends on a fair and functional theory of social justice.

EXERCISES FOR ANALYSIS

EXERCISE 1

The following passages may contain fallacious appeals. Identify them.

1. Female: Personally, I like to have doors opened and dinner checks paid for me. I don't see why people are saying sexism is so bad. (Does the speaker make an assumption about the nature and expression of sexism?)

2. "It is obvious that much of the antisexist feeling is held and advanced by a relatively small number of women known as feminists, but perhaps more rightly termed something less polite. The fact that these women are in the minority is pretty good evidence that the position they advance doesn't deserve much consideration." (Is there an ad hominem appeal here as well as other appeals?)

3. "Everybody knows that all kinds of unfair biases exist in employment practices. And no matter what anyone says, the only way to correct them is through preferential quota hiring."

4. "If we allow women to compete on an equal basis with men for employment, we might as well resign ourselves to a female army."

5. Personnel director to a female applicant: The fact that we have historically hired men for the position of aircraft mechanic suggests that men are better equipped for that job than women.

6. "Some state supreme courts have already ruled that preferential placement is unconstitutional. That's enough for me to say that preferential treatment is immoral."

---

*See Brian Barry, *The Liberal Theory of Justice* (New York: Oxford University Press, 1973).

7. In answer to the criticism that it is inconsistent to advocate preferential hiring to combat unfair employment biases, the arguer says, "The principle of preferential hiring as expressed by guidelines like affirmative action is really different from traditional job-market hiring biases in an important respect—spirit. In preferential hiring, no one even implies that the favored group is inherently superior to the disfavored one. But traditional job-hiring discrimination was intended to keep jobs from people of a group thought to be inherently inferior to the favored group." (Is this a legitimate defense of the apparent inconsistency?)

EXERCISE 2

Fundamental to the issue of quota hiring is the question of sexism, that is, the deliberate discrimination of one person against another solely on the basis of sex. Women in our society obviously have been victimized by this practice on more occasions than males generally, and white males particularly. Although few would seriously argue that sexism is always moral, many argue that it sometimes is. Opposed to this view are those who contend that there is never any justification for sexism, that sexism is inherently immoral. Following are some condensed general arguments against and for sexism. Determine whether the justification for each conclusion is adequate. Also, look for consequential and nonconsequential arguments. You will find that, in general, arguments against sexism are nonconsequential, while arguments for sexism are decidedly consequential.

Arguments against Sexism

1. Surely one of the most fundamental aspects of one's self-concept is sexual. When individuals have what psychologists call a "healthy self-concept," you will invariably find a healthy sense of sexual self-identity. Conversely, where self-image is damaged, you will likely find serious identity problems. When people have a poor self-concept, they experience anxiety and frustration and are unable to attain happiness; indeed, they can hardly pursue happiness. By making individuals feel inferior, inadequate, or incomplete because of their sex, sexists strike at the roots of an inalienable right, the right to a positive self-image. Because sexism is a practice that destroys one's self-concept, it is immoral.

2. By definition *sexism* means that one sex will receive preferential treatment over the other solely for biological reasons. This is inherently unfair because it represents unequal treatment. Equality can only exist where all individuals are treated the same, where they are rewarded or punished to the same degree for the same behavior, regardless of their sex. But sexism precludes this. Therefore, sexism is immoral.

3. A most insidious aspect of sexism is that it wastes human resources. Just think of all the qualified individuals who have not been admitted to medical, dental, or law schools, or into other areas where our nation and world could use all the humanpower it can muster. By restricting a sex to predetermined occupational groups, sexists not only discourage individual ambition and initiative, but they also minimize the total creative output of their societies. Thus, sexism is immoral because it wastes human resources.

Arguments for Sexism

1. Certainly from at least the Middle Ages, the female has held a preferred position in Western society. Our religious legacies portray her not only as the giver of life, but also as the merciful and compassionate element in the cosmic scheme of things. Socioreligiously, the female embodies the principles of love, beauty, and virtue. In short, the female traditionally has symbolized many of the ideals that are the mortar of Western society. It is only natural, therefore, that the female should command a preferred status in society. So, since sexism can have the effect of preserving the preferred values and ideals of a society, it is not always immoral.

2. Because of what many would pejoratively call "sexist attitudes," females today are not expected to perform certain tasks and duties that befall males; the most obvious is the military obligation. Even in cases where females volunteer for military service, they are rarely assigned to combat duty. This does not mean that some women could not meet the requirement. The question is whether females are currently prepared psychologically and culturally to accept roles that have historically befallen their male counterparts. It's doubtful that they are. Because sexism is a practice that can have the effect of protecting persons from great needless physical and psychological harm, it is not always immoral.

3. Let's face it, just as often as not the female benefits from sexist attitudes. When was the last time a disarming smile or a great pair of legs got a man what he wanted? Perhaps this is a fatuous example. Consider, then, other advantages that females often reap. The sexism that supposedly has directed many women into elementary school teaching also has given elementary school girls a decided advantage over boys. The sexism that supposedly keeps women out of the job market actually provides them with more jobs during their high school and college years than their male counterparts. The sexism that supposedly prevents a woman from earning pay equal to a man often reduces her cost of living; her entertainment and transportation bills, for example, are frequently a fraction of the male's. The point is that, at least in the United States, the female is a desired and desirable entity. Because sexism has the effect of providing women with substantial advantages, it is not always immoral.

SELECTIONS FOR FURTHER READING

Social Justice

Barry, B. M. *The Liberal Theory of Justice.* Oxford: Clarendon Press, 1973.

Bedau, H. A., ed. *Justice and Equality.* Englewood Cliffs, N.J.: Prentice-Hall, 1971.

Black, Charles. *The People and the Court.* New York: Macmillan, 1960.

Brandt, Richard. *Ethical Theory.* Englewood Cliffs, N.J.: Prentice-Hall, 1959.

Brunner, E. *Justice and the Social Order.* Translated by M. Huttinger. London: Lutterworth Press, 1946.

Bryson, L., ed. *Aspects of Human Equality.* New York: Harper, 1956.

Ginsberg, M. *On Justice in Society.* Ithaca, N.Y.: Cornell University Press, 1965.

Kelsen, Hans. *What Is Justice?* Berkeley, Calif.: University of California Press, 1957.

Rawls, John. *A Theory of Justice.* Cambridge, Mass.: Harvard University Press, 1971.

Plato. *Republic.* Translated by F. M. Cornford. New York: Oxford University Press, 1945.

Rescher, Nicholas. *Distributive Justice: A Constructive Critique of the Utilitarian Theory of Distribution.* Indianapolis: Bobbs-Merrill, 1968.

Quota Hiring

Amundsen, Kirsten. *The Silenced Majority: Women and American Democracy.* Englewood Cliffs, N.J.: Prentice-Hall, 1971.

Beauvoir, Simone de. *The Second Sex.* Translated by H. M. Parshley. New York: Knopf, 1953.

Bier, Caroline. *Women in Modern Life.* Bronx, N.Y.: Fordham University Press, 1968.

Bird, Caroline, and Briller, Sara Welles. *Born Female: The High Cost of Keeping Women Down.* New York: McKay, 1970.

Doriot, George, ed. *The Management of Racial Integration in Business.* New York: McGraw-Hill, 1965.

Kothe, Charles A. *A Tale of Twenty-Two Cities: Report on Title VII of the Civil Rights Act of 1964.* Washington, D.C.: National Association of Manufacturers, 1965.

Mill, John Stuart, and Mill, Harriet T. *Essays on Sex Equality.* Edited by Alice C. Rossi. Chicago: University of Chicago Press, 1970.

BIRD / *The Case for Equality*

In Born Female: The High Cost of Keeping Women Down, *author Caroline Bird graphically details antifemale discrimination in the job market. In her conclusion, "The Case for Equality," Bird contends that equality ultimately is justified not by appeals to consequence but to principle. Equality, she argues, is not a matter of expedience, but of equity. "The way women are treated is just plain wrong," she says. This reality alone would be enough to demand remedy. Do you agree?*

Is it a good idea to treat men and women exactly alike?

What would happen if we tried it? Is it even possible?

"After all, men and women are different," people argue. "You can't treat them alike!"

Just as we formerly had laws that said that noblemen had certain privileges because of their names, so we now have laws that say that men and women have certain privileges because of their sex. If we think we can't treat men and women alike, it may only be because the law hasn't done it.

But it can be done. In a provocative article in *The George Washington Law Review* of December 1965, Pauli Murray and Mary Eastwood reviewed the laws affecting men and women as separate sexes and reported that all such laws would be either clearer or fairer if rewritten in terms of situations, as all other laws are written. It wouldn't be necessary, they pointed out, to say that the crime of rape could be committed only by men or that maternity benefits could be claimed only by women. By defini-tion, these situations apply to one sex only. A woman can't commit rape. A man can't have a baby. The conditions that seem to require special treatment for men or women can all be defined without mentioning sex. If all persons were liable for military or jury service, for instance, men and women could both claim exemption because they had dependents. Women able to serve would relieve the men for whom the draft is now a real hardship.

There is no reason why women should not be drafted. The crack Israeli Army drafts all boys and single girls at the age of 18. Girls who marry during their draft terms, as three out of ten do, go into the reserves. Pregnant women and mothers are excused, but women officers in the regular army get four months of fully paid leave beginning with the ninth month of pregnancy. Israeli women soldiers have fought in bloody battles in the past, but they are now assigned to handle paperwork, communications, and medical services in units with men.

It isn't necessary to require that

---

husbands support wives in order to protect children. Both partners to a marriage could simply be required to support each other and their children in case of need. There is nothing morally repugnant about requiring money or services from the partner best able to give them, regardless of sex.

Pauli Murray and Mary Eastwood point out that the principle of mutual support legally recognizes the value of women's unpaid domestic services, which economists estimate amounts to at least a fifth of the current Gross National Product. Domestic services are regularly included in the Swedish Gross National Product, and their domestic law specifically mentions the domestic services of the wife as an economic contribution to the marriage partnership.

This recognition clarifies the position of the traditional wife whose years of homemaking experience are not negotiable in the job market if the marriage ends. Our divorce laws now award her alimony, but as Clare Boothe Luce wrote in 1967, it would be more appropriate to recognize her past services by giving her severance pay. Courts could protect rich men from women who marry them only for their money by awarding alimony on the basis of the length of the marriage and the domestic services the wives have actually rendered.

The principle of mutual support would eliminate many other abuses. Family counselors now advise that some children, particularly boys, would be better off with their fathers than with their mothers. To date, divorce courts automatically assume that mothers should always care for children and fathers always pay for them. The reverse would be better for some families.

There is no rhyme or reason to current laws specifying the ages at which a person is permitted to marry, work, or retire. There would be much fairer if the specifications were the same for men and women all the way down the line, just as they are for voting and driving. Boys mature more slowly, so there is no reason why state child labor laws should permit boys to start working younger than girls. A really functional law might require a person to demonstrate fitness to work by physical or mental test, just as we now require driving tests. Functional tests for jobholding might allow girls to work at an earlier age and let them keep working later than law and custom now permit.

The principle of mutual support would give surviving husbands the same pension and insurance benefits that go to widows. Employers could, if they wished, require beneficiaries to pass a means test. Under this system, wives who actually support themselves would not draw benefits any more than do husbands who actually support themselves. This would allow funds committed to these programs to take better care of wives who have no earning power because their lifetime contribution was made in the home, as well as providing support for the substantial number of husbands who, because they are older than their wives, have become disabled.

Ideally, marriage should not alter the civil and legal rights of either husband or wife. Wives should be able to choose a *legal* domicile separate from that of their husbands, if this is what they both want, without this in any way jeopardizing the marriage or rights. This would allow a woman who for business or professional reasons does not live constantly with her husband, at the residence legally his, to maintain her voting rights, as well as letting her hold public office even if her husband doesn't live in the district.

Sex equality would, of course, remove any lingering doubt that a woman has a right to use her maiden name for any legitimate reason. Other countries are more consistent than we in handling names. Spanish cultures add the mother's maiden name to surnames, recognizing both lines of descent instead of the father's alone. We call a married woman "Mrs.," but a "Mr." may be married or single. Much as the Swedes love titles, they are now moving to drop forms of address that identify the marital status of women in situations where the marital status of men is not recognized.

The most widespread changes, of course, would occur in laws affecting employment. Employers would be forbidden to discharge a woman for maternity just as they are now forbidden to discharge a man for military or jury service. If men were not required to support their wives under all circumstances, there would be no reason to protect a man's job and not a woman's. A pregnant woman who loses her job should get unemployment insurance, whether her husband can support her or not, just as a married man gets unemployment insurance, whether or not his wife can support him.

Laws limiting the weight a woman worker may lift are now used to keep women out of jobs that are no more arduous than hauling sacks of groceries from the supermarket or removing a five-year-old from mischief. These laws would be fairer if they required tests of physical ability for jobs requiring strength. Men, after all, are the sex most vulnerable to hernia. Instead of forbidding women to do jobs that are considered hazardous, a really protective law would limit dangerous work to those who had passed a test of skill. There's no reason, for instance, why a woman can't run a drill press as safely as a man, if she is taught how to do it.

Minimum wage and maximum hour laws could apply to both sexes with identical exemptions. Some foreign countries guarantee the right of a mother to time off for family emergencies. American employers expect mothers to take time off, but because it is unofficial, they tend to charge the time lost against women workers in general. It would be fairer as well as better for the children if mothers and fathers were permitted a certain number of days off a year to cope with family problems. Parents could spell each other during a long siege instead of making the wife's employer stand for all the inconvenience.

All these legal inequalities could be remedied, but the real question is: Do we want to do it? Do we really want to treat men and women alike? The only way to find out is to examine, as best we can, what the change would do. The most radical effects would be felt in the field of employment. If access, pay, promotion, and conditions of work for every job were open equally to men and women, as Title VII plainly requires, there would be no legal or moral basis for what

Pauli Murray and Mary Eastwood call ". . . the assumption that financial support of a family by the husband-father is a gift from the male sex to the female sex, and, in return, the male is entitled to preference in the outside world."

Supposing individuals were hired in all occupations without regard to sex. Women would compete with men in areas now closed to them, but they would not compete with each other as much as they now do for "women's jobs." Women who stayed in "women's jobs" would win higher wages. As the wages rose, men would be attracted to these fields. Since the lowest-paying jobs are those dominated by women, equal opportunity would have the same effect as raising the minimum wage.

Thousands of marginal jobs would go out of existence. It would suddenly be profitable to mechanize cherry-picking and sell even more standard items in vending machines. What operations could not be mechanized might well be omitted. Some of us might have to go without lettuce because no one would be willing to pay what it would cost to produce as much lettuce as we now consume if we paid a living wage to the people who cultivate it. We have, of course, survived other such deprivations. No one can afford hand-tooled shoes except the very rich, and they seldom bother with custom-made apparel because fittings take time and clothes are no longer expected to last forever.

If, along with sex equality, we expected all adults to work, women who could not show that they were earning their keep at home would have to find jobs. According to one estimate, full utilization of "woman-power" would add ten million workers to the labor force. If these women could work wherever they were needed, they would free men from the obligation to earn that injures and limits some of them as grievously as the obligation to do housework now injures and limits some women. This is no idle supposition. As we have noticed earlier, under full employment many families find it makes more sense for women to work and support their menfolk.

If women were freer to choose where they worked, they would take a good hard look at some of the chores that now keep them at home. What, for instance, is the actual money value of staying at home all day long to do two hours of cleaning? Of hauling groceries from the supermarket? Of waiting in the pediatrician's office for an hour? In 1968, mothers expect all sorts of people to waste their time. The waste is not necessary, and it is not motherhood.

A woman we know solved the problem of the doctor's waiting room by arranging for a baby-sitter to take her son to the appointment. She found that she could continue working in her office for an hour or more while they waited for his turn. She could earn more at her own trade than she could have saved in cab fare and baby-sitting fees, even though the expense was not deductible. A working woman has to operate a home in a world that assumes that a homemaker's time is worth less than the wages of the lowest-paid worker for money. Deliveries are arranged on the assumption that she can sit home all day long and wait. No one calculates the time cost of shopping, either, especially in crowded discount houses and supermarkets, where women on budgets are forced to shop. No one counts the time cost of toting shoes to and from the repairman, or exchanging goods that may have been ordered by telephone to save time, but weren't right on arrival. Purchasing departments count the cost of the time that clerks use when they check prices and quality before buying, but housewives don't add the cost of their time to the price paid for family purchases.

If all adults were required to work, and free to choose the kind of work they wanted, many women would leave their homes and thereby create more paying jobs. Baby-sitters and service workers, many of them now considered unemployable because of age or lack of education, would be drawn out of their isolation and into the labor force. But all of these newcomers would not necessarily find themselves doing what housewives used to do at home. Many would find jobs in services especially organized to do housework efficiently.

More women could afford housekeeping services that now exist for the very rich alone. More charge-and-deliver grocers would be needed to serve the growing number of housewives who would not mind paying more to save the time they now spend shopping in self-service supermarkets. Cleaning services could contract to keep a house in shape by sending in teams of machine-equipped professionals to tidy for an hour or so every day; maintenance services employing salaried mechanics could keep all household gear operating for a flat annual fee; yard services like those run by teams of Japanese gardeners in Los Angeles could contract to keep lawns mowed and garden beds weeded. Food take-out services and caterers proliferating around the country would increase to serve the growing number of women who like to entertain but don't have time to cook.

These new services would be cheaper in real economic terms, because specialists working at what they enjoy are more efficient than amateurs doing chores they may detest. But the big gain would be a better use of talent. If the born cooks, cleaners, and children's nurses were paid well enough so that they could make careers out of their talents, domestic services would attract women who now enjoy household arts but hesitate to practice them professionally because they don't want to be treated as "servants." Women who have never worked often have trouble with servants because they have never learned how to hold employees to objective standards. If most women worked, domestic service could become more attractive, since, hopefully, domestic workers would begin to be treated more like office workers.

For hundreds of years now, many tasks have been passing from what the economists call "customary" work, done without pay, to wage work. Canning, clothes-making, and the care of the sick now are jobs, not unpaid chores. The hired man has replaced the farmer's son, the paid babysitter has replaced neighborly child-watching, and young people learn to drive, skate, ski, and swim from paid instructors, rather than older relatives. The shift has always increased efficiency and improved the status of the task.

Housekeeping is the last unpaid customary job, and if most women worked, it would be professionalized, too. The errands, the repairs, the appointment-making, the bookkeeping, the snack-making, the chauffeuring and other odd jobs which make women feel disorganized and undervalued, could all be turned into professionally run services. These new businesses would create more part-time, seasonal, odd-hour jobs, which would offer men and women wider choices about when they would—or could—work than the traditional nine-to-five schedule. Odd-hour schedules of work and study beget more odd-hour jobs. Round-the-clock cafeteria workers are needed to feed round-the-clock factory workers, round-the-clock bus services to move round-the-clock cafeteria workers, and so on. In New York City, there are all-night hairdressers, garages, office services, movies, and restaurants for the "night" people. These services were set up for the theatrical community, but they now grow by serving each other.

Mechanization of many routine tasks means that the expensive computers and complicated business machines that are being used more every day must be kept going constantly in order to pay their way. This is one of the reasons why Herman Kahn predicts that there will be much more flexible business schedules in the year 2000 than we now have. He foresees that professional and technical specialists will do much of their work alone at computer terminals installed in their homes. I.B.M. now trains mechanics this way. Instead of traveling to a central school, each student plugs into a nearby machine that is connected with the central computer, whenever he has a free hour, and works as long as he pleases.

Flexible schedules are increasing. More men and women than ever before do work that allows them to determine their own hours. Among them are researchers for professional lawyers and accountants, computer programmers, interviewers for opinion polls, and market research analysts. There is increasing opportunity to do independent work designing everything from radios to gardens, and selling every kind of product from housewares to job printing.

Work of this kind encourages both men and women to try out new divisions of labor within families, new programs of work-and-study or work-and-child-rearing, or work-and-retirement. Women need not retire completely from work while their children are young if work is available when and where and in quantities they can choose. And there is no reason why fathers should work traditional hours, either, if they don't want to.

Work doesn't have to be done in set eight-hour shifts, and at the office or the plant. It can be allocated so that part-time, part-year workers could be used everywhere, without making women do all the "adjusting" required. Professional women have learned to take their work home and do it after the children are in bed, or while they are in school. Many more tasks could be organized this way if employers were willing.

Real sex equality would mean that every institution depending on the "free time of housewives" would undergo radical change. Unpaid welfare work would not rely primarily on the volunteer services of women. Health and welfare responsibilities would be divided equally between the sexes, just as jury duty and military service would be done by both according to ability and availability. Organizations would not have "ladies' auxiliaries" doomed to make-work activities.

There would be fewer hen parties and stag parties, more opportunities for coeducational groupings around a common interest such as cooking, hiking, or painting. Girl reporters would not be dispatched to invent a "woman's point of view" on general news, but would have to report the human point of view in competition with men reporters. The "woman's page" would become a collection of columns for all, on food, fashion, home decoration, child care—presumably all material relating to living problems that would interest either men or women.

Desegregation of the work force would eliminate the advantage Women's Women make of their sex. If clerks were a mixed group of men and women, there would be no particular reason to prefer a woman supervisor. Achieving women would not have to feel so exceptional. If the chores of consumption were shared by men and women alike, advertising and merchandising would lose its feminine orientation. If marriage were not the only or the principal means for women to acquire status, sex appeal would not be the dominant sales appeal for advertising copy.

Real desegregation of work, real enforcement of equal opportunity, would have far-reaching economic consequences. It would threaten labor costs and management incentives. It would compel a radical restructure of work, accelerate mechanization already under way, and destroy the use of women as a labor reserve.

Women are the last labor reserve employers can take for granted; they are the only labor reserve well enough educated to do the white-collar "dirty work." What would happen to the economy of the United States if this reserve disappeared? The question is not academic. Equal opportunity laws work hand in glove with minimum wage laws to make it hard for marginal enterprises to pick up cheap help, and full employment means that there is very little cheap help left. In the 1960s some crops have actually gone to waste because low-cost labor was not, as formerly, instantly available.

More important to the economy, of course, is the effect of big companies. When they figured the cost of expanding or adding new products, they would discover that they would have to pay much more for extra hands than in the past, and this could make such projects look less attractive. Equal opportunity could raise our labor costs, make it harder for us to adjust supply to demand, and reduce the flexibility of our economy. We might slow down as did the socialized British, Germans, and Swedes.

Office work would change if it were not sex-typed. Men bosses could no longer play the role of Victorian patriarch with secretaries. A man could not relegate details to "my girl," and a woman would hardly call her male secretary "my boy." It is an open secret that men whose wives no longer wait on them at home may act like Victorian patriarchs at work. They value secretaries in part for the psychological lift of being served, and may create such work as keeping scrapbooks, writing useless memos, and keeping unnecessary records, to justify their presence. Under equal opportunity, executives would have to get along without servants in the office just as they get along without butlers at home.

Real equality could have unpredictable consequences in fields like public-school teaching, where men and women are employed together. Charles R. Benson, an economist specializing in the problems of schools, analyzes one such problem in a little book optimistically titled *The Cheerful Prospect*. Equal pay, he says, has ruined the morale of the teaching profession, because it fails to recognize that men and women teachers work for different reasons. The men teachers want money and sometimes take on outside jobs after school to get it. If they were paid more, they would take on heavier teaching loads. But if women teachers were required to teach two shifts of children a day, or work through the summer, many of them would drop out. If the women who teach because they can combine it with family duties should quit, Benson writes, there wouldn't be enough men teachers to go around. So we limp along, fearful to demand the productivity from teachers that could raise their wages and reform the system.

The interesting thing about Ben-

son's analysis, of course, is that he assumes that all women have the same motivations. It does not occur to him that some women, as well as some of the moonlighting men, would be glad to work longer and harder for more pay, while others of both sexes would quit teaching. He assumes that all women are only working for their families and cannot be counted on to work for a better school system. Improved teaching, he argues, depends on making the profession attractive to men, but what he really means is that we need more committed teachers. Sex equality, along with higher pay and higher standards, could attract ambitious men and women who now hesitate to go into a profession whose prestige is low because it has been dominated by women.

Desegregation would force companies to re-examine their motives. Frequently men commit company money to beat each other out in order to gain promotion. They are more interested, sometimes, in winning recognition in the organization than in doing what's best for it. Incentives based on brownie points, trips to Hawaii for sales winners, and the gamey pitting of one worker against another may have sold vacuum cleaners, but this warlike spirit is not productive in such modern industries as aerospace research. Even companies selling to consumers sometimes find that the aggressive, old-fashioned sales methods alienate important customers or cost too much to service.

Business is becoming too sophisticated and subtle to be played like a game of football. Men who succeed in technologically advanced work can't afford to waste energy proving that they are masculine. They are interested in responsive teamwork which may seem more feminine than masculine.

And if business is a "game," there is no particular reason to assume that men have a monopoly on the winning tactics. Pentagon researchers have been working with "games" intended to sharpen military thinking. Like poker, these games require the players to anticipate the opposition. In one experiment, John R. Bond and W. E. Vinacke pitted men players against women. They found that the men tried much harder to win, but that they used exploitative tactics, which were self-defeating. The women found ways to reward other players and they won more games.

The "masculine" style can be destructive in projects requiring flexible teamwork and in the expanding fields which provide health, education, and welfare services. American hospitals worry about their cold efficiency. Because American doctors are almost all male, hospitals in this country have become starchy, impersonal factories for processing sick people as if they were things. A patient undergoing surgery is made to feel as if he were on an assembly line.

Prophets generally foresee a world which has less use for the masculine style. The high point of the male mystique may well have been a half-century ago when the great American fortunes were carved out by men who fought each other with money instead of with swords. The enterprises they built have long since become bureaucracies headed by organization men whose main concern is smoothing relations and holding the enterprise together. Responsibility for keeping things going peacefully within the firm or family has traditionally been left to women, but internal relations are now important enough to engage the attention of men.

If there are advantages in taking the sex labels off jobs, there are even more gains in devocationalizing family life. "After all, women should make more concessions in marriage because marriage is a woman's *business*," the editor of a woman's magazine remarked in 1952. The word "business" made me want to ask, "Like prostitution?"

American brides indignantly deny that they are contracting to exchange domestic services and sexual availability for financial support. Yet the vocational obligation remains. An American working wife thinks she should pay for the cleaning woman out of her salary because cleaning the house is her "job." She may try to get home before her husband at night to be sure everything is ready for him. She insists that she is earning "for the family" and boasts that she arranges matters so that they are not inconvenienced in the slightest by her earning for them. Her husband may offer to help with the shopping and the children, but it is a magnanimous free gift. Only financial support is expected of him. One wife actually agreed not to bother her husband for any help in handling the house or children during the five years he gave himself to win promotion to vice president of his company. He was doing it, he firmly believed, because he loved his family.

Love has supplanted the notion of a contract. Marriage now has to be "for love." I heard a great deal about love in discussing the new-style marriage with men and women.

"But wouldn't you rather be loved than be equal?" many people asked, but they never seemed able to explain exactly why love and equality had to be an either-or proposition. In an attempt to find out, I spent hours trying to convince a young man that a relationship recognized as dependent could not properly be described as love. He was not persuaded. A few days later another young man put the old question, "Do you really care about all this equal rights business? Wouldn't you rather be adored?"

My answer was firm. "No, I would rather *not* be adored. It's been tried, but it just makes me nervous."

Love that simply projects a romantic ideal onto another person is not very flattering to the love object. It is irritating to be adored for what one is not, and it is dull to be constrained to serve as a mirror or screen. Furthermore, it is plain wrong for one human being to use another human being as a passive object, and if this sort of relationship is natural, it is that part of nature that civilization should alter. To set the record straight, and only because the issue keeps coming up, I honestly believe that love is a strictly private and personal relationship that cannot exist if it is harnessed to economic or social objectives beyond itself. Institutions of freedom and equality can make love possible, but love itself is not an institution, a motive, a reward, an excuse, or a compensation for giving up something else.

Working women frequently told us that they were happier when they worked, and their husbands frequently confided that they got along better with their wives when both worked. "I urged her to go back after each of the babies," the husband of a department store vice president told us. "She was happier and she was much more fun when she was working."

Women have no monopoly on whining, nagging, complaining, sniping, malingering, sabotage, cattiness, touchiness, suspiciousness, petty attention-getting. Slaves, children, courtiers, male secretaries, and assistants to the president act "just like a woman," too. So do soldiers cooped up in barracks. These unattractive postures crop up whenever people are dependent on other individuals in a close, unequal personal relationship. When husbands say their *wives* are happier when they work, they may really mean that they *themselves* are freed from the demands and, sometimes, the hostilities of emotional dependence.

Marriages have always deviated widely from the model usually presented to boys and girls, but the parents involved have always been made to feel guilty about being different. Women who are dominant feel they must conceal their strength in the interest of public relations, or, worse yet, prove to themselves that they are not unnatural monsters. Men who are constitutionally unaggressive have compensated by unpleasant blustering. The first step is to render unto Caesar those things which belong to Caesar and unto love those things that belong to love. Husbands are not employers. Children are not jobs.

Caring for small children is, of course, productive work. It is usually done by the child's mother, but it is a mistake to confuse mothering with doing the diapers, making the formula, bathing, chauffeuring, dressing, feeding, and stopping backyard fights. All this and more, others can and often do. A mother and a father provide the child with models of what adults are like. Children do not grow up to be like their nurses, but like their parents. Europeans brought up by nannies say that the moral influence of their parents was stronger because their parents were not involved in their day-to-day physical care.

A generation of over-mothered children has convinced a great many armchair advisers on family affairs that fathers are needed at home as much as mothers, although perhaps at different stages of a child's development.

Young men and women would have to be educated to accept this kind of partnership, but the strongest argument for desegregation is that the public schools treat boys and girls in much the same way until they are in their teens. Why not continue this approach into adult life? The change would have to start with retraining vocational guidance counselors who now have the embarrassing job of preparing girls for the limitations of the job market.

Desegregating all education would end schools for one sex on the ground that they overemphasize sex roles. Children who profit by boarding school—and there are always some—might profit even more by coeducational institutions like Putney, in Vermont, where girls and boys get some of the social advantages of very large families or old-fashioned neighborhoods, where

children did not have to be chauffeured to each other for casual play.

But the important change in education is one that the graduate school couples are pioneering already. Ever since the GI Bill of Rights, wives have been earning while their husbands go to school. If desegregation of employment offered financial rewards to women achievers which were equal to those of men, it would encourage husbands to pay their wives back by allowing them to go back to school. A working wife is now one of the principal sources of funds for the medical education of future doctors. Even if all higher and continuing education is eventually subsidized by the Government with family allowance grants, husbands and wives will have to take turns at home if careers are going to require the amount of continual retraining that planners see ahead. The U-shaped career may soon become the fate of every first-class earner.

All this sounds fine, but do women want it? Doesn't this radical reallocation of responsibilities overemphasize work? Won't the world of the future have to cope with leisure rather than stimulate achievement? Don't we need the special talents of women to reform business and public life, and won't we lose their special gifts if we bring them up to be exactly like men? And finally, won't there be more family quarrels and ground for conflict when men and women do exactly the same things? And what about chivalry? Doesn't the financial support men give to women catalyze something in their relationship that is valuable?

The objections are formidable. The most thoughtful idealists of 1968 often defend the contribution of womanliness on esthetic and even spiritual grounds.

"The future of mankind may well depend on the fate of a 'mother variable' uncontrolled by technological man," Erik Erikson, lecturer in psychiatry at Harvard writes. Like many sensitive people appalled at the mechanical, crowded, impersonal society we are building, Erikson hopes that the compassion and humanity of women can save us. Idealists who look to women for salvation are often less interested in man-woman relations than in using women as a natural resource against the collapse of human values under the impact of technological advance. This is, of course, a New Masculinist attitude.

The most fervent of these idealistic New Masculinists are men. In 1964, Vermont Royster, the chief editor of the business-oriented *Wall Street Journal*, attacked the "Work Mystique" which in his opinion was misleading women into equating self-fulfillment with employment. Work is not all that important, he insisted. In 1967, a *Reader's Digest* editor, Charles W. Ferguson, articulated this New Masculinist appeal in his book, *The Male Attitude*, which blamed the parlous state of the world squarely on stag rule and urged society to save itself, before it was too late, by making greater use of the neglected insights of women.

What these people are saying is that women are better than men because less tainted with power. They have revived the Victorian notion of the pure woman, the madonna redeeming an evil world. The trouble with this flattering assumption is that women are no purer than they ever

were and the history of their behind-the-scenes or from-the-side influence is as uneventful as their impact on politics. Women are uncommitted and unorganized and hence a tempting target for politicians and reformers, but they have, so far, resisted all attempts to make themselves better than men. Today's women can't pioneer leisure styles of living for men any more than yesterday's women could appreciate art and music for men. There is no male side or female side to the war in Vietnam. A father's son dies for every mother's son who dies.

With us still are the Old Masculinists who argue that real equality would leave women worse off than before. And it's true. Laws that classify by sex are largely designed to protect women from desertion. They date from the days when marriage, with its consequent exposure to childbearing, was the only way a woman could earn a decent living. But family-support laws are becoming dead letters, and in any case they bear more heavily on the rich who own property than on the poor who don't have assets worth attaching. Desertion is the poor man's divorce.

More serious is the possibility that real desegregation would develop conflicts of interest between husbands and wives that now occur only rarely. In 1962, the London Stock Exchange turned down the application of Elisabeth Rivers-Bulkeley for membership because her husband, a Lloyd's insurance broker, was "at business in risk" and she might have a "moral obligation" to meet his debts. But such problems can be solved. If Carolyn Agger, the Washington lawyer, had a case that went to the Supreme Court of the United States, her husband Justice Fortas might elect not to hear the case, or she might get another lawyer to argue it.

A more serious problem for two-income families is our increasing mobility. Salaried workers are frequently moved by their organizations or offered better jobs elsewhere. In Asiatic cultures, separation of the husband and wife for periods is not regarded as serious. Family ties are not personal but legal. In our American upper classes, as in others, husbands and wives often go on separate trips and do not feel that they must be together all the time in every phase of their marriage.

But in a society where men and women are treated equally a wife would not be forced to follow a husband if he were better able to make the sacrifice of location than she, and the move made sense for the partnership, as well. In some cases, key men have refused to move to a new place unless suitable jobs could be found for their wives. Employers could do more of the accommodating than it occurs to them to do now. Federal and state services might lead the way by adopting a policy that the spouse of a transferred worker be given priority on appropriate job openings in the new area; that husbands and wives employed by the service be transferred, insofar as possible, together; and that refusal to move because of employment of a husband or wife may not be held against a civil servant in considering him for promotion.

Finally, there is no avoiding the fact that there are drawbacks. If boys and girls are not to form their charac-

ters around the need to be "manly" and "womanly," they will need other models, other motivations. It is realistic to urge a boy to do a dull job because it will benefit him in the future, but it is easier to get him to "act like a man." And because of its visibility, sex difference is a handy way to decide small matters, such as who gets named first in a social introduction. The brave new world of sex equality would be a world of frequent divorce. Divorces increase in good times and decline in bad times, suggesting that many more couples would like to separate than are financially able to. Regardless of cause or effect, the marriages of career women are less stable than the marriages of women financially dependent on their husbands.

Vanguard couples have taken turns working and going to school, but all pioneering requires thought and planning which tradition and habit settle with less effort. The answer is easier to find when the answer is the same for all; if grandmother's marriage seemed calmer, it may have been only that it required fewer personal decisions and women had to make more accommodations. The colleague marriage may be "better" if it comes off, but it takes more energy. It's risky, and it fails noisily.

Parallels to the dangers of choice in family roles are the uncertainties of choice in vocation. When asked why they marry, men often answer "to have something to work for." When asked what they would do if they had enough money to live without working, they say they would continue to work. In the Old Masculinist morality, women symbolize the goal. When a man has a woman to work for, he doesn't have to think any further. Without her, he has to examine his real feelings and motivations.

American women are already confused by the choices they now have of work and home and various combinations of each. Are we to impose this kind of choice on men, too? There is evidence that the intrinsic interest of the work is more important to girls choosing professions than the money they can earn. If boys as well as girls were free to choose work that interested them, we might have a hard time getting dull jobs done. What if everybody wanted to act in television, an occupation which need not increase proportionately to population, while fewer and fewer wanted to become nurses and teachers, occupations which parallel population growth?

The real argument for equality cannot be made on the basis of expedience. The compelling reason is equity. The little jokes the New Masculinists love to make about the New Feminists imply that the difference between the sexes is so beautiful, so rewarding, so deeply rooted, so innocent, and so much fun that it is worth enhancing at the expense of considerable inequity.

Yet equity is not to be dismissed so lightly. It is the sort of blessing that doesn't count when you have it, but ruins everything if you don't. Most Americans are now aware of the enormous social, psychic, and economic cost of Negro slavery. These costs became widely apparent only when the inequity of slavery aroused indignation and set people thinking.

Billions of words and hours of thought have been expanded on the complexities of race relations. Progress, said the sophisticated, will have to be slow. You cannot change a way of life overnight. Yet today it is clear that however agonizing the changes have been, the problem has never been all that complicated. What we did to the Negroes was just plain wrong, and everybody knew it.

So with the employment of women. Relations between the sexes are complicated, and change is hard, but the way women are treated is just plain wrong.

It is wrong to make aspiring women prove they are twice as good as men.

It is wrong to pay women less than men for the same work just because they will work for less.

It is wrong to exclude women from work they can do so that they have to work for less in the jobs open to them.

It is wrong to make aspiring women pay the penalty of women who are content to be used as a labor reserve.

It is wrong to assume that because some women can't do mathematics, *this* woman can't do mathematics.

It is wrong to expect women to work for their families or the nation and then to step aside when their families or the nation want them out of the way.

It is wrong to deny individuals born female the right to inconvenience their families to pursue art, science, power, prestige, money, or even self-expression, in the way that men in pursuit of these goals inconvenience their families as a matter of course.

It is wrong to impute motives to women instead of letting them speak for themselves.

It is wrong to ridicule, sneer, frighten, or brainwash anyone unable to fight back.

It is wrong, as well as wasteful and dangerous, to discourage talent.

All these things are wrong, and everybody knows it. And just as "separate but equal" schools limited white children as well as Negroes, so the doctrine that women are different but equal limits men. Mary Wollstonecraft, John Stuart Mill, George Bernard Shaw, and President Goheen of Princeton were all concerned, and some of them primarily with the damage inequity does to men. David Reisman points out that every boundary we impose on women we impose on men also.

Equity speaks softly and wins in the end. But it is expedience, with its loud voice, that sets the time of victory. The cotton gin did not make slavery wrong, but it helped a lot of Southerners to *see* that slavery was wrong. The immigrant vote did not make woman suffrage right, but it frightened politicians into enfranchising women on the theory that the educated women of politically conservative old American stock would vote more readily than the submissive women of politically unpredictable ethnic groups.

So with equal opportunity for women. Conditions conspire to help people see the inequity and the advantages of ending it. First the pill gives women control over their fate so that they can be as responsible as men. Then modern medicine prolongs the lives of women so that all now have decades of potential working life, beyond child-rearing age, during which none of the limitations imposed on women make sense. Next, modern technology takes their work out of the home and invites them to do it elsewhere, and for pay. It frees more mothers of the work of bringing up children, and gives it to schools. Meanwhile, the new technology is less and less a respecter of old-fashioned sex differences. It eliminated the need for physical strength very rapidly and is now eliminating the need for "detail work."

What the new technology needs is educated manpower that can learn new skills. What it doesn't need is more ordinary people without skills. Both needs strengthen the case for equal opportunity for the underprivileged majority of Americans who were born female.

NEWTON/*Reverse Discrimination as Unjustified*

Lisa Newton, who delivered a version of the following essay at a meeting of the Society for Women in Philosophy in 1972, argues that reverse discrimination cannot be justified by an appeal to the ideal of equality. Indeed, she argues that reverse discrimination does not advance but actually undermines equality, because it violates the concept of equal justice under law for all citizens.

She further contends that the implications of reverse discrimination are serious. Among these is that reverse discrimination must be used to wipe out a history of discrimination. Since virtually everyone is a member of some minority or oppressed group, she asks, does this mean that everyone has a rightful claim to preferential treatment? Her conclusion: reverse discrimination destroys justice, law, equality, and citizenship itself.

Central to Newton's analysis is her definition of justice. Do you agree with it? If you don't, how would you alter it? Although Newton is opposed to reverse discrimination, she is obviously opposed to discrimination for the same reasons. How do you think, then, she would attempt to remedy the sexual imbalance in the job market that has resulted from discrimination?

I have heard it argued that "simple justice" requires that we favor women and blacks in employment and educational opportunities, since women and blacks were "unjustly" excluded from such opportunities for so many years in the not so distant past. It is a strange argument, an example of a possible implication of a true proposition advanced to dispute the proposition itself, like an octopus absentmindedly slicing off his head with a stray tentacle. A fatal confusion underlies this argument, a confusion fundamentally relevant to our understanding of the notion of the rule of law.

Two senses of justice and equality are involved in this confusion. The root notion of justice, progenitor of the other, is the one that Aristotle (*Nichomachean Ethics* 5. 6; *Politics* 1.2; 3. 1) assumes to be the foundation and proper virtue of the political association. It is the condition which free men establish among themselves when they "share a common life in order that their association bring them self-sufficiency"—the regulation of their relationship by law, and the establishment, by law, of equality before the law. Rule of law is the name and pattern of this justice; its equality stands against the inequalities—of wealth, talent, etc.—otherwise obtaining among its participants, who by virtue of that equality are called "citizens." It is an achievement—complete, or, more frequently, partial—of certain people in certain concrete situations. It is fragile and easily disrupted by powerful individuals who discover that the blind equality of rule of law is inconvenient for their interests. Despite its obvious instability, Aristotle assumed that the establishment of justice in this sense, the creation of citizenship, was a permanent possibility for men and that the resultant association of citizens was the natural home of the species. At levels below the political association, this rule-governed equality is easily found; it is exemplified by any group of children agreeing together to play a game. At the level of the political association, the attainment of this justice is more difficult, simply because the stakes are so much higher for each participant. The equality of citizenship is not something that happens of its own accord, and without the expenditure of a fair amount of effort it will collapse into the rule of a powerful few over an apathetic many. But at least it has been achieved, at some times in some places; it is always worth trying to achieve, and eminently worth trying to maintain, wherever and to whatever degree it has been brought into being.

Aristotle's parochialism is notorious; he really did not imagine that persons other than Greeks could associate freely in justice, and the only form of association he had in mind was the Greek *polis*. With the decline of the *polis* and the shift in the center of political thought, his notion of justice underwent a sea change. To be exact, it ceased to represent a political type and became a moral ideal: the ideal of equality as we know it. This ideal demands that all men be included in citizenship—that one Law govern all equally, that all men regard all other men as fellow citizens, with the same guarantees, rights, and protections. Briefly, it demands that the circle of citizenship achieved by any group be extended to include the entire human race. Properly understood, its effect on our associations can be excellent: it congratulates us on our achievement of rule of law as a process of government but refuses to let us remain complacent until we have expanded the associations to include others within the ambit of the rules, as often and as far as possible. While one man is a slave, none of us may feel truly free. We are constantly prodded by this ideal to look for possible unjustifiable discrimination, for inequalities not absolutely required for the functioning of the society and advantageous to all. And after twenty centuries of pressure, not at all constant, from this ideal, it might be said that some progress has been made. To take the cases in point for this problem, we are now prepared to assert, as Aristotle would never have been, the equality of sexes and of persons of different colors. The ambit of American citizenship, once restricted to white males of property, has been extended to include all adult free men, then all adult males including ex-slaves, then all women. The process of acquisition of full citizenship was for these groups a sporadic trail of half-measures, even now not complete; the steps on the road to full equality are marked by legislation and judicial decisions which are only recently concluded and still often not enforced. But the fact that we can now discuss the possibility of favoring such groups in hiring shows that over the area that concerns us, at least, full equality is presupposed as a basis for discussion. To that extent, they are full citizens, fully protected by the law of the land.

It is important for my argument that the moral ideal of equality be recognized as logically distinct from the condition (or virtue) of justice in the political sense. Justice in this sense exists *among* a citizenry, irrespective of the number of the populace included in that citizenry. Further, the moral ideal is parasitic upon the political virtue, for "equality" is unspecified—it means nothing until we are told in what respect that equality is to be realized. In a political context, "equality" is specified as "equal rights"—equal access to the public realm, public goods and offices, equal treatment under the law—in brief, the equality of citizenship. If citizenship is not a possibility, political equality is unintelligible. The ideal emerges as a generalization of the real condition and refers back to that condition for its content.

Now, if justice (Aristotle's justice in the political sense) is equal treatment under law for all citizens, what is injustice? Clearly, injustice is the violation of that equality, discriminating for or against a group of citizens, favoring them with special immunities and privileges or depriving them of those guaranteed to the others. When the southern employer refuses to hire blacks in white-collar jobs, when Wall Street will only hire women as secretaries with new titles, when Mississippi high schools routinely flunk all the black boys above ninth grade, we have examples of injustice, and we work to restore the equality of the public realm by ensuring that equal opportunity will be provided in such cases in the future. But of course, when the employers and the schools *favor* women and blacks, the same injustice is done. Just as the previous discrimination did, this reverse discrimination voilates the public equality which defines citizenship and destroys the rule of law for the areas in which these favors are granted. To the extent that we adopt a program of discrimination, reverse or otherwise, justice in the political sense is destroyed, and none of us, specifically affected or not, is a citizen, a bearer of rights—we are all petitioners for favors. And to the same extent, the ideal of equality is undermined, for it has content only where justice obtains, and by destroying justice we render the ideal meaningless. It is, then, an ironic paraodx, if not a contradiction in terms, to assert that the ideal of equality justifies the violation of justice; it is as if one should argue, with William Buckley, that an ideal of humanity can justify the destruction of the human race.

Logically, the conclusion is simple enough: all discrimination is wrong prima facie because it violates justice, and that goes for reverse discrimination too. No violation of justice among the citizens may be justified (may overcome the prima facie objection) by appeal to the ideal of equality, for that ideal is logically dependent upon the notion of justice. Reverse discrimination, then, which attempts no other justification than an appeal to equality, is wrong. But let us try to make the conclusion more plausible by suggesting some of the implications of the suggested practice of reverse discrimination in employment and education. My argument will be that the problems raised there are insoluble, not only in practice but in principle.

We may argue, if we like, about what "discrimination" consists of. Do I discriminate against blacks if I admit none to my school when none of the black applicants are qualified by the tests I always give? How far must I go to root out cultural bias from my application forms and tests before I can say that I have not discriminated against those of different cultures? Can I assume that women are not strong enough to be roughnecks on my oil rigs, or must I test them individually? But this controversy, the most popular and well-argued aspect of the issue, is not as fatal as two others which cannot be avoided: if we are regarding the blacks as a "minority" victimized by discrimination, what is a "minority"? And for any group—blacks, women, whatever—that has been discriminated against, what amount of reverse discrimination wipes out the initial discrimination? Let us grant as true that women and blacks were discriminated against, even where laws forbade such discrimination, and grant for the sake of argument that a history of discrimination must be wiped out by reverse discrimination. What follows?

First, are there other groups which have been discriminated against? For they should have the same right of restitution. What about American Indians, Chicanos, Appalachian Mountain whites, Puerto Ricans, Jews, Cajuns, and Orientals?

And if these are to be included, the principle according to which we specify a "minority" is simply the criterion of "ethnic (sub) group," and we're stuck with every hyphenated American in the lower-middle class clamoring for special privileges for *his* group—and with equal justification. For be it noted, when we run down the Harvard roster, we find not only a scarcity of blacks (in comparison with the proportion in the population) but an even more striking scarcity of those second-, third-, and fourth-generation ethnics who make up the loudest voice of Middle America. Shouldn't they demand *their* share? And eventually, the WASPs will have to form their own lobby; for they too are a minority. The point is simply this: there is no "majority" in America who will not mind giving up just a bit of their rights to make room for a favored minority. There are only other minorities, each of which is discriminated against by the favoring. The initial injustice is then repeated dozens of times, and if each minority is granted the same right of restitution as the others, an entire area of rule governance is dissolved into a pushing and shoving match between self-interested groups. Each works to catch the public eye and political popularity by whatever means of advertising and power politics lend themselves to the effort, to capitalize as much as possible on temporary popularity until the restless mob picks another group to feel sorry for. Hardly an edifying spectacle, and in the long run no one can benefit: the pie is no larger—it's just that instead of setting up and enforcing rules for getting a piece, we've turned the contest into a free-for-all, requiring much more effort for no larger a reward. It would be in the interests of all the participants to reestablish an objective rule to govern the process, carefully enforced and the same for all.

Second, supposing that we do manage to agree in general that women and blacks (and all the others) have some right of restitution, some right to a privileged place in the structure of opportunities for a while, how will we know when that while is up? How much privilege is enough? When will the guilt be gone, the price paid, the balance restored? What recompense is right for centuries of exclusion? What criterion tells us when we are done? Our experience with the Civil Rights movement shows us that agreement on these terms cannot be presupposed: a process that appears to some to be going at a mad gallop into a black takeover appears to the rest of us to be at a standstill. Should a practice of reverse discrimination be adopted, we may safely predict that just as some of us begin to see "a satisfactory start toward righting the balance," others of us will see that we "have already gone too far in the other direction" and will suggest that the discrimination ought to be reversed again. And such disagreement is inevitable, for the point is that we could not *possibly* have any criteria for evaluating the kind of recompense we have in mind. The context presumed by any discussion of restitution is the context of the rule of law: law sets the rights of men and simultaneously sets the method for remedying the violation of those rights. You may exact suffering from others and/or damage payments for yourself if and only if the others have violated your rights; the suffering you have endured is not sufficient reason for them to suffer. And remedial rights exist only where there is law: primary human rights are useful guides to legislation but cannot stand as reasons for awarding remedies for injuries sustained. But then, the context presupposed by any discussion of restitution is the context of preexistent full citizenship. No remedial rights could exist for the excluded; neither in law nor in logic does there exist a right to *sue* for a standing to sue.

From these two considerations, then, the difficulties with reverse discrimination become evident. Restitution for a disadvantaged group whose rights under the law have been violated is possible by legal means, but restitution for a disadvantaged group whose grievance is that there was no law to protect them simply is not. First, outside of the area of justice defined by the law, no sense can be made of "the group's rights," for no law recognizes that group or the individuals in it, qua members, as bearers of rights (hence *any* group can constitute itself as a disadvantaged minority in some sense and demand similar restitution). Second, outside of the area of protection of law, no sense can be made of the violation of rights (hence the amount of the recompense cannot be decided by any objective criterion). For both reasons, the practice of reverse discrimination undermines the foundation of the very ideal in whose name it is advocated; it destroys justice, law, equality, and citizenship itself, and replaces them with power struggles and popularity contests.

10

PERSONAL CONCERN
of deciding to decide
SOCIAL RESPONSIBILITY

Back in the 1960s a tragic event made the front pages of our newspapers. It involved a young woman named Kitty Genovese, who was stabbed to death in New York City. The murder was not in itself so unusual. Sadly, many of these occur daily in cities and towns across the United States. What was peculiar was that thirty-eight of Kitty Genovese's neighbors witnessed her brutal slaying. In answer to her pitiful screams of terror, they came to their windows at 3 A.M., where they remained for the thirty minutes it took for her assailant to slay her. Of the thirty-eight, not one attempted to intervene in any way; no one even phoned the police. Why didn't they act?

Perhaps they were groggy, too sleepy to realize what was happening. After all, it is not easy to be awakened from a deep sleep and act efficiently. A possible explanation, but unfortunately it does not explain such indifference at high noon, at which time Eleanor Bradley, while shopping along Fifth Avenue, again in New York City, tripped, fell, and broke her leg. Before being assisted, she lay on the sidewalk for forty minutes while scores of pedestrians stopped, gawked, and went about their business. Surely they were not half asleep.

Maybe it is just big-city dwellers. Maybe they have just become hardened to the physical and mental horrors that they are exposed to daily. Perhaps if Kitty Genovese had been attacked in a small town in the Midwest or if Eleanor Bradley had tripped in a rural town in the South, people would have reacted differently. Perhaps. But interviews with eyewitnesses to the Genovese murder contradict this hypothesis. Rather than being unmoved or impervious to the event, they were horrified. Then why didn't they react?

Psychological experiments suggest a possible answer: the more people there are watching a distressing event, the less likely the victim is to receive aid. In other words, there may be an inverse correlation between the number of witnesses to a tragedy and the assistance that is rendered. Behind this hypothesis are some interesting social comments.

Apparently, it is generally considered unsophisticated in our society to reveal emotions publicly. Thus, we try to appear less excited, less anxious, less eager, less aroused, and less distressed than we do privately. Have you ever studied men thumbing through *Playboy* or *Penthouse* in a drug store? If you just judged from their reactions, you'd probably swear they were gazing at *Reader's Digest*. Maybe you've turned your ankle walking down a crowded street. What was your reaction? You probably felt rather foolish and conspicuous. But you surely wouldn't if you turned your ankle in the privacy of your home; in fact, you'd probably cry out or deliver a pain-relieving round of expletives. Similarly, it is thought inappropriate for others to show deep concern for our condition. In short, when in public we frequently allow other people to define the appropriateness of our behavior, even in supportive situations. Conformity is the rule, not the exception, and often conformity means nonintervention.

This tendency to remain uninvolved is, perhaps, the most serious obstacle to overcome in formulating a useful and satisfying code of ethics, because it betrays a lack of concern. *To be concerned is to perceive the importance of something to one's own life or to the lives of others, to perceive a personal responsibility for the direction that the object of our concern takes, and to make an effort to translate these perceptions into appropriate action.* Without concern, we cannot formulate a moral position on any issue. As a result, we remain morally uninvolved.

There seems to be a large measure of this unconcern these days. It is difficult to isolate what is fostering it, but one phenomenon is a likely candidate—the fear of decision making. We may fear to make decisions because we do not wish to look foolish if we err, we are not sure of our position, or we have never really had to make a decision for ourselves. The reasons are properly evaluated by psychologists and sociologists. But one thing is clear: if we fear to make decisions, then we can never formulate a moral code; for any moral code presumes a decision about what is right and wrong and an intention to act on that decision.

So, the willingness to make a decision is basic to any moral code. Unfortunately, many of us dread making decisions. It follows, therefore, that many of us do not formulate our own moral codes. This is a serious matter, and this is why the last chapter of this book is devoted to the subject of decision making.

Some may wonder why, if decision making is basic to a moral code, the subject was not undertaken earlier, perhaps at the outset of our study. The primary reason is because now that you have been exposed to considerable ethical thought and codes, you probably feel thoroughly undecided about your own moral stand. In a curious way, you may feel less certain though more informed than when you began the study. This is entirely understandable, for at the outset you were probably committed to assumptions that you now question.

But this state of indecision is also risky because it can itself become a convenient excuse for making no commitment, for leaving yourself in an ethical limbo. At first glance, taking no moral stand may appear a thoroughly sophisticated attitude for an enlightened person of the latter twentieth century. But before this chapter is finished, you should see why it is no more than a convenient and acceptable way to avoid making a decision. Since it comes at the end, this chapter on decision making should have more of an impact than if it had appeared earlier. It should stand as a kind of caution to this last temptation, the temptation to remain uncommitted.

We will see ways in which we avoid decisions and how these undermine the formulation of a moral code. Remember in the first chapter we talked about logical fallacies. In the subsequent chapters and in exercises we saw frequent examples of these, even in the thought of ethicists. You could call the devices that we use to avoid decision making *psychological fallacies*, which occur as frequently as logical fallacies. We will also see why there is reason for optimism amidst the welter of often conflicting ethical thought that we have studied, and most important, how we can go about evaluating our own morality.

AUTONOMY

To begin our discussion of decision making, let's talk about autonomy. In his book *From Decidophobia to Autonomy Without Guilt and Justice,* Princeton University professor of philosophy Walter Kaufman defines *autonomy* as "making with open eyes the decisions that give shape to one's life."* You might think that in this sense everyone wishes to be autonomous. But as Kaufman points out, "The fear of autonomy is a nameless dread, which leaves me free to coin a name for it: decidophobia."† By *decidophobia* Kaufman means the fear of choosing fateful alternatives with your eyes wide open, fully aware of the risks.

A good example of decidophobia is the character Grand in Albert Camus's novel *The Plague.* Grand is a writer at work on a novel. But the first sentence of his novel is so bothersome that he keeps rewriting it, spending weeks on a single word. True, the proper choice of words is obviously crucial to a good novel. But Grand is so bogged down on a single word that the novel goes begging. Likewise, we can become so immersed in microscopic moral distinctions that we avoid making ethical decisions with any care or close our eyes to the major ethical alternatives. We can best see how we avoid decisions, specifically moral decisions, by considering the major obstacles to autonomy.

OBSTACLES TO AUTONOMY

Kaufman cites what he believes are common strategies by which we avoid autonomy. They can be summarized as: (1) avoiding fateful decisions (which

---

*Walter Kaufman, *From Decidophobia to Autonomy Without Guilt and Justice* (New York: Delta, 1975), p. 2.
†Kaufman, *Decidophobia,* p. 3.

includes strategies involving recourse to authority and strategies that do not which are compatible with going it alone), (2) stacking the cards to make one alternative clearly right and thus removing all risk, and (3) declining responsibility.

AVOIDING FATEFUL DECISIONS

Authority

One clear way to avoid making our own moral decisions is to rely on authority to decide for us. Authority, as we have seen, can take many forms—religious, political, philosophical, and educational. Let's take educational authority as an example.

Right now you find yourself at a college. How did you get there? Primarily by accidents of geography and financial condition. It is possible that you never considered the alternative of going elsewhere, and it is likely you never considered who composed the faculty. And it is almost certain that you never thought about what books and ideas you would be exposed to. Yet, for the next several years all these factors will wield an authoritative influence over your life. In some instances this influence will last a lifetime.

Let's say that while in college the only ethics course you ever take is taught by an act utilitarian. If the instructor vigorously presents act utilitarianism and is highly critical of opposing views, there is a good chance that your subsequent ethical perceptions will betray a strong act utilitarian basis. Again, let's say a philosophy course that you found particularly stimulating was taught by an existentialist. Should that be your only exposure to philosophy, it would not be unusual for you to subsequently identify yourself with the existential school of thought.

If you doubt that education can wield this kind of influence, ask yourself how seriously you have ever thought about socialism, communism, fascism, libertarianism, or anarchism as alternative political lifestyles. Probably not much, because the authoritative educational influences in your life have not carried these biases, nor have any other authoritative influences for that matter. As a result, you probably don't consider these alternatives seriously, if at all. But *don't* does not mean *can't*. That's the point. By locking into authorities, we equate *don't* with *can't*. The result is often an evasion of moral autonomy, an avoidance of making with open eyes the moral decisions that shape our lives—a convenient way to remain uninvolved.

On the other hand, some of us reject authority and attempt to go it alone. The result can be drifting.

Drifting

We all know people who would rather go along with the way things are than choose their own lifestyles, places to live, pastimes, and moral values. Perhaps you know people who watch a lot of television. Commercial television is currently glutted with two kinds of programs—police dramas and situation comedies. When was the last time anybody you know wrote to a network and asked for different programming? Perhaps they genuinely like such programming. But perhaps they are resigned to the *status quo,* to what there is, to what somebody is giving them. Maybe they are so accepting of the way commercial television is that they do not consider the alternatives. They drift until next season or the season thereafter when something else becomes fashionable.

But this kind of drifting can take a more subtle form, a form with serious implications for moral decision making. Take the case of Frank and Jean Baker, a young married couple with a four-year-old son, Timmy. Like many other couples, the Bakers work hard during the day and at night just like to take it easy. Now that they have Timmy they do not go out as much as they did when they were in school, contenting themselves mostly with chatting, watching television, and having some friends over. In recent months this routine has begun to bother Jean. She can't put her finger on it, but she senses that something important is missing from their lives.

On the particular evening that we join them, they're relaxing after having put Timmy to bed.

Jean: Frank, I'm worried.
Frank: About what?
Jean: About us.
Frank: What about us?
Jean: It's hard to pin down exactly. But when I picked Timmy up at the nursery today I had this strange, unsettling feeling. I know this is going to sound crazy, but as I watched him and the other children playing in the yard today I felt that somehow we were failing them.
Frank: How?
Jean: I don't know exactly. But I thought that somehow we just weren't doing enough for them, that somehow we just didn't care enough.
Frank: But we're giving Timmy a good home, plenty of love and attention.
Jean: I know we are. It's not that. It has to do with the world that they're going to live in when we're not here, a world that they are not responsible for making.
Frank: I don't quite understand.
Jean: Just think of all the things that are happening, all the things that we hear and see on the news every night. Nuclear proliferation, environmental pollution, rising crime, overpopulation, depletion of natural resources, the list goes on and on.
Frank: But, Jean, there's not a heckuva lot an individual can do about those things. I mean those problems are so monstrously large and complex that—
Jean: I know what you're going to say—that governments must determine their solutions.
Frank: Well, they must.

Jean: But that's the point. I felt so pitifully helpless this afternoon. I found my-self thinking that I shouldn't be worried because there was nothing that I as an individual could do to help any of them, that the problems were bigger than any individual, that all I could do was to make sure Timmy had lots of love, a good home, a proper upbringing—whatever that is. And you want to know the worst part? None of that seemed to matter, because all the way home I was thinking that even if we do give Timmy all those things, what's the point if we're turning him out into a world that isn't fit to live in?

Frank: I see what you're saying. But what can we do about it?

Jean: I have no idea. But I can no longer accept that convenient bromide that it's not my problem, that I don't have any responsibility to the Timmies for the kind of world they'll inherit.

Frank: Now aren't you being a little harsh on yourself? I mean we keep abreast of what's going on. There isn't a documentary that goes by that we don't watch. Just in the area of pollution alone—how many TV specials have we watched this year about the environment?

Jean: Dozens. And what have we done afterwards? Turned on the late-night news, got a little high, and gone to bed.

Sadly, Jean's feelings of helplessness are shared by many people today, but unfortunately not enough of us share her spirit to change things. Others share Frank's illusion of an involvement that is actually nonintervention and drifting. The electronic media are accomplices to this illusion.

There is no question that the electronics explosion has made us more aware of problems than any generation before us. But there are three woefully over-looked by-products of this information cornucopia. First, we can easily begin to suffer from "information overload." By this is meant that we can be bombarded by more information than we are able to understand, assimilate, and process. The result is that, almost as a defense mechanism, we begin to shut down. We listen but do not hear; we are aware but remain uninvolved; we know but remain inert. We disengage rather than become involved.

The "information explosion" can produce another effect with the same result. We can become so overexposed to a problem that it no longer seems a problem. Remember the story of the boy who cried "wolf" too often; when the wolf finally came, nobody believed his cry. Perhaps you remember people saying, "I'm sick of hearing about the Vietnam war" or, "I'm fed up with all this talk about Watergate." The point is that we can become inured to issues and problems simply because we have heard about them so often.

A final side effect of media overexposure is that, because the problems of the day can occupy 25 percent of our waking hours, we can easily think that we are actively engaged in resolving them. But, this can be an illusion. Like Frank, we can have the impression of involvement when, as Jean senses, we are in fact passive receptacles of information. In short, we are drifting without even knowing it.

All of these real threats of media overkill leave us feeling powerless and dispirited; the problems are just too awesome to cope with. The result is a kind of moral paralysis, rooted in a fear of doing anything or deciding any issue. As Jean experiences it, this feeling is perhaps more terrifying than the problems themselves. Thus, we can easily surrender our decision-making capacity to the "powers that be" and "the people who know better," to agencies, governments, and institutions. In short, we can acquiesce to any power that we perceive as powerful enough to direct our course.

Feeling this way, some choose to drift by turning their backs on the status quo, on tradition, and the so-called establishment. They accept no values, codes, purpose, or plan. They simply "drop out," becoming society's flotsam. In living by chance and whim, they still the dizziness of making decisions with open eyes. But in living this way, they drift with authority as much as others yield to it.

Although drifting is perhaps the most common way to avoid moral authority, it is hardly the only way. Another involves stacking the cards so that we leave ourselves with no real moral decisions at all.

STACKING THE CARDS

Many people insist on making decisions but load the choices so as to avoid the pain of really choosing. Let's say that you're offered two plates of food. One is tasty and healthful, the other distasteful and poisonous. The choice is obvious— the first dish. That choice was not hard to make because the "deck was stacked." In a similar way many of us stack the choices that profoundly affect us as moral agents.

Frank: Consider for a minute any one of the problems you mentioned. Let's take the environment.
Jean: All right, let's talk about the environment.
Frank: I agree that something must be done about air pollution. If it goes unchecked, by the time Timmy's grown up it won't be fit to breathe. But do you realize what we're up against in terms of economic vested interests? And I'm not talking just about the oil and automobile industries. I'm talking about everyone who's plugged into our technoautomotive economy.
Jean: What you're really saying is that to change our driving habits or fuel consumption would require a reevaluation of our values.
Frank: You bet it would.
Jean: But if that's the only way we're going to leave behind us some breathable air, don't you think we have an obligation to begin that reevaluation?
Frank: But you and I can't solve the problem alone.
Jean: But does that make our responsibility any less? I mean, open marriages are pretty popular in this neighborhood, too. But because we disapprove of it we don't practice open marriage. We'd think it was pretty ridiculous if we disapproved of open marriage but practiced it.
Frank: It's not the same thing.
Jean: No, it's not exactly the same thing. But what I'm saying is that when you clearly see your moral obligation, you have a responsibility to discharge it.

And I think we both agree that we have a moral obligation to Timmy and the generations to come to preserve this air, the environment, and to do whatever we can personally and collectively to accomplish that.

The only alternatives that Frank can visualize are to revolutionize the value system or to do nothing. In effect, he is saying that if we can't change the whole thing immediately, there is nothing we can do. Obviously, since we cannot change everything immediately, the choice is clear-cut; and it promises indecision, irresponsibility, and the ultimate surrender of personal responsibility.

The flaw in Frank's thinking is that there is no middle ground. Of course the value system cannot be changed overnight, not even in a generation or two. But we can begin, first in our personal lives and then on a collective level. Frank has allowed the size of the problem to preclude a consideration of alternative ideas. Worse, the size of the problem has made him rationalize away any personal responsibility for resolving it and perhaps for causing it. This suggests a third way that we avoid making moral decisions.

DECLINING RESPONSIBILITY

Frequently today we avoid moral decisions simply by declining responsibility. Let's see how this works.

Frank: All right, give me an example of what you're talking about.
Jean: Gladly. What did you do before dinner?
Frank: Before dinner? I went and got a paper.
Jean: You *drove.*
Frank: So I drove.
Jean: So you didn't have to drive. You could have walked. And I could have walked to the nursery as well. It's only three blocks away, but I didn't. I drove, too.
Frank: Do you think that's going to save the environment?
Jean: That alone won't. But that multiplied countless times over throughout this country, plus hundreds, perhaps thousands, of more inventive and courageous personal and collective efforts will at least raise our consciousness of the problem to the point where we can solve it. And even if we never do, the important thing for me is that at least we will not have presided over our own extinction. Frank, you can't remain neutral. Either you're part of the problem or part of the solution. And I don't want our children and theirs to look back and view us as silent partners to their begrimed legacy.

Jean has an important insight. If we are to solve the problems that beset us, from crime in the streets to air pollution, we must develop a deep sense of personal moral responsibility. She seems to have it; Frank does not. This does not mean that individually we are the cause of social problems. But if we have concern we must be part of the solution simply because we are aware of the problems and can do something, however small, to alleviate them. Granted, the thirty-eight who eyewitnessed the slaying of Kitty Genovese may not have been able to do a lot to prevent it. But they could have done something; they at least could have phoned the police before dropping their shades.

How crucial this sense of personal morality is is difficult to understand with respect to the environmental problem because of its enormous scope, the self-sacrificial implications of any solution, and because most of us living now would probably not be around should the earth's ecosystem collapse. But most of all, we probably do not see our own complicity in this ongoing problem.

The fact of the matter is that each of us must be responsible for spelling out moral priorities, points of emphasis, and courses of action. This is basic. Nevertheless, leaving the basis for moral decisions at this would be merely to avoid the issue. Fortunately, from our introduction to ethics we can establish some reasonable parameters by which to make moral decisions. Although the nature of these considerations is general, they are nonetheless useful. At the same time, these criteria leave much latitude for individual value selection, emphasis, and execution. We can call these criteria *intention, means,* and *ends.*

ELEMENTS OF MORAL DECISION MAKING

INTENTION

Intention refers to a person's motives, the reasons behind the actions. We previously noted that it is rarely easy to isolate motives, and we can never be certain of them. However, it is probably safe to say that when persons inquire about what is the right thing to do in a particular situation, they are attempting to purify their motives or intentions.

In the course of this text, we have seen a number of persons trying to do this. One was a reporter under pressure to reveal her confidential sources of information. Another was a young woman contemplating an abortion. In this chapter's dialogue, Jean is pondering what is the right thing to do with respect to future generations. As Immanuel Kant and most religious moralists have pointed out, intentions are fundamental in determining morality. In brief, only the action that springs from a good intention may be approved without reservation.

Consideration of intention is what is sometimes known as *subjective rightness.* Subjective rightness concerns the individual's will. As Kant pointed out, mere conformity is not sufficient to make an act right or moral. An action performed only out of fear, for social approval, or even for beneficial consequences cannot be considered in the highest sense moral. Indeed, even when an act leads to unfortunate and unforeseen consequences, if that action was inspired by a good motive, then we understandably are less harsh in our disapproval; for we know that the individual meant well. It is true, as meta-ethicists tell us, that it is very difficult to determine what a good intention is. But helping us in this matter, which admittedly cannot be completely resolved, is a consideration of the second element affecting moral decisions, means.

MEANS

By means we mean the way, the method, the procedure, or the action taken to effect the intention. Previously we met a young student who plagiarized a term paper in order to satisfy a graduation requirement. There is little question that his intention was good: he intended to fulfill a graduation requirement. But the means he took are deplorable: he stole someone else's work. Therefore we cannot approve of his action without reservation.

On some occasions, however, we might approve of the means employed that under other conditions we would condemn. Take, for example, the case of an airline pilot who knows that his aircraft is seriously damaged and is in imminent danger of crashing. Knowing that an announcement of a severe problem has panicked his passengers and caused them great emotional, even physical harm in the past, the pilot announces a false reason for a forced landing at an airfield miles from the intended destination. As a result, he lands the plane without emotional or physical injury to his passengers. Although we might generally disapprove of lying, we excuse it in this case because of the pilot's intention.

This does not mean that under any circumstances intention justifies means. But it does recognize that under certain conditions an action that would usually be considered wrong is justified by the probable beneficial results for all concerned. Perhaps we could apply this reasoning to the case of the experimental psychologist we met who told harmless lies to his test subjects because that was the only way to conduct an experiment with highly beneficial social consequences. Obviously the means are directly related to the consequences, the third element for making moral decisions.

ENDS

By ends is meant the results, effects, or consequences of our actions. Surely consequentialists are correct in arguing that humans rarely approve of an action that produces evil results. The action that we approve without reservation is one whose results are good. When the results are not good we rarely approve of the action. But, again, there are times when we do approve the action with undesirable consequences.

For example, we would undoubtedly approve of a surgeon who operates on a patient as the only measure to save the person's life, even if the patient dies. On the other hand, we would likely condemn the action of a district attorney who framed a notorious criminal, even though the action benefited society.

By including consequences among the criteria for judging an action good without reservation, we are introducing an objective element into moral decisions. This is crucial, for in the last analysis whether an action is good or bad must be determined by an appeal to human experience and to all the evidence at hand. Experience may be limited, vision constrained, and perception incomplete. But that seems to be part of the human condition. We still must ultimately assess intention, means, and ends as comprehensively as we can according to the depth and breadth of human experience. Thus, Jean recommends that when she and Frank don't absolutely need to drive their car, they should not. Suppose that in walking to the store to buy a paper, Frank is struck by an automobile and killed. We would hardly consider her or his action as immoral, for the test of human experience suggests that both the intention and means were sound.

Obviously, then, intention, means, and ends are intimately wed. In recognizing this we also acknowledge the dynamic, functional, and experimental nature of morality. Moral judgments are never easy. They grow out of the stuff of life, which is constantly changing and thus altering our concepts of morality. Thus, we recognize an element of truth in moral relativism. Undoubtedly, there is a personal, relativistic element in moral decisions.

Thus, if I can swim and you cannot, then I have an obligation to attempt to save the life of a drowning person, but you probably do not. At the same time, we must reject the more extreme claims of moral relativism where it equates morality with convention or custom, for in doing this moral relativists in effect exonerate one from personal responsibility and allow continuation of blatant injustices. Thus, had he been a relativist, as a Southerner, Martin Luther King would not have protested racial injustices, but acquiesced to the custom of racial discrimination.

In conclusion, the right action is the one that springs from a good intention, is executed by the best available means, and produces good consequences. Again, these are admittedly broad factors, perhaps painfully so. But they at least provide a framework within which to make moral decisions. Of course, to reassert the predominant theme of this final chapter, the formulation of moral decisions presumes moral sensitivity, concern, commitment, and a deep sense of personal responsibility for one's own life and the lives of others. None of these is possible without a code of values.

VALUES

The selection of values is a matter of hot debate. In our opening chapter we saw Martin Luther King choose the value of racial equality over civil order. In another chapter we saw a young woman arguing for immediate sexual equality while a young man argued for justice. Just what should we value?

There is general agreement that certain groups of values, such as moral, political, esthetic, religious, and intellectual values, exist, and that genetic, biological, and cultural influences produce many of these values. But there is little agreement about the nature of these values, their relative importance, or their relationship to one another. Nevertheless, we can isolate three principles that should prove helpful in determining values. In raising these, let's return to Jean and Frank several days after their conversation.

1. *We should prefer values that are productive and lasting to ones that are not.*

> **Frank:** I've been thinking about what you said the other night about our values. And it seems to me that that conversation bears directly on our decision not to have any more children.
>
> **Jean:** Just how exactly?
>
> **Frank:** Well, remember how we decided that by not having any more we'll be able to provide Timmy and ourselves with more of the material things of life?
>
> **Jean:** And now you don't think that's the right decision?
>
> **Frank:** I'm not sure anymore. I mean, what's more important, giving Timmy a new bike or car or vacation, or giving him the opportunity to form a life-long bond of affection and love with a brother or sister? And the same applies to us. We're comfortable enough; we're not hurting. We don't need the additional wealth that not having a child provides any more than we need the additional time that we might get out of driving the car when we don't really have to. Sure, maybe we shouldn't have any more kids. But I'm no longer sure that our reason is any good.

Frank and Jean must choose between two values—having another child or the material wealth that will accrue from not having one. At least part of Frank's concern is about the relative productive and lasting merits of the alternatives. In brief, physical and material values are generally less productive and long-lived than social, artistic, intellectual, and religious values. Long after a new automobile has worn out or a fortune has been spent, a genuine friendship or one's personal integrity persists.

2. *In choosing between two values, we should prefer the greater.*

> **Jean:** Frank, if we choose to have another child, let's adopt one.
>
> **Frank:** I never even considered that.
>
> **Jean:** Well, why don't we consider it? I couldn't agree more with what you've said about values. But if we do choose to have another child, let's really examine the relative merit of having our own as opposed to adopting one.
>
> **Frank:** Well, one thing's for sure. If we adopt one we won't be adding to the population explosion.
>
> **Jean:** And we'll not only be adding to our own happiness and joy by having a child, but we'll also be bringing a lot of happiness and love into the life of another person who otherwise might not get that.

Jean has introduced another dimension to their decision—the choice between having their own child or adopting one. She seems to think that adoption is the greater value of the two. What's more, she can make a rather strong case for that value, especially since they already have a child of their own and there are countless thousands of needy children throughout the world. Ethicists are generally agreed that in debating two values, we should choose the one that is greater. Obviously what is "greater" is itself a relative and subjective determination. But the point remains that where there is concern there is profound consideration and assessment of alternatives. Having decided which is the greater of the values, we should choose it.

3. *We should choose our own values based on our own goals and ideals.*

> **Frank:** What you say makes a lot of sense.
> **Jean:** Let me throw out something else. You know, every time I pick up Timmy at the nursery I marvel at how well the children get along, no matter what their color, religion, or nationality, economic or social backgrounds.
> **Frank:** I know. That's struck me, too. It's too bad it can't last.
> **Jean:** Look, we both consider social harmony an important ideal to pursue, don't we?
> **Frank:** Sure. But what does that have to do with adoption?
> **Jean:** If we decide to adopt, why don't we let that decision reflect our ideal of social harmony? Why don't we at least think about adopting a child of another race?

Notice that arising here is a value that springs from Jean's own goals and ideals. One of the most insidious problems in the world today is separatism, which is at the root of most hatred, injustice, inequality, and war. Contributing to this separatism is the conviction that some people are intrinsically better than others. Where do we get this idea? Probably we inherit it, in the sense that our provincial upbringings spawn it. For many, separatism is a value that they have accepted and will pass on to their own offspring.

Jean, on the other hand, has a vision of social harmony. Consequently she presents the value of an interracial adoption. True, most people do not choose interracial adoptions; most adoption agencies, in fact, are scrupulous in "matching" a child with prospective parents, and there are good reasons for this. Nevertheless, Jean recognizes that other people's values are not necessarily based on her own goals and ideals, and she is right in concluding that she should choose her own values which are.

Finally, observe again the concern that has fostered this exchange. Jean and Frank are now deeply interested in their own lives and the lives of others. They realize that the actions that they take can bear directly on the happiness or suffering of those around them. With this realization comes the responsibility of courageously developing a code of values upon which they automatically make moral decisions.

A BASIS FOR DECISION

Having considered the alternative ethical codes vying for your loyalty, it is entirely possible, indeed likely, that you are still in doubt about which you should follow or how to use them in formulating your own code. How do you decide? Sadly, there is no one principle that we can apply in choosing from among ethical codes. Does this mean that any ethical position is ultimately arbitrary? No.

It is true that a person would probably be making an arbitrary choice if that person decided that, since all ethical codes generally agree on basic ideals, it does not matter which one is followed. Such a position would be incorrect as well, because it is based on a questionable assumption. The fact is that a commitment to act utilitarianism is different from a commitment to rule nonconsequentialism. In other words, although there may be principles and ideals that most ethical codes share, there is frequently radical disagreement in executing these. Which ethical code, then, is correct? There is no scientific way to prove that one is correct and the others are not. In short, we simply cannot avoid a personal choice. When we root this choice in a consideration of all the alternatives, then the choice cannot be arbitrary. On the contrary, it is one based on the best evidence available. This point is made by British philosopher R. M. Hare:

> To describe such ultimate decisions as arbitrary . . . would be like saying that a complete description of the universe was utterly unfounded, because no further fact could be called upon in corroboration of it. This is not how we use the words 'arbitrary' and 'unfounded.' Far from being arbitrary, such a decision would be the most well-founded of decisions, because it would be based upon a consideration of everything upon which it could possibly be founded.*

Thus, if you are trying to formulate a responsible moral commitment to a way of life, then thoughtful consideration of all available options will make a good beginning. But such an investigation will not prescribe which option to choose or how to use it. To a large extent your choice will be influenced by your view of human nature. Just how do you see yourself and other humans? Is there a basic human nature common to all? In answering such questions, we must consult the natural and social sciences, indeed any discipline that helps reveal us to ourselves. For any code of ethics that asks of us more than it is possible for us to achieve would be of little use.

At the same time, although the final decision as to a moral code is strictly your own, it is helpful to isolate any principles that all or nearly all ethical codes share. In so doing, we stand a good chance of erecting our own codes on a firm basis, since we would be using the distilled ideas of centuries of profound ethical thought that rests on a careful and at times agonizing analysis of moral behavior. Are there any such basic principles?

---

*R.M. Hare, *The Language of Morals* (Oxford: Clarendon Press, 1952), p. 69.

BASIC MORAL PRINCIPLES*

Surely among the principles for constructing a code of ethics is one that recognizes the inherent value and worth of human life. It is hard to imagine an ethical system that lacks some reference to the respect and reverence life deserves. This does not mean that no one may ever commit suicide, perform an abortion, or choose euthanasia. It simply recognizes that without some such principle there would be little logical basis for ethics. (Of course, some might argue that there should be no ethical codes, which will not be argued here.) After all, ethics is concerned with moral human conduct, at least in relation to other people. Any moral code, therefore, that ignores the moral importance of human life would founder on a grave inconsistency. On the one hand it would purport to be concerned with the moral behavior between humans, while on the other it would ignore what figures prominently in those relations, human life itself.

Another principle common to all ethical systems is one that deals with rightness. The principle of rightness or goodness means that we are morally obliged to do what is right and avoid what is wrong. Clearly what is right and wrong is open to interpretation. But once we perceive what is good, we are obliged to promote it; once we perceive what is bad, we have an obligation to avoid, prevent, or minimize it. Without such a principle, a code of morality seems hopelessly incomplete, for while the code would propose what is right and wrong, it would not be obligating anyone to do right and avoid wrong. What, then, would be the point of formulating statements about right and wrong to begin with?

A third principle you would be wise to include is a justice principle. In effect, this principle asserts that all people should be treated equally in the distribution of goodness and badness. For example, suppose that there are a number of people in need of heart transplants for survival. Donors are limited; some of the patients will inevitably die. Problem: what will determine who gets an available donor's heart? In resolving terrible dilemmas like this, we must try to act fairly, that is, we must attempt to distribute equally the goodness, in this case the donor's heart.

Some say that distribution is fairest when it is based on a merit system: people should get what they deserve. But it is very difficult to evaluate precisely what this would be. Others argue that distribution should be based on what people need or perhaps what they are capable of. The problem in our illustration is that all parties are in need. Another possibility, and one that avoids the difficulties of the first two, is to view equal distribution as one in which all involved stand an equal chance of receiving the goodness or badness. Thus, in this case, a lottery system probably would be thought the fairest way to determine heart recipients.†

---

*These have been adapted from Jacques Thiroux, *Ethics* (Encino, Calif.: Glencoe, 1977), ch. 6, pp. 102–16.
†See Thiroux, *Ethics,* pp. 87–88.

Whatever the justice principle, there is a good and understandable reason for including it in any ethical code. Moral issues frequently involve questions of who gets what. Without some basic principle to direct such moral decisions, we introduce an element of bias and caprice that is bound to undermine the impartiality and disinterestedness that fair decisions require.

Finally, it seems that you should take heed of some principle relating to personal moral freedom which recognizes that in moral matters all people have equal rights until they prove otherwise. This obviously does not mean that people are equally talented, imaginative, or intelligent. Rather it recognizes that people must be free to choose their own ways of being moral, thus respecting the multitude of differences that exist among people. Without some such principle, we ignore the essence of morality—free choice. Moreover, the freedom to make for ourselves the fateful decisions of our lives is probably as dear as life itself, for it is the stuff from which life takes on definition and meaning. To disregard such a principle, therefore, is to disregard a necessary condition for the human to function as a complete being.

It should be obvious that this last principle is not intended to permit licentiousness, for example to condone someone's "freedom" to drive on whichever side of the road the individual chooses. To behave in such a way would clearly disregard the first three principles, for such an individual would willfully be endangering human life and treating himself or herself as an exception rather than an equal. In effect, the moral freedom principle recognizes the worth of Kant's claim that a human should never be considered as a means to an end but as an end itself. It also recognizes the validity of the golden rule, which would have us treat others as we would want to be treated. In brief, we must treat others as moral equals.

Assuming we now have some basic ethical principles, how can we use them and the other broad observations we have drawn from our study of ethics in some code of moral obligations? This is not easy to answer. First, we must distinguish between positive obligations, things we should do, and negative obligations, things we should avoid doing. The diversity of moral situations makes it impossible to specify what we must do. Individual circumstances, situations, and issues all will affect what we view as positive moral obligations. In general, however, our second principle would impose an obligation to promote goodness over badness and to prevent badness or harm. Obviously, what's good and bad is debatable. But the positive moral obligation is that, having determined what the good is, we must promote it; having determined what the bad is, we must prevent or at least minimize it. Although these are general obligations, it does seem that being any more dogmatic would tend to compromise the fourth principle, personal moral freedom. Nevertheless, we can throw additional light on positive obligations by considering negative obligations. These are easier to enumerate, especially by applying our basic ethical principles.

NEGATIVE OBLIGATIONS

What follows may be viewed as a suggested scheme for determining what we must avoid as being immoral.* Note that there is much room for personal evaluation and interpretation as each occasion for a moral decision would demand. The following three negative obligations are proposed to illustrate how one can employ the essentials of any moral decision—intention, means, and ends— together with basic ethical principles in some practical format for avoiding unethical conduct. It is based generally upon a synthesis of traditional ethical thought; it recognizes that no code by itself is so comprehensive that it accounts for the full range of human experiences and moral considerations. Finally, it is a scheme that rests on the assumption that it is easier to determine what we should not do than what we should do, although the two are obviously related.

1. *It is wrong to will, as a means or an end, the violation of a basic ethical principle.* Clearly, if an ethical principle is so basic that it is necessary for an ethical code, it follows that willing a violation of it is a serious evil. To illustrate, I could not willingly imprison an unsavory character for a crime the person did not commit, simply because I believed such an action was in the social interest. To do so would be to violate at least a principle of justice. Similarly, if I voted for a proposition that I knew was calculated to restrict a group's right to free speech on political affairs, I would be acting immorally, for I would have willed the violation of personal moral freedom.

Of course, these examples are extremely general, and situational nuances could change the evaluation. Notice that in each case I am willing the evil means or ends. But violations of basic ethical principles do not always result from what I will or intend, but from what I risk or allow to happen.

2. *It is wrong to risk or permit a violation of a basic ethical principle without a proportionate reason.* By *risk* is meant to foresee an evil as probable but not to will it either as a means or an end. *Permit* means to allow an evil but not to will it either as a means or an end. But undoubtedly the operative phrase in this second negative obligation is *proportionate reason*. For the obligation means that I may risk or allow a violation of a basic ethical principle when I have a proportionate reason. But what is a proportionate reason?

This is a difficult question to answer. In general, though, a *proportionate reason* exists when the intended result of an action is equal to or greater than the evil (the violation of a basic ethical principle) that is being risked or permitted, but not willed.† In other words, I am not morally responsible for side effects that I do not will, provided I have a sufficient reason for risking or allowing them. It is essential to understand this principle, lest it be used to mask unethical behavior.

---

*This treatment is indebted to Thomas M. Garrett, *Business Ethics* (Englewood Cliffs, N.J.: Prentice-Hall, 1966), ch. 1, pp. 3–20.

†*See* Garrett, *Business Ethics*, pp. 9–11.

Note that this proportionality principle is not the same as saying the end justifies the means, for under no circumstances can I ever *will* or intend a violation of a basic ethical principle. For example, I cannot use the proportionality principle to conduct medical experiments on the mentally retarded in my charge, even if the results would benefit countless thousands of persons. Presumably, I would have to conduct the experiments without the subjects' informed consent, which I would clearly have to assume. (Let's dismiss for the sake of argument the presence of parents, relatives, or guardians who might voice consent, for this raises additional questions.) To assume their consent in such a circumstance seems a violation of the moral freedom principle and, depending on the nature of the experiments, perhaps the reverence-for-life principle as well.

At the same time, the proportionality principle does recognize the value of consequential ethics by conceding that sometimes the consequences are great and desirable enough for one to *risk* or *permit* (never will) the violation of a basic ethical principle. For example, I could risk my life by rushing into a burning building to save a small child trapped inside. Here the child is not saved by my losing my life. In other words, losing my life is not the means by which I shall save the child or be helped in saving the child. Clearly, then, I do not will the loss of my life. I am risking its loss, and in such a case it seems I have a proportionate reason, the life and safety of the child.

At this point it will be helpful to acknowledge that often there is some question about whether I am willing or risking an evil means. A helpful way to ease this problem is to ask, "Can I achieve the end even if the unwilled evil does not occur?" If the answer is yes, the evil is probably not the means. If the answer is no, the evil is the means and the principle of proportionality does not apply. Thus, because I can save the child without losing my life, I am not willing my death.

Another more troublesome problem, however, is what constitutes a proportionate reason. This is impossible to answer precisely. But we can suggest some things to consider in determining whether we can risk or allow a violation of a basic ethical principle.

First, it seems we should consider whether the goodness intended is necessary or useful. A necessary good is something a person needs to be a person, keeping in mind the basic ethical principles. In the preceding example, clearly the entrapped child needs its life. In contrast, a useful good is one that, while helpful for a person to function, is not necessary. For example, generally speaking, entertainment is a useful but not necessary good. A necessary good, of course, would take precedence over a merely useful one. Suppose, for example, in an attempt to entertain a bored four-year-old, I decided to take her for her first motorcycle ride. She has no helmet, but nevertheless I perch her atop the gas tank and then speed off, confident that this will entertain the tyke. The useful good desired here, the child's entertainment, does not equal or outweigh the harm risked—serious injury to the child.

Another factor affecting proportionality is the urgency of the good desired. While *necessity* refers to the quality of the good, *urgency* refers to its immediacy.

If a good is needed immediately or very soon, if it cannot be delayed or postponed without serious harm resulting, then it is urgent. Again, the child trapped in the burning building needs immediate rescue. The entertainment of the child in the second example is not urgent.

A third factor to consider in proportionality is the certainty of the good. A good that is certain would count for more in determining proportionate reason than one that is not certain. Again, if I executed my rescue attempt properly I would stand a very good chance of saving the child in the building. Suppose, on the other hand, I suffered from a heart condition. This would reduce the likelihood of my rescuing the child and thus weaken my justification for risking my life. As for entertaining the child with a motorcycle ride, it is highly questionable that the child would be entertained; she would just as likely be frightened.

Finally, in determining proportionality, I must remember that I have a positive obligation to avoid or minimize evil wherever possible. This means that I should consider alternatives. If some alternative will achieve the same desired and desirable result but run less a risk of violating a basic ethical principle, then I should choose it. Thus, if I can safely summon a fire rescue specialist, I should do that rather than risk my own life. Likewise, if I can entertain the child in some safer way than taking her for a motorcycle ride, I should do that.

This last suggestion, together with the preceding three, will not make decisions about proportionate reasons easy. The illustrations provided here have been intentionally simple and general. Moreover, assigning relative weights to these four factors will always be problematic. Nevertheless, considering them in determining when you have proportionate reason for risking or permitting the violation of a basic ethical principle should be easier than if you ignored them.

3. *It is wrong to will, risk, or permit without proportionate reason an evil that does not violate a basic ethical principle.* This final negative obligation recognizes that not all evils are violations of basic ethical principles. Some evils are minor in the sense that they do not injure life, justice, or moral freedom. For example, probably most people would consider so-called white lies as minor evils. Suppose, for example, strictly in order to save a person from great emotional harm, I told that person a lie that in no way injured the person or anyone else. This third negative obligation would allow such willful behavior provided there was a proportionate reason for it. If, of course, there was no proportionate reason for it, then I would not be justified in performing even a minor evil. Again, this negative obligation, like the second, recognizes the worth of consequential thought. Note also that it allows one to will, as well as risk or permit, a minor evil for proportionate reason.

A concluding word about these obligations. Observe that the first is especially mindful of nonconsequential ethics. It recognizes that some evils may never be willed—those that violate basic ethical principles. The second and third obligations, on the other hand, acknowledge the value of consequentialism by noting conditions under which violations may be risked or permitted, and when evils that are not violations of basic ethical principles may be willed, risked, or permitted. It seems that at this point in the study of ethics we cannot get more specific. Using these negative obligations and basic ethical principles, however, should prove helpful when we do find ourselves thrown into the thick of some specific moral issue, for example, premarital sex, civil disobedience, abortion, or privacy.

SUMMARY AND CONCLUSIONS

In this final chapter we noted the importance of autonomy in formulating and implementing an ethical code. For a number of reasons many people purposely try to avoid autonomy by relying on authority or drifting, stacking the cards in favor of one decision, or denying responsibility. A most dangerous factor about these devices to avoid autonomy is that society frequently approves them.

The result of avoiding autonomy is that we frequently have moral decisions made for us or simply allow them to transpire. Although this is deplorable, it is understandable, for by avoiding autonomy we do not develop our own values upon which to base moral decisions.

Gaining autonomy, with our accompanying capability to develop moral values and courage to make moral decisions, presupposes concern. When we are genuinely concerned we perceive the importance of something to our lives and the lives of others. Perceiving its importance, we also recognize our personal responsibility for the direction that the object of our concern takes. Finally, we attempt to translate this awareness of responsibility into appropriate action.

In short, the beginning of any ethical code is personal concern. This concern is basic to a consideration and implementation of the essentials of any moral decision (intention, means, and ends), of the general ethical principles (life, goodness, justice, and moral freedom), and of the positive and negative moral obligations.

Also implied in this chapter is the importance of this concern relative to the environment. By the *environment* we mean the total circumstances surrounding an organism or group of organisms (specifically, the combination of external physical conditions that affect the growth and development of organisms) and the complex of social and cultural conditions affecting the nature of an individual or community. Thus, Jean recognized that emphasis by Frank and her on luxury and personal convenience is playing a part, however small, in air pollution. Later, both also recognized that an addition to their family, a seemingly personal decision, is unavoidably tied to problems like overpopulation and racial separatism.

The point is that without that personal concern vital to any ethical code, our own values and those of our society are likely to remain underdeveloped, for personal and social values are inextricably joined. Much hinges on personal concern—much for you, much for me, much for those to come.

EXERCISES FOR ANALYSIS

EXERCISE 1

What do you think is the morally right thing to do in the following situations? Justify your reply.

1. Night is falling. You're leisurely driving when suddenly you are startled by something in the road. You slow down and see a sharp piece of jagged metal. "Boy," you think as you negotiate around it, "I'm sure glad it wasn't any darker. I would have hit that thing." It dawns on you that maybe you should return to remove the vehicular menace to prevent potential injury to an unsuspecting motorist. But then you think that it's not your responsibility, it's really a job for highway authorities. What should you do?

2. You're the fiction editor of a widely circulated and respected literary magazine. You acquired the position some years before through the kind intervention of a friend. One day this friend approaches you with a story that his son has written; he informs you that his son, who has always dreamed of having something published, is terminally ill. Seeing the story published would greatly please the son and, of course, your friend. You read the story and decide that it is hardly up to the standard of your magazine; in fact, it's a hopelessly inferior piece of writing. You want to publish the work, but feel a responsibility to your readers, who trust you, not to publish what you consider poor work. What should you do?

3. You're a pharmacist's assistant whose job mainly consists of putting up prescriptions. One day while you're going through some old records, you're horrified to discover that the mysterious death of a local businessperson was caused by a mistake you made while compounding a prescription. The error occurred nine years before. Since then you have married and have two small children. The case has been closed for several years, but a shroud of suspicion has always hung over the businessperson's partner. What should you do?

4. You're an actor or actress. The break that you have been awaiting for years has finally come. Unfortunately, the role you must play is a moral outrage to you. In fact, you're convinced that the production itself is totally immoral. You realize that if you refuse the part you will at best be setting back your career, at worst destroying it. At the same time, you know the film will be produced with or without you. What should you do?

5. You are part of a church committee that has received an extraordinarily generous contribution from a man notorious for his underworld associations, immoral behavior, and criminal activities. You're convinced that the money constitutes ill-gotten goods. At the same time you realize that such an enormous contribution will itself be sufficient to construct a badly needed hospital that otherwise will not be built for some years. Members of the committee are in a moral quandary. What should you do?

6. You're a social worker. After a thorough investigation of a case, you decide that an individual is a malingerer and thus not entitled to any welfare claims. So, you cut off the individual's payments. The individual appeals your decision and it is reversed. Outraged, you ask your superior for an explanation. You're told that the individual is in fact a malingerer and undeserving of anything, but that cutting off the individual's payments could produce much unfavorable publicity for the welfare program. You're convinced that your superior is spineless and, in effect, an accomplice to fraud. You have a good mind to quit or go above your superior. But you need your job and fear that any additional action will jeopardize your position. What should you do?

7. You are an airline pilot. Between annual company physicals, you develop severe headaches that your physician attributes to elevated blood pressure. The cause is unknown, but the hypertension could easily be connected with some personal domestic troubles you're having. You know that it is airline policy to ground pilots with blood pressure as high as yours simply as a precaution. You think that you should report your condition to airline authorities. On the other hand, if it's just a passing problem, as it likely is, you don't see any sense in imperiling your livelihood. What should you do?

8. Your spouse is hospitalized. Because you're an X-ray technician, you just happen to know many of the hospital's personnel. Feeling an obligation to do all you can for your spouse, you're tempted to approach the staff involved and secure preferential treatment. But you realize that because the hospital is understaffed, preferential treatment for one patient means probable neglect of another. What should you do?

9. You are working as a psychological counselor for a public agency designed to provide counseling and treatment for anyone who is needy and desirous of help. The number of needy people who apply are far more than you can handle. Should you provide a very small amount of time for each applicant, in which event it is highly unlikely that you will substantially improve the lot of more than a handful? Or should you provide substantial treatment for a smaller number and only token treatment for the others?

EXERCISE 2

Do humans bear any moral obligations with respect to the environment? How we answer this question may affect what we choose to do to solve our environmental problems, the urgency with which we do it, and one's own environmental habits. Following are some condensed general arguments for and against the belief that we have moral obligations with respect to the environment. Notice that opponents do not necessarily encourage a prodigal and senseless use of the environment. They simply contend that morality and moral obligations just do not enter into environmental questions. Determine whether the justification for each position is adequate. As usual, pick out fallacies.

Arguments for Environmental Moral Obligations

1. The relationship between human life and the environment is one of a most sensitive and delicate balance, as we are sadly learning in the last quarter of the twentieth century. To treat this relationship with calloused indifference is wrong, not only because such treatment is a direct threat to life itself, but because that delicate balance is life generating, sustaining, and fulfilling. Thus, because a natural relationship exists between a human being and the environment, moral obligations exist for the human being with respect to the environment.

2. As a member of the human species, each of us has certain duties toward each other. One of these is a duty of noninjury; we should not needlessly hurt, injure, jeopardize, or kill another human being. But one of the biggest threats to human life is environmental pollution. Not only does it threaten individual lives, but also the very survival of the species. The obligations we have to future generations, therefore, have the effect of imposing obligations on us with respect to the environment.

Arguments against Environmental Moral Obligations

1. Those who talk of environmental moral obligations do not really understand the nature of obligations. Obligations by definition are duties that spring from relationships that one human being or human institution has with another human being. So, to speak of one's "obligation" to a lake or tree is really nonsensical. This does not mean that developing environmental concern is not necessary, desirable, or prudent, or that we do not have obligations to each other that involve the environment. It simply means that we are under no moral obligation to the environment per se.

2. Only those who are foolish, ignorant, or irrational would seriously argue that we should not be concerned about our environment. Of course we should; our very survival depends on it. What reasonable people disagree about, however, is precisely how we should go about improving and conserving our biosphere. Priorities, costs, risks—all these factors enter into the proposed solutions. These are difficult enough to assess without introducing the intangible dimension of morality. The only questions to debate are: What must be done? What will it cost? And who will pay the bill? Difficult to answer as these questions are, contrast them with the insoluble one of determining whether we have any moral obligations with respect to the environment. The fact is that such a question is meaningless in the sense that answering it will not at all affect what we do, how much it costs, and who pays the bill. So, since the issue of environmental moral obligations makes no concrete difference in the way people behave to correct the problem, no moral obligations can be said to operate with respect to humans and the environment.

SELECTIONS FOR FURTHER READING

Personal Concern

Frankl, Victor. *Man's Search for Freedom.* New York: Pocket Books, 1965.

Kierkegaard, Sören. *Fear and Trembling.* New York: Anchor, 1954.

Laing, R. D. *The Divided Self.* New York: Pantheon, 1969.

May, Rollo. *Man's Search for Himself.* New York: Signet, 1967.

Miller, Arthur. *Death of a Salesman.* New York: Viking, 1941.

Social Responsibility

Hoffer, Eric. *The True Believer.* New York: Harper & Row, 1966.

Kaufman, Arnold S. *The Radical Liberal: The New Politics in Theory and Practice.* New York: Simon & Schuster, 1968.

Marcuse, Herbert. *One-Dimensional Man: Studies in the Ideology of Advanced Industrial Society.* Boston: Beacon Press, 1965.

Pappenheim, Fritz. *The Alienation of Modern Man.* New York: Monthly Review Press, 1959.

Plato. *The Republic.* Translated by F. M. Cornford. Oxford: Oxford University Press, 1945.

Riesman, David. *The Lonely Crowd.* New Haven, Conn.: Yale University Press, 1950.

Slater, Philip. *The Pursuit of Loneliness: American Culture at the Breaking Point.* Boston: Beacon Press, 1971.

Wilson, Colin. *The Outsider.* New York: Delta, 1967.

READING

SARTRE/*Existentialism*

Perhaps no writer has more fiercely addressed the problems of autonomy, including the accompanying anguish and isolation, than the French existentialist Jean-Paul Sartre. In the passage that follows, taken from his Existentialism and Human Emotions, *Sartre claims that we are nothing else but what we make of ourselves. Once thrown into the world, we are responsible for everything we do. Note, however, that for Sartre a choice that is "personal" is at the same time a social choice, in that we are choosing for everyone. Why does he say this? In his example of the young man, does Sartre accurately typify a large number of moral decisions? Does he typify many of those that we encountered in this text? Sartre concludes, "No general ethics can show you what is to be done; there are no omens in the world." Do you think he means that questions of values and morality are, therefore, meaningless, useless to ponder? That we should not concern ourselves with them? Or is he characterizing the state of most moral decision making?*

Man is nothing else but what he makes of himself. Such is the first principle of existentialism. It is also what is called subjectivity, the name we are labeled with when charges are brought against us. But what do we mean by this, if not that man has a greater dignity than a stone or table? For we mean that man first exists, that is, that man first of all is the being who hurls himself toward a future and who is conscious of imagining himself as being in the future. Man is at the start a plan which is aware of itself, rather than a patch of moss, a piece of garbage, or a cauliflower; nothing exists prior to this plan; there is nothing in heaven; man will be what he will have planned to be. Not what he will want to be. Because by the word "will" we generally mean a conscious decision, which is subsequent to what we have already made of ourselves. I may want to belong to a political party, write a book, get married; but all this is only a manifestation of an earlier, more spontaneous choice that is called "will.". . .

. . . When we say that man chooses his own self, we mean that every one of us does likewise; but we also mean by that that in making this choice he also chooses all men. In fact, in creating the man that we want to be, there is not a single one of our acts which does not at the same time create an image of man as we think he ought to be. To choose to be this or that is to affirm at the same time the value of what we choose, because we can never choose evil. We always choose the good, and nothing can be good for us without being good for all. . . .

. . . The existentialists say at once that man is anguish. What that means

Abridged from Jean-Paul Sartre, *Existentialism and Human Emotions*, Citadel Press, 1971. Reprinted by permission.

is this: the man who involves himself and who realizes that he is not only the person he chooses to be, but also a lawmaker who is, at the same time, choosing all mankind as well as himself, can not help escape the feeling of his total and deep responsibility. Of course, there are many people who are not anxious; but we claim that they are hiding their anxiety, that they are fleeing from it. Certainly, many people believe that when they do something, they themselves are the only ones involved, and when someone says to them, "What if everyone acted that way?" they shrug their shoulders and answer, "Everyone doesn't act that way." But really, one should ask himself, "What would happen if everybody looked at things that way?" There is no escaping this disturbing thought except by a kind of double-dealing. A man who lies and makes excuses for himself by saying "not everybody does that," is someone with an uneasy conscience, because the act of lying implies that a universal value is conferred upon the lie.

Anguish is evident even when it conceals itself. This is the anguish that Kierkegaard called the anguish of Abraham. You know the story: an angel has ordered Abraham to sacrifice his son; if it really were an angel who has come and said, "You are Abraham, you shall sacrifice your son," everything would be all right. But everyone might first wonder, "Is it really an angel, and am I really Abraham? What proof do I have?" . . .

Now, I'm not being singled out as an Abraham, and yet at every moment I'm obliged to perform exemplary acts. For every man, everything happens as if all mankind had its

eyes fixed on him and were guiding itself by what he does. And every man ought to say to himself, "Am I really the kind of man who has the right to act in such a way that humanity might guide itself by my actions?" And if he does not say that to himself, he is masking his anguish.

There is no question here of the kind of anguish which would lead to quietism, to inaction. It is a matter of a simple sort of anguish that anybody who has had responsibilities is familiar with. For example, when a military officer takes the responsibility for an attack and sends a certain number of men to death, he chooses to do so, and in the main he alone makes the choice. Doubtless, orders come from above, but they are too broad; he interprets them, and on this interpretation depend the lives of ten or fourteen or twenty men. In making a decision he can not help having a certain anguish. All leaders know this anguish. That doesn't keep them from acting; on the contrary, it is the very condition of their action. For it implies that they envisage a number of possibilities, and when they choose one, they realize that it has value only because it is chosen. We shall see that this kind of anguish, which is the kind that existentialism describes, is explained, in addition, by a direct responsibility to the other men whom it involves. It is not a curtain separating us from action, but is part of action itself. . . .

. . . Man is condemned to be free. Condemned, because he did not create himself, yet, in other respects is free; because, once thrown into the world, he is responsible for everything he does. . . .

To give you an example which

will enable you to understand for-lornness better, I shall cite the case of one of my students who came to see me under the following circumstances: his father was on bad terms with his mother, and, moreover, was inclined to be a collaborationist; his older brother had been killed in the German offensive of 1940, and the young man, with somewhat immature but generous feelings, wanted to avenge him. His mother lived alone with him, very much upset by the half-treason of her husband and the death of her older son; the boy was her only consolation.

The boy was faced with the choice of leaving for England and joining the Free French forces—that is, leaving his mother behind—or remaining with his mother and helping her to carry on. He was fully aware that the woman lived only for him and that his going-off—and perhaps his death—would plunge her into despair. He was also aware that every act that he did for his mother's sake was a sure thing, in the sense that it was helping her to carry on, whereas every effort he made toward going off and fighting was an uncertain move which might run aground and prove completely useless; for example, on his way to England he might, while passing through Spain, be detained indefinitely in a Spanish camp; he might reach England or Algiers and be stuck in an office at a desk job. As a result, he was faced with two very different kinds of action: one, concrete, immediate, but concerning only one individual; the other concerned an incomparably vaster group, a national collectivity, but for that very reason was dubious, and might be interrupted en route. And, at the same time, he was wavering between two kinds of ethics. On the one hand, an ethics of sympathy, of personal devotion; on the other, a broader ethics, but one whose efficacy was more dubious. He had to choose between the two.

Who could help him choose? Christian doctrine? No. Christian doctrine says, "Be charitable, love your neighbor, take the more rugged path, etc., etc." But which is the more rugged path? Whom should he love as a brother? The fighting man or his mother? Which does the greater good, the vague act of fighting in a group, or the concrete one of helping a particular human being to go on living? Who can decide *a priori*? Nobody. No book of ethics can tell him. The Kantian ethics says, "Never treat any person as a means, but as an end." Very well, if I stay with my mother, I'll treat her as an end and not as a means; but by virtue of this very fact, I'm running the risk of treating the people around me who are fighting, as means; and conversely, if I go to join those who are fighting, I'll be treating them as an end, and, by doing that, I run the risk of treating my mother as a means.

If values are vague, and if they are always too broad for the concrete and specific case that we are considering, the only thing left for us is to trust our instincts. That's what this young man tried to do; and when I saw him, he said, "In the end, feeling is what counts. I ought to choose whichever pushes me in one direction. If I feel that I love my mother enough to sacrifice everything else for her—my desire for vengeance, for action, for adventure—then I'll stay with her. If, on the contrary, I feel that my love for my mother isn't enough, I'll leave."

But how is the value of a feeling determined? What gives his feeling for his mother value? Precisely the fact that he remained with her. I may say that I like so-and-so well enough to sacrifice a certain amount of money for him, but I may say so only if I've done it. I may say "I love my mother well enough to remain with her" if I have remained with her. The only way to determine the value of this affection is, precisely, to perform an act which confirms and defines it. But, since I require this affection to justify my act, I find myself caught in a vicious circle.

On the other hand, Gide has well said that a mock feeling and a true feeling are almost indistinguishable; to decide that I love my mother and will remain with her, or to remain with her by putting on an act, amount somewhat to the same thing. In other words, the feeling is formed by the acts one performs; so, I can not refer to it in order to act upon it. Which means that I can neither seek within myself the true condition which will impel me to act, nor apply to a system of ethics for concepts which will permit me to act. You will say, "At least, he did go to a teacher for advice." But if you seek advice from a priest, for example, you have chosen this priest; you already knew, more or less, just about what advice he was going to give you. In other words, choosing your adviser is involving yourself. The proof of this is that if you are a Christian, you will say, "Consult a priest." But some priests are collaborating, some are just marking time, some are resisting. Which to choose? If the young man chooses a priest who is resisting or collaborating, he has already decided on the kind of advice he's going to get. Therefore, in coming to see me he knew the answer I was going to give him, and I had only one answer to give: "You're free, choose, that is, invent." No general ethics can show you what is to be done; there are no omens in the world.

READING

CAMUS/*The Myth of Sisyphus*

There comes a time when even someone morally committed asks, "Why? What's the point?" Any number of things may provoke this question—uncertainty, frustrating failure to be true to one's own code, the rebuke of others, or just plain weariness. This despair is a normal, almost predictable reaction that the thoughtful, sensitive moral agent must anticipate. If not, then the commitment needed for a personal code of ethics will probably be undermined, the autonomy subverted.

Albert Camus engages this problem of meaning and purpose in what has become a classic, "The Myth of Sisyphus." Condemned to push a rock to the top of a hill, whereupon the rock always rolls back, Sisyphus epitomizes the absurd hero. But Camus makes more of him than that, and it seems that we as students of morality should as well. For Sisyphus's tragedy and salvation lie in his being conscious of his plight. This consciousness somehow lifts him above the futility of it all. It impresses on him that his fate belongs to him, and that there is no higher destiny.

So, lacking meaning, purpose, and clear justification, Sisyphus nevertheless goes on. For us, Sisyphus should stand as a testament to the sense of commitment, autonomy, and responsibility that we must cultivate, despite the obstacles, in order to function as moral beings. At the same time Sisyphus stands as a sympathetic companion for us who are on the hill behind the rock.

The Gods had condemned Sisyphus to ceaselessly rolling a rock to the top of a mountain, whence the stone would fall back of its own weight. They had thought with some reason that there is no more dreadful punishment than futile and hopeless labor.

If one believes Homer, Sisyphus was the wisest and most prudent of mortals. According to another tradition, however, he was disposed to practice the profession of highwayman. I see no contradiction in this. Opinions differ as to the reasons why he became the futile laborer of the underworld. To begin with, he is accused of a certain levity in regard to the gods. He stole their secrets. Ægina, the daughter of Æsopus, was carried off by Jupiter. The father was shocked by that disappearance and complained to Sisyphus. He, who knew of the abduction, offered to tell about it on condition that Æsopus would give water to the citadel of Corinth. To the celestial thunderbolts he preferred the benediction of water. He was punished for this in the underworld. Homer tells us also that Sisyphus had put Death in chains.

Pluto could not endure the sight of his deserted, silent empire. He dispatched the god of war, who liberated Death from the hands of her conqueror.

It is said that Sisyphus, being near to death, really wanted to test his wife's love. He ordered her to cast his unburied body into the middle of the public square. Sisyphus woke up in the underworld. And there, annoyed by an obedience so contrary to human love, he obtained from Pluto permission to return to earth in order to chastise his wife. But when he had seen again the face of this world, enjoyed water and sun, warm stones and the sea, he no longer wanted to go back to the infernal darkness. Recalls, signs of anger, warnings were of no avail. Many years more he lived facing the curve of the gulf, the sparkling sea, and the smiles of earth. A decree of the gods was necessary. Mercury came and seized the impudent man by the collar and, snatching him from his joys, led him forcibly back to the underworld, where his rock was ready for him.

You have already grasped that Sisyphus is the absurd hero. He *is,* as much through his passions as through his torture. His scorn of the gods, his hatred of death, and his passion for life won him that unspeakable penalty in which the whole being is exerted toward accomplishing nothing. This is the price that must be paid for the passions of this earth. Nothing is told us about Sisyphus in the underworld. Myths are made for the imagination to breathe life into them. As for this myth, one sees merely the whole effort of a body straining to raise the huge stone, to roll it and push it up a slope a hundred times over; one sees the face screwed up, the cheek tight against the stone, the shoulder bracing the clay-covered mass, the foot wedging it, the fresh start with arms outstretched, the wholly human security of two earth-clotted hands. At the very end of his long effort measured by skyless space and time without depth, the purpose is achieved. Then Sisyphus watches the stone rush down in a few moments toward that lower world whence he will have to push it up again toward the summit. He goes back down to the plain.

It is during that return, that pause, that Sisyphus interests me. A face that toils so close to stones is already stone itself! I see that man going back down with a heavy yet measured step toward the torment of which he will never know the end. That hour like a breathing-space which returns as surely as his suffering, that is the hour of consciousness. At each of those moments when he leaves the heights and gradually sinks toward the lairs of the gods, he is superior to his fate. He is stronger than his rock.

If this myth is tragic, that is because its hero is conscious. Where would his torture be, indeed, if at every step the hope of succeeding upheld him? The workman of today works every day in his life at the same tasks, and this fate is no less absurd. But it is tragic only at the rare moments when it becomes conscious. Sisyphus, proletarian of the gods, powerless and rebellious, knows the whole extent of his wretched condition: it is what he thinks of during his descent. The lucidity that was to constitute his torture at the same time crowns his victory. There is no fate that cannot be surmounted by scorn.

If the descent is thus sometimes performed in sorrow, it can also take place in joy. This word is not too much. Again I fancy Sisyphus returning toward his rock, and the sorrow was in the beginning. When the images of earth cling too tightly to memory, when the call of happiness becomes too insistent, it happens that melancholy rises in man's heart: this is the rock's victory, this is the rock itself. The boundless grief is too heavy to bear. These are our nights of Gethsemane. But crushing truths perish from being acknowledged. Thus, Œdipus at the outset obeys fate without knowing it. But from the moment he knows, his tragedy begins. Yet at the same moment, blind and desperate, he realizes that the only bond linking him to the world is the cool hand of a girl. Then a tremendous remark rings out: "Despite so many ordeals, my advanced age and the nobility of my soul make me conclude that all is well." Sophocles' Œdipus, like Dostoevsky's Kirilov, thus gives the recipe for the absurd victory. Ancient widsom confirms modern heroism.

One does not discover the absurd without being tempted to write a manual of happiness. "What! by such narrow ways—?" There is but one world, however. Happiness and the absurd are two sons of the same earth. They are inseparable. It would be a mistake to say that happiness necessarily springs from the absurd discovery. It happens as well that the feeling of the absurd springs from happiness. "I conclude that all is well," says Œdipus, and that remark is sacred. It echoes in the wild and limited universe of man. It teaches that all is not, has not been, exhausted. It drives out of this world a god who had come into it with dissatisfaction and a preference for futile sufferings. It makes of fate a human matter, which must be settled among men.

All Sisyphus' silent joy is contained therein. His fate belongs to him. His rock is his thing. Likewise, the absurd man, when he contemplates his torment, silences all the idols. In the universe suddenly restored to its silence, the myriad wondering little voices of the earth rise up. Unconscious, secret calls, invitations from all the faces, they are the necessary reverse and price of victory. There is no sun without shadow, and it is essential to know the night. The absurd man says yes and his effort will henceforth be unceasing. If there is a personal fate, there is no higher destiny, or at least there is but one which he concludes is inevitable and despicable. For the rest, he knows himself to be the master of his days. At that subtle moment when man glances backward over his life, Sisyphus returning toward his rock, in that slight pivoting he contemplates that series of unrelated actions which becomes his fate, created by him, combined under his memory's eye and soon sealed by his death. Thus, convinced of the wholly human origin of all that is human, a blind man eager to see who knows that the night has no end, he is still on the go. The rock is still rolling.

I leave Sisyphus at the foot of the mountain! One always finds one's burden again. But Sisyphus teaches the higher fidelity that negates the gods and raises rocks. He too concludes that all is well. This universe henceforth without a master seems to him neither sterile nor futile. Each atom of that stone, each mineral flake of that night-filled mountain, in itself forms a world. The struggle itself toward the heights is enough to fill a man's heart. One must imagine Sisyphus happy.

INDEX

A

Abortion, 193–194
  arguments for and against, 207–209
  in Jane Roe case, 193–195
  related to criminal acts, 194
  related to privacy, 193
  as therapeutic, 194
Absolutism, moral, 49–51
  contrasted with relativism, 51, 58
  defined, 50, 57
  objections to, 51–53
  objections to, summarized, 57
Act nonconsequentialism theories
(act deontology), 234–235
  defined, 234
  objections to, 235–237
Act utilitarianism, 160–161
  defined, 160
  objections to, 161–164
  objections to, summarized, 168
Ad hominem fallacy, 10
Affirmative action, 301–302. *See also*
Social justice
Agape, 197–199
  defined, 197
Ambiguity
  defined, 11
  in moral discourse, 11–12
  related to King's moral justification,
19, 21

Amoral, defined, 5. *See also* Ethics
Analogy, 163
Anarchy, State and Utopia (Nozick), 317n
"Animal Liberation" (Singer), 173–185
"Antidotes for the New Puritanism"
(May), 145–153
Antinomian, 195
  as related to situational ethics, 195
A priori, defined, 53
Argument
  defined, 7
  example of, 7
  logical fallacies in, 10–18
  in reasoning, 7
  truth in, 9
Arguments
  for and against civil disobedience,
23–25
  for and against environmental moral
obligations, 367–368
  for and against euthanasia, 59–60
  for and against human experimentation without informed consent,
170–171
  for and against premarital sex,
137–138
  for and against restrictive abortion
legislation, 207–209
  for and against sexism, 321–322
  for and against war, 275–277

Arguments from ignorance
  defined and illustrated, 14–15
  related to act utilitarianism, 163
  related to analogies, 163
Aristotle
  act nonconsequentialism in thought of, 235
  Nichomachean Ethics, 128
Atkins, Susan, 233
Authority
  false appeal to, 15–16
  as an obstacle to decision making, 348
Autonomy, 347–348
  importance of, summarized, 364
  obstacles to, 347–353
  related to environmental concerns, 364

B

Bailey, F. Lee, in Hearst case, 88
Bakersfield, California, 236
Barry, Brian, *The Liberal Theory of Justice*, 320n
Begging the question
  in contra-causal freedom argument, 92
  defined and illustrated, 14
Being and Nothingness (Sartre), 101–106
Beneficence, duties of, 269–270
Benn, Stanley, 247n
Bentham, Jeremy
  contrasted with Mill, 159
  hedonistic calculus of, 159–160
Berkeley, George, advancing rule utilitarianism, 165
Binkley, Luther, 197n, 198n, 199n
Bird, Caroline, "The Case for Equality," 324–338
Blackmun, Justice, 193
Brandt, R. B., 165n
  act utilitarianism of, 165
Brave New World (Huxley), 186–191
"The Burning" (Cady), 75–82
Business Ethics (Garrett), 361

Busing, related to civil disobedience, 11
Butler, Joseph, 235n

C

Cady, Jack, "The Burning," 75–82
Caldwell Decision, 250–260
Calley, Jr., Lt. William L., 263–264
  case related to freedom, 90
  case related to moral responsibility, 88
  case related to *prima facie* duties, 265
Campbell, C. A. 90–91, 92n
Camus, Albert, "The Myth of Sisyphus," 373–376
  The Plague, 347
"The Case for Equality" (Bird), 324–338
Categorical imperative, 239–243
  defined, 241
  objections to, 242–243
  objections to, summarized, 244
  related to good will, 239–240
Certainty, as a factor in proportionality, 363
Christian situational ethics. *See* Situational ethics; Fletcher, Joseph
Civil disobedience, 3–26
  arguments for and against, 23–25
  busing and, 11
  defined, 4
  freedom riders in, 3
  Jesus as practicing, 3
  King as practicing, 3
  Socrates as practicing, 3
Civil Disobedience (Thoreau), 38–44
Common practice appeal. *See* Two wrongs-make-a-right
Concern, defined, 346–347
Connor, Eugene "Bull," 3
Consequentialism (deontology), 122–123
  hedonism in, 126–127
  theories of, 123–125
Consistency, related to Kant's categorical imperative, 240

Contra-causal freedom, 91–92
Contract theory, 307
    Hobbes's, 305
    Locke's, 305–307
    Rousseau's, 305
The Crito (Plato), 27–37

D

Death, defined, 48
"A Defense of Abortion" (Thomson),
210–224
Democracy, appeal to. *See* Authority,
false appeal to
Deontology. *See* Nonconsequentialism
Determinism, 88–90
    contrasted with indeterminism, 89
    defined, 88
    evidence for, 97
    hard, defined, 95
    in Skinner's psychological
    behaviorism, 89
    in social sciences, 89
    soft, defined, 96
Deterrent view of punishment. *See*
Punishment
Difference principle, 312–314. *See also*
Rawls, John
Divine command theory (theological
voluntarism)
    defined, 237
    objections to, 238–239
    objections to, summarized, 244
    related to golden rule, 238
    whom it excludes, 239–240
Douglas, William O., 233
Drifting, as obstacle to decision making,
348–349
Duties
    actual, 266
    prima facie, 266
Duty, as related to Kant's categorical
imperative, 241–242

E

Egoism, 126–130
    defined, 126, 135
    impersonal, 126
    in moral counsel, 133–134
    objections to, 130–134
    objections to, summarized, 135
    personal, 126
    psychological, 128–129
    related to moral point of view, 134
    related to moral responsibility, 87
Ellis, Albert, *Sex Without Guilt*, 140–144
Empiricism
    defined, 52
    related to absolutism, 52
Ends, as an element in moral decisions,
354–355
Environment, defined, 364
Environmental moral obligations,
arguments for and against, 367–368
Equality, as used by Rawls, 310
Equal liberty principle, 310–311. *See also*
Rawls, John
Equal Rights Amendment, related to
ad hominem appeal, 10
Ethical principles, 359–362
Ethics
    absolutism in, 50
    defined, 5, 21
    implications of, 4
    main classifications in, 22
    and morals, 5
    nature of concerns in, 5
    nonconsequential (deontological)
    defined, 234
    non-normative (meta), 5
    normative, 5–6
    practical nature of, 4
    relativism in, 50
Euthanasia
    active, 47
    arguments for and against, 59–60

Euthanasia (*continued*)

  involuntary, 47

  morality of, 47–48

  passive, 47

  voluntary, 47

Evils

  minor, 363

  as violations of basic ethical principles, 363

Ewing, A. C., 164n

  criticizing act utilitarianism, 164

Existential, as synonymous with antinomian, 195

Existentialism and Human Emotions (Sartre), 369–372

F

False appeal to authority. *See* Authority; Logical Fallacy

Farr, William, 233, 235

Fidelity, duties of, in Ross, 268

Fletcher, Joseph, 194–205

  agape, 197–199

  antinomian ethics, 195–196

  as approving summary rules, 202

  legalistic ethics, 195–196

  main situational tenets, 199

  position on general rules, 203

  Ramsey on, 203

  situational approach, 194–199

  Situation Ethics, 195

Fourteenth Amendment, in *Roe vs. Wade*, 193

Freedom, 90–91

  as compatible with determinism, 92–95

  in conditions for excusing behavior, 90

  contra-causal, 91–92

  as incompatible with determinism, 91–92

  as used in ethics, 90

  See also Inquiry

From Decidophobia to Autonomy Without Guilt or Justice (Kaufman), 347

G

Garrett, Thomas, 361n

General rule, defined, 203

Geneva Convention on the Law of War, 264

Genovese, Kitty, 345

God

  in divine command theory, 237–238

  related to concept of just law, 20

Golden rule, 238

Graham, Virginia, 233

Gratitude, duties of, in Ross, 268

Growing Up in America (Hechinger), 85

H

Hague Convention of Land Warfare, 264

Hard determinism

  defined, 95

  objections to, summarized, 95–96

Hare, R. M., *The Language of Morals*, 358

Hearst, Patty, related to freedom, 90, 97

Hechinger, Fred M., 85

Hedonism, 125–126

  defined, 125

Hedonistic calculus, 159–160

Hitler, Adolf, 236

Hobbes, Thomas

  contract theory of, 305–307

  Leviathan, 305

  Rawls's criticism of, 308–309

  related to Rawls, 308–309

Hospers, John, "What Means This Freedom?" 107–118

Human experimentation

  arguments for and against, 170–171

  related to informed consent, 169

Humanism, in psychology, 128

Human life, as a value, 359

Huxley, Aldous, *Brave New World*,
186–191

I

Impersonal egoism, defined, 126, 135
Inconsistency, fallacy of
    defined, 13
    in personal egoism, 130–131
    in Rawls's maximin principle, 317
    in relativism, 56
    in rule utilitarianism, 167
    in soft determinism, 96
Indeterminism
    defined, 89, 96
    objections to, summarized, 96
Informed consent, related to human
experimentation, 169
Intention (will)
    defined, 353
    in moral decisions, 353–354
    in negative obligations, 361
Inquiry, arguments for the general
freedom of, 248
Invincible ignorance, fallacy of, defined
and illustrated, 12

J

Johnny Got His Gun (Trumbo), 293–296
Justice, 302–305
    duties of, in Ross, 269
    as a moral principle, 359
    sexism and, 301–303
    See also Social justice
Justification, moral, 8–10
    defined, 8, 10, 22
    illustrated, 10
    logical fallacies appearing in, 10–18

K

Kamisar, Yale, "Some Non-Religious
Views against Proposed Mercy-Killing
Legislation," 62–74

Kant, Immanuel, 239–243
    three conditions for a moral rule,
    241–242
    See also Categorical imperative
Kaufman, 347n
King, Martin Luther
    and "Bull" Connor, 3
    concept of justice, 4
    distinction between just and unjust
    laws, 2–21
    "Letter from a Birmingham Jail," 3
    moral justification, 3–4
    moral justification of civil
    disobedience, 19–21
    normative position of, 6
    values of, 355
Knowledge
    related to *a priori*, 53
    related to rationalism, 53

L

Legalistic
    contrasted with situational, 195
    position in ethics, 195
Leviathan (Hobbes), 305
Logical fallacy, 10–18
    ad hominem, 10
    ambiguity, 11–12
    argument from ignorance, 14–15
    begging the question, 14
    defined, 10
    false appeal to authority, 15–16
    invincible ignorance, 12
    provincialism, 16
    questionable claim, 12–13
    slippery slope, 17
    two-wrongs-make-a-right, 17
Logic, described, 10
Los Angeles Herald Examiner, 233

M

Magruder, Jeb Stuart, related to moral

responsibility, 88

Manson, Charles, 233

Maslow, Abraham, 128

Maximin principle
    defined, 308–309, 318–319
    objections to, 315–318
    objections to, summarized, 318–319

May, Rollo, "Antidotes for the New Puritanism, 145–153

Means, defined, 354

Medlin, Brian, 134n

Meta-ethics, defined, 6

Milgram, Stanley, 155

Milgram studies, 155–156
    as atypical, 171

Mill, John Stuart
    concept of quality, 159
    contrasted with Bentham, 159
    See also Utilitarianism

Moore, G. E., 157n
    utilitarianism of, 157

Moral
    contrasted with nonmoral, 124
    point of view, 134
    words, 7

Moral counsel, in egoism, 33–34

Moral decisions
    ends as a factor in, 354–355
    factors in making, 355–356

Moral judgments (statements)
    defined, 7
    importance of context in making, 8
    nature of, 9
    related to justification, 8

Moral principles, 359–360

Moral reasoning, the three don'ts of, 18–19

Moral relativism. *See* Relativism

Morals, defined, 5. *See also* Ethics

Moral theories
    absolutism, 49–51
    relativism, 49–51

See also Consequentialism;
    Nonconsequentialism

My Lai, 263

"The Myth of Sisyphus" (Camus), 373–376

N

Narveson, Jan, "Pacifism: A Philosophical Analysis," 279–292

Natural right, related to contract theory, 306

Necessity, as a factor in proportionality, 362–363

Negative obligations, 360–364
    related to consequentialism (teleology) and nonconsequentialism, 363–364

Newton, Lisa H., "Reverse Discrimination as Unjustified," 339–343

Nichomachean Ethics (Aristotle), 128

Nonconsequentialism (deontology)
    contributions to ethical thought, 244–245
    defined, 234, 243
    theories, 234–243

Nonmaleficence, duties of in Ross, 271–272

Nonmoral, concerns in consequentialism, 124–125

Normative, defined, 22

Normative ethics
    main classifications in, 6
    positions in, illustrated, 5–6

Nozick, Robert, 317n

Nuremberg, 264

O

Older, Judge Charles, 233

One Man's Watergate (Magruder), 88

Original position, defined, 309

P

"Pacifism: A Philosophical Analysis" (Narveson), 279–292

Personal concern, 345–364
Personal egoism, defined, 135
Plagiarism, 85–88
   common justifications, 87
Plague, The (Camus), 347
Plato
   contract theory of, 305
   The Crito, 27–37
   Rawls's criticism of, 309
   Republic, 128
Popularity. *See* Authority, false appeal to
Preferential hiring, defined, 301. *See also* Social justice
Prima facie duties (Ross), 263–272
   of beneficence, 269–270
   defined, 266, 273
   distinguished from actual duties, 266
   of fidelity, 268
   of gratitude, 268
   of justice, 269
   of nonmaleficence, 271–272
   objections to, 272–273
   of self-improvement, 270
Privacy, 233–234
   arguments for the principle of, 247–248
   in *Roe vs. Wade* decision, 193
   See also Caldwell decision
Proportionate reason, in negative obligations, 361–362
Provincialism, fallacy of, defined and illustrated, 16
Psychological behaviorism, 89
   objections of, to contra-causal freedom, 92
Psychological egoism, 128–130
Psychological fallacies, 347
Punishment
   deterrent view of, defined, 99
   retributivist view of, defined, 99
   therapeutic view of, defined, 99

Q

Questionable claim
   defined and illustrated, 12–13
   inconsistency version of, 13
   in Rawls's maximin principle, 314–315
   related to King's moral justification of civil disobedience, 19, 21
Quinlan, Karen Ann, 47
Quota hiring, 301. *See also* Social justice

R

Racism. *See* Social justice
Ramsey, Paul, 203n
   criticizing Fletcher, 203
Rashdall, Hastings, 157n
   utilitatianism of, 157
Rationalism
   in absolutism, 52
   defined, 52
Rawls, John, 308–319
   concept of practice, 310
   concept of reciprocity, 313
   contributions summarized, 319–320
   difference principle, 312–314
   equal liberty principle, 310–311
   ideal observer, 309
   maximin principle, 308–310
   objections to maximin principle of, 314–318
   original position, 309–310
   A Theory of Justice, 308–314
   veil of ignorance, 309
   view on Plato, 309
Reasoning
   in argument, 7
   defined, 7
Reciprocity, in Rawls, defined, 313
Rehnquist, Justice, 193–194

Social responsibility, 345–364
Sociological relativism, 54–55
Socrates, 3
Soft determinism
  defined, 96
  objections to, 93–95
  objections to, summarized, 96
  in Sartre, 92
"Some Non-Religious Views against
Proposed Mercy-Killing Legislation"
(Kamisar), 62–74
Summary rule, defined, 202

T

Taylor, Paul, 90n, 95n
Teleology. *See* Consequentialism
Theological voluntarism. *See* Divine
command theory
A Theory of Justice (Rawls), 308
Therapeutic view of punishment. *See*
Punishment
Thiroux, Jacques, 359n
Thomson, Judith Jarvis, "A Defense of
Abortion," 210–224
Thoreau, Henry David, *Civil
Disobedience*, 38–44
Tillich, Paul, 200n
  on situational ethics, 200
Traditional wisdom. *See* Authority, false
appeal to
Trumbo, Dalton, *Johnny Got His Gun*,
293–298
Truth, defined, 9. *See also* Argument
Two-wrongs-make-a-right, 17

U

Urgency, as a factor in proportionality,
362–363
U.S. Constitution, basis on contract
theory, 387

U.S. Supreme Court
  Caldwell decision, Douglas opinion,
  256–260
  Caldwell decision, White opinion,
  251–255
  in Manson case, 233
  Roe vs. Wade decision, 193
Utilitarianism, 155–167
  act, defined, 160
  in Fletcher, 205–206
  Hastings Rashdall's, 157
  Moore's, 157
  objections to act, 161–164
  objections to act and rule,
  summarized, 168
  pluralistic (ideal), 157
  points of clarification about, 157–159
  rule, 164–167

V

Validity
  defined, 8
  and truth, 8–9
  See also Argument
Values, 355–358
  areas of, 3, 355–356
  conflicting, 4
  defined, 3
  determining, 356–357
  moral, 3
  as uniquely human, 3–4

W

War
  laws of, 264–265
  prima facie duties in, 263–274
Wasserstrom, Richard, 264
Wellman, Carl, 23n, 137, 207n
"What Means This Freedom?"
(Hospers), 107–118

White, Justice, 193–194

Will, as used by Kant, 240.
See also Intention

Z

Zahn, Gordon C. "A Religious Pacifist
Looks at Abortion," 225–231